MODERN LEGAL

FAMILY, LAW AND RELIGION

AUSTRALIA
The Law Book Company
Brisbane ● Sydney ● Melbourne ● Perth

CANADA
Ottawa ● Toronto ● Calgary ● Montreal ● Vancouver

AGENTS
Steimatzky's Agency Ltd., Tel Aviv;
N.M. Tripathi (Private) Ltd., Bombay;
Eastern Law House (Private) Ltd., Calcutta;
M.P.P. House, Bangalore;
Universal Book Traders, Delhi;
Aditya Books, Delhi;
MacMillan Shuppan KK, Tokyo;
Pakistan Law House, Karachi, Lahore

MODERN LEGAL STUDIES

FAMILY, LAW AND RELIGION

by

CAROLYN HAMILTON, LL.B.

*Senior Lecturer in Law and
Director of the Children's Centre,
University of Essex*

LONDON
SWEET & MAXWELL
1995

Published in 1995 by
Sweet & Maxwell Limited of
South Quay Plaza, 183 Marsh Wall, London E14 9FT
Computerset by Interactive Sciences, Gloucester
Printed in England by Clays Limited, St. Ives, plc

No natural forests were destroyed to make this product;
only farmed timber was used and replanted.

A CIP catalogue record for this book is available from
the British Library

ISBN 0 421 45860 7

© Carolyn Hamilton, 1995

In this, the United Nations Year of Tolerance, this book is dedicated to my father, David, saved from religious intolerance by the Kindertransport, and in memory of Hannah, who was not.

Preface

The rise of multi-cultural societies in the western world has rekindled the debate about religious freedom. While those of us living in England and the United States are frequently told that we are living in a secular age, conflicts such as those in Bosnia and Northern Ireland remind us that the tensions of religious conflict can very quickly surface as a focus of discontent. This book seeks to discover how attempts to provide for religious freedom at both national and international level affect the family, particularly families from minority religious groups who seek to live according to their religious values and beliefs.

Over the years many academics, politicians, political theorists and others have emphasised the need for a written constitution in the United Kingdom. Many argue that such a constitution is a necessity if religious and other fundamental freedoms are to be assured to each and every member of society. This book examines that idea in relation to the family, and, in particular, whether the English legal system can provide the protection afforded by a written constitution. In the debates on a written constitution, few speakers have identified a need for separate provisions upholding the rights of children, as distinct from the rights of their families. As a lawyer primarily interested in child law, I was particularly concerned to see whether a written constitution really does provide greater protection for children than the common law, or whether a written constitution places too great an emphasis on parental rights and too little on the need for flexibility in dealing with the changing needs of children and the changing concept of family. Among other goals, this book attempts to answer that question.

The book examines a number of themes relating to religious freedom, but does not purport to be an exhaustive legal textbook on the subject, particularly in relation to the vast jurisprudence on this subject in the United States.

I would like to thank various people who have helped in the development of this book; James Busittil and Sheldon Leader for reading and commenting on specific chapters, to my children, Sarah, Lucy and Rachel for giving me the time to write the book and to Diane Tan, Claire Thomas and Clara Gore for helping in many ways. In particular, I would like to thank Martin Harris and the University of Essex for their support and for the study leave which enabled me to complete the project, and Dame Brenda Hale and Professor David McLean not only for their invaluable comments, but for the time that they gave me in discussing both ideas and details in the book. Lastly, I would like to thank my husband and colleague Professor James Gobert, who now knows more about religious freedom than he ever wanted to know, for his time, his patience, his interest and his generous help with the more intractable areas of American constitutional law. Any errors remain, of course, mine alone.

CAROLYN HAMILTON

Contents

Table of Cases

U.K. and European Cases

U.S. Cases

Other Cases

Table of Legislation

United Nations Instruments

Chapter One

Introduction: the development of religious freedom

It has been argued that no society without a written constitution can adequately ensure the preservation of its citizens' rights. This monograph does not seek to determine whether England needs a written Bill of Rights, but to explore the truth of this hypothesis in relation to freedom of religion. It will examine the extent to which the laws of England, with its Established Church and without a written constitution, allow families to regulate their lives and relationships according to their religious beliefs and values. It will compare the legal position in England with that in the United States, with a written constitution providing specifically for free exercise of religion and prohibiting the government from establishing any church. The basic aim is to determine whether a written constitution makes a difference.

A second aim is to examine the role of international law in this area. Since the Second World War, there has been a proliferation of international instruments confirming freedom of religion as one of the basic human rights. This book will examine the extent to which these instruments have been incorporated into the domestic laws of England and the United States, and the degree to which domestic law accords with each country's international obligations. A separate question is the effect of such instruments on judicial decisions.

The vast majority of the populations of England and the United States would no doubt agree that families should be able to regulate their lives according to their religious beliefs, and that the State should tolerate diversity. While the concept of tolerance in earlier centuries meant little more than allowing people to belong to a different religion other than that endorsed by the State, the concept of

1

toleration is interpreted today as providing equal respect and recognition to all religions. In neither England nor the 50 States that make up the United States, however, does the family have complete autonomy in its self-regulation. Claims for freedom of religion have to be balanced against the duty of the State to protect the weak and vulnerable members of society. The problem to be faced by the courts is whether religious practices which are regarded by them as discriminatory against women, in conflict with social norms or human rights norms or not in the best interests of the child, should be tolerated in the name of religious freedom. Competing claims as to the "rights" to be enforced may arise between the family and the State, or between family members themselves, particularly where parents have different religious beliefs, or one has no religious beliefs. In the latter instance, the courts may be faced with the additional problem of the weight that should be given to competing religous beliefs.

The book will examine how the legal systems and legislatures balance competing religious claims, and whether it is possible to delineate a limit of "tolerance" in the courts, a point at which the courts will not tolerate religious practices or permit families to conduct their lives according to their religious beliefs.

This chapter concentrates on the development and interpretation of the term "religious freedom", both in domestic law and international law. The later chapters will specifically address the issues raised in the context of the family; marriage and divorce, the upbringing of children, custody and contact with children when a relationship breaks down, adoption and education.

The Development of Religious Freedom

Before examining the attitude and approach of the two legal systems to religious disputes which arise within the family context, whether between family members themselves or between the family and the state, it is necessary to lift the curtain on current judicial thinking and appreciate the history that lies behind the law. This requires an understanding of the historical development of the relationship between Church and State, the development of "freedom of religion" within the two legal systems, and the role of international standards and norms in relation to freedom of religion. Religious freedom within the two societies needs to be clearly defined, divided as it is between freedom of conscience, (or the right to freedom of belief), and freedom to manifest religious belief or conduct one's life in a particular manner according to religious practices and traditions.

Judicial attitudes to religious disputes in families have, over the last two centuries, reflected the historical relationship between Church and State. The nature of the relationship between a state and a religion may take a number of forms. Partsch[1] postulated four types of possible relationship between the state and religious communities:

1. where the civic community and the religious community are identical and the law is based on, and reflects, religious beliefs[2];
2. where the state and the religious community are formally separated but where one creed dominates the public philosophy[3];
3. where the population belong to more than one religion or confession (or some to none at all), and religious freedom is fully recognised with the separation of state and religion a reality[4];
4. where atheism is the official policy but religion is more or less tolerated.

These four models may, however, be insufficiently flexible to cover all existing arrangements between Church and State. Elizabeth Odio-Benito as Special Rapporteur on the Elimination of all forms of Intolerance and Discrimination based on Religion or Belief, provided a wider range of possible models in her report based on information supplied by the governments of 37 states.[5] The data identified eight possible relationships that currently exist between State and Church. In all of them there is a freedom to practice religion, although in some states certain religions are regarded

---

[1] Partsch, "Freedom of Conscience and Expression and Political Freedom" in *The International Bill of Rights: The Covenant on Civil and Political Rights* (Henkin ed. 1981).

[2] A model which reflects the English experience up until the 18th century.

[3] The present English model.

[4] The present position in the U.S.

[5] Reproduced or summarised in App. A of Elizabeth Odio-Benito, *Elimination of all Forms of Intolerance and Discrimination based on Religion or Belief* (1989).

as predominant. Thus a State may adopt an official religion, such as is the case in Pakistan, where Islam is the state religion. Secondly, States may follow the model of an Established church, but nevertheless recognise freedom of religion, the current position in England. Thirdly, States may be neutral or secular as regards religion,[6] or have no official religion.[7] A fifth model is that of separation of Church from State, the model followed by the United States. A number of states have agreements with the Catholic Church[8] or protect legally-recognised religious groups.[9] Lastly, there is the "Millett" model, where a state recognises a number of religious communities, allowing them to follow their personal religious law in family issues.[10]

The different relationships between Church and State that exist in England and the United States owe much to the political and historical development of the two nations.

HISTORICAL DEVELOPMENT IN ENGLAND

For many centuries England was a part, albeit an outlying part, of the universal, and later the Western, church. In England, as elsewhere in Europe, there were tensions between the authority of the Papacy and that of secular rulers. The "Investiture Controversy" of the eleventh and twelfth centuries (which concerned lay rights of nomination to church offices, and in particular the claims of princes to invest Bishops with insignia of office and receive their homage) showed itself in the dispute between St. Anselm, Archbishop of Canterbury, and King Henry I; in the end the King's rights were limited to receiving homage for the temporalities of the bishop's office (a practice still followed in the Church of England). Under Edward III there was an issue as whether the representatives of the clergy should continue to sit in their Convocations or become part of what is now the House of Commons; the Convocations survived (and survive to this day). Various statutes passed in the fourteenth century, the Statutes of Praemunire and Provisors, sought to limit the jurisdiction of the Papal courts as against those of the

---

[6] *e.g.* Turkey.
[7] As in Italy, Spain or Germany.
[8] Bolivia, Poland, Portugal, Spain and Italy.
[9] Cape Verde, Italy, Portugal and Spain.
[10] As happens in Israel.

King, and to check Papal intervention in the appointment to bene-
fices in England. Finally, King Henry VIII repudiated Papal authority altogether and secured for himself recognitions as Supreme
Head on Earth of the Church of England. Although the concept
would not have been understood at the time, this can be seen as the
"establishment" of the Church of England as a church which was a
part of the structure of the state.

Despite the brief restoration of Papal authority under Queen
Mary I, the "Elizabethan Settlement" consolidated the process
begun under Henry VIII and continued under Edward VI. The Act
of Supremacy 1559 made the monarch the Supreme Governor of
the Church of England, Cranmer's Prayer Book (with some alter-
ations) was prescribed by the Act of Uniformity of the same year
and the Thirty-Nine Articles defined the theological position of the
Church. Adherence was seen as a test of loyalty for the Queen's
subjects, but there continued to be dissent both from those who
remained faithful to Roman obedience (and who became known as
Roman Catholics) and from Puritans or Independents, who for
theological reasons wanted greater change in the Church's struc-
tures and liturgy. Elizabeth and her advisers viewed these Protestant dissenters, whose religious inspiration came in part from
Geneva, as no less a threat to the security of the Kingdom than the
Catholics who looked to Rome. Action was eventually taken to
neutralise Protestant influence and organisation by the Act against
Seditious Sectaries in 1593. The State imposed severe punishment
or imprisonment, banishment and even death for those who
refused to attend the church of England or who attended Convent-
icles.[11]

After the Civil War, during the Commonwealth period, political
change was once more reflected by religious adherence. During this
period there was "toleration" of dissenting religious groups. The
exceptions to this "toleration" were Roman Catholics and Anglicans, who were seen as supporters of the monarchy. After the restoration of the monarchy, the Church of England regained its pre-
eminent position.[12] Although initialy, through the Declaration of
Breda in 1660, Charles II appeared willing to allow some measure

---

[11] Meetings of the Protestant dissenters.
[12] Charles, in restoring the Anglican Church to its former position, was once more
consolidating political power, filling the Church with his supporters, and undermining the influence and political power of the dissenters.

of religious toleration, this was short lived. The Clarendon Code, consisting of a number of Acts, placed religious and political restrictions on Roman Catholics and the dissenters, the latter representing the former holders of political power.

The Corporation Act 1661 required all those holding civic office to be communicants of the Church of England. The Act of Uniformity in 1662 and the Conventicle Act of 1664 made it illegal for anyone over the age of 16 to attend any "assembly, conventicle or meeting, under colour or pretence of any exercise of religion, in other manner than according to the liturgy and practice of England".

These Acts sought to solidify the position of the Anglican Church.[13] In the Five Mile Act of 1666 non conformist ministers were forbidden from living or visiting within five miles of any place in which they had previously worked, unless they took a special oath of loyalty, which most could not. In 1673 the Test Act required all those holding any civil or military office to receive the Holy Communion according to the rites of the Church of England, to denounce the doctrine of transubstantiation, and to take the oaths of Supremacy and allegiance. The Test Act was aimed at both Roman Catholics and dissenters. The philosophical position of the Anglicans post-restoration, was that adherence of the population to more than one religion would result in weakness in the body politic. They were unable to imagine that there could be more than one expression of religion in any cohesive state. Thus, early relationships between Church and State had much more to do with the reduction of political threat than religious doctrine.

The Act of Uniformity, the Conventicle Act and the Five Mile Act were all repealed in 1689,[14] when a Protestant King and Queen came to the throne. The Toleration Act was also enacted in 1689. It allowed most dissenters to have their own places of worship, provided that they met with doors unlocked and notified the bishop or his representative of their exercise. The Act did not go as far as

---

[13] This activity was largely restricted to other Christian sects, Jews appearing to be exempt from these restrictions. In 1655, Robles, a Portuguese Jewish refugee won a court case which established his right to practice his religion and bury his dead according to his beliefs.

[14] In 1687 and the following year James II issued Declarations of Indulgence in which, largely for the sake of trade and encouraging immigrants, he declared his protection for the Established Church but at the same time suspended all penal laws against nonconformists, Roman Catholic and otherwise.

removing civil disabilities on dissenters or treating the free churches, as they were known, on equal terms with the Church of England. Neither did these concessions apply to Roman Catholics or Unitarians.

Religious toleration continued to follow political allegiances in the early eighteenth century. The right of even the dissenters to follow their religion without suffering disabilities was fragile, and subject to political change.[15] Roman Catholics were still regarded as a danger to the security of the State,[16] while Quakers, who refused to pay tithes or bear arms for the country, were regarded as both anti-social and dangerous.

By the late eighteenth century a slow, but significant change had occurred. Non-Anglicans were seen as very much less of a threat, and were increasingly allowed freedom of worship. However, they were still disqualified from holding public office. Following an influx of French refugees from the Revolution in France, there was also less hostility and even a degree of sympathy for Roman Catholics.[17]

The eventual move towards full religious freedom began in England in the nineteenth century. A large number of diverse factors contributed towards this change. These included the effect of the French Revolution, a change in philosophical and political thinking brought about by the Enlightenment, the dwindling political power of the Papacy, the wealth and influence of the dissenters, many of whom had grown rich from the industrial revolution, the

---

[15] For instance, in 1711 the Tory government of the day passed the Occasional Conformity Act. Until this Act a number of dissenters occasionally took communion in the Anglican Church so that they could hold civic office. This Act decreed that anyone holding any office, civil or military, who "shall at any time . . . resort to or be present at any Conventicle, Assembly or Meeting . . . for the exercise of Religion in other manner than according to the Liturgy and Practice of the Church of England . . . shall forfeit £40". (a huge amount of money at this time.) Three years later in 1714 the Schism Act forbade nonconformists to have their own schools. This was passed with the aim of keeping nonconformists out of the professions. These Acts were both repealed in 1718 by a Whig government.

[16] In 1778 a Bill was introduced for the Relief of Roman Catholics. Although the Bill was passed, it led to such serious rioting (the Gordon riots) that it was withdrawn. An attempt was made in 1753 to lessen the religious disabilities on Jews. The Naturalisation Bill would have allowed Jews both to reside in England and to own land. Up until this time any Jew who wished to be naturalised had to take the sacraments of the Church of England. The Bill was passed and immediately repealed as a result of protest.

[17] An Act for the Relief of Roman Catholics was passed in 1791.

effect of the industrial revolution itself, and an increasing number
of adherents to an increasing number of Christian denominations.
By 1791, when John Wesley died there were said to be 70,000 registered Methodists in England.

An Act for the Relief of Roman Catholics, admitting Roman
Catholics to the legal profession, allowing Roman Catholic schools
and places of worship, and relieving them from the Oath of
Supremacy was passed in 1828. In the same year, the Test and Corporation Acts were repealed. As a result, Protestant non-
conformists were finally allowed to hold public office without
swearing to a religious test contrary to their consciences. Catholics
became eligible for public office the following year.[18] The repeal of
the requirements of the Test and Corporation Acts 1828 did not,
however, apply to Jews. In 1830 a bill which would have permitted
the admission of Jews to Parliament, similar in form to the Catholic
Emancipation Act, was defeated by 228 votes to 165. Most of those
who objected to the admission of Jews did so on the ground that
their admission was incompatible with the Christian character of
the Constitution.[19] It was not until 1858 that Jews were able to
enter Parliament[20] and 1888 that atheists could affirm rather than
swear an oath of allegiance to become a member of Parliament.[21]

With an increase in tolerance for non-Anglicans came a weaken-
ing of the bonds between Church and State. The Church of Ireland
was disestablished in 1869 and the Church of Wales in 1914.[22] Control over universities passed from the hands of the Church of England in 1871, when all religious qualifications were removed. The
argument for preserving Anglican control in the universities was
the same as that put forward in the 1830's when refusing Jews the
right to sit in Parliament: not the need to preserve Anglicanism *per
se*, but the need to preserve the Christian character of national insti-

---

[18] The Roman Catholic Emancipation Act 1829 made Catholics eligible for state and
municipal office.

[19] See Norman, *Church and Society in England 1770–1970*, p.116.

[20] The Jewish Relief Act 1858. This Act was passed after an agreement by both
Houses of Parliaments to draw up an oath acceptable to both Christians and Jews:
the Oaths Act of 1888.

[21] Affirmation rather than the swearing of an oath was also allowed for witnesses
giving evidence in court under the Oaths Act 1888, which could be regarded as
ending civil disabilities.

[22] This did not come into force until March 31, 1920, when four dioceses were cut
off from the province of Canterbury to form the Church of Wales.

tutions. This was perhaps a more fruitful line of argument given the fall in public support and practice of Anglicanism itself. The religious census of 1851 showed that 66 per cent of seats in Anglican churches were unoccupied on a Sunday. 3,773,474 people attended the Church of England on census day, while nearly as many, 3,487,558 attended Catholic or dissenting churches. While there was some sympathy for preserving the Christian character of national institutions, the numbers of formal adherents to non-Christian religions or atheism were so small, as not to be regarded as a threat to the state or to its ethos or national character.

HISTORICAL DEVELOPMENT IN THE UNITED STATES

The degree of tolerance practised by the early States depended largely on the founding fathers of those States. Early Anglican settlers in Virginia, Puritan settlers in New England, and Catholic settlers in Maryland, denied religious freedom to those who did not follow the founders' religion. They continued to adhere to Old World practices of restricting electoral franchise to members of the church, enforcing church attendance, civil disabilities, test oaths for public offices and the imposition of taxes to support the church.[23] On the other hand, a few colonial settlements, primarily in Pennsylvania and Rhode Island[24] were notable for a degree of religious toleration. Under the Great Law enacted in 1682 in Pennsylvania, no person who acknowledged one God and agreed to live "peaceable and just under the civil government" was to be disturbed because of his religious faith or worship, or compelled to attend any religious service other than that of his own choice.[25] The

---

[23] See the Fundamental Orders of Connecticut 1639. Thorpe, *The Federal and State Constitutions* (1909), Vol. 1, p. 519; the General Laws and Liberties of the Massachusetts Colony 1646, and Maryland, "Act Concerning Religion" (1649) in *American State Papers on Religious Freedom* (1949); "Virginia Lawes Divine, Moral and Martial" in *The Rise of Religious Liberty in America* (S. H. Cobb, 1902).

[24] See Charter of Rhode Island and Providence Plantations 1663. *American State Papers on Religious Freedom* (1949), pp. 53–54.

[25] See Pfeffer, *Religious Freedom* (1977), p. 10.

religious freedom offered here was, however, more apparent than real and was limited to other Protestant sects. Neither Jews nor Catholics had complete freedom of worship, and Sunday observance was still required.

Post-independence, most state constitutions guaranteed the right to freedom of belief and freedom of worship in their new constitutions. Some, however retained test oaths, establishment and restrictions on religious practices.

The political and philosophical change towards religious freedom was spurred on by the War of Independence, new nationhood and the need to provide a Code of laws for the newly federated states. The framers of the United States Constitution did not, however, provide for freedom of religion. The assumption appeared to be that religion was outside the ambit of government. The only clause contained in the Constitution of 1787 relevant to religious freedom, was Clause VI,[26] the federal test oath clause, which provided that federal and state officials "shall be bound by oath or affirmation to support this Constitution; but no religious test shall ever be required as a qualification to any office or public trust under the United States".[27] This clause did not, however, end the practice. Test oaths endured in a number of States well into the nineteenth century and until 1961 in Maryland, when the United States Supreme Court invalidated a Maryland law which required notary publics to declare a belief in God.[28]

The absence of a Bill of Rights was a cause of concern to the State ratifying Conventions. For a number of States, consent to the Constitution was conditional on a future amendment of the Constitution to include a Bill of Rights. A committee was appointed, headed by Madison, to draft a Bill of Rights. In 1791, the First Amendment to the Constitution was approved; "Congress shall make no law respecting the establishment of religion or prohibiting the free exercise thereof." While the amendment prohibited the federal legislature from establishing a church or placing any form of restriction on the free exercise of religion, individual states were not under the same

---

[26] The Federal Constitution, of which this Article is part, was signed in 1787.
[27] U.S. Const. Art. VI, Cl.3. State constitutions enacted during the war commonly required test oaths for public office. See Adams and Emmerich, *A Nation Dedicated to Religious Liberty* (1990), p. 14.
[28] *Torcaso v. Watkins* 367 U.S. 488 (1961).

obligations.[29] Indeed the last state to disestablish a church did not do so until 1833.[30] It was not until 1868 that the Fourteenth Amendment prohibited any state from depriving a person of "life, liberty or property without due process of law", and not until 1923 that the United States Supreme Court held specifically that the free-exercise clause was applicable to the States because it fell within the definition of the term "liberty" in the Fourteenth Amendment.[31]

The dichotomy between the freedom of religion contained in the federal Constitution and the practices of individual states, raises doubts as to whether religious freedom really developed much earlier in the United States than it did in England. However, more interestingly for the purposes of this book, is the fact that moves towards religious freedom in the two nations were based on different political premises. Religious freedom in England took place within the context of an established Church, the Church of England. Indeed, it has been argued that the growth of religious tolerance was, in effect, a leave granted by a religious majority to a religious minority to practice some or all of their religious practices, and was not to be equated with true religious freedom.[32] Religious freedom in the United States on the other hand, developed out of the premise that all religions were to be regarded as equal, and that the State had no role to play in religion, or the Church in government. This book, in exploring the extent to which there is religious freedom in family life, will seek to ascertain whether the different political and philosophical foundations in the two countries are reflected in modern decisions of the courts and the Acts of the legislature, and the extent to which establishment affects family life and legal regulation.

---

[29] See *Permoli v. New Orleans* 44 U.S. (3 How.) 589 (1845) where a Roman Catholic priest was fined under an ordinance which prohibited the performing of funeral rites in a Catholic Church. The Court stated that:

"The Constitution makes no provision for protecting the citizens of the respective states in their religious liberties; this is left to the State Constitutions and laws: nor is there any inhibition imposed by the Constitution of the United States in this respect on the States."

[30] Massachusetts was the last State to do away with its established Church when the State adopted a new constitution.

[31] *Meyer v. Nebraska* 262 U.S. 390 (1923). See also *Cantwell v. Connecticut* 310 U.S. 296 (1940). In *Everson v. Board of Education* 330 U.S. 1 (1947) the court held that the Establishment Clause also fell within the Fourteenth Amendment.

[32] Kurland, "The Religion Clauses and the Burger Court" (1984) 34 Cath.U.L.Rev. 1, 2–3. This is an argument dealt with below in Chap. Seven on religious education.

Establishment and Free Exercise

"By (establishment) is meant the erection and recognition of a State Church, or the concession of special favours, titles and advantages to one Church which are denied to others."[33]

The prohibition against establishment contained in the First Amendment to the Constitution of the United States was explained by Justice Black in *Everson v. Board of Education*.[34]

"The 'establishment of religion' clause of the First Amendment means at least this: Neither state nor the Federal Government can set up a church. Neither can pass laws which aid one religion, aid all religions, or prefer one religion over another. Neither can force nor influence a person to go or remain away from church against his will or force him to profess a belief or disbelief in any religion. No person can be punished for entertaining or professing religious beliefs or disbeliefs, for church attendance or non-attendance. No tax in any amount, large or small, can be levied to support any religious activities or institutions, whatever they may be called, or whatever form they may adopt to teach or practice religion. Neither a state nor the Federal government can, openly or secretly, participate in the affairs of any religious organisations or groups and vice versa. In the words of Jefferson, the clause against establishment of religion by law was intended to erect a 'wall of separation between church and state.' "

Free exercise is a much more difficult term to define. The Supreme Court in *Reynolds v. United States*[35] held that the clause protected freedom of belief from any state interference. However, continued the Court, free exercise could not be equated with the freedom to engage in all forms of religious practice. These remained subject to the regulation of society, and would be restricted if they were inimical to the interests of society. How would a follower of a minority religion know whether the practices of his or her religion would be inimical to the interests of society? According to the court in *Wisconsin v. Yoder*, "only those interests of the highest order not otherwise served can overbalance legitimate claims to the free exercise of religion".[36]

---

[33] Quick and Garran, *Annotated Constitution of the Australian Commonwealth* (1901).
[34] 330 U.S. 1, 15–16, 67 S.Ct. 504, 511, 91 L.Ed. 711 (1947).
[35] 98 U.S. 145 (1878).
[36] 406 U.S. 205, 32 L.Ed. 2d. 15, 92 S.Ct. 1526 (1972).

Does the very presence of an established church mean that families from religions other than that endorsed by the State will be discriminated against? Krishnaswami, in presenting his report on Discrimination in Religious Rights and Practices[37] in 1955 as the Special Rapporteur to the Sub-Commission on Prevention of Discrimination and the Protection of Minorities, devoted a full chapter to the status of religions in relation to the State. He concluded that toleration and non-discrimination depended on the legal arrangements in a State rather than whether there was an established church.

> "one cannot spell out discriminatory treatment . . . merely because the state establishes a religion or belief, or recognizes a number of religions or beliefs."[38]

The general view that establishment is not *per se* discriminatory or intolerant is reflected in the definition articles of both the draft Convention drawn up by the Sub-Commission and the draft Convention adopted by the Commission on Human Rights.[39]

> "article 1(a)
> (for the purpose of the Convention) neither the establishment of a religion nor the recognition of a religion or belief by a State nor the separation of church and State shall by itself be considered religious intolerance or discrimination on the ground of religion or belief; provided that this paragraph shall not be construed as permitting violation of specific provisions of this Convention."[40]

Elizabeth Odio-Benito in her report in 1987 as Special Rapporteur to the same Sub-Commission was not so clear that establishment was not discriminatory:

> "It would appear . . . that practices such as the establishment of a religion or belief by the State do in fact amount to certain preferences and

---

[37] UN doc. E/CN. 4/Sub.2/200/Rev. 2 and official UN Publication No. 60.XIV.2.
[38] UN doc. E/CN.4/Sub.2/L.124/Add.1.
[39] On the basis of a proposal put forward by Krishnaswami.
[40] The Commission did not in the end pursue a Convention in this area, deciding that for the present a Declaration was more appropriate. Since it was felt inappropriate for a Declaration to contain a definition article, this article was not included in the Declaration on the Elimination of all forms of Intolerance and of Discrimination Based on Religion or Belief 1981.

privileges being given to the followers of that religion or belief, and are, therefore, discriminatory. While such practices may not *per se* constitute intolerance, they tend to lead various authorities, organizations or groups to claim rights or to take other action which may indeed amount to further and more accentuated discrimination against particular religions or beliefs."[41]

The converse question also needs to be addressed: whether separation of Church and State is sufficient to ensure non-discrimination. On this issue Krishnaswami concluded that relationships between Church and State were complex and the mere fact of separation of Church and State was not sufficient to ensure non-discrimination.[42] He felt it was impossible to draft a rule for relationships between Church and State which would ensure tolerance and non-discrimination and could not recommend a particular form of judicial relationship.[43]

"in view of the variety of considerations involved, it is difficult to formulate a rule of general applicability, even though it would be desirable to affirm once more the principle that every religion should be accorded the greatest possible freedom in the management of its religious affairs."[44]

International Instruments guaranteeing religious freedom

The idea that an individual has a right to freedom of conscience or belief in international law, has developed largely as a result of European and American thought and experience.[45] The genocide of the Second World War and the oppression of minorities throughout the first half of the twentieth century, provided the impetus for international regulation and protection of minorities, and consensus on the need to articulate fundamental rights and freedoms that

---

[41] Odio-Benito recommended that a further study of the relationship between Churches and States should be undertaken.
[42] See p. 46 of the report.
[43] UN Doc. E/CN.4/Sub.2/200.Rev.1. para. 48.
[44] *ibid*. para. 51.
[45] See Boyle, "Seminar on Freedom of Conscience, University of Leiden" (November 12–14, 1992), Council of Europe.

should apply in all states. The first international instrument to contain the right to freedom of religion was the Universal Declaration of Human Rights[46] adopted by resolution of the General Assembly of the United Nations in 1948. Article 18 provides:

> "everyone has the right to freedom of thought, conscience and religion; this right includes freedom to change his religion or belief and freedom, either alone or in community with others and in public or private, to manifest his religion or belief in teaching, practice, worship and observance."

The right to freedom of religion has developed further since 1948 in two different directions: the "negative" one of outlawing discrimination on the basis of religion, and the "positive" path of adopting and promoting international agreements that incorporate the right to freedom of religion.[47]

The positive right to freedom of religion contained in the Universal Declaration is also to be found in slightly varying forms in other international and regional instruments: in the International Covenant on Civil and Political Rights,[48] to which both the United Kingdom and the United States are signatories; the Declaration on the Elimination of All Forms of Intolerance and of Discrimination based on Religion or Belief,[49] the European Convention on Human Rights which follows the wording of the Universal Declaration and to which the United Kingdom is a signatory,[50] the American Charter on Human Rights[51] and the African charter on Human and Peoples Rights.[52] The standards of freedom of religion are also part of international humanitarian law.[53]

Article 18 of the International Covenant on Civil and Political Rights differs from the Universal Declaration in relation to the right to change religion, referring only to the right to "have or to

---

[46] See Neff, "An Evolving International Legal Norm of Religious Freedom: Problems and Prospects" (1977) 7 Calif. Western Int. Law J. (No. 3) p. 550 and Boyle, "Seminar on Freedom of Conscience, University of Leiden" (November 12–14 1992), Council of Europe.

[47] See Boyle, *ibid.*

[48] In Art. 18.

[49] Adopted by the General Assembly on November 25, 1981 (resolution 36/55).

[50] In Art. 9.

[51] In Art. 12.

[52] In Art. 8.

[53] The Geneva Conventions of 1949 and the 1967 Protocols contain specific and detailed provisions guaranteeing religious freedom to protected persons.

adopt" a religion, the right to change religion being a matter that it was impossible to achieve consensus on:

> "18(1) Everyone shall have the right to freedom of thought, conscience and religion. This right shall include freedom to have or to adopt a religion or belief of his choice, and freedom, either individually or in community with others and in public or private, to manifest his religion or belief in worship, observance, practice and teaching.
> 18(2) No-one shall be subject to coercion which would impair his freedom to have or to adopt a religion or belief of his choice."

The Declaration on the Elimination of All Forms of Intolerance and of Discrimination based on Religion or Belief follows the other instruments in stating that everyone shall have the right to freedom of thought, conscience and religion, but provides only that "this right shall include freedom to have a religion or whatever belief of his choice" and makes no mention of the right to change religions or adopt a different religion. The right to change religions was not unanimously acceptable to the General Assembly,[54] and was omitted to ensure the acceptability of the Declaration.

The negative approach to religious freedom is also to be found in these instruments. The Universal Declaration and the Covenant on Civil and Political Rights both provide that the rights of individuals shall be respected without distinction of any kind, such as religion. Article 14 of the European Convention similarly provides that:

> "the enjoyment of the rights and freedoms set forth in this Convention shall be secured without discrimination on any ground such as . . . religion . . . "

Article 2 of the Declaration on the Elimination of All Forms of Intolerance and of Discrimination based on Religion or Belief has a rather wider requirement of non-discrimination, extending beyond a duty on the state to encompass groups and even individuals:

> "1. No one shall be subject to discrimination by any State, institution, groups of persons, or person on grounds of religion or belief."

These positive and negative rights to religious freedom are not

---

[54] The Islamic countries, in particular, objected to the inclusion of a right to change religion.

overriding and are subject to limitations. All these instruments, other than the Universal Declaration, contain clauses which allow the restriction of religious freedom in certain circumstances. Thus the International Covenant on Civil and Political Rights[55] and the Declaration on the Elimination of All Forms of Intolerance and of Discrimination based on Religion or Belief[56] provide that;

> "Freedom to manifest one's religion or beliefs may be subject only to such limitations as are prescribed by law and are necessary to protect public safety, order, health or morals and the fundamental rights and freedoms of others."

Article 9(2) of the European Convention similarly provides that:

> "freedom to manifest one's religion or beliefs shall be subject only to such limitations as are prescribed by law and are necessary in a democratic society in the interests of public safety, for the protection of public order, health or morals, or for the protection of the rights and freedoms of others."

The Status of International Instruments

Both England and the United States have ratified the Covenant on Civil and Political Rights[57] and the United Kingdom has ratified the European Convention on Human Rights[58] and the United Nations Convention on the Rights of the Child.[59]

THE UNITED KINGDOM

When the United Kingdom ratifies a Convention or Covenant, it is not legally bound to uphold the provisions contained in them. England is a "dualist" legal system and thus, before courts can enforce the provisions of treaties, as these instruments are collec-

---

[55] Art. 18(3).
[56] Art. 1(3).
[57] The U.K. ratified the Convention in 1976 with some reservations. The U.S. ratified in September 1992, again with a number of reservations.
[58] The U.K. ratified the Convention in February 1951. The Convention has not been given statutory form.
[59] Ratified by the U.K. in December 1991. The U.S. has recently signed, but has not, as yet, ratified this convention.

tively known, the provisions must be transformed into domestic legislation through the passing of a statute by Parliament.[60] While Parliament should seek not to enact legislation contrary to its international obligations, and while the English courts will, where possible, construe a statute so as to give effect to the United Kingdom's treaty obligations, the provisions of a treaty will give way where Parliament's intent is clearly expressed and to the contrary.[61] Thus, in *R. v. Chief Immigration Officer Heathrow Airport ex parte Salamat Bibi*[62] the Court refused to allow the provisions of the European Convention on Human Rights to take precedence over domestic legislation, even though the domestic legislation was clearly contrary to the provisions laid down in the Convention.[63] However, the courts have taken the provisions of the European Convention "into account as guide-lines to statutory interpretation or even to fill in gaps in the common law".[64]

The Universal Declaration of Human Rights, passed by the General Assembly of the United Nations is also regarded as a treaty. Its status in English law is unclear. Although not technically legally binding, the general view is that either the Declaration is an authoritative interpretation of the Charter declared by one of its organs, in this case, the General Assembly, or that the Declaration is a part of customary international law. Customary international law is deemed to be part of English law and statutes are to be inter-

---

[60] In the absence of such transformation, the rules contained in these international treaties have no legal force. See *Maclaine Watson v. Department of Transport and Industry* [1989] 3 All E.R. 523, *per* Lord Oliver at 544–5 and Lord Templeman at p. 526. For an example of where Parliament has directly incorporated a treaty see the Child Abduction and Custody Act 1985 which directly incorporates the Hague Convention on Civil Aspects of International Child Abduction, thus giving the Convention the force of law.

[61] See Davidson, *Human Rights*, (1993), Chap. 3, for a clear discussion of the status of treaty obligations.

[62] [1976] 1 W.L.R. 979.

[63] For a further discussion on this issue see *Brind and Others v. Secretary of State for the Home Department* [1991] 1 All E.R. 720 where the House of Lords held that the United Kingdom's courts would seek to interpret domestic legislation in accordance with the Convention where this was possible, but there was no corresponding presumption that the courts would review the exercise of administrative discretion on the basis that the discretion has to be exercised in conformity with the Convention. Lord Ackner, reinforcing the view that Conventions only have legal force if contained in a statute passed by Parliament, commented that to do otherwise would incorporate the Convention into English law by the back door.

[64] See Fawcett, *The Application of the European Convention on Human Rights* (1987), and *Waddington v. Miah* [1974] 1 W.L.R. 683.

preted so as not to conflict with customary law. Again, however, if a treaty is in direct conflict with an English statute, the statute will take precedence.[65]

The rights provided for in the ratified international instruments are unenforceable in a court of law, with the exception of the provisions of the European Convention of Human Rights. An individual may make an application to the European Commission on Human Rights in Strasbourg claiming that one or more rights contained in the European Convention on Human Rights has been violated, provided that domestic remedies have already been exhausted.[66] However, even if legally unenforceable, these international instruments provide a very useful and important standard by which domestic policies and legislation can be measured.

THE UNITED STATES

The United States, as a non-unitary State has more problems with the implementation of international instruments, deciding as it must do, the extent to which a treaty binds all the constituent units of a federal state. If a treaty is self-executing, it becomes the "Supreme Law of the Land" equivalent to a federal statute, as a result of Article VI of the United States Constitution. Where, however, a treaty is not self-executing, legislation must be enacted to implement it. With regard to the Covenant on Civil and Political Rights, Articles 1–27 of the Covenant were declared to be non-self-executing by the United States government.[67] This does not affect the international obligations of the United States, or restrict the undertakings accepted by the United States under the Covenant, but it does mean that the private rights created by the Covenant are not enforceable in United States courts. Where changes are needed, and most of the rights and freedoms contained in the Covenant are already embodied in the Constitution, these changes will have to be made by Congress.

The status of Resolutions and Recommendations from inter-

[65] For a further, and much more detailed, discussion of the role of customary law, see Starke, *Introduction to International Law*, I. Shearer (11th ed.).
[66] See Arts. 25 and 26.
[67] For a greater explanation of the implementation of the Covenant on Civil and Political Rights see Stewart, "U.S. Ratification of the Covenant on Civil and Political Rights: The significance of the reservations, understandings and Declarations" (1993) 14 H.R.L.J. 77.

national organisations, particularly those of the United Nations are
unclear. The general view is that while Declarations, Resolutions
and Recommendations do not constitute binding international obligations, they may be cited as evidence of customary international
law.[68] The 1986 revision of the American Law Institute's Restatement of Foreign Relations Law suggests that customary law will
supersede inconsistent obligations created by earlier agreement if
the parties so intend and the intention is clearly manifested.
Whether a United Nations Resolution contributes to customary
law depends on a number of factors, such as the subject matter of
the resolution, whether it purports to reflect legal principles, how
large a majority it commands, how many states dissented and
whether it is later confirmed by other practice.[69]

In assessing the rights of families to religious freedom in the following chapters, this book will be concerned with the extent to
which international instruments have been ratified and implemented in the two jurisdictions, and whether relevant Declarations,
Recommendations and Resolutions of the United Nations have
been acknowledged and/or considered by the courts.

Defining and interpreting the right to religious freedom

In looking at the European cases and the discussions and reports of
the European Parliament and the Council of Europe, as well as the
domestic decisions of the courts in the United States and England, it
is clear that religions basically fall into three broad groupings. The
first of these may be referred to as main-stream Judaeo-Christian.
When the American Constitution guaranteed free exercise of religion, and the English Parliament repealed legislation restricting
the practice of non-Anglican religions, and both countries

---

[68] See Lillich and Newman, *International Human Rights: Problems of Law and Policy*
(1979), pp. 65–66. This approach has, however, been contested. See Schachter,
"*International Law in Theory and Practice*", Recuel des Cours (Kluwer, 1982–V).
[69] Reporters notes to s.102 of the 1986 revision of the American Law Institute's
Restatement of Foreign Relations Law.

lifted civil disabilities against members of minority religions, the main beneficiaries were Roman Catholics, Protestant dissenters, and Jews.[70] These religions represented, at the time, the minority religions.

During the nineteenth century, the nature of English and American religious society began to change. There was a resurgence of interest in religion, a growing interest in evangelism, a desire for social reform and a desire, particularly in England, to reach out and involve the working classes in the practice of Christianity. The nineteenth century saw a growth in what might be termed "new Christian sects".[71] The Plymouth Brethren originated in 1827, Spiritualism was founded by Kate Fox in 1847, the Salvation Army by Booth in 1865, Christian Science by Mary Baker Eddy in 1875, Seventh Day Adventism by William Miller in Pittsburgh in 1844, Jehovah's Witnesses by Charles Taze Russell in Pittsburgh in 1872 and the Church of Latter Day Saints or Mormonism by Joseph Smith in Utah in 1837.[72] Recognition of some of these new sects was extremely slow. The practices of a number, particularly the Mormons, Jehovah's Witnesses and the Plymouth Brethren were challenged in the courts of both jurisdictions. Their right to religious freedom and the right of the State or other family members of a different religion, to restrict their freedom, is still the subject of debate and litigation in Europe, England and the United States.

A further change in the religious make-up of the populations of the United States and England has taken place since the Second World War. Part of this change has been due to an increase in immigration from non-Christian countries, particularly from the Asian sub-Continent. This immigration has resulted, in England, in a large Muslim community as well as sizeable Sikh

---

[70] Atheists and agnostics also benefited, although reforms did not have them primarily in mind.

[71] The term "new Christian Sects" is a convenient term, though possibly not a particularly precise one. However, it is not the intention of the author to address the question of whether some of the sects are so far removed from main-stream Christainity that the term might be judged inappropriate.

[72] Theosophy and the Baha'i Faith (a syncrestistic faith, largely from Islam but with Christian elements) could be included in the same general grouping as having a 19th century provenance. While not major faiths they are nevertheless not perceived as having some of the controversial characteristics of the category of New Religious Movements.

and Hindu populations. However, a further phenomenon has contributed to the change: the growth in "new religious movements" or cult religions. Barker[73] defines the term "new religious movement" as "covering a disparate collection of organisations, most of which have emerged in their present form since the 1950s and most of which offer some kind of answer to questions of a fundamental, religious, spiritual or philosophical nature".[74] Within this term fall those groups sometimes termed "alternative religions", "unconventional religions", "non-conventional religions", "cults" or "contemporary sects". Beckford points out that the reason for adopting the term New Religious Movement has also:

> "to do with the perception that many of the innovations in belief and ritual which attracted public attention in the West in the 1960's for the first time had been imported from, or influenced by, non-Christian and non-western sources. The movements conveying them were not, therefore, modifications or permutations of the kind of ideas and sentiments that had inspired earlier deviations from mainstream churches and denominations. They were perceived to be radically new in that they drew on completely alien cultural and social traditions."[75]

These new religious movements, while very disparate in nature, share the philosophical premise that formal or traditionally inspired religions have failed in their task and that society requires a fresh approach.

While still battling with acceptance of what we have termed the "second" grouping of religions, (the new Christain sects), the courts in England and the United States as well as the European Court of Human Rights, have also had to face the challenge of ensuring religious freedom for new religious movements. Many of these are both disliked and disapproved of by the general public and politicians alike. The response of the courts to these challenges will be discussed in the context of family issues in the ensuing chapters. At this point, it is intended only to take a brief look at attempts to restrict freedom of religion and to determine whether, if at all, there is any justification for restricting religious freedom in relation

---

[73] Eileen Barker, *New Religious Movements* (1989).
[74] *ibid.* at p. 7.
[75] James A. Beckford, *Cult Controversies* (1985).

to certain religions falling into these groups. On the international front, there has been little in the way of legal interpretation of the right to religious freedom as, apart from the European Convention on Human Rights, the relevant Covenants, Conventions and Declarations have no enforcement procedure. However, the definition and interpretation of religious freedom has been aided by the decisions of the European Commission and Court of Human Rights on Article 9 of the European Convention on Human Rights, as well as by European Parliament Working Documents, Council of Europe[76] Recommendations and Resolutions and a General Comment adopted by the Human Rights Committee under Article 40, paragraph 4, of the International Covenant on Civil and Political Rights.[77]

Restricting Religious Freedom

New Christian sects and new religious movements have generally been regarded with initial suspicion in both England and the United States, particularly insofar as they are perceived to be in conflict with the norms of society. Challenges to the right to freedom of religion for followers of these religions have come in a number of guises. Interestingly, in the United States, the argument was often put forward that the religious views of certain movements posed a threat to the unity of the country. In support of their attempts to restrict religious freedom, States urged that the doctrines and tenets of the religion if permitted, would produce potentially disloyal citizens.[78] This was strikingly similar to the English argument for restricting religious freedom in the late seventeenth century. Thus Jehovah's Witnesses who refused to salute and pledge allegiance to the American flag on the basis that to do so would infringe their religious belief, were initially regarded as disloyal. The United States Supreme Court upheld the decison of the Supreme Court of Georgia that the State had a right to compel them to do so.[79] The United States Supreme Court in the later case

---

[76] The Council of Europe has 32 members. Albania, Belarus, Croatia, Latvia, Moldova, Russia and the Ukraine have also made applications to become members.

[77] CCPR/C/21/Rev.1/Add.4.

[78] See, *e.g.* the arguments put forward by the state in *Farrington v. Tokushige* 273 U.S. 284 (1927) and *Stainback v. Po* 336 U.S. 368 (1949).

[79] *Leoles v. Landers* 302 U.S. 658 (1937).

of *Minersville School District v. Gobitis*[80] justified their finding that
the State could compel school children to salute the flag by holding
that the "freedom to follow conscience" is not unlimited, but must
be reconciled with other freedoms and interests which make up
constitutional democracy.

> "The mere possession of religious convictions which contradict the rel-
> evant concerns of a political society does not relieve the citizen from the
> discharge of political responsibilities . . . National unity is the basis of
> national security."[81]

The decision was the subject of much criticism, from both
religious groups and constitutional lawyers. When the same issue
came before the Supreme Court in *West Virginia State Board of Education v. Barnette*[82] two years later, the Court overruled its previous
decision by a majority of six to three, although it found the compulsory flag saluting to be unconstitutional on the basis that it violated freedom of expression rather than freedom of religion.
However, Justice Jackson, the author of the majority opinion, did
address the issue of when the state may restrict religious freedom:

> "The right of a State to regulate, for example, a public utility may well
> include, so far as the due process test is concerned, power to impose all
> the restrictions which a legislature may have a "rational basis" for adopt-
> ing. But freedoms of speech and of press, of assembly and of worship
> may not be infringed on such slender grounds. They are susceptible of
> restriction only to prevent grave and immediate danger to interests
> which a state may protect."[83]

In their concurring opinions, Justices Black and Douglas agreed
that freedom of religion was not an absolute freedom:

> "No well-ordered society can leave to the individuals an absolute right
> to make final decisions, unassailable by the State, as to everything they
> will or will not do. The First Amendment does not go so far. Religious
> faiths, honestly held, do not free individuals from responsibility to con-

---

[80] 310 U.S. 586 (1940).
[81] It is interesting to note that after this judgment, there were numerous attacks on
Jehovah's Witnesses, who were perceived as disloyal. See, for further discussion
of this decision and earlier ones, Pfeffer, *Church, State and Freedom* (2nd ed., 1967),
Chap. 15.
[82] 319 U.S. 624 (1943).
[83] *ibid.*

duct themselves obediently to laws which are . . . imperatively necessary to protect society as a whole from grave and pressingly imminent
dangers . . . But we cannot say that a failure, because of religious scruples, to assume a particular physical position and to repeat the words of a
patriotic formula creates a grave danger to the nation."

Other grounds of challenge to the practices of the second grouping
of religions in the United States have focussed on protecting public
morals, leading to a finding that the Mormons could not be
allowed to practice polygamy,[84] preserving public peace,[85] protecting and regulating the use of public[86] and private property[87] and the
prevention of fraud.[88]

Although England does not have a written constitution, it has
ratified the European Convention on Human Rights. This document provides, among other rights, for the right to religious freedom. The findings of the European Court and Commission, along
with the Parliamentary debates of the European Parliament and the
Council of Europe, are instructive in indicating the limitations on
religious freedom likely to be applied in England.[89] Up until 1993
neither the European Commission nor the Court of Human Rights
had found a violation of Article 9, guaranteeing religious freedom.
The Commission and Court had, however, previously found it
permissible to restrict manifestation of religious beliefs where such
was likely to provoke "indignation with the public"[90] or in the
interests of public safety or public order,[91] or where such a mani-

---

[84] See *Reynolds v. United States* 98 U.S. 145. (1978), *Davis v. Beason* 133 U.S. 333
(1890). For a further discussion of this issue see Chap. 2, below.

[85] See *Cantwell v. Connecticut* 310 U.S. 296 (1940) and *Chaplinsky v. New Hampshire*
315 U.S. 568 (1942).

[86] See *Cox v. New Hampshire* 312 U.S. 413 (1941), *Schneider v. Irvington* 308 U.S.
147 (1939).

[87] *Marsh v. Alabama* 326 U.S. 501 (1946).

[88] *United States v. Ballard* 322 U.S. 78 (1944).

[89] While domestic legislation takes precedence over the European Convention, the
Courts have taken the provisions of the European Convention "into account as
guide-lines to statutory interpretation or even to fill in gaps in the common law".
See Fawcett, *The Application of the European Convention on Human Rights* (1987)
and *Waddington v. Miah* [1974] 1 W.L.R. 683.

[90] *App. No. 9820/82 v. Sweden.*

[91] *App. No. 9813/82 v. U.K.* It was permissible to restrict the applicant from attending services at chapel with other prisoners. The applicant was a Category A pris-
oner, guilty of six murders, and had given evidence against other criminals. His
presence at the Chapel was thought likely to cause a disturbance by prison officers.

festation would be in breach of a contract freely and voluntarily entered into by the applicant.[92]

The case of *Kokkinakis v. Greece*[93] in 1993 was the first in which the Court of Human Rights gave serious attention to the limits on religious freedom provided for in Article 9(2) and the needs of a democratic society. The applicant in the case was a Greek national and a Jehovah's Witness. After being invited into the home of a Greek Orthodox lady, he proceeded to enter into a discussion with her. He was later arrested and convicted of proselytising, an offence under Greek law. While the Greek Constitution provides for freedom of religion, both the Constitution and a legislative statute prohibit proselytism.[94] The Court of Human Rights found that the sentence passed by the Greek court had infringed Mr Kokkinakis' right to freedom to manifest his religion or belief. The Court accepted that the measure complained of was "prescribed by law" within the meaning of Article 9(2) of the Convention and was in pursuit of a legitimate aim, namely the protection of rights and freedoms of others. The crucial question was whether the measure was necessary in a democratic society. While allowing a certain margin of appreciation to the Contracting State, the Court's task was to determine whether the measures taken at national level were justified in principle and proportionate. In reaching their decision, the majority weighed the requirements of the protection of the rights and liberties of others against the conduct of which the applicant stood accused. Rather than treating this issue as a matter of general principle, the majority looked at the impugned judicial decisions against the background of the case as a whole, and noted that:

---

[92] *Ahmad v. United Kingdom* (1981) 4 E.H.R.R. 25. At the time of accepting a teaching contract, Ahmad did not reveal that he would require time off to attend the Mosque on a Friday, and the education system as a whole could not cope with absences from a post when a teacher was on a full-time contract.

[93] Series A, No. 260-A Application No. 14307/88 May 25, 1993. (1993) 17 E.H.R.R. 397.

[94] Art. 13. Proselytism was further defined by s.2 of Act 1672/1939:
   "by Proselytism is meant, in particular, any direct or indirect attempt to intrude on the religious beliefs of a person of a different religious persuasion, with the aim of undermining those beliefs, either by any kind of inducement or moral support or material assistance, or by fraudulent means or by taking advantage of his inexperience, trust, need, low intellect or naivety."
   The offence of proselytism was originally to prevent the conversion of children from the dominant Greek Orthodox Church.

"a distinction had to be made between bearing Christian witness and improper proselytism. The former corresponds to true evangelism, which a report drawn up in 1956 under the auspices of the World Council of Churches describes as an essential mission and a responsibility of every Christian and every Church. The latter respresents a corruption or deformation of it. It may, according to the same report, take the form of activities offering material or social advantages with a view to gaining new members for a Church or exerting improper pressure on people in distress or in need; it may even entail the use of violence or brain-washing; more generally, it is not compatible with the respect for the freedom of thought, conscience and religion of others."

In the instant case, the Greek court had not sufficiently specified in what way the accused had attempted to convince his neighbour by improper means. That being so, the Court of Human Rights found it was not shown that the applicant's conviction was justified by a pressing social need. The contested measure did not, therefore, appear to have been proportionate to the legitimate aim pursued, or consequently "necessary in a democratic society".

Kokkinakis v. Greece is the first major case brought before the European court concerning freedom of religion, and it is to be regretted that the majority judgment was such a narrow holding, turning on the unique facts of the case: whether "improper" proselytism had been proved. By so doing, the majority failed to address the broader issue; to what extent should a democratic society be allowed to restrict religious freedom. The majority judges were taken to task by Judge Pettitti in his partly concurring opinion for failing to clarify the meaning of proselytism and the scope of the right to freedom of religion. He expressed concern that the majority limited themselves to, in effect, controlling the domestic court. The Judge argued that proselytism, even "improper proselytism", was the basis of the expression of freedom of religion, and a fundamental right and liberty which must be allowed to all religions and beliefs. He believed that, not only was the wording of the Greek law itself contrary to Article 9, but even if the law did not fall foul of Article 9, legislation should not be kept in force that is restricted to vague incriminations and where conviction depends on the subjective evaluation of the judge.

The only limits to the exercise of the right of religious freedom, including proselytism, that could be envisaged by the Judge were respect of others' rights. These, he found, would be exceeded by any attempt to force the consent of an individual or to use manipulative behaviour. Other practices, such as brain-washing, attacks on the right to work, attacks on public health and incitement to vice, occasionally practiced by certain pseudo-religious groups, should be dealt with by the general criminal law of a State. The State should not forbid all proselytism as a way of controlling such abuses.

Judge Martens in a partly dissenting opinion, concentrated on what is meant by religious freedom and the right of the State to interfere in the exercise of this freedom.[95] To Judge Martens the right to freedom of thought, conscience and religion enshrined in Article 9(1) is absolute, and there is no room whatsoever in the Convention for interference by the State. As these absolute freedoms explicitly include the freedom to change one's religion and beliefs, whether or not somebody intends to change religion should be of no concern to the State. Consequently, it likewise should not be the State's concern if somebody attempts to induce another to change his religion. But is there a duty on the State to act to prevent "improper proselytism" where this impinges on other freedoms? Contrary to the majority judges, Judge Martens found that the State had no such duty. First, respect for human dignity and human freedom implies that the State is bound to accept that in principle everybody is capable of determining his fate in the way he deems best, thus there is no justification for the State to use its power to "protect" the proselytised. Secondly, the "public order" argument cannot justify use of coercive State power in a field where tolerance demands that "free argument and debate" should be decisive. Thirdly, under the Convention all religions and beliefs should, as far as the State is concerned, be equal.[96]

While accepting that the freedom to proselytise may be abused, Judge Martens did not see the criminal law as an appropriate remedy to prevent such abuses for two reasons. The first is that the state, being bound to strict neutrality in religious matters should not set itself up as arbiter for assessing whether particular religious

[95] Martens dissents from the majority in that he finds Art. 9 does not allow Member States to make it a criminal offence to attempt to induce somebody to change his religion.

[96] That is also true where, as in the present case, one particular religion has a dominant position; as the drafting history of Art. 9 confirms, the fact of one religion having a special position under national law is immaterial to the State's obligation under that Article.

behaviour is "proper" or "improper". The absence of a touchstone cannot be made good (as the Court attempt to do) by resorting to the quasi-neutral test of whether or not the proselytism in question was "compatible with respect for the freedom of thought, conscience and religion of others". The second reason is that the rising tide of religious intolerance makes it imperative to keep the state's powers in this field within the strictest possible boundaries. According to Judge Martens the court achieves quite the reverse when it attempts to settle those boundaries by means of so elusive a notion as "improper proselytism", especially where there is no attempt to define the term.

One may conclude from the *Kokkinakis* case that there is a pressing need for the European Court of Human Rights to clarify the extent to which a State may restrict freedom of religion. Judge Martens and Pettitti take the discusson on freedom of religion to a new plane, but unfortunately, as neither of them are majority judges their remarks must be regarded as obiter. It is to be hoped that these arguments will be further addressed and thoroughly debated in subsequent cases before the Court of Human Rights.

The General Comment on the meaning of freedom of religion in Article 18 of the Covenant on Civil and Political Rights, adopted by the Human Rights Committee in 1992,[97] tends towards the view expressed by Judge Pettitti in the *Kokkinakis* case. Proselytism may be barred where it involves coercion, including the use, or threat of, physical force or penal sanctions, or refusal of access to education, medical facilities, employment and other rights in order to persuade an individual to adopt or keep a religious belief. However, the Comment does not stipulate what form of action the prevention of coercion may take. The General Comment would also allow religious freedom to be restricted in order to protect other rights guaranteed under the Convention, although limitations must be imposed by law, and must not vitiate the rights guaranteed in Article 18. Limitations may only be imposed on the grounds specified within the article: to protect public safety, order, health or morals or the fundamental rights and freedoms of others. The Comment is subject to the same criticisms made by Judge Martens in the *Kokkinakis* case. The terms used are inexact. For instance, there is no definition of what constitutes a threat to public safety or

---

[97] 1993 CCPR/C/48/CRP 2/Rev.1.

the freedoms of others. Neither is it clear on what basis a state would decide that a particular religion was a threat to morals. While it is possible to contemplate that a religion which espoused child prostitution as an essential part of its religious practices could be regarded as a threat to morals, what of a religion which blasphemed others or demanded that all members have a right to abortion on demand? Such inexactitude raises the possibility of discrimination against minority or unpopular religions.

The *Kokkinakis* case, while concerned with proselytising by a Jehovah's Witness follower, has much wider ramifications. By discussing improper proselytism the court is revealing a deeper concern, relating particularly to the practices of the new religious movements. In 1984, the European Parliament, following two resolutions expressing concern at the activities of the Unification Church, asked the Committee on Youth, Culture, Education, Information and Sport, to examine the lawfulness of the practices of the new religious movements. To this end the Cottrell Committee were appointed.

The Cottrell Report[98] did not propose control or regulation of belief, but was concerned only with the secular consequence of involvement with the new religious movements. The Cottrell Committee were presented with evidence that parents had lost contact with their children, sometimes for years. Other children, on their infrequent visits to family homes, seemed strage and distant and reluctant to stay. There were accusations before the Committee that recruits were virtually brainwashed into dependence on a new faith, for example, by control of diet; isolation from parents, friends and outside contact of all forms, disturbed sleeping patterns, being awoken at irregular hours to chant, sing and pray. This, it was claimed, was nothing more than a process of indoctrination which led to total subservience to a movement and its controllers and created a willingness to obey.

The Cottrell Committee stressed that full freedom of religion is a principle within the community, and that institutions have no right to judge the value of either religious beliefs in general or other individual religious practices. After considering the evidence, and bearing in mind the need to preserve religious freedom, the Committee

---

[98] European Parliament Working Documents 1984–85 Doc. 1–47/84.

concluded that existing legal measures in Member States were sufficient to control any abuses, and that what was required was the development of an atmosphere of "co-existence". The Committee emphasised that they were not attempting to proscribe or control religious belief, or indeed the privacy of belief, but were concerned instead with matters of human rights. They were in no doubt that the phenomenon of new religious movements would remain a strong feature of the social landscape, and that Member States should look to the prospect of integrating them into society. At the same time, the new religious movements should respect human rights which "are enshrined without question at every other level of society and every other area of public activity". Rather than suggesting any new form of legislation, the Committee suggested voluntary guide-lines. The committee considered it necessary that:

(a) persons under the age of majority should not be induced on becoming a member of a movement to make a solemn long-term commitment that will determine the course of their lives;

(b) there should be an adequate period of reflection on the financial or personal commitment involved;

(c) after joining an organization contacts must be allowed with family and friends;

(d) members who have already commenced a course of education must not be prevented from completing it;

(e) the following rights of the individual must be respected;
— the right to leave a movement unhindered,
— the right to contact family and friends in person or by letter and telephone,
— the right to seek independent advice, legal or otherwise;
— the right to seek medical attention at any time;

(f) no-one may be incited to break any law, particularly with regard to fund-raising, for example by begging or prostitution;

(g) movements may not extract permanent commitments from potential recruits, for example students or tourists, who are visitors to a country in which they are not resident;

(h) during recruitment, the name and the principles of the movement should always be made immediately clear;

(i) such movements must inform the competent authorities on

request of the address or whereabouts of individual members;

(j) new religious movements must ensure that individuals dependent on them and working on their behalf receive the social security benefits provided in the Member States in which they live or work;

(k) if a member travels abroad in pursuit of the interests of a movement, it must accept responsibility for bringing the individual home, especially in the event of illness;

(l) telephone calls and letters from member's families must be immediately passed on to them;

(m) where recruits have children, movements must do their utmost to further their education and health, and avoid any circumstances in which the children's well-being may be at risk.

In addition to the guide-lines, the Cottrell Committee called on the Commission to compile data on the new religious movements, particularly the international ramifications of new religious movements. Their activities in the Member States should be noted, as well as measures taken by government bodies, especially the police and the courts, in response to infringements of the law by these movements. The findings of government commissions of investigation into certain new religious movements should also be added. The Commission once in receipt of the information, were asked to submit proposals to the Council of Ministers responsible, with a view to securing the effective protection of community citizens.

The Committee also considered that a common approach within the context of the Council of Europe would be desirable and called on the governments of the Member States to press for appropriate agreements to be drawn up by the Council of Europe which would guarantee the individual effective protection from the machinations of these movements and their physical and moral coercion.[99]

While declaring that there was no intention to restrict religious freedom in any way, the Report is extremely hostile to new religious movements. The guide-lines must be regarded as placing considerable restriction on the activities of some of the new

---

[99] The Cottrell Committee Report was duly accepted by the full Committee on Youth, Culture, Education, Information and Sport other than one member who abstained from voting on the Resolutions contained in the Report.

religious movements. The restirctions, however, are indiscriminate and appear to apply to all new religious movements, whether the subject of controversy or not. Further, no reason is given to indicate why such restrictions should only apply to new religious movements and not to all religions. It would also appear that the remedy suggested is disproportionate to the problem. It is not wholly clear that the alarm felt by the Cottrell Committee in relation to recruitment was justified. While there has been concern at the recruiting methods of certain new religious movements, there has been little firm evidence that these practices are harmful, improper or criminal. Judge Martens points out in the *Kokkinakis* case[1] that the existence of such practices as brain-washing had not been proved, and that a report in 1984 commissioned by the Netherlands Parliament, concluded after extensive research that, as far as the Netherlands was concerned, there was no such evidence. Eileen Barker in her research on new religious movements similarly finds no firm evidence for improper practices.[2] The Report did not, unfortunately, address an issue of rather more concern, that of the treatment of children in new religious movements.[3]

The Cottrell Report, with a few minor amendments was presented to the European Parliament in 1984[4] and adopted in the form of a Resolution. Although the United Kingdom decided not to implement the Resolution through legislation,[5] a private members

---

[1] In *Kokkinakis v. Greece* Series A, No 260–A Application No. 14307/88 May 25, 1993. (1933) 17 E.H.R.R. 397.

[2] There is a substantial body of research showing that most people are perfectly capable of rejecting the overtures of the new religious movements if they want to. Of 1,000 people who became sufficiently interested in the Unification Church (the Moonies) to attend a residential workshop in the London area in 1979, a time when accusations of brain washing as a method of recruiting were frequent, approximately 90 per cent resisted the proselytising efforts and declined to have anything more to do with the Church. See Barker, *New Religious Movements* (1989), p. 18. See also Beckford, *Cult Controversies* (1985), and Galanter, "Psychological Religious Induction into the Large Group: Findings from a Modern Religious Sect" (1980) American Journal of Psychiatry. Vol. 137, No. 12, p. 1575.

[3] See Chaps. 4 and 5. See also Barker *ibid*. Chap. 7.

[4] On March 23. The Resolution was renamed and entitled "Concerning Common Action on the Part of the European Member States with Regard to the Violations of the Law on the Part of New Organizations Acting Under the Cover of Religious Freedom."

[5] The Home Office and the Foreign Office informed the English Council of Churches that they would not be implementing the Resolution in England. See Turner, "New Religious Movements and the Law in Britain" (1987), pp. 48–55.

Bill was introduced into Parliament in England by David Alton[6] in 1984, seeking to implement a small part of the Resolution, that of allowing parents and next of kin rights of access to relatives who have joined religious cults. The Bill was not, however, enacted.

Although the Council of Europe were invited to consider the problems presented as a result of activities of sects and new religious movements, it was not until 1987 that two Resolutions[7] were placed before the Council in relation to the implementation of the European Parliament's earlier Resolution and not until 1992 that the Council of Europe debated the issue of implementation. The Resolutions of 1987, while concerned as to whether the Cottrell Report Resolution infringed the right to religious freedom and the right to privacy under the European Convention, still expressed concern about the activities of new religious movements and also of deprogrammers hired by families to "cure" members of their attachment to one of the new religions.

In 1992 the Parliamentary Assembly of the Council of Europe finally concluded in Recommendation 1178, that the provisions of Article 9 made major legislation restricting the activities of new religious movements undesirable. The Recommendation, while continuing to express concern at the activities of new religious movements, did not adopt the guide-lines recommended by the Cottrell Committee and previously adopted by the European Parliament. Instead, the Recommendation required that existing legislation concerning the protection of children should be more rigourously applied, and that those belonging to a sect should be informed that they had a right to leave.[8] The Recommendation also

---

[6] Hansard October 24, 1984, 707. David Alton also pointed out that The Cottrell Report's suggested guide-lines for cults had not been adopted in England, and that this should be a matter for consideration by the Select Committee on Home Affairs.

[7] Parliamentary Assembly of the Council of Europe, Motion for a Resolution on Religious Freedom. Presented by Mr Elmquist and others. May 6, 1987, Doc. 5737. Parliamentary Assembly of the Council of Europe, Motion for a Resolution on Freedom of Religion. Presented by Mr. Cifarelli and others. July 28, 1987, Doc 5767.

[8] The Recommendation also required that persons working for sects should be registered with social welfare bodies and guaranteed social welfare coverage, and that such coverage should also be available to those deciding to leave a sect. It is interesting to compare Parliamentary Assembly of the Council of Europe Recommendation no. 1202 (1993) on Religious Tolerance in a Democratic Society concerned with the Prevention of Xenophobia.

called for member states to educate their populations on the nature of the new religious movements.

The last ten years in Europe have been characterized by attempts to restrict the activities, in particular active recruitment, of the new religious movements. The aim of the guide-lines, Resolutions and Recommendations has been to remedy what were perceived as abuses. Whether these attempts are compatible with the international obligations on both England and the United States to ensure religious freedom is highly debatable, especially in the light of the General Comment on Article 18 of the Covenant of Civil and Political Rights adopted by the Human Rights Committee.[9] The General Comment makes it clear that freedom of religion is not limited in its application to traditional religions, or to religions and beliefs with institutional characteristics or practices analogous to those of traditional religions. The Human Rights Committee viewed with concern a tendency to discriminate against any religion for any reason, including the fact that they are newly established, or represent religious minorities that may be the subject of hostility by a predominantly religious community.

The following chapters will seek to explore the extent to which the concerns expressed in relation to new religious movements and the new Christian sects are reflected in decisions reached by the courts. These are of particular importance in the chapters dealing with upbringing and custody, where the best interests of the child is an additional factor to be weighed in the balance of religious freedom. Thus, for instance, where religious teaching demands that parents pray for a sick child rather than seek medical treatment, the court will be asked to balance the best interests of the child against the right of the family to religious freedom.

It is outside the scope of this book to undertake a review of religious freedom within the two societies generally. Instead, the book concentrates on those issues which effect the family most: the upbringing of children, arrangements for children after separation or divorce of the parents, adoption, marriage and divorce. It is in the area of education, and religious education in particular, that the general divergence between practices in the United States and Eng-

---

[9] General Comment adopted by the Human Rights Committee under Art. 40, para. 4 of the International Covenant on Civil and Political Rights. UN Doc. CCPR/C/21/Rev.1/Add.4.

land is most obvious, and the role played by establishment most clear.

It will be obvious to the reader that this book contains no definition of religion. This is a deliberate omission. The Declaration on Elimination of all Forms of Intolerance and Discrimination based on Religion or Belief does not define religion or belief, although the Draft Convention drawn up by the Sub-Commission on Prevention of Discrimination and Protection of Minorities and the Draft Convention drawn up by the Commission on Human Rights defined religion or belief as including theistic, non-theistic and atheistic beliefs. Special Rapporteur Odio-Benito in her report,[10] in the absence of definition, suggested as a working definition of religion, an explanation of the meaning of life and how to live accordingly. Every religion has a creed, a code of action and a cult. This book takes as its definition of religion that of the draft Convention, bearing in mind the working definition of the Special Rapporteur.[11]

---

[10] UN Doc E./CN4./Sub.2/1987/26.

[11] For an excellent discussion of the Declaration on the Elimination of all Forms of Intolerance and of Discrimination based on Religion or Belief see Donna Sullivan American J. of International Law (1988) Vol. 82, 487. Sullivan attributes the lack of definition of religion to the difficulty of formulating a definition of religion or belief broad enough to be acceptable to a large number of states but sufficiently specific to expand the protections afforded. She postulates that a lack of definition may prove more conducive to the protection of freedom and belief than any definition.

Chapter Two

Marriage

Article 16 of the Universal Declaration of Human Rights provides that men and women, of full age, without any limitation due to race, nationality or religion shall have the right to marry and found a family. Such rights are also recognised in other human rights instruments.[1] Both England and the United States regard marriage and the establishment of a family unit as an essential and integral part of society,[2] necessary amongst other things for mutual support and the nurturance of the family. Religions also place great emphasis on family formation.

This chapter will concentrate on the ability of parties to form and celebrate marriages according to their religious traditions. The vast majority of religions regard the formation of marriage and its surrounding traditions as an essential part of their culture, and most have detailed, specific rules relating to both marriage and divorce. Religious traditions relating to marriage can, however, on occasions, conflict with state regulation. While both England and the United States permit and, to a large extent, recognise, religious marriage, the legislatures and courts in both jurisdictions have shown a much greater concern over the last two centuries to regulate the formation and registration of marriage. Both States have been faced with the need to decide whether religious practices relating to marriage can be tolerated, or whether society requires that

---

[1] *e.g.* the European Convention on Human Rights, and the International Covenant on Civil and Political rights.

[2] For the importance of the family to the American constitution, see Heymann and Barzelay "The Forest and the Trees: *Roe v. Wade* and its critics" (1973) 53 B.U.L. Rev. 765. See also Art. 10(1) International Covenant on Economic, Social and Cultural Rights.

certain religious practices be restricted. The justification for restrictions vary: from the need for protection of the vulnerable, to the need for certainty and equality between men and women, and the need to ensure public morality. International regulation placing restrictions on marriage concentrates largely on protection of the young and equality between the sexes, and is itself in conflict with religious tradition in certain instances.

Preliminaries to Marriage

In the United States, regulation of marriage has always been in the control of the civil authorities rather than ecclesiastical authorities. Indeed, in many States, statute expressly provides that marriage is a civil contract. This is in direct contradiction to the view of most Christian churches that marriage is a sacrament. Parties may solemnise their marriage by means of a civil ceremony or a religious ceremony. In either case, the State requires the fulfilment of certain preliminaries. The nature of these preliminaries depend on the nature of the ceremony. Apart from various statutory regulations imposed on couples wishing to marry, such as the need for a medical examination or the imposition of a waiting period,[3] the laws of all States require the parties, whatever their intended mode of solemnisation, to procure a licence before a marriage takes place.[4]

Entering into marriage is not a uniform procedure in England. If the parties intend to marry in the Church of England, banns are published in the parish church where each resides[5] on three Sundays preceding the marriage.[6] This stands in place of obtaining a

---

[3] *In Griswold v. Connecticut* 381 U.S. 479, 85 S. Ct. 1678, 14 L.Ed 2d 510 (1965) the Supreme Court held that the State may not intervene in the area of sexual relations within marriage without showing a subordinating State interest which is compelling. However, requirements of licence, various kinds of pre-marital examination or counselling, etc., appear to be constitutional.

[4] There are exceptions to this in a small number of states; *e.g.* California does not require that a licence be obtained if the parties have previously been living together as husband and wife without being married.

[5] The reading of banns involves reading aloud a form of words giving notice of intended marriage, identifying the couple, and asking anyone who knows of any impediment to make this known. If the parties wish to be married in another church, in an area where neither resides, then the banns must be published there as well.

[6] The marriage must take place within three months of the publication of the banns.

licence. However, parties may obtain a common licence[7] in place of the publication of banns. The licence allows a marriage to be celebrated in the parish church in the area in which at least one party has resided for 15 days, provided that the parties can satisfy the grantor that there is no impediment to the marriage, and that the residence qualifications are satisfied.[8] It is also possible to marry in the Church of England following the grant of a special licence by the Archbishop of Canterbury or a Superintendent Registrar's certificate.[9] For all other forms of marriages, whether the parties intend to marry by a civil ceremony alone, or by a religious ceremony or by both, it is necessary to obtain a Superintendent Registrar's certificate.[10]

THE VALIDITY OF A MARRIAGE SOLEMNISED BY A RELIGIOUS CEREMONY, BUT WITHOUT A LICENCE

Where a religious marriage takes place, but the parties have failed to fulfil the preliminary civil requirements, the question arises whether the state will recognise this ceremony as conferring the status of marriage on the parties. In both the United States and England, the law favours the validity of marriage, particularly where the parties have not knowingly and wilfully contracted a marriage in defiance of the legal requirement to obtain a licence. In the United States, the validity of a religious marriage contracted without a licence depends on the language of the statute. Some licensing statutes make it plain that no marriage is valid without a licence, and, if so, the courts will hold the unlicensed marriage

---

[7] This is a not infrequent practice. The licence is obtained from the office of the Surrogate.

[8] The couple may prove either that one of them has resided in the area for 15 days or that the church where the ceremony is to be held is the regular place of worship for one of them.

[9] The granting of such a licence is discretionary. Marriage in the Church of England may also be celebrated following the grant of a Superintendent Registrar's certificate, the same formality as for non Church of England marriages. In practice, few Church of England marriages are authorised by this method.

[10] Such certificates may be issued with or without a licence. The obtaining of a licence merely does away with the need to wait three weeks before the marriage is celebrated. The term certificate is somewhat confusing as, in reality, this is a licence.

invalid.[11] Where the licensing statute does not expressly state this, "the cases find the policy favouring marriage sufficiently strong to justify upholding the ceremony of marriage".[12] The court is particularly reluctant to find such a marriage invalid where the issue is raised long after the alleged marriage, the parties have acted on the assumption that the marriage is valid and subsisting and when the legitimacy of children is involved.[13] There is little point in these cases in finding the marriage void, although the courts recognise that such a marriage may well be voidable.[14] Arguably, the appropriate remedy is to make it a criminal offence for an authorised person to celebrate a marriage without ensuring that the civil preliminaries have been complied with.

The English courts are not, however, prepared to overlook a flagrant disregard of the appropriate civil formalities to marriage. They will not treat a religious marriage, even one valid according to the particular religious law, celebrated in the absence of these, as creating a marriage at all.[15] This would mean that the possibility of nullity proceedings, even to declare the marriage void, would not be open nor, therefore, would the possibility of claiming some form of matrimonial relief. This is clearly illustrated in the case of *R v. Bham*.[16]

The appellant in this case was a Muslim and leader of his community. He was charged and initially found guilty of knowingly and wilfully solemnising a marriage in a place other than a registered building specified in the notice of marriage.[17] The groom, a 24 year old Muslim had tried to obtain a Registrar's certificate as required under the Marriage Act 1949, but the Superintendent

---

[11] Unless the parties believed that they were married and acted on this basis. See n. 52.

[12] See Clark, *The Law of Domestic Relations in the United States* (2nd ed., 1988). The New York statute expressly provides that the lack of a licence will not invalidate a ceremonial marriage.

[13] See *Sanders v. Sanders* 52 Ariz. 156, 79 P. 2d 523 (1938) *Dunham v. Dunham* 162 Ill. 589, 44 N.E. 841 (1896) annot. 74 A.L.R. 138 and *Sy Joc Lieng v. Sy Quia* 228 U.S. 335 (1913).

[14] This appears to be the case where there is no express language declaring the marriage void for failure to observe statutory requirements. See *Gould v. Gould* 78 Conn. 242, 61 A. 604 (1905), *Hames v. Hames* 163 Conn. 588, 316 A 2d 379 (1979), *Perlstein v. Perlstein* 152 Conn. 152, 204 A. 2d 909 (1964).

[15] See *R. v. Bham* [1965] 3 All ER 124.

[16] *ibid.*

[17] An offence regarded as a felony and carrying the possibility of imprisonment up to a maximum of five years.

Registrar refused to accept the notice or issue a certificate because the man could not satisfy him that he was single. The ceremony of marriage was performed by Bham in a private house, which was not a registered building for the purposes of marriage according to Islamic traditions. The Court of Criminal Appeal found that the provisions of the Marriage Act 1949 prescribe and control the manner in which a marriage may be solemnised. It did not seem to the Court that the provisions of the 1949 Act had any relevance or application to a ceremony which was not, and did not purport to be, a marriage of the kind allowed by English domestic law. Unless the marriage purporting to be solemnised under Islamic law is also a marriage of the kind allowed by English law, it was not a marriage with which the Marriage Act 1949 is concerned, and, therefore, the appellant was not guilty of any offence.

This decision is perhaps more easily explained by the references to the earlier case of *R v. Ali Mohammed*[18] The important point here was whether the parties believed that a valid marriage under English law was being created. In this case the husband was already married, and both the husband, the lady that he was marrying and Ali Mohammed knew that the marriage would not be valid under English law. Ali Mohammed nevertheless performed the ceremony as he was obliged to do under Islamic law to salve the husband's conscience as he and the lady were going to live as man and wife. In both cases, it was accepted by the court that neither the parties nor the celebrants intended to effect a valid English marriage, only an Islamic one. The court held in *Bham* that, for the Act of 1949 to have any application, the ceremony "must be at least [one] which will prima facie confer on them that status by English law and, in our judgment, it did not constitute the solemnisation of a marriage within s.75(2), and the conviction must be quashed".[19]

The decision leaves the law in a rather uncertain position. The result appears to be that parties who have gone through a religious ceremony without first fulfilling the civil preliminaries, will be treated as never having contracted a marriage, if the parties knew that the marriage would not be valid under English law. The case does not deal with the situation where the parties marry in this

---

[18] [1964] 1 All E.R. 653. [1964] 2 Q.B. 350.
[19] [1965] 3 All E.R. 124, *per* Thompson J. at p. 129. Similar judgment was given by Humphrey's J. in *R. v. Ali Mohammed* [1964] 1 All E.R. 654 at 656; [1964] 2 Q.B. 350 at 352.

form believing that they are contracting a valid marriage according to both their religious traditions and English law. While any child of such a marriage would be legitimate if both or either of the parties reasonably believed that the marriage was valid,[20] it is not clear whether the marriage would be treated as valid for all purposes. It may well be that English judges would reach the same conclusion as the Connecticut court in the case of *Carabetta*.[21] The court found that the Carabetta's had married in a Roman Catholic ceremony but had failed to obtain a licence. In holding their marriage was not invalid, Associate Judge Bogdanski found that marriage was strongly favoured by the law and that the presumption of marriage is very strong. "It is a presumption that grows stronger with the passage of time, is especially strong when the legitimacy of children is involved and can only be negated by disproving every reasonable possibility that it is valid."

Solemnising and Registering Marriage

The history of solemnisation of marriages in England is chequered. Up until the time of Lord Hardwicke's Marriage Act of 1753, there were various ways of solemnising a valid marriage, not all of which required that there be a religious ceremony. While a marriage ceremony in church conducted by a clergyman after the publication of banns, was a valid marriage, so too were declarations of marriage made by the parties. A declaration *per verba de praesenti*, "I do take thee to my wife or husband" resulted in a binding marriage of immediate effect. A couple could also bind themselves to a marriage in the future *per verba de futuro*, the marriage taking effect when there was consummation. The Church of England sought to exert more controls over solemnisation of marriage in the seventeenth century, by insisting that certain preliminaries were fulfilled.[22] However, marriages solemnised by clergymen which did

---

[20] s.1(1) Legitimacy Act 1976. To confer legitimacy one or both of the parents must have reasonably believed the marriage to be valid at the time of the act of intercourse resulting in the birth. The section applies only where the father of the child was domiciled in England or Wales at the time of the birth, or if he died before the birth, was so domiciled immediately before his death.

[21] 182 Conn. 344, 438 A 2d 109 (1980).

[22] That marriages took place in the church in the parish where one of the couple resided, after the banns had been read for three weeks, and between the times of 8 a.m. and noon.

not meet these requirements, although illegal, were still valid marriages. By the middle of the eighteenth century the law of marriage was recognised as unsatisfactory and uncertain, if not scandalous. There was no public registration of marriages *per verba de praesenti* or *per verba de futuro*, and clandestine marriages were easy to contract and often kept secret. The result of such practices, and the unavailability of divorce, was bigamy on a considerable scale. It was not uncommon for a spouse, on the death of the other, to discover that their partner had previously been married clandestinely, that the marriage was invalid, the children illegitimate, and that there was no possibility of inheriting the deceased spouse's estate. A further dissatisfaction was that these illegal but valid marriages did not require that parental consent be obtained where one or both of the parties was under the age of 21. Parents could find their children married to spouses they considered undesirable, a matter of particular concern when the common law rule was that all property of the wife vested in the husband on marriage.[23]

The effect of Lord Hardwicke's Marriage Act of 1753 was to regularise the performance and registration of marriages. Responsibility for the preliminaries to marriage was placed in the hands of the State, while responsibility for the solemnisation of marriage was placed in the hands of the Church. To effect a valid marriage the Act required that the marriage be solemnised, according to the rites of the Church of England, in the parish church of the parish in which one of the parties resided, in the presence of a clergyman and two witnesses. Marriages which did not meet these requirements were to be regarded as invalid, as were marriages of persons under the age of 21 where there was no parental consent. To foster greater certainty as to the status of individuals, marriages were to be entered into the parish register and signed by both parties. The only groups exempted from these requirements were the Quakers and the Jews who were allowed to marry according to their own customs and usages. Other religious groups, such as the Catholics and Protestant dissenters were not granted such exemptions. For them, the only way of contracting a valid marriage was to marry according to Anglican rites, in an Anglican church, a restriction which remained in force until the Marriage Act of 1836.

---

[23] For an informative and entertaining description of the difficulties of the marriage system of this time, see Lawrence Stone, *The Family, Sex and Marriage 1500–1800* (1979).

After the passing of the 1836 Act, parties were able to marry through a completely civil ceremony in the presence of a superintendent registrar, a registrar of marriages and two witnesses after obtaining a licence. The Act also recognised the rights of Catholics and Protestant dissenters and permitted the registration of places of worship other than Anglican churches for the purpose of the solemnisation of marriage. The previously disenfranchised groups could now marry in a "registered building" in accordance with the religious ceremony of the denomination to which they belonged, provided that there was, at some stage, a declaration *per verba de praesenti*, that the parties took each other as husband and wife. While these amendments were aimed at the Catholics and the Protestant non-Conformists, the provisions have been of use to other minority religions wishing to celebrate marriages according to their own religious traditions and ceremonies.

In the United States, unlike England, the recognition of informal, or "common law" marriages as valid continued far longer.[24] In a small number of states a marriage can still be contracted by agreement followed by the open assumption of the marital relationship.[25] Most States, however, require both the obtaining of a licence and solemnisation for there to be a valid marriage.[26] All States have statutes governing the solemnisation of marriage. Couples may solemnise their marriage through a purely civil ceremony, or through a religious ceremony. Some States require, as does England, that the parties declare in the presence of the presiding official and the required witnesses that they "take each other as husband and wife".[27] Further, in both jurisdictions there is a requirement that the marriage be solemnised by an authorised per-

---

[24] Common law marriages contracted abroad and valid by the *lex loci domicilii* will still be recognised in England in some circumstances, but have not been recognised if contracted in England since Lord Hardwicke's Act of 1753. A number of the States of the U.S. continued to regard such marriage as valid after independence from England. See Koegel, *Common Law Marriages*, (1922), pp. 54–90 and Weyrauch, "Informal and Formal Marriage—an appraisal of Trends in Family Organization" (1960) 28 Univ. Chi. L.Rev. 88. Thirteen States and the District of Columbia continue to recognise common law marriage.

[25] See generally Annot. 133 A.L.R. 758 (1941). Also, *United States Fidelity and Guaranty Co. v. Britton* 269 F.2d 249 (D.C.Cir.1961); *National Union Fire Ins. Co. v. Britton*, 187 F. Supp. 359 (D.C.C.1960), judgment affirmed 289 F.2d 454 (D.C.Cir 1961). *Beck v. Beck* 286 Ala. 692, 246 So. 2d 420 (1971).

[26] But see pp. 39–40.

[27] See N.Y. Dom. Rel. Law para. 12.

son, either a specified religious minister or a specified civil officer. In England, the authorised person will normally be a Minister of the particular religion appointed by the trustees or governing body of the religious organisation.

To what extent do these requirements impose a restriction on religious groups? International instruments support the right of the State to legislate on formalities prior to marriage and in relation to the solemnisation of marriage, and recognise the right of States to insist on the registration of marriages. Thus religious groups will have difficulty arguing that their religious ceremonies are sufficient to create a valid marriage of itself, and that they should not be requested to comply with state legislation in relation to marriage. The Convention on Consent to Marriage, Minimum Age for Marriage and Registration of Marriage[28] adds to Article 16 of the Universal Declaration of Human Rights in stating in Article 1 that:

> 1. No marriage shall be legally entered into without the full and free consent of both parties, such consent to be expressed by them in person after due publicity and in the presence of the authority competent to solemnize the marriage and of witnesses, as prescribed by law.

Article 3:

> All marriages shall be registered in an appropriate official register by the competent authority.

One of the effects of Article 1 is to stop proxy marriages, marriages where the parties do not appear together in front of the competent authority for the marriage ceremony, but are represented by a third party. Such marriages are recognised in Islamic law and have, on occasion, been recognised when performed in the United States, although it has been argued that proxy marriages fail to meet the statutory requirements for valid ceremonial marriages.[29] However, proxy marriages are disliked by the civil authorities in England and the United States as it cannot be ascertained that there

---

[28] Opened for signature and ratification by General Assembly Resolution 1763 A (XVII) of November 7, 1962. Entered into force: December 9, 1964, in accordance with Art. 6. The Convention was ratified by the U.K. in 1970. The U.S. is not a party to the Convention.

[29] Howery, "Marriage by Proxy and other Informal Marriages" (1944) 13 U. Kan. City L. Rev. 48. For cases recognising proxy marriages, see *Barrons v. U.S.* F.2d 92 (9th Cir. 1951), *State v. Anderson* 230 Or. 200, 396 P 2d 558 (1964).

has been full and free consent to marriage by both parties.[30] Not-withstanding the dislike of proxy marriages, such marriages will be valid in England and the United States if valid under the law of the *lex loci celebrationis*, even if one of the parties is domiciled and resident in England.[31]

The Convention on Consent to Marriage has been reinforced by a United Nations General Assembly Resolution; Recommendation on Consent to Marriage, Minimum Age for Marriage and Registration of Marriage[32] which recommends that Member States should enact legislation to this effect if they have not already done so.

COMPETENT AUTHORITIES

In the United States, problems have arisen as to the "authority competent to solemnise the marriage". States normally require that a religious minister of the relevant religion solemnise a religious marriage. Some statutes attempt to define what is meant by a religious leader or minister, but where this is done, a broad definition is the norm. For instance, the Wisconsin statute[33] provides that,

"unless the context clearly indicates otherwise, 'clergyman' in this chapter means spiritual adviser of any religion, whether he is termed priest, rabbi, minister of the gospel, pastor, reverend or any other official designation."

The freedom of denominations to solemnise marriages when every member of that denomination is regarded as a Minister, has been challenged. However, in *State ex rel Hayes v. O'Brien*[34] it was held

---

[30] See Pearl, *Textbook on Muslim Law* (1987), p.42.
[31] See *Dicey and Morris on the Conflict of Laws* (12th ed., 1993), p. 643. Such marriages are not regarded as contrary to public policy, as "the method of giving consent, as distinct from the fact of consent, is essentially a matter for the *lex loci celebrationis'* and does not raise a question of capacity . . . or essential validity". *Apt v. Apt* [1948] P. 83, C.A. See also *Luder v. Luder* [1963] 4. F.L.R. 292 and "In the Marriage of Barriga" (No.2) (1981) F.L.C. paras. 91–088.
[32] General Assembly Resolution 2018 (XX) of November 1, 1965.
[33] Wis. Stat. Ann. para. 765.002 (Supp 1984).
[34] 160 Ohio St. 170, 114 NE 2d 729 (1953).

that a member of the Jehovah's Witnesses could perform marriages since all members of the sect were designated as ministers. More recently, though, members of the Universal Life Church who, under the rules of that sect may become ministers for life merely by asking to be ordained, and without any qualifications, were held not to be eligible to perform marriages under a statute which required proof that ordinands were in regular communication with their religious society.[35] The opinion in this case indicated that this denomination has over one million ordained persons for only 9,000 churches.[36] However, in some States, special statutes have been passed to deal with those religious denominations which do not have an identifiable religious leader within the community. Thus, for instance, Colorado and Massachussets have specific statutes permitting the solemnisation of marriages between members of denominations which are known to have no ministers, such as the Quakers or the Ethical Culture Society.[37]

Registered Buildings

In England, the requirement that non–Anglican, Quaker or Jewish marriages take place within a registered building or approved premises[37a] is a matter of contention for many minority religious groups. In 1991, 306,576 people got married in England; 155,423, over 50 per cent, marrying in a religious ceremony.[38]

---

[35] See also *State v. Lynch* 301 NC 479, 272 S.E. 2d 349 (1980) *Cramer v. Commonwealth* 214 Va. 561, 202 S.E. 2d 911 (1974) cert denied 419 US 875, 95 S.Ct. 137, 42 L. ed. [2d 114 (1974)].

[36] See also *Ravenal v. Ravenal* 72 Misc. 2d 100, 338 NYS 2d 324 (1974) *Paramore v. Brown* 84 Nev. 725, 448 P 2d 699 (1968).

[37] *e.g.* Colorado (Colo. Rev. Stat. para. 14–2–109 (1984) Mass. Gen. L. Ann., Chap. 207, para. 38 (Supp. 1984).

[37a] See s.2b(i)(bb) Marriage Act 1949 as amended by the Marriage Act 1994.

[38] The other 151,333 married in a civil ceremony at a registry office. See *Marriage and Divorce Statistics OCPS 1991* HMSO (1993). The numbers marrying religiously rather than civilly are noticeably higher in the lower age groups. Only when the parties are over the age of 30 does the civil rate of marriage outweigh the religious. This might be accounted for by the number of second marriages in this group who are not able to remarry religiously. The figures for all marriages have dropped over the last two years from a total of 346,697 in 1989 of whom 180,046 married in a religious ceremony.

Of those who married in a religious ceremony, 102,840 were
Church of England or Wales, and 19,551 were Roman Catholics. A
further 31,069 belonged to Christian congregations of various
denominations.[39] 969 Jews also married under religious auspices,
but only 994 people belonging to "other bodies" married in a
religious ceremony.[40] The "other bodies" include Muslims, Hindus and Sikhs. While there were 15,064 Methodist marriages for a
population of approximately 466,000 Methodists, there were fewer
than nine hundred Muslim marriages[41] for a population of nearly a
million.

This anomalous statistic may be attributable to the requirement
that the building in which a marriage takes place must be registered
or approved. The Marriage Act 1949 provides for registration of a
building which has been certified as a place for religious worship,[42]
under the Places of Worship Registration Act 1855. This has been
interpreted as excluding a building used by the Scientologists, as
Scientology is not recognised as a religion under this Act.[43] While
there is no reason why Mosques, Hindu and Buddhist[44] Temples
and Sikh Gudawaras should not be certified as registered buildings,
in fact, few are. Only 74 mosques were registered for marriages in
1991,[45] although there are 452 mosques certified as places of
worship,[46] as against 952 Exclusive Brethren buildings,

---

[39] This consisted of 15,063 Methodists, 829 Congregationalists, 3,275 Baptists, 404
    Calvanistic Methodists, 5,901 United Reformed Church and 5,597 other Chris-
    tian bodies. This latter category includes such groups as the Salvation Army,
    Society of Friends, Unitarians, Plymouth Brethren and Jehovah's Witnesses all of
    whom have buildings registered for marriages. See OCPS statistics ibid.
[40] The figures in 1989 reveal a drop in 1991 marriages for all groups except Jews and
    "other bodies", both of which showed an increase.
[41] The statistics do not breakdown "other bodies" into the different religious deno-
    minations, and it is not possible, therefore, to discover how many of the 867 mar-
    riages were Muslim.
[42] s.41(1) Marriage Act 1949, unless it is a Roman Catholic Chapel. See Marriage
    Acts Amendment Act 1958 s.1(1).
[43] See ex p. Segerdal [1970] 2 Q.B. 697. See also Re South Place Ethical Society [1980] 1
    W.L.R. 1565.
[44] Lord Denning stated in Segerdal (ibid.) that Buddhist temples are properly des-
    cribed as places of meeting for religious worship, despite the fact that mainstream
    Buddhists do not apparently revere a deity.
[45] As compared to 61 in 1989. See Marriage and Divorce Statistics OCPS (1991) (1993)
    HMSO.
[46] Even this number is low, as there are estimated to be nearer 1,000 mosques.
    However, some may be just a room in a house and is not a building as such. Only
    452 are certified as places of worship.

3,697 Roman Catholic buildings, 879 Jehovah's witness buildings and 152 Sikh buildings.[47]

It has been suggested[48] that one of the reason why there are so few non-Christian buildings registered is that the building has to be shown to be a place of public religious worship.[49] This phrase has never been defined, but it was held in *Church of Jesus Christ and the Latter Day Saints v. Henning*[50] that public religious worship connoted corporate worship and that the place of worship had to be "open to all properly disposed persons who wish to be present". It is not enough for the place to be public, as opposed to private, in the minds of those worshipping. Specifically, the phrase was said not to encompass a Mormon temple where worshippers could only be present if they had a "recommend" from their Bishop. In *Broxtowe Borough Council v. Birch*[51] the *Henning* principle was extended to include buildings which, although open to all, had no "open invitation or notification of permission to attend services". The invitation test was held, in this case, to exclude a meeting hall owned by the Exclusive Brethren, which had nothing about it, by way of architectural design or notice, to indicate that it was a place of worship open to the public; this, despite the fact that members of the public were not, in fact, formally excluded.[52]

It is unlikely that these are the sole reasons for the low number of minority religious buildings that are registered. It may be partly

---

[47] Up from 745 in 1989. Only an extra 22 mosques were certified during this period, compared to an extra 403 Roman Catholic buildings, 203 Exclusive Brethren buildings, 155 Jehovah's Witness buildings and 51 Sikh buildings. Marriages according to the usages of Jews or the Society of Friends do not have to be solemnised in a registered building.

[48] Bradney, "How Not to Marry People: Formalities of the Marriage Ceremony" [1989] Fam. Law. 408.

[49] At one time the building had also to be a "separate" building used specifically for religious worship. This caused difficulties in registration when the place of worship was also used as a community centre or school or general meeting place, a regular occurrence with minority religious groups, such as Muslims, Hindus and Sikhs. This requirement was done away with by the Marriage (Registration of Buildings) Act 1990. However, there is still a noticeable difference between the number of buildings certified as a place of worship by minority religious groups, and the number of buildings registered for marriage by those groups. See *Marriage and Divorce Statistics* OCPS (1991) tables 3.11 (a) and (b), *ibid.*

[50] (Valuation Officer) [1964] A.C. 420.

[51] [1983] 1 W.L.R. 314.

[52] For a good discussion of this issue see Bradney, "How Not to Marry People: Formalities of the Marriage Ceremony" [1989] Fam. Law 408. There are, however, 952 Brethren buildings certified as places of worship.

due to lack of knowledge that the Marriage (Registration of Buildings) Act 1990 now allows buildings to be registered even if they are used for purposes other than religious worship. Previously, the fact that a mosque was used as a community centre or a school as well as a place of worship, would have prevented registration as it was not a "separate" building for religious worship. However, the lack of registration of buildings is more likely to be a product of earlier non-recognition of potentially polygamous marriages in England. Thus, Muslim and Hindu couples have become accustomed to marrying first in a civil ceremony, to ensure compliance with civil marriage laws, and then attending at the mosque or temple, for a traditional, religious wedding.[53] The OCPS statistics do not indicate how many couples marry in two ceremonies, a civil ceremony followed by a religious wedding and thus, to an extent, give a misleading picture of minority religious marriages. If a couple marry in a civil ceremony first, this is the only ceremony of marriage recorded for that couple, thus there is no knowledge of the real level of celebration of religious marriages amongst "other bodies".[54] It is, however, likely to be very much greater than that indicated by the statistics.

Minority religious groups in England have complained of discrimination in relation to the formality and solemnisation requirements placed on them, and those placed on the adherents of the Church of England, the Quakers and the Jews, arguing that if these groups are free to follow their own traditions and usages, that other religions should have the same privilege. The Law Commission[55]

---

[53] There are elements of traditional Muslim marriages, such as proxy marriage, which would amount to an invalid marriage ceremony in England. However, once there has been a civil ceremony of marriage, the religious ceremony can be as traditional as required, as it does not have the legal effect of marrying the couple. Another possible reason for the low rate of Muslim marriages is that Muslims are deliberately circumventing marriage laws and are marrying according to Muslim custom with no registration of marriage. There is however no evidence to this effect.

[54] The non-recording is due to the fact that the marriage in the religious building will not need to be registered, the couple having already married under a civil ceremony. This miscounting of figures can also be applied to Anglican marriages where one of the parties is divorced. Many are not able to marry in the Anglican church, and marry first in a civil ceremony, and then receive a blessing in church. This is bolstered by the fact that older people are more likely to marry in civil ceremony, but are also more likely to have been divorced.

[55] *Report on Solemnisation of Marriage* (1973) Law Com. No. 53, para. 16.

in their Report on the Solemnisation of Marriage, took the view that it would be impossible to adequately reform the present system unless uniform civil preliminaries were made compulsory in the case of all marriages, and unless the civil preliminaries were themselves reformed. This is far from being a novel or revolutionary suggestion. When the Marriage Bill was introduced in 1836 it in fact provided for civil preliminaries to all marriages. The clause which required this in the case of Church of England marriages was removed during the course of the Bill's passage so that the major reforms contained in the Bill could be assured of swift enactment. But the government of the day expressed the view then, that it would be necessary on a future occasion to carry the whole of the original plan into effect.

The recommendations of the Law Commission have never been the subject of legislation, although the government has subsequently reviewed possible procedural changes to civil marriages and religious marriages outside the Church of England in a discussion paper on Registration in 1988,[56] and a subsequent White Paper, Registration: Proposals for Change in 1990.[57] The Green Paper accepted that the government had no plan to review fundamental marriage law or make any proposals concerning the Established Church, nor did it touch on the issue of civil preliminaries.[58] The purpose of the review was a desire on the part of the government to simplify procedures and to allow the public a greater degree of choice. It also reflected a concern that couples only enter into marriages which are valid in law and are recorded accurately. Proposals made to facilitate the registration of buildings have been brought into effect, but no action has been taken on the other recommendations contained in either of the papers.[59]

---

[56] *Registration: a Modern Service*, Cm. 531 (1988).

[57] Cm. 939 (1990). A number of the proposals made in the Green and White Papers reflected the recommendations of the Law Commission made in 1973 in their report on Solemnisation of Marriage.

[58] This was a matter which had been considered by the Working Party established by the Standing Committee of the General Synod of the Church of England, *An Honourable Estate* (1988).

[59] Proposals made to facilitate the registration of buildings were put into effect by the Registration of Buildings (Public Worship) Act 1990. Changes have been made under the Marriage Act 1994 allowing civil marriages to take place in "approved" premises as well as registry offices.

Substantive Requirements

Apart from procedural preliminaries and solemnisation, all of
which relate to the actual marriage service, both the United States
and England impose certain substantive requirements for a marriage to be valid.

PARTIES TO A MARRIAGE MUST BE MAN AND WOMAN

In England, it has been held that marriage can only take place
between a man and a woman, and not between two parties of the
same gender. Gender is assigned at birth and, at present, a transsexual (a person who, during his or her lifetime, changes gender), is
still to be regarded as retaining the gender he or she was born
with.[60] While the American courts have been willing to recognise
transsexual marriage, such flexibility has not been extended to marriages between two persons of the same gender.[61] Not all the
American states explicitly prohibit such marriages,[62] but when the
validity of same gender marriages has been tested before the courts,
recognition of their validity has been denied and the marriages
declared void.[63] Chief Judge Hill in *Adams v. Howerton*[64] found
that:

> "the definition of marriage, the rights and responsibilities implicit in that
> relationship, and the protections and preferences afforded to marriage,

---

[60] See *Corbett v. Corbett* [1970] 2 W.L.R. 1306, [1970] 2 All ER 33. The U.K.'s refusal to recognise transsexual marriage has been upheld by the European Court of
Human Rights in *Cossey v. U.K.* [1991] 2 FLR 492 and was not regarded as a violation of the European Convention of Human Rights.

[61] In *MT v. JT* 140 N.J. Super 77, 355 A 2d 204 (1976) the court was willing to recognise the gender reassignment of the wife. Although she had been born a male,
the court was willing for the purposes of the hearing to treat her as a female.
Weyrauch and Katz in their book *American Family Law in Transition* (1983), suggest that this case can be distinguished on its particular facts. The husband in this
case paid for the "wife's" operation to remove male genitalia and the construction
of female genitalia, and was, in effect, estopped from later denying the validity of
the marriage. Such a result may not occur again.

[62] Although an increasing number are explicitly barring same gender marriages to
avoid confusion.

[63] See Rivera, "Our Straight-Laced Judges: The Legal Position of Homosexual Persons in the United States" 30 Hastings L.J. 799.

[64] 486 F. Supp. 1119 (C.D. Cal. 1980).

are now governed by the civil law. The English civil law took its attitudes and basic principles from Canon law, which, in early times, was administered in the ecclesiastical courts. Canon law, in both Judaism and Christianity could not possibly sanction any marriage between persons of the same sex because of the vehement condemnation in the scriptures of both religions of all homosexual relationships. Thus there has been for centuries a combination of scriptural and canonical teaching under which a 'marriage' between persons of the same sex was unthinkable and, by definition, impossible."

Added to this, the societal view of marriage has resulted in a strong federal policy against marriages between persons of the same gender. But not all religious groups take the same view. A few, recognising that societal attitudes towards homosexuals have changed, marry such couples. Although validly married according to religious law, it is unlikely that such marriages will be accorded recognition in any of the American States.[65]

In 1984 the Unitarian Universalist Association General Assembly, the governing body of the Unitarian Church in America affirmed the growing practice of some of its ministers of conducting services of union of gay and lesbian couples and urged member societies "to support their ministers in this important aspect of our movement's ministry to the gay and lesbian community". A claim has been made that such marriages should be granted recognition on the basis of the right to free exercise of religion. However, such an argument is extremely unlikely to be successful. In *Jones v. Hallahan*,[66] in upholding a decision of the lower court in which two women were refused a licence to marry each other, the court invoked the authority of the Supreme Court in *Reynolds v. U.S.*[67] This case made clear that the claim of religious freedom could not be extended to make the professed doctrines of a particular religious group superior to the law of the land, and in effect to permit every citizen to become a law unto himself. Marriage was to be treated as the union of one man and one woman and could not be extended to marriages between two persons of the same gender.

---

[65] Although no State as yet, to the authors knowledge allows same gender marriage (except in the case of transsexuals), Denmark and Sweden recognise registered partnerships between two people of the same gender, which are, in essence, marriages. These partnerships while conferring some of the benefits of marriages do not confer all.

[66] 501 S.W. 2d 388 (Ky. 1973).

[67] 98 U.S. (8 Otto) 145 (1878).

AGE OF MARRIAGE

The age at which parties may marry has been the subject of legislation in both England and the United States. In fixing a minimum
age of marriage, the interests of the State differ from traditional
religious views, which were initially common to all the major
world religions. For the mediaeval church, the main function of
marriage was to remedy and avert loose living and concupis-
cence.[68] This view, a dislike of extra-marital sexual relations, and a
belief that once puberty has been reached, marriage is appropriate,
was, and to some extent still is, reflected in other religious traditions, such as Islam, Judaism and Hinduism.[69] The encouragement of early marriage is reflected in the common law, which
treated children as being capable of rationally consenting to marriage at the age of seven, although the marriage remained voidable
so long as either of the parties was below the age at which it could
be consummated.[70] A canonical presumption taken over later by
the common law fixed the age at which consummation could take
place (in effect the age of puberty) at 14 for boys and 12 for girls,
but this was rebuttable on the facts in any given case.[71]

Modern justifications for establishing a minimum age of marriage address rather different concerns. In both England and the
United States it is accepted that marriages entered into at a young
age, during the teenage years, are statistically far more likely to end

---

[68] See Exhortation at the beginning of the marriage service in the *Prayer Book* of
   1662 and the omission proposed in 1928 (Cambridge University Press) pp.298,
   303.
[69] While such an approach was traditionally taken by these religions, not all necessarily encourage such an approach today; *e.g.* Judaism encouraged marriage once
   the age of puberty was reached, but even in Israel the minimum age of marriage is
   17. The Roman Catholic church sets the age of marriage at 16 for boys and 14 for
   girls, but accepts that these age limits are subject to the civil law regulations of the
   country in which the person is living. Islamic law sets the age of capacity as the
   age of puberty. The presumption is that puberty is reached at 15, but evidence can
   be produced that puberty has been reached earlier than this. Minimum ages
   appear to be 12 in the case of males and 9 in the case of females. See Pearl, *A Textbook on Muslim Personal Law* (1987), p. 42.
[70] In other words during the time before the boy reached 14 or the girl reached 12,
   the marriage could be annulled.
[71] In such cases, when consummation took place, the marriage was treated for all
   purposes as a valid marriage.

in divorce than marriages contracted at a more mature age.[72] There are, however, other reasons, some national, some international, for restricting the age at which parties can marry. On a national level, the need to educate children to participate in the modern, technological State, has meant that the time-span of "childhood" and economic dependence has been extended, certainly up until the end of the period of compulsory schooling. Early marriage and childbirth would interfere with this necessary educational process. A further justification was provided by Pearce J. in *Pugh v. Pugh*[73]:

> "The 'mischief and defect for which the common law did not provide' was, according to modern thought, that it is socially and morally wrong that persons of an age at which we now believe them to be immature and provide for their education should have the stresses, responsibilities and sexual freedom of marriage and the physical strain of childbirth."

On both the national and international level, an imposed minimum age has also been seen as effective in reducing the birth rate which, while not a great point of issue currently in England and the United States, is still relevant in the developing world. Such a restriction also has the side effect of reducing the physical stress on women of a long period of child-bearing, and thus improving their general health.

Internationally, there is a perceived need for a minimum age of marriage to prevent trafficking in children, normally for the purposes of prostitution, to prevent the exploitation of young girls, and thus protect them and promote their welfare. Attempts to establish an international standard minimum age of marriage began with the Declaration on the Elimination of Discrimination against Women Article 6(3),[74] which provided that;

> "Child marriage and the betrothal of young girls before puberty shall be

---

[72] See, *e.g.* Schoen, "California Divorce Rates by Age at First Marriage and Duration of First Marriage" (1975) 37 J. of Marriage and the Family 548.

[73] [1951] P. 482, [1951] 2 All E.R. 680.

[74] Proclaimed by General Assembly resolution 2263 (XXII) of November 7, 1967. It is worth remembering that Declarations are regarded as setting a standard to which all countries should seek to aspire.

prohibited, and effective action, including legislation, shall be taken to specify a minimum age for marriage . . . "[75]

The Convention on Elimination of Discrimination against Women,[76] opened for signature some 13 years after the Declaration makes the dislike of early marriages even clearer by declaring in Article 16(2) that:

"The betrothal and marriage of a child shall have no legal effect, and all necessary action, including legislation, shall be taken to specify a minimum age for marriage . . . "

Neither the Declaration nor the Convention define the word "child". While the Declaration envisages the age of puberty being the minimum age, this was considered unsatisfactory. In 1965 the United Nations issued a Recommendation on Consent to Marriage, Minimum Age for Marriage and Registration of Marriage[77] in which it recommended that:

"Member States shall take legislative action to specify a minimum age for marriage, which in any case shall not be less than fifteen years of age; no marriage shall be legally entered into by any person under this age, except where a competent authority has granted a dispensation as to age, for serious reasons, in the interests of the intended spouses."

This recommendation was reinforced once more in the Convention on Consent to Marriage, Minimum Age for Marriage and Registration of Marriages[78] which exhorts States yet again to take legislative action to specify a minimum age for marriage.[79]

The minimum age of marriage in England was raised in 1929 from the old common law ages of 14 for boys and 12 for girls, to 16

---

[75] The Reporter's Notes to s.102 of the 1968 Revisions of the American Institutes Restatement of Foreign Relations Law recalls a memorandum of the Office of Legal Affairs of the UN Secretariat: "in view of the greater solemnity and significance of a 'Declaration' it may be considered to impart, on behalf of the organ adopting it, a strong expectation that members of the international community will abide by it." Consequently, insofar as the expectation is gradually justified by State practice a Declaration may, by custom, become recognised as laying down rules binding upon states.

[76] Adopted and opened for signature, ratification and accession by General Assembly Resolution 34/180 of December 18, 1979.

[77] General Assembly Resolution 2018 (XX) of November 1, 1965. Principle II.

[78] Opened for signature and ratification by General Assembly Resolution 1763A (XVII) of November 7, 1962.

[79] In Art. 2.

for both.[80] Interestingly, one of the principal reasons for raising the minimum age was Britain's desire to assist the League of Nations in raising the minimum age overseas, to prevent trafficking in children.[81] The House of Lords Select Committee[82] reported:

> "It may be difficult to prove that, in Great Britain, the disparity between the legal age of marriage and the facts of national life impede the progress of morality. But there is evidence that it does impair the influence of Great Britain in co-operating in the work of the League of Nations for the protection and welfare of children and young people and does prejudice the nation's effort to grapple with the social problems arising from the early age at which marriages are contracted in India."[83]

Any marriage that takes place in England where either of the parties are under the age of 16 will be void, regardless of the circumstances.[84] Where either party to a marriage is between the age of 16 and 18, the under-age party needs the consent of any person with parental responsibility for them. If a parental responsibility holder refuses to grant such consent, the child may seek the consent of the court instead. Failure to obtain such consent renders the marriage voidable rather than void.[85]

The majority of States in the United States have statutes setting the age at which parties may get married without parental consent, at 18. A marriage celebrated under this age is not, however, necessarily invalid. Many States also allow marriage under the age of 18 if parents consent, and provided that the child is above the minimum age.[86] In the event that parents refuse their consent,

---

[80] Age of Marriage Act 1929 s.1 now re-enacted in the Marriage Act 1949 s.2.

[81] See Cretney, *Principles of Family Law* (4th ed., 1984), p.56.

[82] 74 H.L. Official Report (5th Series) Col 259.

[83] There has been legislation since 1929 imposing a minimum age of marriage in the Indian Subcontinent. In India the minimum age is now 21 for a male and 18 for a female; Child Marriage Restraint (Amendment) Act 1978, and 16 for a girl and 18 for a boy in Pakistan and Bangladesh; Muslim Family Laws Ordinance (1961) s.12.

[84] Matrimonial Causes Act 1973 s.11(a)(ii).

[85] See Marriage Act 1949, s.3.

[86] It is not always clear what the minimum age is. In these instances, common law must be assumed to apply: 14 for boys and 12 for girls. Theoretically, there could be marriage of children so young that the marriage should have no effect for any purpose. (*i.e.* it should be void.) In fact, such marriages are so rare as not to be a factor in legislative regulation. Sanctions preventing such marriages are in any event provided by the delinquency and contributory delinquency statutes. See Clark, *The Law of Domestic Relations in the United States* (2nd ed., 1988), Chap. 2:10.

some statutes give minors the right to seek the consent of the court instead. If parties to the marriage are under 18 and did not obtain parental consent, the marriage is more likely to be treated as voidable than void.[87] This is partly due to the fact that many statutes do not specifically provide that such marriages are invalid, and partly to the reluctance of the courts to treat a marriage as void without a clear statutory mandate.[88] If a marriage is initially defective, due to the fact that one or both of the parties were under age at the time it was contracted, it becomes wholly valid if there is cohabitation beyond the age of consent.[89] Some non-age statutes expressly enact this rule, but it is followed whether expressed in the statute or not, and whether the statute makes such marriages voidable or wholly void. It is recognised that this practice is inconsistent with the characterisation of non-age marriages as void, but is very much in line with common law tradition.[90]

(i) Where one or both of the parties is domiciled in England or the United States.[91]

If a party domiciled in England or the United States[92] marries in a religious ceremony in another country or state, the question of the validity of the marriage in the home state arises, particularly where one of the parties to the marriage is under the minimum age of capacity set by the home state. Where one of the parties was domiciled in England at the time of the marriage, the marriage will be invalid if either of the parties was under the age of 16, even if the State, the *lex loci celebrationis*, in which the marriage took place,

---

[87] In a number of States, marriages may be validly contracted by children under the minimum age set by statute if the girl is pregnant and the court agrees.

[88] For further discussion of the validity of non-age marriages, see Clark, *The Law of Domestic Relations in the United States* (2nd ed., 1988), Chap. 2:10.

[89] *i.e.* for most States, at 18.

[90] The old common law view was that marriages of children over the age of 7 could be confirmed by cohabitation after the age of puberty. See, *e.g. Kibler v. Kibler* 180 Ark. 1152, 24 S.W.2d 867 (1930), *Jones v. Jones* 200 Ga. 571, 37 S.E. 2d 669 (1955), *Powell v. Powell* 97 N.H. 301, 86 A 2d 331 (1952), *Jimenez v. Jimenez* 93 N.J. Eq. 257, 116 A. 788 (1922). Annot. 159 A.L.R. 104 (1945).

[91] The reference to the United States only applies to those States which have a minimum age of capacity statute: approximately 40 States.

[92] U.S. citizens are recognised as being domiciled in one particular State, rather than in the U.S. itself. For the purposes of this book, and to make the text flow more easily, the convenient short-hand term of referring to persons as being domiciled in the U.S. is employed. For the actual domicile of a U.S. citizen, readers are asked to refer to the cases.

recognises the marriage as valid. The extension of authority to cover foreign domiciliaries as well as English domiciliaries who marry abroad, was justified in *Pugh v. Pugh* by Pearce J.:[93]

"It must be remembered that personal status and capacity to marry are considered to be the concern of the country of domicil. It is right and reasonable that the country of domicil should . . . from time to time vary and affect the personal status of its subjects and their capacity to marry as changing religious, moral and social conditions may demand. . . .

Child marriages, by common consent, are believed to be bad for the participants and bad for the institution of marriage. Acts making carnal knowledge of young girls an offence are an indication of modern views on this subject. The remedy 'the Parliament has resolved' for this mischief and defect is to make marriages void where either of the parties is under sixteen years of age. To curtail the general words of the Act so that a person can evade its provisions by merely going abroad, entering into a marriage where one of the parties is under sixteen in some country . . . where Canon law still prevails,[94] and then returning to live in this country after the marriage seems to me to be encouraging rather than suppressing 'subtle inventions and evasions for the continuance of mischief' . . . In my view, by the Age of Marriage Act 1929 it [*Parliament*] deliberately legislated on a matter that is its own particular concern, namely, the personal status of His Majesty's subjects and their capacity to contract marriage. This Act was intended . . . to affect that capacity in all persons domiciled in the United Kingdom wherever the marriage might be celebrated."

Most American States take a rather different attitude, recognising as valid an under-age marriage contracted in a different State, unless the home State has a statute which expressly declares that under-age marriage by a domiciliary is void, even though celebrated in a place that would permit the marriage. Occasionally, such as in the case of *Wilkins v. Zelichowski*[95] there is an echo of the view expressed in *Pugh*, and a reluctance to allow the evasion of well-considered social policy by recognising an out of State under-age marriage. However, on the whole, under-age marriage is not seen as a pressing problem. The National Conference of Commissioners on Uniform State Laws at one time promulgated the Uniform Mar-

---

[93] [1951] P. 482, [1951] 2 All E.R. 680.
[94] *i.e.* the minimum age of marriage is less than 16.
[95] 26 N.J. 370, 140 A 2d 65 (1958).

riage Evasion Act, which was designed to prohibit marriage outside the State where this was primarily to avoid marriage restrictions in the home State, but interest in adopting this statute was
sparse, and the statute was eventually withdrawn.

(ii) Where neither party is domiciled in England or the United States. If
neither party to a marriage is domiciled in England at the time of
marriage, but one of the parties is under the age of 16 when the
marriage is celebrated, such a marriage will be regarded as valid in
English law if the marriage is valid under the *lex loci domicilii* of each
party (and perhaps also under the *loci celebrationis*). The relaxation
of the stringent requirements on age was explained by the English
High Court by Pearce J. in *Pugh v. Pugh*[96]:

> "I see no reason to put on the words [*i.e. the requirement that both parties
> must be at least 16 years old*] any other limitation than the obvious one that
> they are not intended to apply to marriages abroad of persons who are
> not domiciled here and are not the concern of or subject to the laws of
> Parliament."

The recognition of such marriages has been challenged, however,
where the marriage conflicts with cultural notions of childhood.
The most notorious English case is that of *Alhaji Mohamed v.
Knott.*[97] The 25 year old husband married his 13 year old bride in a
Muslim ceremony in Nigeria where both were domiciled. The ceremony was recognised as a valid form of marriage. After the ceremony, both came to live in England while the husband completed
his studies. While the marriage was undeniably a valid marriage
according to the *lex loci celebrationis*, the court was asked to determine whether, given her age, the wife was in need of care, protection or control under the then current legislation.[98] The
magistrates, before whom the case was initially heard, found that
the wife was exposed to moral danger, and was in need of care and
control:

> "Here is a girl aged thirteen or possibly less, unable to speak English,
> living in London with a man twice her age to whom she has been mar-
> ried by Moslem law. He admits having sexual intercourse with her at a
> time when according to the medical evidence the development of

[96] [1951] P. 482, [1951] 2 All E.R. 680.
[97] [1969] 1 Q.B. 1 [1968] 2 All E.R. 563.
[98] s.2 Children and Young Persons Act 1963.

puberty had certainly not begun. He intends to resume intercourse with her as soon as he is satisfied that she is adequately protected by contraceptives from the risk of pregnancy. He admits that before the marriage he had intercourse with a woman by whom he has three illegitimate children. He further admits that, since the marriage, . . . he has had sexual relations with a prostitute in Nigeria from whom he has contracted venereal disease. In our opinion a continuance of such an association notwithstanding the marriage, would be repugnant to any decent minded English man or woman. Our decision reflects that repugnance."

On Appeal, Lord Parker C.J. found that the justices had misdirected themselves. They had only considered the view of an Englishman or woman in relation to an English girl and a western way of life. What was necessary was to look at the upbringing and way of life that the wife had experienced within her Moslem culture, in which it was quite acceptable to marry at that age. It could only be said that she was in moral danger if one was considering somebody brought up in, and living, an English way of life. While it is an offence to have sexual intercourse with a girl under 16,[99] this was not applicable in a case of this nature where the parties were married. The wife could not be said to be exposed to moral danger just because she was carrying out her wifely duties. In justifying this decision Lord Parker found that it was natural for a Nigerian girl to marry at that age, and also expressed the opinion that Nigerian girls develop sooner, and that there is nothing abhorrent in their eyes in a 13 year old girl marrying a 25 year old man.

Both this case and the case of *Pugh* raise the difficult question of whether it is right for a State to tolerate under-age marriage, even though acceptable to, and performed under the auspices of, the parties religion, when it is considered highly undesirable for their own citizens. It is difficult to balance opposing needs. On the one hand there is a need to tolerate religious practices, while on the other there is a need to bear in mind international regulation[1] and the need to offer protection to young, and often very vulnerable and socially isolated, girls. Jaffey[2] suggests that English law was wrong

---

[99] Sexual Offences Act 1956, s.6(1).
[1] The UN Recommendation on Consent to Marriage, Minimum Age for Marriage and Registration of Marriage, passed by the General Assembly. G.A.Res. 2018 (XX) of November 1, 1965. Principle II sets 15 as the minimum age of marriage.
[2] Jaffey, "The Essential Validity of Marriage in the English Conflict of Laws" (1978) 41 M.L.R. 38.

in *Pugh*. He postulates that the purposes of a rule, prescribing a minimum age for marriage are, first, to protect an immature person from the hazards of a premature marriage and, secondly, in the public interest, to prevent marriages which are likely to be unstable. As regards the first purpose, it can hardly be the purpose of English law to protect a foreign domiciliary, whose own law does not regard him as needing such protection. As for the purpose of preventing marriages which are likely to be unstable, English law should not be concerned unless England is the matrimonial home. Jaffey follows Lord Parker's view that children may develop socially, emotionally and even physically, at different rates in different environments. It is, therefore, sensible for English law to rely on the judgment of the law of the country in which a party is domiciled for the decision whether he or she is mature enough to marry. While this is certainly the view taken by the court in *Mohamed v. Knott*, it does not take into account current thinking on the undesirability of early marriages. Lord Parker's view that children in cultures permitting early marriage mature earlier, is not borne out by the evidence in *Mohamed v. Knott*. The magistrates commented specifically that the wife had not reached the age of puberty at 13 when she was married. There is little evidence to show that girls from Muslim countries reach menarche at an earlier stage than girls in the west. Indeed, due to poor nutrition, they may well reach puberty rather later than their well fed western counterparts. As for the view that one should rely on the judgment of the law of the country to which the person belongs for the decision on whether she is mature enough to marry, this takes no account of the international view that marriage below the age of 15 should be forbidden. Given that the United Nations did not view earlier marriage as sensible for any girl, and indeed regarded it as harmful, one cannot necessarily impute "sense" to those countries and cultures which permit marriage earlier. England certainly has the power and the duty to ward any child who arrives in the country if there is a need to protect them, and ought to consider very carefully both their national and international legal obligation to protect children.[3]

---

[3] Recommendations and Declarations are standard setters only, and therefore, not binding. However, Declarations may be seen as expressing customary law, see n. 75. The U.K. is also a signatory to the UN Convention on the Rights of the Child and has ratified the Convention.

PROHIBITED DEGREES

Prohibition of incestuous marriages and marriages between close relatives are to be found in both State laws[4] and religious laws, although the definition of prohibited relationships differ. All agree that marriages between a man and his mother and immediate female ascendants, or his daughter and female descendants, or between brother and sister is prohibited, and will be void both in England[5] and the United States.[6] The extent of prohibition of marriage based on consanguinity[7] and affinity[8] rules varies between different religious groups.

One notable area of difficulty is the recognition of marriages which take place abroad between foreign domiciliaries, which are valid by the parties' religious law, but invalid according to American and English legislation.[9] The question for the courts in England is whether such marriages, although technically valid in England, can be tolerated, or are quite simply, too offensive. The issue has arisen particularly in relation to marriage between an uncle and a niece. Such a marriage falls under the prohibited degrees in

---

[4] State prohibition was originally based on religious requirements contained in the biblical book of Leviticus, although the extent of the prohibition has been somewhat reduced.

[5] The list of prohibited degrees of relationship are contained in the Marriage Act 1949, First schedule, as amended by the Children Act 1975 and the Marriage (Prohibited Degrees of Relationship) Act 1986. The Matrimonial Causes Act 1973 s.11(a)(i) states that any marriage which is not a valid marriage under the Marriage Act 1949 will be void. Such marriages have also been described as "contrary to religion, morality, or to any of its fundamental institutions". *Brook v. Brook* (1861) 9 HLC 193, 212. The invalidity of such marriages extends to marriages within the prohibited degrees celebrated abroad by British domiciliaries, even if valid by the *lex loci celebrationis*; *Re De Wilton* [1900] 2 Ch. 46; 108 L.J. Ch. 717; 83 L.T.70; 11 Digest 416.

[6] All States in the U.S., except Alabama, have a statute prohibiting such marriages, which will be void. See Clark, *The Law of Domestic Relations* (2nd ed., 1988), para.2.9, pp. 83–85, and *Catalano v. Catalano* 170 A.2d 726 (Conn.) 1961. For further information see Bratt, "Incest Statutes and the Fundamental Right of Marriage: Is Oedipus Free to Marry" (1984) 18 Fam. L.Q. 257.

[7] *i.e.* blood relations. 30 States in the U.S. ban marriage between first cousins, whereas England permits such marriages.

[8] A relationship through marriage. 15 States continue to forbid marriage between persons related by marriage. There is no absolute prohibition against affinity marriages in England. See Marriage (Prohibited Degrees of Relationship) Act 1986 s.1(1); Marriage Act 1949 s.78 (as amended) and 1986 Act s.1(3),(4); Marriage Act 1949 s.1(4),(5) and Sched. 1, Pt. III (as amended).

[9] The general rule is that a marriage celebrated abroad is valid if each party has the capacity to marry the other by the law of his or her antenuptial domicile.

England and some of the States in the United States, but is a valid marriage under, for example, Jewish law. Interestingly, the relevant Rhode Island statute excepts Jews from the prohibition against uncle-niece marriages on the ground that such marriages are permitted by the religious traditions of that group.

In *Cheni v. Cheni*[10] the parties, who were uncle and niece, had contracted a valid marriage in Egypt in 1924, according to Jewish rites. The parties later settled in England. In 1961 the wife filed a petition seeking a declaration that the marriage was null and void on the ground of consanguinity. Counsel for the wife accepted that the marriage was valid by the law of the parties' domicile, by which capacity to marry is to be tested.[11] But, it was argued that there was an exception to this "dual domicile" rule, where the marriage was regarded as incestuous by the general consent of all Christendom. Counsel preferred the term "the general consent of civilised nations or by English public policy", rather than the general consent of Christendom, possibly because, in fact, the marriage was not invalid in all Christian countries, but was invalid under Islamic and Hindu law. Counsel for the husband pointed out that it was not an offence for an uncle to have sexual intercourse with his niece[12] and it would be strange if public policy demanded the rejection of marriages constituted by a relationship of which the criminal law took no notice. Sir Jocelyn Simon P. pointed out that the exception as to marriages incestuous by the general consent of Christendom, had never been applied to invalidate a marriage good by the law of its domicil, and that, in his opinion, the exception did not represent the law. Expressing irritation with the notion of the general consent of "Christendom" or "civilised nations" rather than the principles of private international law, he held:

> "Whatever test is adopted, the marriage in the present case was, in my judgment, valid. I do not consider that a marriage which may be the subject of papal dispensation and will then be acknowledged as valid by

---

[10] [1965] P. 85, [1962] 3 All E.R. 873, [1963] 2 W.L.R. 17.

[11] This capacity rule is clearly illustrated in *Sottomayor v. De Barros* (No.1)(1877) 3 P.D.1. The parties, who were first cousins and both Portuguese subjects and Portuguese domiciliaries married in England. After the marriage, the parties lived together in England for six years. Although marriage between first cousins was valid in England, it was not under Portuguese law. Because the parties were at the time both Portuguese domiciliaries, the failure to fulfil the capacity requirements of their domiciles resulted in the marriage being void.

[12] Under the Sexual Offences Act 1956.

all Roman Catholics, and without any such qualification is acceptable to Lutherans, can reasonably be said to be contrary to the general consent of Christendom . . . If the general consent of civilised nations were to be the test, I do not think that the matter can be resolved by, so to speak, taking a card vote of the United Nations and disregarding the views of the many civilised countries by whose laws these marriages are permissible. As counsel for the husband observed, Egypt, where these people lived and where the marriage took place, is itself a civilised country. If public policy were the test, it seems to me that the arguments of the husband, founded on such inferences as one can draw from the scope of the English criminal law, prevail. Moreover, they weigh with me when I come to apply what I believe to be the true test namely whether the marriage is so offensive to the conscience of the English court that it should refuse to recognise and give effect to the proper foreign law. In deciding that question the court will seek to exercise common sense, good manners and a reasonable tolerance. In my view, it would be altogether too queasy a judicial conscience which would recoil from a marriage acceptable to many people of deep religious convictions, lofty ethical standards and high civilisation. Nor do I think, that I am bound to consider such marriages merely as a generality. On the contrary, I must have regard to this particular marriage, which has stood, valid by the religious law of the parties' common faith and by the municipal law of their common domicil unquestioned for thirty-five years . . . In my judgment, injustice would be perpetrated and conscience would be affronted if the English court were not to recognise and give effect to the law of the domicil in the present case."[13]

In reaching his decision, Sir Jocelyn Simon P. focussed on the notion of tolerance. In balancing what could be regarded as competing religious claims, he found that this was not a marriage which broke through the limits of tolerance as defined by the court. There was no reason for not respecting the religious law or municipal law of the parties' domicile, even if the marriage would not be acceptable to the Established Church in England or valid if celebrated in England.

The United States has taken the same view. The Second Restatement of Conflict of Laws[14] provides that the validity of marriage is to be determined by the law of the State which has the most signifi-

---

[13] The petition to have the marriage declared null and void was rejected. The decision would, of course, have been quite different if the parties had been domiciled in England at the time of the marriage.

[14] Restatement (Second) of Conflict of Laws s.283 (1971).

cant relationship to the spouses and the marriage. It further provides that a marriage valid by the law of the place in which it was contracted will be valid elsewhere, unless it violates the strong public policy of another state which has the most significant relationship to the spouses and the marriage.

POLYGAMOUS MARRIAGES

In both England and the United States marriage is still defined as a monogamous union between one man and one woman,[15] although both jurisdictions are now willing to recognise polygamous marriages contracted by non-domiciliaries abroad.[16] Recognition of the validity of these polygamous marriages was slow to develop, even though polygamy[17] was recognised by other major world religions as acceptable under certain circumstances and conditions. Judaism,[18] Islam, Buddhism and Hinduism[19] have all allowed polygamy in the past, and most Islamic countries continue to do so.[20] Polygamy is also a well-recognised custom in large parts

---

[15] All States in the U.S. have legislation which restricts the number of spouses a person may marry at any time. Any attempt to marry a second spouse while still married to the first will result in the marriage being void and a possible charge of bigamy. Matrimonial Causes Act 1973, s.11(b) provides that for England and Wales a marriage will be void if, at the time of the marriage, either party was already lawfully married.

[16] Provided that these meet the requirements for validity of the *lex loci celebrationis* and the parties domiciliary law. It should be remembered that:
   (a) a marriage celebrated in a form that is monogamous under the law of the place of celebration is a monogamous marriage, whatever the personal law of the parties at the time of marriage.
   (b) A marriage celebrated in a form which is polygamous under the law of the place of celebration is a polygamous marriage whatever the personal law of the parties at the time of the marriage.
   See *Dicey and Morris on the Conflict of Laws* (12th ed., 1993), r. 71, p. 678.

[17] The general term polygamy is used, though in fact, polygyny, the marriage of a man to more than one woman is the more accurate term. Polyandry, the marriage of a woman to more than one man is rare. The term polygamy is more commonly used and covers both situations.

[18] An edict by Rabbi Gershom Ben Juda in the eleventh century ended polygamy amongst European Jews although it continued amongst Sephardic Jews for rather longer.

[19] The majority of Hindus reside in India, and are now covered by the Hindu Marriage Act which made all Hindu marriages in India monogamous from 1955.

[20] The practice of polygamy has, however, been restricted in a number of Islamic countries, including Turkey, Morocco, Iraq, Pakistan and Singapore.

of Africa and South-East Asia. Neither England nor the United States, however, allow polygamous marriages to be contracted within the jurisdiction, regardless of the religious beliefs and practices of the intended spouses.

The nineteenth century courts of both England and the United States expressed a very clear dislike of polygamy. This expression was most intense in relation to cases involving Mormons in the United States. The Mormons, a break-away Christian sect founded by Brigham Young in the nineteenth century, regarded polygamy as an essential part of their religious practices, a practice totally unacceptable to the United States Supreme Court;

> "Polygamy has always been odious among the northern and western nations of Europe and, until the establishment of the Mormon Church, was almost exclusively a feature of the life of Asiatic and of African people. At common law the second marriage was always void (2 Kent Com. 70) and from the earliest history of England polygamy has been treated as an offence against society."[21]

Other cases heard at the latter end of the nineteenth century indicate that the dislike of polygamy in the United States was based on its perceived affront to Christianity and to Christian social organisation.[22] Mr Justice Field revealed such an attitude quite clearly in the American case of *Davis v. Beason*.[23]

> "Bigamy and polygamy are crimes by the laws of all civilized and Christian countries . . . They tend to destroy the purity of the marriage relation, to disturb the peace of families, to degrade women and to debase man. Few crimes are more pernicious to the best interest of society and receive more general or more deserved punishment. To extend exemption from punishment for such crimes would be to shock the moral judgment of the community. To call their advocacy a tenet of religion is to offend the common sense of mankind."

---

[21] *Reynolds v. U.S.* 98 U.S. (8 Otto) 145 at p. 164. (1878) See also *Potter v. Murray City* 585 F.Supp. 1126. (D. Utah 1984).
[22] Although, interestingly, it would appear that monogamy was established in western Europe even before the advent of Christianity, see Stone (1961) 24 M.L.R. 501.
[23] 133 U.S. 333, 10 S. Ct. 299, 33 L. Ed. 637 (1890).

His view was mirrored in England by Lord Penzance in his judgment in *Hyde v. Hyde*[24];

> "We have in England no law framed on the scale of polygamy, or adjusted to its requirements. And it may well be doubted whether it would become the tribunals of this country to enforce the duties (even if we knew them) which belong to a system so utterly at variance with the Christian conception of marriage, and so revolting to the ideas we entertain of the social position to be accorded to the weaker sex."

In America, the Mormons, in raising a defence to charges of bigamy arising from marrying more than one wife, or resisting charges of breaches of the Mann Act[25] or challenging restrictions on voting rights, pleaded the First Amendment right allowing free exercise of religion by all, and preventing the establishment of any religion. The courts, in disallowing such defences and justifying the imposition of laws forbidding polygamy, drew a distinction between the freedom to profess a religious belief and the freedom to carry out religious practices. Chief Justice Waite found in the case of *Reynolds v. U.S.*[26] that:

> "Laws are made for the government of actions, and while they cannot interfere with mere religious belief and opinions, they may with practice. Suppose one believed that human sacrifices were a necessary part of religious worship, would it be seriously contended that the civil government under which he lived could not interfere to prevent a sacrifice? Or if a wife religiously believed it was her duty to burn herself upon the funeral pile of her dead husband, would it be beyond the power of the civil government to prevent her carrying her belief into practice? So here, as a law of the organization of society under the exclusive dominion of the United States, it is provided that plural marriages shall not be allowed. Can a man excuse his practices to the contrary because of his religious belief? To permit this would be to make the professed doctrines of religious belief superior to the law of the land, and in effect to permit every citizen to become a law unto himself. Government could exist only in name under such circumstances."

---

[24] (1866) LR 1 P & D 130.

[25] See *Cleveland v. U.S.* 329 U.S. 14 (1946). The Mormons in this case were found guilty of violating the Mann Act in that they had taken women across State lines for the purpose of making them plural wives, which amounted to transportation for "any other immoral purpose" and was a breach of the Act.

[26] 98 U.S. (8 Otto) 145 (1878). Reynolds was charged with bigamy after following the Mormon practice of marrying more than one wife.

The Supreme Court in *Davis v. Beason*[27] agreed:

"With man's relation to his Maker and the obligations he may think they impose, and the manner in which an expression shall be made by him of his belief on those subjects, no interference can be permitted, provided always the laws of society, designed to secure its peace and prosperity, and the morals of its people, are not interfered with. However free the exercise of religion may be, it must be subordinate to the criminal laws of the country, passed with reference to actions regarded by general consent as properly the subject of punitive legislation . . . Probably never before in the history of this country has it been seriously contended that the whole punitive power of the government, for acts recognized by the general consent of the Christian world in modern times as proper matters for prohibitory legislation, must be suspended in order that the tenets of a religious sect encouraging crime may be carried out without hindrance."

Until after the Second World War, the English courts would not recognise either an actually polygamous marriage (where the husband had married more than one wife) nor a potentially polygamous marriage (one where it was possible to take more than one wife, but in fact no second wife had been married at the time of the case). Wives of such marriages were not able to seek any form of matrimonial relief from the English courts.[28]

After the Second World War, however, with an increasing number of immigrants arriving from countries where polygamy was an accepted way of life, the refusal of any remedies to such wives was seen to operate extremely harshly. In *Srini Vasan v. Srini Vasan*[29] the court, in recognising an earlier Hindu marriage in India as a valid marriage, notwithstanding its potentially polygamous character, and granting the petitioner a declaration that her later marriage to the respondent was null and void held that:

---

[27] 133 U.S. 637, 10 S. Ct. 299, 33 L. Ed. 637 (1890). The statutes of Idaho forbade polygamists or bigamists to vote. Davis was charged with conspiracy to unlawfully pervert and obstruct the due administration of the laws in the Territory in that he sought to unlawfully register himself as a voter, when he was forbidden to do so because he was a member of the Mormon Church which supported polygamy.

[28] See *Re Bethell* (1888) 38 Ch. D. 220 and *Re Naguib* [1917] 1 K.B. 359. *Re Bethell* is, however, an unsatisfactory case and it is not entirely clear what constituted the *ratio decedendi*. For a greater discussion of polygamous marriages see Poulter, *English Law and Ethnic Minority Customs*, Chap. 3. and Bromley's *Family Law* (8th ed., 1991), Chap. 2.

[29] [1946] p. 67.

"To deny recognition of a Hindu marriage for the purpose in hand,
would, in my opinion, be to fly in the face of common sense, good manners and the ordered system of tolerance on which the Empire is based;
and, as I decide, to deny such recognition would be bad law."

The last 50 years has seen an increasing liberalisation in the law
relating to polygamy and also an increased tolerance towards non-
Christian cultural traditions. English law now recognises both
potentially polygamous and actually polygamous marriages contracted by foreign domiciliaries abroad, and is willing to grant
matrimonial relief or a declaration concerning the validity of the
marriage notwithstanding that it is polygamous.[30] However, a
polygamous marriage contracted in England or contracted abroad
by a person domiciled in England is still void.[31]

In the United States, there has again been a willingness to recognise a potentially polygamous marriage[32] as valid, and even an
actually polygamous marriage. In *Re Dalip Singh Bir's Estate*, the
Californian court, in resolving how to distribute the deceased's
estate, decided that the deceased Hindu's two wives should share
the estate equally. For this purpose the court were willing to recognise the polygamous marriage, finding that such a decision did not
breach California's public policy. However, the Court went on to
say that the State's policy would be violated if a polygamist tried to
bring several of his wives into the State, and attempted to cohabit

---

[30] Initially under the Matrimonial Proceedings (Polygamous Marriages) Act 1972,
repealed and re-enacted in Matrimonial Causes Act 1973 s.47.

[31] See *Hussain v. Hussain* [1983] Fam. Law 26; [1982] 1 All E.R. 369. The husband,
domiciled in England, went through a potentially polygamous marriage ceremony in Pakistan. The marriage was regarded as monogamous by the English
courts, because a Muslim man domiciled in England has no capacity to take a
second wife by reason of s.11(b) Matrimonial Causes Act 1973, and a wife cannot
take a second husband under Muslim law. There was, therefore, no possibility of
the marriage ever being polygamous. Possible reform of this aspect of the law
was considered by the English Law Commission in Law Com. W.P. No 83 and
Law Com. Report No. 146 (1985). The Law Commission recommended that the
Matrimonial Causes Act 1973 s.11(d) should be amended so as to prohibit only
actual polygamous marriages. Thus a potentially polygamous marriage would be
treated as valid, but any subsequent marriage would be treated as void. This
would extend the judgment of *Hussain* to cover instances where the wife rather
than the husband is domiciled in England. See Poulter, *English Law and Ethnic
Minority Customs*, Chap. 3.14.

[32] *Royal v. Cudahy Packing Co.* 195 Iowa 759, 190 N.W. 429 (1922).

with them, in which case the marriages would not be regarded as valid.[33]

While the attitude of both the United States and the English legal systems might be said to have grown more tolerant towards recognition of polygamy, neither are prepared to countenance such practices among their domiciliaries, even where this is an accepted practice for the particular religious groups to which the party belongs. Both the United States and England are majority Christian countries, but they both contain, particularly England, sizeable minorities to whom polygamy is a socially and religiously acceptable practice. A nineteenth century argument that polygamy is an anathema and offensive to Christian concepts of marriage, is not sufficient, in the face of human rights instruments, to deny these religious groups the right to live according to their religious beliefs. The Universal Declaration on Human Rights,[34] the European Convention on Human Rights[35] and the International Covenant on Civil and Political Rights[36] all provide for the right of freedom of religion and the right to manifest religion in practice. Each allow the State to restrict religious freedom, but only to the extent that such limitations are prescribed by law and are necessary in a democratic society in the interests of public safety, for the protection of public order, health or morals, or for the protection of the rights and freedoms of others.[37]

Can a restriction on the religious practice of polygamy be justified under these limitations? Such a restriction might open the western State to an allegation that a refusal to recognise polygamy as an acceptable form of family unit is based on racial discrimination. After all, as was pointed out in *Reynolds*,[38] most of those who practice polygamy come from the Middle-East, Africa and

---

[33] Such a decision would operate very harshly against a second or subsequent wife, and might result in her suffering grave economic and social hardship. She would presumably have no remedy against her "husband" if the marriage were declared void.

[34] Art. 18.

[35] Art. 9.

[36] Art. 18. Both the U.K. and the U.S. are signatories to this Covenant, although the U.S. has entered numerous reservations.

[37] See Art. 18(3) International Covenant on Civil and Political Rights, Art. 1(3) of the Declaration on the Elimination of all forms of Intolerance and of Discrimination based on Religion or Belief.

[38] 98 U.S. (8 Otto)145 (1878).

South East Asia. The Proclamation of Teheran[39] reinforced the
need for every nation to grant freedom of religion, and provided
that all ideologies based on racial superiority and intolerance should
be condemned and resisted. If England and the United States are to
counteract possible allegations of racial discrimination, a positive
reason, justifying a restriction on polygamy must be shown. This
could be done on two grounds. Western, Christian societies could
argue that a ban on polygamous marriages is necessary for the protection of morals within their societies. It can clearly be argued that
such marriages are alien to British or American social policy, but
are they immoral? The American judge in the nineteenth century
case of *Davis v. Beason*[40] quite clearly saw this as one reason for
holding such marriages invalid and liable to the criminal charge of
bigamy. It is, however, extremely difficult to show that such a ban
is necessary for the protection of morals today when both countries
allow what is termed "serial monogamy"; marrying a second or
subsequent spouse after divorcing the previous spouse. There is
also no restriction on polygamous cohabitation in either country,
even though it is known that this takes place.

There is, though, a much more serious argument for limiting
polygamy, which is that such a practice effects the rights of others,
in this case women.

The International Covenant on Civil and Political Rights, article
23(4) provides that States Parties shall take appropriate steps to
ensure equality of rights and responsibilities of spouses as to marriage. But, more important in this area, is the Convention on the
Elimination of All Forms of Discrimination against Women; article
15 requires that States Parties shall accord women equality with
men before the law, while article 16 provides that States Parties
shall take all appropriate measures to eliminate discrimination
against women in all matters relating to marriage and family relations and, in particular, shall ensure, on a basis of equality of men
and women, "the same right to enter into marriage."[40a]

It is difficult to see how polygamy would fit into this Convention. Even if the wife agrees to the husband taking a second wife,
this does not amount to equality of rights in entering into marriage.
The husband is able to take more than one wife, but the wife is not

---

[39] Proclaimed by the International Conference on Human Rights at Teheran on May
    31, 1968.
[40] 113 U.S. 637 (1889). See also p. 69.
[40a] The U.K. is a contracting party to this Convention.

entitled to take more than one husband. The standard set by this Convention[41] can be used to show that permitting polygamous marriages to take place within the jurisdiction of either country would effect the rights of women to equality with men. In this regard, it is extremely likely that both the United Kingdom and the United States would be justified in prohibiting polygamy within their jurisdiction. It would, however, be difficult to justify refusing to recognise polygamous marriages entered into by foreign domiciliaries which take place abroad. To do so might be to deny vulnerable wives economic and social protection. England has remedied its early refusal to provide relief to polygamous marriages of this nature. However, it is not at all clear whether the United States give full recognition to such polygamous marriages.[42]

Consent to Marriage

Apart from compliance with substantive requirements and formalities laid down in statutes, the consent of both parties has always been necessary for a valid marriage in both England and the United States. It is also recognised as a requisite for a valid marriage in international human rights instruments. The Covenant on Political and Civil Rights, for example, provides that no marriage shall be entered into without the free and full consent of the intending spouses.[43]

It is quite common in England and the United States for parties to a marriage to agree that they will marry twice; first in a civil ceremony, followed shortly afterwards by a religious ceremony of marriage. It can be inferred from the OCPS statistics[44] that most Sikhs, Moslem and Hindu marriages follow this pattern. There

---

[41] To which both the U.K. and the U.S. are signatories.

[42] For an interesting note on attempts to reform polygamy laws, see Anderson, "Presidential Address" (1969), Vol. X. Journal of the SPTL, pp. 249–251. Attempts to change laws permitting polygamy in Ghana in the early 1960s were socially unacceptable within Ghana as providing too little protection for "second" wives.

[43] Both the U.K. and the U.S. are signatories to this Convention. The requirement of free and full consent by the parties is also contained in the Convention on Consent to Marriage, Minimum Age for Marriage and Registration of Marriage and the Recommendation on Consent to Marriage, Minimum Age for Marriage and Registration of Marriage General Assembly Resolution 2018 (XX) of November 1, 1965.

[44] See p. 47–48.

may be pressing reasons why a civil marriage, which is quick to arrange, should take place before the religious marriage. These range from immigration restrictions[45] to advantages in gaining a mortgage or a business arrangement.[46] Alternatively, there may be concern about the official validity of a religious ceremony, or, in England, there may not be a convenient registered building or an authorised person to conduct the marriage.

Once a civil ceremony of marriage takes place, the couple are, in the eyes of the State, validly married. Such a marriage may not, however, be regarded as valid by certain religious authorities, which require that a marriage be performed according to religious rites. Further, many religious couples do not regard themselves as truly married until after the religious marriage, and, indeed, do not cohabit or consummate the marriage until the religious marriage ceremony has been performed. When a second marriage does not take place, the question may arise as to the effect of the first, civil marriage. First, does the civil marriage demonstrate full and free consent to the marriage, or is consent conditional upon the second ceremony and, second, where the second wedding does not take place is consent to be regarded as incomplete.

Where one of the parties refuses to go through a religious wedding ceremony after the civil marriage has taken place, both spouses may be left in a state of limbo. They are married in the eyes of the State, but not in the eyes of their religious community. Most will not have consummated the marriage and are not likely to do so. Indeed, they may never have spent any time with their spouse since the wedding day. The response of the courts, when presented with a petition for a decree of nullity[47] in this situation has varied. The English courts have commonly ignored the issue of consent and granted a decree of nullity on the basis that the respondent spouse has wilfully refused to consummate the marriage.[48] Courts in the United States on the other hand, have preferred to find a breach of the contract of

---

[45] See *Jodla v. Jodla* [1960] 1 All ER 625, [1960] 1 W.L.R. 236. [H.C.]

[46] *Kelly v. Kelly* (1933) 148 L.T. 143. (High Court).

[47] The cases that are reported are those where a decree of nullity is sought rather than a divorce. This is partly due to the age of the cases, most reports are from a time when there were restrictive divorce laws in both England and the United States, and nullity was an obvious course of action. But others, particularly the Roman Catholics, did not wish to have the stigma of divorce against them when there had never been a "marriage" in the full sense of the word.

[48] Matrimonial Causes Act 1973 s.12(b).

marriage, which invalidates consent, on the ground of fraudulent misrepresentation, at least where there has been an explicit agreement that a religious ceremony will occur.[49] In all instances, however, the courts are sensitive to the public policy issues that arise when parties wish to dissolve marriages which are perfectly valid in the eyes of the State, although not in the eyes of the parties or their religious authorities.

There is some indication that the courts are willing to look at religious custom in deciding whether the parties intended to give full and free consent to marriage at the civil ceremony. In the English case of *Neuman v. Neuman (otherwise Greenberg)*[50] Lord Merrivale granted a decree of nullity in respect of a register office ceremony on the ground that, being orthodox Jews, neither party believed that the civil ceremony alone effected a valid marriage. Their common objective was to marry in accordance with Jewish law and not English law. In the slightly later case of *Kelly (otherwise Hyams) v. Kelly,*[51] heard again before Lord Merrivale P., the plaintiff wife, an orthodox Jew, sought to prove that she had believed that the civil marriage was merely a betrothal ceremony. To this end, she introduced evidence before the court that it was unusual for Jewish couples to marry by a civil ceremony in a registry office. The President took into account the alleged beliefs of the wife as to the nature of the ceremony, but was heavily influenced in reaching his decision to grant a decree of nullity by the fact that the parties had never cohabited, nor was the marriage consummated.[52]

> "That fact in this case, coupled with the facts of their Jewish origin and racial community, justify me in saying that the petitioner when she went through the form or ceremony was not aware that it was a ceremony which would make her and the respondent man and wife."

Later English cases appear to ignore the issue of full and free consent in the face of failure to arrange a second, religious ceremony.

---

[49] This agreement must have been reached before the civil marriage, but need not be in written form. It will, however, have to be proved, normally by oral evidence, although conduct, particularly non-consummation may be used as evidence of such an agreement.

[50] *The Times*, October 15, 1926.

[51] (1933) 148 L.T. 143, H.C.

[52] Evidence was given that the civil ceremony was intended to facilitate a business agreement by which the father of the bride would convey a shop to the couple, which he wished to do in the one common surname.

Instead, they have concentrated on the lack of consumption of the marriage, finding that refusal on the part of the respondent to arrange, or participate in, the agreed upon religious ceremony constitutes wilful refusal to consummate the marriage,[53] a ground on which a nullity decree may be granted.[54]

Cases in the United States have focussed almost exclusively on whether a refusal to arrange a religious marriage ceremony, in the face of an ante-nuptial agreement that such a ceremony would take place, constitutes a fraudulent misrepresentation, such that it vitiates the contract of marriage.[55] In the case of *Di Lorenzo*[56] the Court of Appeals found that:

> "the free and full consent, which is of the essence of all ordinary contracts, is expressly made by the statute necessary to the validity of the marriage contract. The minds of the parties must meet in one intention. It is a general rule that every misrepresentation of a material fact, made with the intention to induce another to enter into an agreement and without which he would not have done so, justifies the court in vacating the agreement. It is obvious that no one would obligate himself by a contract, if he knew that a material representation, entering into the reason for his consent, was untrue. There is no valid reason for excepting the marriage contract from this rule . . . If the plaintiff proves to the satisfaction of the court that, through misrepresentation of some fact, which was an essential element in the giving of his consent to the contract of marriage and which was of such a nature as to deceive an ordinarily prudent person, he has been victimized, the court is empowered to annul the marriage."

The willingness to annul is aided by the fact that in many cases and texts on voidable marriage, an unconsummated marriage is regarded as little more than an agreement to marry. Where effected with fraud, which would render a contract voidable, the marriage

---

[53] Matrimonial Causes Act s.12(b) provides that a marriage shall be voidable if it has not been consummated owing to the wilful refusal of the respondent to consummate it.

[54] See *Jodla v. Jodla* [1960] 1 All E.R. 625, [1960] 1 W.L.R. 236, H.C. and *Kaur v. Singh* [1972] 1 All E.R. 292, C.A. and *Mohd Tariq Malik v. Secretary of State for the Home Department.* [1981] Imm. A.R. 134. (Immigration Appeal Tribunal.)

[55] See *Aufiero v. Aufiero* 222 A.D. 479; 226 N.Y.S. 611, Supreme Court of New York, Appellate division (1928) and *Watkins v. Watkins* 197 A.D. 489; 189 N.Y.S. 860, Supreme Court of New York appellate division (1921). Ante-nuptial agreements to arrange a religious marriage after the civil ceremony may be oral or written.

[56] 174 N.Y. 467 at 471, 472.

is voidable at the option of the injured party if it is promptly disaffirmed before any change of status has occurred.[57] Where the marriage has been consummated, a greater degree of fraud has to be shown, going to the essentials of the marriage but is not fatal to the obtaining of a decree of nullity. In *Bilowit v. Dolitsky*,[58] a New Jersey case, misrepresentation by the husband that he was an orthodox Jew was held to go to the essentials of marriage. The court reasoned that an orthodox Jewish woman could not properly perform her duties as a wife and mother, following the rules and teachings of her faith, without the support of a husband holding the same beliefs. The fraud was said to be "gross and far-reaching".

Poulter[59] asks the question whether the English courts, as a matter of policy, should uphold foreign customs and attitudes. He points out that the courts have increasingly pursued an enlightened and tolerant approach to foreign culture, recognising *talaq* divorces and instant consensual divorces, foreign marriages which are contrary to rules governing capacity, polygamy and the stigma of divorce in certain religious communities. Ought such tolerance to be extended to recognition of the incomplete nature of marriage where it has been agreed that a religious ceremony will take place after the civil ceremony? Early English case-law would not have supported such an approach. Lord Merrivale, while granting a decree of nullity in the *Kelly* case, expressed concerns about such annulments on public policy grounds:

> "In a country like ours, where the marriage status is of very great consequence and where the enforcement of marriage laws is a matter of great public concern, it would be intolerable if the marriage law could be played with by people who thought fit to go to a register office and subsequently, after some change of mind to affirm that it was not a marriage because they did not so regard it."[60]

---

[57] See *Akrep v. Akrep* 1 N.J. 268; 63 A.2d 253. Supreme Court of New Jersey. (1949). A similar argument was put forward in *Lorifice v. Lorifice* 148 N.Y.S. 2d 578, Supreme Court, Special Term. (1956) but was rejected.

[58] See *Bilowit*, falsely known as *Ann Dolitsky v. Michael Dolitsky* 124 N.J.. Super 101; 304 A.2d 774 (1973) Superior Court of New Jersey.

[59] Poulters, "Definition of Marriage in English Law" (1979) 42 M.L.R. 409.

[60] (1933) 148 L.T. 143. See also the American case of *Mirizio v. Mirizio* 242 N.Y. 74; 150 N.E. 605; 44 A.L.R. 714 (1926) Court of Appeals, where Chief Judge Hiscock found that private agreements between the parties which made consent at the time of the civil marriage, conditional, could lead to results which are unjust and unfortunate.

Although courts in the United States initially expressed similar public policy concerns, the courts were willing[61] on the basis of *Di Lorenzo*,[62] to find that there was no violation of public policy in granting a remedy where the marriage was unconsummated, and the respondent offered no defence. The existence of the concept of fraudulent misrepresentation gives the court much more flexibility in granting relief where there is a failure to go through the agreed-upon second, religious marriage. It recognizes the simple truth that the spouse seeking nullity would not have agreed to the civil ceremony unless a religious ceremony was to follow. Indeed, this approach has been extended to cases where a party promises to convert to the other spouse's religion after civil marriage and then go through a religious ceremony.[63] Where fraud such as to induce a party to the marriage is proved, consent initially freely and fully given is vitiated.

England, unfortunately, has not taken this path, preferring instead to grant a decree of nullity on the basis of wilful refusal to consummate the marriage.[64] Such an approach fails to recognise the religious values of a number of religious minorities, and the importance that is attached by these groups to the religious ceremony of marriage. It also pays scant heed to the issue of consent. Where parties have agreed that there will be a second, religious ceremony, and that only after this event will they cohabit, it is difficult to assert that their consent to the civil marriage is anything other than conditional upon the performance of the religious ceremony.

One could argue that the time has come for the English courts to recognize the validity of ante-nuptial agreements, either written or oral, which stipulate that a second, religious marriage will take place, and treat failure to organize such a ceremony as vitiating consent to the marriage. Public policy has little interest these days in upholding such "limping" marriages,[65] particularly where the parties have never cohabited or consummated the marriage. No legislative change would be required as section 12(c) of the Matrimonial

---

[61] See, *e.g. Watkins v. Watkins* 197 A.D. 489; 189 N.Y.S. 860 (1921) Supreme Court of New York.

[62] 174 N.Y. 467.

[63] See *Rutstein* 221 A.D. 70; 222 N.Y.S. 688 (1927) Supreme Court of New York.

[64] Under Matrimonial Causes Act 1973 s.12(b).

[65] In this case, marriages which are recognised as valid by the state, but as incomplete and invalid by at least one of the parties to the marriage, and his or her religious community.

Causes Act 1973 provides that a marriage "shall be voidable if either party did not validly consent to it, whether in consequence of duress, mistake, unsoundness of mind or otherwise." When a party enters a civil marriage believing that a religious ceremony will follow, and that the marriage will only then be a "full" marriage, failure of the other party to arrange or participate in such a ceremony should fall within the definition of "otherwise" in Section 12(c). These parties could undoubtedly, in time, obtain a divorce. However, where a marriage has never even started, the possibility of a nullity decree should be available. As the Law Commission pointed out in their Report on Nullity of Marriage[66] a decree of nullity recognises the existence of an impediment which prevents the marriage from becoming effective. This is a matter of essence to Roman Catholics who wish to contract a second marriage within the church, and also avoids the stigma of divorce, important to many minority religious groups.

Conclusion

In both England and the United States, Christian ideals and morals infused the common law and later legislation on marriage.[67] This fact has meant that establishment or non-establishment of a church has, in practice, made little difference to legislation on marriage in the two jurisdictions. The main effect of establishment in England is that those who chose to solemnise their marriage according to the rites of the Church of England do not need to fulfil civil preliminaries: a necessity for other forms of marriage. While a distinction, it is hard to argue that this discrimination causes undue hardship.[68]

The domestic laws of England comply with international Conventions, Declarations and Recommendations. A number of States in the United States do not, however, comply with the Recommendation on Consent to Marriage, Minimum Age of Marriage and Registration of Marriage.[69] Not all States have legislated to set

---

[66] 1970 Law Com. No 33.

[67] It is not being argued that other religious groups do not also hold these values and beliefs, but it is Christianity which has informed the common law.

[68] Marriages according to the usages of Jews or the Society of Friends do not have to be solemnised in a registered building.

[69] See n. 74. The U.S. is not a party to the Convention on Consent to Marriage, Minimum Age for Marriage and Registration of Marriage.

a minimum age of marriage of not less than 15 years of age. In reality, however, such marriages are extremely rare.

Parties may solemnise their marriages through a religious or a civil ceremony. However, domestic religious ceremonies are only valid in so far as they comply with legislation.[70] Marriage laws in both England and the United States reflect Christian ideals and traditions. Those parties whose religious traditions conflict with Christian traditions may find, not only that their marriages will not be recognised, but that they are liable to criminal prosecution. Thus, parties marrying in England or the United States must be above the minimum age set by legislation, regardless of religious tradition, must not be within the prohibited degrees, be of the same gender or already married. While, therefore, there appears to be religious freedom to celebrate marriages according to religious belief, in fact tolerance of different religious traditions is limited to those practices acceptable to a western, Christian State.

It is undoubtedly the case that the marriage laws of England and the United States limit the religious freedom of adherents of certain religious groups to marry according to their traditions and beliefs. This raises the question whether such restrictions on religious freedom are justifiable. While in early times the justification for refusing to recognise religious marriages which conflicted with English and American common law and legislation on marriage, was that it would be offensive to the Christian world,[71] later refusals are based on the need to preserve equality amongst men and women, and the need to recognise fundamental and essential rules of social organisation within the United States and the United Kingdom. In this they are largely supported by international human rights instruments. It can be argued that such restrictions are, therefore, justified, and that tolerance does not necessarily require recognition of all religious practices. It may be concluded that States, such as England and the United States are entitled to reject the right of some religious groups to marry according to their religious beliefs, customs and traditions where such traditions are seen as causing harm or

---

[70] Marriage laws also effect the validity of marriages celebrated abroad by English or US domiciliaries. See pp. 39–42.

[71] Even the U.S. with its First Amendment prohibition of establishment of religion and constitutional free exercise of religion refused to acknowledge polygamous marriages as valid on the basis that they were an affront to Christian nations. See *Davis v. Beason* 133 U.S. 333, 10 S. Ct. 299, 33 L. Ed. 637 (1890).

inequality, provided that the State does not restrict the right of one religious group to marry and found a family any more than another, and this does not breach international instruments governing marriage.

Chapter Three

Divorce

"Between the reformation in the 1530's and the Divorce Act of 1857, the laws governing separation and divorce were those which had come down unaltered from the Middle Ages. This legal situation, which was unique in the non-Catholic Christian world may be described as Protestant reactionary. After 1604 it was virtually identical to the Catholic position."[1]

Divorce laws in both England and the United States developed as the bonds between Church and State weakened. The jurisdiction of ecclesiastical authorities over family matters, particularly in England, was gradually taken over by the State. There were a number of reasons for the loss of church authority, but amongst them was the inability of the majority Christian churches to respond to the growing demand for an easing of the restrictions on divorce and remarriage.

Most religions, and certainly all the major religions, seek to regulate family relationships, particularly marriage, divorce and remarriage. As in the case of marriage, religious divorce laws are not always compatible with State divorce laws. While it would appear that in both England and the United States parties are free to divorce and remarry according to their religious traditions, such divorces and remarriages are unlikely to be recognised by the law of the State. Without such recognition, the parties are still bound by State law, still obliged to obtain a civil divorce in order to contract a second, valid marriage, and are not able to regulate their lives solely in accordance with their religious beliefs and traditions.

---

[1] Stone, *Road to Divorce England in 1530–1987* (1990).

This chapter, will first examine the development of secular divorce laws, and the effect of establishment. Secondly, it will explore the extent to which religious divorces, obtained domestically or abroad, are recognised. The problem for England and the United States is, once more, what degree of recognition should be given to religious divorces which, by national standards, are discriminatory, usually against women. Both States must balance the requirements of their own, secular systems of divorce and the requirement of international instruments that men and women should have equal rights on dissolution of marriage,[2] with the need to ensure religious freedom for their residents.

Recognition of religious divorces depends largely on where and by whom they are obtained. However, the courts in both England and the United States have shown great reluctance to cede any of their authority over domestic divorces to religious courts.

Within the area of divorce there is a further dilemma for the courts. This dilemma is, essentially, the extent to which religious laws and traditions should be accommodated within the secular divorce system. Should the courts or the legislature seek to encourage, or indeed, enforce, compliance with appropriate religious divorce laws. While under State law, parties only need a civil divorce in order to remarry, under religious law, spouses may require a religious divorce. A failure to obtain one may mean that the religious spouse is not able to marry again within her community. Should the State be under a duty to ensure that, in granting a civil divorce, all barriers to remarriage have been removed? International instruments offer little help here. It is up to the State to decide whether religious freedom requires that positive aid should be lent by the secular law to enforce religious law, and thus enable spouses to follow their religious traditions.

Historical Development

At the time that the United States were being colonised by the British, both England and the fledgling states of America regarded

---

[2] See the covenanant on Civil and Political Rights, art. 23(4), and the convention on the Elimination of All Forms of Discrimination against Women, arts. 15 and 16.

marriage as an indissoluble union lasting for as long as the spouses remained alive. It was possible in certain circumstances to obtain what was in effect, a legal separation: divorce a *mensa et thoro*, but such a decree did not allow for the possibility of remarriage. The Anglican ecclesiastical courts, guided by ecclesiastical law, had exclusive jurisdiction in relation to marriage and its annulment. The civil courts had no jurisdiction at all, and there was no civil legislation of any form allowing the state to end a marriage.

During the seventeenth century a number of influential writers sought to convince the Church that their stand on indissolubility of marriage was both too harsh and not scripturally justified. However, such attempts were always strenuously resisted by the Church, which made no compromise towards those seeking the possibility of divorce and remarriage.[3] When divorce did become a legal reality in England and the United States, it was not through any change of policy on the part of the Anglican Church in England but through political action. The need for divorce in both jurisdictions was felt most keenly by those who had property which they wanted to pass on to a child of their own. Those men whose marriages had failed and had no children wanted the opportunity to produce an heir with a second wife. Those who had children, but knew that they were the children of another man, also sought the possibility of remarriage with a declaration that the children were not their legitimate heirs. The acceptance that such a need existed, and in some cases was justifiable, and the refusal of the Anglican church to accept anything other than the indissolubility of a valid marriage, resulted in the English Parliament itself being presented with, and granting, private Acts of Divorce.[4] Although the procedure was expensive and slow, it provided a possibility of divorce to the rich in England that otherwise did not exist until the Matrimonial Causes Act of 1857 removed the divorce jurisdiction from the hands of the ecclesiastical courts and gave it to the civil courts.

---

[3] For anti-divorce literature supporting the then status quo in the Church of England, see Dove, "Of Divorcement: A Sermon preached at St. Paul's Cross the 10 of May 1601" (London 1601), and Howson, *Uxore simissa propter fornicationem aliam non licet superinducere* (Oxford, 1602). Phillips points out in his book *Putting Asunder* (1988) that no bishop or incumbent of other high office in the Church of England in the first half of the 17th century supported the legalisation of divorce.

[4] Divorce by private Act of Parliament was hardly a panacea for those seeking divorce. Only 325 were granted during the whole period 1670–1857.

During the Colonial period in America, the South did not permit divorce,[5] but New England developed divorce laws in the seventeenth century.[6] To what extent this was an improvement on English legislative divorce is unclear; divorces were given on grounds such as bigamy, non-consummation or fraudulent contract, which would have been grounds for an annulment within the Church of England and would, if successful, have freed the spouses to marry again. Some States sought to develop a legislative divorce system of their own, but such developments were disapproved of by the English Privy Council who, in the 1770's disallowed legislative divorces in Pennsylvania, New Jersey and New Hampshire.[7]

After Independence, the States of the United States were free to develop their own divorce laws, without being restricted by the Anglican establishment.[8] In the South, development of divorce was extremely slow. Where divorce was permitted, it was once more through the development of legislative divorce. In the North, developments were far faster, and all the New England States had a divorce law before 1800, as did Pennsylvania, New York, New Jersey and Tennessee. However, judicial divorce only became the norm from about 1850 onwards as the numbers seeking divorce increased.

With the passing of the Matrimonial Causes Act 1857 in England, jurisdiction over matrimonial causes was transferred from the ecclesiastical courts to the civil courts. The grounds for divorce under the new Act were limited to those circumstances which had previously served as the basis for a legislative divorce. A husband could apply for divorce on the basis of his wife's adultery, but the wife could only apply on the ground of adultery aggravated by

---

[5] Indeed, South Carolina still had no divorce law by the end of the 19th century.
[6] New England was, in its colonial phase, Puritan. In other words the dominating religions were dissenting Protestant groups, rather than Anglican, and not so wedded to the theory of indissolubility of marriage.
[7] See, for more detail, L. M. Friedman, *A History of American Law* (1973).
[8] It is not at all clear that the New England colonies took a more liberal view of marriage breakdown. Adultery could attract capital punishment in the early 17th century and was not abolished as a punishment until the 1670s. For a much more detailed description of the American divorce laws see Phillips, *Putting Asunder* (1988), particularly Chap. 11.8.

some other conduct, such as desertion.[9] The loss of jurisdiction over family issues by the ecclesiastical courts was inevitable, and due to a range of factors. The refusal of the Anglican church to permit divorce was an attitude out of line with the accepted view of Parliament that divorce should be granted in certain instances. The nineteenth century was also a period of increased secularisation of society, and a time when the numbers belonging to religious minorities grew. Secular marriage had been introduced in 1836, and it was recognised that with a more religiously mixed population, one that included a sizeable minority of Catholics, dissenters and Jews, exclusive jurisdiction in the Church of England over family matters was unsatisfactory. Procedure in the ecclesiastical courts was also the subject of much unfavourable comment[10] and there was an acceptance that the time had come for reform of family jurisdiction.

While these views were given credence and reflected in the legislature, reforms to the divorce system were, nevertheless, the subject of dire warnings in both England and the United States in the nineteenth century; not only because such divorce went against Christian religious teaching, but also because divorce was seen as a social curse and a danger to society.[11] While it was possible after the passing of the Matrimonial Causes Act of 1857 for the Church of England to argue that the new secular law was only applying a possible interpretation of the scriptures,[12] such a claim became more difficult when the grounds of divorce were extended in England by the Matrimonial Causes Act of 1937.[13] After this Act the

---

[9] Other aggravating grounds were incestuous adultery, adultery coupled with cruelty, desertion for two years or upwards, or on the ground of sodomy or bestiality. The grounds on which husbands and wives were able to petition for divorce were not the same for men and women until 1923.

[10] These courts reached decisions purely on the basis of written testimony, and did not see or examine witnesses.

[11] The absence of an established church in the U.S. did not prevent opposition to any liberalisation of the divorce laws from virtually all Christian sects. For more detail see Phillips, *Putting Asunder* (1988), Chap. 11.9.

[12] See Phillips, App. A, para.14, SPCK 1966. *ibid.*

[13] This Act implemented the recommendations of the Report of the Royal Commission on Divorce, chaired by Lord Gorell (1912) Cd. 6478. When the Gorell Commission recommended the extension of the grounds of divorce, the Church of England were unequivocal in their opposition. In 1912 the Lower House of the Convocation of York resolved that "the law of the Church of England being what it is, namely, that marriage is indissoluble, we cannot give our support to increased facilities for divorce other than judicial separation". Two years later the

Church of England decided that, as a rule of discipline, a divorced person should not be permitted to remarry within the rites of the church.[14] In 1951 a further Royal Commission, the Morton Commission, again considered the law of divorce.[15] A memorandum submitted by the Church to the Royal Commission conceded that the existence of a plural society made it impossible for the commission to base its recommendations on Christian doctrine alone. Nonetheless, the Church opposed any extension of the divorce grounds to allow divorce by consent, as this would conflict with the essential Christian view that marriage was intended as a life-long union.[16]

While initially hostile to divorce, the Church of England has accepted its inevitability and has lately supported non-adversarial and no-fault divorce.[17] The change of attitude was heralded in the Archbishop of Canterbury's report, *Putting Asunder*,[18] in which the Archbishop's group made it clear that Church of England doctrine fully recognised that it was right and proper for the State "to make provision for divorce and remarriage"[19] and that "there is nothing to forbid the Church recognising fully the validity of a secular divorce law within the secular sphere". By reason of its legal establishment the group argued that the Church of England has a special interest in what happens to the secular matrimonial law and a

---

Lower House of Canterbury also affirmed its opposition to the majority report of the Gorell Commission.

[14] This rule still exists, but it is only a rule of discipline and not a rigid rule of prohibition. In some circumstances, clergy are willing to remarry divorcees in church.

[15] *Report of the Royal Commission on Marriage and Divorce* (Chairman: Lord Morton of Henryton) Cmnd.9678 (1956).

[16] In April, 1963 in the face of a Bill presented by Leo Abse M.P. which would have granted divorce after a period of separation, the Archbishop of Canterbury, the Archbishop of York and Wales, the Roman Catholic Archbishop of Birmingham and the Moderator and General Secretary of the Free Church Federal Council issued a joint statement opposing the provision for divorce after seven years separation on the ground that it would "introduce a dangerous new principle into our marriage laws".

[17] The Church of England Board for Social Responsibility in it's response to Law Commission Report, *Family Law, the Ground for Divorce* No. 192 (1990) thought the concept of divorce as a no-fault process over time was an attractive concept and worthy of further consideration. This approach to divorce reform was also supported by the Mothers' Union (Anglican), the National Board for Catholic Women and the Board of Deputies of British Jews.

[18] Report of a group appointed by the Archbishop of Canterbury. London SPCK (1966).

[19] *ibid.* at para. 14.

special duty to concern itself with that law's improvement. But in so doing, "the only Christian interests that need to be declared are the protection of the weak and the preservation and strengthening of those elements in the law which favour lasting marriage and stable family life".[20] Establishment appears to have had little discernible effect on modern divorce law, although it initially hindered the development of a divorce law in England. Christian churches in both jurisdictions were influential in the early stages of divorce law, and retain a degree of influence over contemplated changes. Divorce is, however, regarded by both jurisdictions as a matter for the secular law and is not seen as falling within the religious sphere.

The Church of England has now taken great steps to accommodate divorced members of the church, and does not impose any impediments to their full participation in the Church, even if they have remarried.[21] Other religions, however, have been unable to accommodate civil divorce in the same way. The Catholic church does not regard civilly divorced spouses as being divorced in Catholic ecclesiastical law, as marriage is indissoluble in Catholic doctrine.[22] Unlike the Church of England, the Catholic Church still requires those wishing to marry a second time to obtain a decree of nullity, in respect of the first marriage, from the Catholic ecclesiastical courts. Without such a decree a remarried divorcee may not be admitted to the Eucharist. Both Muslims[23] and Jews also require their adherents to obtain a religious decree of divorce before they can remarry in a religious ceremony. If a second marriage is to be recognised under Jewish law, the wife, if previously married in a

---

[20] The Archbishop's Report also influenced developments in the U.S. towards no-fault divorce in the late 1960s and 1970s. It is interesting to note that divorce reform also occurred in France and Germany at this time. See generally, Glendon, *State, Law and Family: Family Law in Transition in the United States and Western Europe*, (1977); Eekelaar and Katz, (eds.), *Marriage and Cohabitation in Contemporary Societies*, (1980).

[21] The Church is willing to bless a couple in church after their wedding, if it is a second marriage for one or both and the previous spouse is still alive. Some ministers are even willing to marry a divorced person in church in appropriate circumstances. The Church does not require a decree of nullity from the ecclesiastical courts before a couple may be blessed.

[22] It is possible to have the marriage annulled by the Catholic church on a number of grounds, including affinity, consanguinity or no true consent. Such an annulment allows the parties to marry again in the church.

[23] In the case of women, and, in Islamic jurisdictions where polygamy is not allowed, in the case of men as well.

Jewish ceremony, must obtain a *get*, while under Islamic law there must be a *talaq or khul*.

Recognition of Religious Divorces

While a couple may fulfil the requirements of their appropriate religious divorce law, and be granted a divorce, they may not fulfil the necessary conditions under civil law for the granting of a divorce. Such spouses, having obtained a religious divorce, may regard themselves as able to contract a valid second marriage. However, the State, in the absence of a civil divorce, will regard the parties as still legally married and a second marriage as bigamous. The religious law may regard the children of any second marriage after a religious divorce as legitimate, while the state will regard them as illegitimate. It is important to know what status the civil law gives to religious divorces, and to what extent they will be regarded as a valid and a legally recognisable method of dissolving a marriage. Uncertainty as to their effectiveness can cause problems relating to personal status, including inheritance and immigration.

DOMESTIC DIVORCES

The English courts have jurisdiction to grant a divorce if, and only if, either of the parties to the marriage, is domiciled in England on the date when proceedings begin, or was habitually resident in England for one year prior to the initiation of proceedings.[24] In the United States, nearly all States impose a residence requirement before the court has jurisdiction to grant a divorce.[25]

Where a party to a marriage seeks to divorce and contract a second valid marriage in either jurisdiction, the divorce must be a judicial divorce obtained under the secular divorce laws of the State. Without a judicial divorce, a second marriage[26] would raise

---

[24] See Domicile and Matrimonial Proceedings Act 1973 s.5(2). See also *Dicey and Morris on the Conflict of Laws*, (12th ed., 1993), r. 77, p. 712.

[25] Alaska and Washington appear not to have any durational residence requirement. See Clark, *The Law of Domestic Relations in the United States*, (2nd ed., 1988), Chap. 12.2.

[26] The term "second marriage" is used for convenience and to reduce confusion in the text. It is recognised that the same problems could apply with a third or subsequent marriage.

the possibility of being prosecuted for bigamy.[27] While Jews or Muslims or members of the Greek orthodox church may obtain a religious divorce under their relevant religious law, such a divorce will not be recognised by the State. Remarriage after a religious divorce alone will not be valid in either jurisdiction, even if the marriage is valid according to religious law.[28]

The non-recognition of extra-judicial religious divorces is a matter of concern to religious minorities,[29] particularly those who have come from countries where a pluralistic legal regime exists.[30] In many areas of the Middle East, Africa and Asia, personal law depends on traditional custom or the religious affiliation of the couple. Thus, for Muslims living within the country, the law relating to divorce is Islamic law, for Chinese residents, Chinese customary law, etc. When England was a colonial power it recognised the validity of this system of differing personal laws in some of its colonies, known as the Millet system, and left it in place. Accordingly, in the case of *Sasson v. Sasson*[31] a *get* obtained by a Jewish couple in Egypt was held to be a valid divorce. The couple, domiciled in Egypt, but British citizens, could not have obtained a divorce in England on the grounds put forward. However, they were able to obtain a Jewish divorce[32] under the law prevailing in Egypt at the time. The question arose as to whether the court should recognise the validity of the Jewish divorce given that the parties were British citizens. Ottoman Order in Council 1910[33] Article 90 provided that:

"subject to the provisions of this Order, the civil jurisdiction of every court shall, as far as circumstances admit, be exercised on the principles

---

[27] Under the Family Law Act 1986, s.44(1), no divorce or annulment shall be regarded as effective in any part of the U.K. unless granted by a court of civil jurisdiction. For an explanation of why American courts only recognise civil divorce and not religious divorce see *Falkoff v. Sugarmann* 26 Ohio N.P. (n.s.) 81 (1925). See also *Shikoh v. Murff* 257 F.2d 306 (2nd Cir. 1958).

[28] See In re *Spiegel* 24 F.2d 605 (S.D.N.Y. 1928) and *Petition of Horowitz* 48 F.2d 652 (E.D.N.Y. 1931).

[29] See Union of Muslim Organisations, *Why Family Law* (1983).

[30] Such a regime may be described as one in which a number of different legal systems operate. Which applies to a particular individual, depends on that person's religious or ethnic affiliation.

[31] [1924] A.C. 1007.

[32] A *get* or Jewish divorce is obtained on the basis of mutual consent.

[33] Ottoman Order in council 1910 Art. 55.2 gave jurisdiction to the Supreme Court of Alexandria as to all personal and proprietary rights of British subjects.

of, and in conformity with, English law for the time being in force. Pro-vided that in all matters relating to marriage, inheritance or other ques-tions involving religious law or custom, the court shall, in the case of persons belonging to non-Christian communities, recognise and apply the religious law or custom of the person concerned.''

Here, the court accepted that the proper and only court was that of the domicil, and that religious law applied to the couple whose Jewish divorce should be recognised as valid.

The Millet system is not, of course, without its problems, as shown by the many cases in India, the greatest user of the Millet system. In India, as in many countries, the Millet system gives little choice as to which personal law applies. By the secular law of the land if a person is born into a given religion, and has not undergone formal conversion to another religion before marriage, the law of that religion applies. Whether the couple wish to adhere to the par-ticular religion, or whether they are practising members of that religion is not relevant. Thus if two Hindus married, and the wife later converted to Islam and sought a divorce, the courts have held that the governing law should be Hindu law and not Islamic law.[34] In a country where the relevant divorce law depends on the religious affiliation of the couple, a religious divorce is sufficient and is recognised by the State.

Neither England nor the United States have any tradition of a pluralistic legal system, largely because at the time of the formation of the common law, very few religious minority groups existed in either country.[35] Further, when a divorce law was developed, in the face of religious opposition from the churches,[36] it was a secular law designed to be accessible to all within the jurisdiction, regard-less of their religious or ethnic origin. It is known, however, that Jews domiciled in England did divorce under their own system of

---

[34] See *Farooq Leivers v. Adelaide Bridget Mary* 1958 PLD (WP) Lah. 431 and *Syed Ali Nawaz Gardezi v. Lt. Col. Muhammed Yusif* 1963 PLD SC 51. See generally, Pearl, *A Textbook on Muslim Personal Law* (1987), Chap. 10. See also *Seth v. Seth* 694 S.W. 2d 459 (Tex. App. 1985) where the Texan court held that it would not rec-ognise a *talaq* after the husband converted to Islam.

[35] There was a community of Jews in England from the 11th Century, but they were expelled from England in 1290 and did not return until Charles II took the throne in the 17th century.

[36] Particularly the Church of England and the Catholic Church.

religious law before judicial divorce became available in England in
1857. It is debatable to what extent such divorces between couples
domiciled in England were regarded as valid under English law.
Breitowitz has suggested[37] that these divorces were accorded pre-
sumptive validity. It is difficult, however, to find any evidence of
this. The case of *Moss v. Smith*[38] is often cited as authority for this
proposition, but is unclear. The judge in the case, which was concerned with bailment of goods, found that no Jewish divorce could
be proved in the absence of the production of the written *get* itself.
However, Erskine J. did not go on to discuss whether the divorce
would have been treated as a legal divorce if the document had been
produced.

Even after the 1857 Act gave civil courts the power to grant divorces where adultery was proved,[39] Jewish couples still continued
to divorce by means of a *get*, which was absolutely necessary for
them if they were to remarry under Jewish law. The validity of
such divorces in English law was settled in 1866 when the Registrar–General decided that, as a matter of law, he could not recognise
a Jewish divorce as valid.[40] A similar restriction would apply to any
other divorce granted by a religious body within England.

In the United States, none of the States recognise the efficacy or
validity of a religious divorce obtained within the United States.[41]
To do so would conflict with the establishment clause of the First
Amendment, which requires a "wall of separation between Church

---

[37] Breitowitz, *Between Civil and Religious Law; The Plight of the Agunah in American
Society* (1993).

[38] 1 Man & G 228. See also *Har-Shefi v. Har-Shefi* [1953] All E.R. 783. The English
court was willing to grant recognition of a *get* written and delivered in London,
on the ground that the divorce was valid in Israel where the husband was, at all
times, domiciled.

[39] The court had jurisdiction only over those domiciled in England.

[40] See Poulter, *Ethnic Minorities and the Law* (1986) and Maidment, "The Legal Effect
of Religious Divorce" (1974) 37 M.L.R. 611 at 620. This does not mean that the
obtaining of a *get* is necessarily irrelevant in a case. It may be used to show that
there was agreement to desertion, or that the wife agreed to the husband's adultery or behaviour. See *Joseph v. Joseph* [1953] 1 W.L.R. 1182. Since the Registrar-
General's ruling it has become the practice of the Jewish authorities never to grant
a *get* unless and until the marriage has been dissolved by decree absolute from the
English courts.

[41] Although, like England, the U.S. may well recognise a religious divorce obtained
by foreign domiciliaries in the *lex domicilii*.

and State".[42] To allow religious bodies to establish the criteria for divorce would be to confer a benefit or impose a burden on a particular group, neither of which are permissible under the First Amendment prohibition against Establishment.[43]

It can be argued that, since both United States law and English law are prepared to accept the validity of religious marriage, there is little logic or reason for refusing to accept the validity of religious divorces. Further, it could be argued that the non-recognition of religious divorces at present reflects only historical accident rather than any legal necessity and, therefore, religious divorces should be recognised.[44]

Such arguments raise two questions. The first of these is one purely of recognition. If the parties were to obtain a religious divorce, could the civil law treat this as sufficient, without the need to obtain a civil divorce? This leads on, however, to a second issue. Underlying such an argument appears to be an assumption by those arguing for the recognition of religious divorce, that those who were married religiously should be required to obtain a religious divorce rather than a civil divorce. Are those arguing for recognition of religious divorces really asking for a return to the Millet system, requiring parties to adhere to the personal law of the religion in which they married? Evidence that this is so is provided by the Union of Muslim Organisations in their formal resolution in England in the 1970's to seek recognition of a separate system of Islamic family law.[45] Similar arguments have been made by members of the Jewish community.[46]

There are a number of considerations underlying the demand by

---

[42] *Everson v. Board of Education* 330 U.S.1 (1947) p. 16 (quoting Thomas Jefferson).

[43] See Kurland, "Of Church and State and the Supreme Court" (1961) 29 Univ. Chic. L. Rev. 1 and Kurland" (1961); "The Irrelevance of the Constitution: The Religion Clauses of the First Amendment and the Supreme Court", (1978) 24 Vill. L.Rev. 3.

[44] It might also be argued that non-recognition of religious divorces obtained abroad was justified in England up until 1984 to protect the economic interests of divorced wives. Where an overseas religious divorce was obtained, wives resident in England were unable to obtain ancillary relief. This justification is probably a much later argument for non-recognition, and has now been remedied by the Matrimonial and Family Proceedings Act 1984.

[45] *Why Muslim Law for British Muslims* (1983).

[46] Berkovits, "*Get* and *Talaq* in English Law: Reflections on Law and Policy" in *Islamic Family Law* (Mallet & Connors eds. 1990). Rabbi Berkovits is a dayan (judge) at the Religious Court of the Federation of Synagogues in London.

the Union of Muslim Organisations.[47] For many religious minority groups, particularly non-western immigrant groups, maintaining their religious way of life means adhering to traditional customs, moral values and legal principles. Complying with civil legal requirements in relation to the regulation of the family may upset these traditional beliefs, and weaken the religious bonds within the community. Many minority religious groups have a rather stricter attitude towards morality and the family than that exhibited by the civil system of family law, and fear that their standards of morality will decline if their members are subject only to the requirements and values of the civil system. Further, immigrant communities from countries with a plural legal system find it difficult to see why western nations cannot accommodate such legal pluralism. They point to the fact that Britain in its colonial period accepted such a system, and see no reason why, now that there are substantial religious minorities in England, such a system could not be introduced. For many this is seen as an issue of religious freedom and religious toleration, and a matter of free exercise of religion.

None of the international instruments concern themselves specifically with the freedom to live by religious law or with the recognition of religious divorces, but they do provide for freedom of religion. Article 18 of the Universal Declaration of Human Rights declares that:

> "Everyone has the right to freedom of thought, conscience and religion; this right includes freedom to change his religion or belief, and freedom, either alone or in community with others and in public or private, to manifest his religion or belief in teaching, practice, worship and observance."

The International Covenant on Civil and Political Rights contains a similar Article,[48] as does the European Convention on Human

---

[47] These are explained in more detail in Poulter, "The Claim to a Separate Islamic System of Personal Law for Muslims" in *Islamic Family Law* (Mallet & Connors (eds.) 1990). The same could be argued for other ethnic religious minority groups.

[48] Art. 18(1) "Everyone shall have the right to freedom of thought, conscience and religion. This right shall include freedom to have or adopt a religion or belief of his choice and freedom, either individually or in community with others and in public or private, to manifest his religion or belief in worship, observance, practice or teaching." Both the U.K. and the U.S. are Signatories to the International Covenant on Civil and Political Rights. The United States only ratified the Covenant in 1992.

Rights[49] and the Declaration on the Elimination of All Forms of Intolerance and Discrimination Based on Religion or Belief.[50] Both England and the United States allow their Jewish and Muslim communities freedom to manifest their religion in teaching, worship and observance, and allow them to practise their family law. The crucial question is whether the freedom to practise religion should extend to the State's recognition of religious divorces or are there competing considerations which would justify the state in not recognising religious divorces.

Judaic law provides that the husband and wife may obtain a divorce by mutual consent, but it is in fact the husband who must initiate the procedure and who ultimately serves the *get* on his wife. The wife cannot initiate the procedure herself, and in the face of the refusal of her husband to obtain a *get* she is powerless, and must remain married to her husband, albeit in name only, with no possibility of remarriage. Similarly, Islamic law gives the right to obtain a divorce to the husband through the pronouncement of a *talaq*. It is possible for a wife to obtain a divorce herself, through suspension or delegation of the husband's right of *talaq*, but this is rare and must normally be stipulated for in the marriage contract. Under classical Hanafi[51] law the parties may also mutually consent to divorce, but this normally requires payment by the wife of a certain sum of money.[52] Neither of these religions, therefore, offer divorce on an equal basis to men and women. However, the various international instruments which the United Kingdom and the United States have ratified , and the Declarations of the United Nations,[53] require that States offer equality to men and women, not only in political rights, but also in relation to civil rights, such as marriage and the dissolution of marriage. The Universal Declaration of Human Rights provides in Article 16(1) that:

"Men and women of full age, without any limitation due to race, nation-

---

[49] Art. 9.

[50] See Art. 1 which is almost identical to the clause in the International Covenant of Civil and Political Rights.

[51] One of the four Sunni schools of Islamic law. Hanafi law is recognised by countries who were formerly part of the Ottoman Empire and also by the Indian subcontinent.

[52] See Pearl, *A Textbook on Muslim Personal Law* (1987), pp. 120–121.

[53] Declarations set minimum standards of rights which the UN expects Member States to aspire to.

ality or religion,[54] have the right to marry and to found a family. They
are entitled to equal rights as to marriage, during marriage **and at its
dissolution**."

The International Covenant on Civil and Political Rights, to which
both the United Kingdom and the United States are signatories,
echoes the need for equality in Article 23(4):

"States Parties to the present Covenant shall take appropriate steps to
ensure equality of rights and responsibilities of spouses as to marriage,
during marriage **and at its dissolution**."[55]

Article 16 of the Convention on the Elimination of All Forms of
Discrimination Against Women[56] provides similarly:

1. States Parties shall take all appropriate measures to eliminate discrimination against women in all matters relating to marriage and family relations and in particular shall ensure, on a basis of equality of men and
women:

. . .

(c) The same rights and responsibilities during marriage and at its dissolution."[57]

The right to equality at dissolution of marriage is difficult to
balance with a right to freedom of religion, where there is an inherent inequality between men and women within that religion. Both
the United States and England have systems of civil divorce which
comply with the requirements of the various Covenants and Declarations, and divorce is equally available to men and women. If a
plural, Millet, legal system were to operate and authority was
ceded by the state to Islamic or Jewish religious authorities, women
would not be in an equal position as far as the right to dissolution
was concerned. This would leave the State in obvious violation of
the requirement of equal rights on dissolution of marriage. Such a
potential breach of international standards provides very adequate

---

[54] Islamic law would appear to be in breach of this article as Muslim women are forbidden to marry a non-Muslim.

[55] Art. 5 of Protocol 7 of the European Convention on Human Rights also provides
for equality between spouses on dissolution of marriage. The U.K. has not ratified this Protocol.

[56] To which the U.K. is a contracting party.

[57] Egypt, Bangladesh, Iraq, Jordan, Tunisia and Turkey have all entered reservations to Art. 16.

justification to both countries in their refusal to allow a plural legal system to apply with regard to family law, and to turn down demands from such organisations as the Union of Muslim Organisations for a separate system of family law.

It does not, however, necessarily preclude the State from operating a dual system of divorce, separating the legal termination of marriage from its practical consequences. Under a dual system of divorce, just as with marriage, the State could recognise the religious ceremony as ending a marriage. Civil divorce would be an available option for all, but those couples who jointly agreed would be permitted to obtain a religious divorce instead of a civil divorce. This option, however, raises the question of whether the State has an overriding interest in limiting divorce to civil divorce.

The arguments against recognising religious divorces, even where they have been obtained with the mutual consent of both parties, have centred largely on perceived inadequate protection for women. There is a general dislike of unilateral repudiation by the husband of his wife, which in Islamic law takes effect almost immediately,[58] and a distrust of extra-judicial divorces, which do not involve judicial proceedings or judicial intervention.[59] One can counter such arguments by pointing out that both English and United States divorce laws already permit unilateral repudiation, albeit with a longer waiting time before the divorce takes effect. It would, also, be possible to split the obtaining of a divorce from ancillary relief so that while the divorce itself was granted by the religious body, all matters relating to property, maintenance or children were dealt with by the secular civil system. It could also be provided that the effect of the divorce would be delayed until such time as the ancillary issues were satisfactorily resolved.[60] Lack of judicial intervention in the obtaining of the divorce itself is hardly a draw-

---

[58] See Pearl, *Textbook on Muslim Personal Law* (1987), pp. 101–104. The period of time before a *talaq* becomes effective depends on the form of *talaq*. The longest period of time before the divorce is effective appears to be three and a half months.

[59] See, *e.g.* the different criteria for recognition of divorces obtained overseas through proceedings and those obtained otherwise than by proceedings under Family Law Act 1986, s.46.

[60] This would satisfy the argument that the state needs to maintain some involvement in the divorce process, to ensure that a party does not become a charge on the state through inadequate maintenance or division of property, and that adequate safeguards are provided for the children. See Law Com. Rep. No. 170, *Facing the future: A Discussion Paper on the Ground of Divorce* (1988).

back, as in both England and the United States the vast majority of divorces are undefended and the actual granting of a divorce is largely an administrative task, which does not involve judicial inquiry.

However, any demand for the recognition of religious family law raises immediate practical problems, particularly in relation to jurisdiction. For instance, if a couple agreed to obtain a religious divorce, which religion would have jurisdiction? Would it be the religion that they professed at the time they wished to divorce, the religion that they were born into, or the religion under whose auspices the marriage service was performed? Would a couple be allowed to opt for a religious divorce when they had no obvious affiliation with that religion? How could one be assured that there was true mutual consent to the obtaining of a religious divorce rather than a civil divorce? A further practical difficulty would arise in deciding which religious groups would be allowed to maintain their own divorce jurisdiction. In the event that the couple agreed to submit themselves to the appropriate religious jurisdiction, would there be a right of appeal to a civil court? Article 6(1) of the European Convention on Human rights provides that:

> "In the determination of his civil rights and obligations . . . everyone is entitled to a fair and public hearing within a reasonable time by an independent and impartial tribunal established by law."

If parties were to appear before a religious court to obtain a divorce, the words "independent and impartial tribunal" in Article 6(1) would seem to require that there be a right of review or appeal to a civil court. Alternatively, if a religious tribunal were to be regarded as an "independent and impartial tribunal", England would need to legislate for the creation of such tribunals to meet the requirement "established by law". Were England to contemplate establishing a series of religious courts, this would amount to recognition of the legal authority of religious law, without attending to the inequalities inherent in religious law. Once more England would be in breach of those Conventions which require that there be equality between men and women on dissolution of marriage.

While the United States is not bound by the requirements of the European Convention, the same problems would inevitably arise. It is difficult to envisage a delegation of civil authority to religious tribunals, without the possibility of an appeal from the decision of that tribunal, whether this be on the substantive issue, or procedure. Apart from the practical problem of finding judges sufficiently versed in different religious laws to sit on such a court, any attempt by judges in the United States to interpret religious law would amount to excessive entanglement with religion and would be in breach of the Establishment Clause of the First Amendment.

Apart from the intransigent problem of sexual inequality, and the practical difficulties, there are also policy considerations which militate against recognition of religious divorce as a substitute for civil divorce. Perhaps the most obvious is that both the United States and England believe in the principle that one set of laws should apply to all. If divorce were to be dictated by religious law, this unitary system of law would be replaced by a multitude of laws. A further consideration is that once religious laws were recognised this would make it extremely difficult for the state to change its laws. There would be immense pressure to maintain the status quo. The risk is that the professed doctrines of a particular religious group might become superior to the law of the land, and in effect permit every citizen to beome a law unto himself.[61]

Constitutional law in the United States prevents any recognition of religious divorces as a substitute for civil divorce. There can be no doubt that to allow people to choose, or be allocated to a religious system of family law, rather than be subject to a secular civil legal system, would amount to an undue entanglement of Church and State and would be a breach of the Establishment Clause. There is no such constitutional restriction in England. Nevertheless, it is exceedingly unlikely that religious divorces would ever be regarded as an appropriate substitute for civil divorce. The major problem faced by those religions seeking recognition of religious divorces, is the immutability of their religious laws, areas of which conflict with the fundamental rights and freedoms of the individual in a western, democratic society. Even where Islamic religious law is the governing law, a number of countries have reformed family law through legislation.[62]

The argument that both England and the United States recognise religious marriage, and, therefore should logically recognise

---

[61] See *Reynolds v. U.S.* 98 U.S. (8 Otto) 145 (1878.)
[62] *e.g.* Pakistan, Tunis and Egypt. See generally Pearl, *A Textbook on Muslim Personal Law* (1987).

religious divorce, is fallacious. Both jurisdictions have a secular law of marriage and divorce, the latter of which came into existence through legislation. Although both recognise a religious ceremony as a legally binding marriage if certain formalities are fulfilled, the legal effect does not derive from the religious law, but from the fact that recognition of religious marriages has been incorporated into the legislation of England and the United States.

Most States seek to encourage marriage and the creation of a family unit. Families are viewed as the basic unit of society and the ideal environment for the procreation and upbringing of children. Article 16(3) of the Universal Declaration of Human Rights recognises that:

> "the family is the natural and fundamental group unit of society and is entitled to protection by society and the state."

This is echoed in the Covenant on Civil and Political Rights.[63] While liberal divorce laws exist in both the United States and England, society is not in favour of divorce. Ever since the first reforms allowing judicial dissolution of marriage, divorce has been regarded as a necessary evil, and an area of law that should remain firmly under the control of the State. It is difficult to foresee a time when either the United States or England would be prepared, either politically or legally, to release control over the family to any religious group.

DIVORCES OBTAINED ABROAD

While England and the United States may be able to justify their refusal to countenance religious rather than State control of divorce within their own jurisdiction, such justification becomes more difficult when a divorce is obtained outside the country under the authority of religious bodies. At common law, both the United States and England have been willing to recognise a foreign decree of divorce if it was validly obtained by parties who were both domiciled in the granting country, provided of course, that this was not contrary to public policy. While England developed further rules of recog-

---

[63] Art. 23(1).

nition, both at common law and through legislation, the United States have been reluctant to follow suit and develop a coherent policy of recognition of foreign divorces. This might seem rather surprising given that America has a high rate of immigration from a very wide mix of cultures and religious groups. There appear to be a number of reasons for the lack of development in the common law of the United States. First, the individual States were concerned during times when there were restrictive divorce laws, to prevent their domiciliaries from evading State law by travelling to another State with more liberal divorce law and obtaining a "quickie" or "mail order" divorce.

The concentration on evasion resulted in strict retention of the domicile rule for recognition until fairly recently.[64] Further, where it appeared that a foreign divorce was not obtained with evasive intent, the United States courts hardly ever questioned recognition.[65] Secondly, it is suggested that the issue of recognition of foreign religious divorces does not arise with the same frequency in the United States.[66] Juenger[67] attributes this to the ease with which the parties are able to obtain a marriage licence as against the greater scrutiny of personal status when granting a licence in England. Recognition problems tend to arise, therefore, not when parties wish to remarry, but when a second or subsequent marriage breaks down. One party may then allege that there was never a marriage due to the invalidity of the first, foreign, divorce. The issue may also arise when a party to the marriage dies, and his or her estate is contested with regard to the validity of the marriage.

The courts in both England and the United States are willing to recognise foreign divorces obtained by couples domiciled abroad even though a divorce would not have been granted on the same grounds or by the same procedure at home. The basis of this recog-

---

[64] This meant that the only those domiciled in a state could apply for a divorce there. Habitual residence was not sufficient to constitute "domicile".

[65] See Baade, "Marriage and Divorce in American Conflicts Law: Governmental-Interests Analysis and the Restatement" (1972) (Second). 72 Colum.L.Rev. 329.

[66] As late as 1978 the Supreme Court of Tennessee found no single case from Tennessee dealing with the recognition of judicial decrees of any kind from foreign nations. See Weyrauch and Katz, *American Family Law in Transition* (1983).

[67] Juenger, "Recognition of Foreign Divorces—British and American Perspectives" (1972) 20 Am.J. Comp.L. 1.

nition is comity,[68] defined in the United States case of *Hilton v. Guyot*[69] as falling somewhere between obligation and courtesy. A further reason is the prevention of "limping marriages" whereby parties are regarded as married to each other in one State and as legal strangers in another.

Recognition Before 1970

Where both parties to a marriage were domiciled in the overseas country granting the divorce, courts in England and the United States were willing to recognise the divorce as valid, even where the nature of the divorce was religious, and was obtained by extra-judicial or non-judicial means.[70] Although, under common law, the courts could refuse to recognise a marriage on public policy grounds, neither jurisdiction found any public policy objection to recognising Jewish divorces obtained in such circumstances. Thus, in *Ganer v. Lady Lanesborough* in 1790[71–72] the English court was willing to accept the evidence of the former wife of John King that she and her husband were divorced by the Rabbi at Leghorn in Italy according to Jewish rites and customs. The Court was further willing to recognise this as a valid divorce, and to treat John King's second marriage, celebrated in England, as valid.[73] Similarly, in *Sasson v. Sasson*[74] the English court was willing to accept the validity of a *get* obtained in Egypt by Egyptian domiciled Jews. No insuperable public policy arguments arose, even though the ground of divorce, mutual consent, was not permitted in England at the time. In *Har-Shefi v. Har-Shefi*[75] the English court was even willing to grant recognition of a *get* written and delivered in London on the ground that the divorce was valid by the law of the husband's

---

[68] Comity is a doctrine whereby every sovereign will admit that a law which has already operated in the country of origin shall retain its force everywhere provided that it does not unjustly prejudice the subjects of the sovereign whose recognition is sought. See Butterworths Family Law service, Div. C para.51. Comity is the ruling principle in American law.

[69] 159 U.S. 113 (1895)

[70] These terms are used interchangeably.

[71–72] (1790) 1 Peake 25 (170) E.R. 66.

[73] The case is, however, of limited use for assessing the likelihood that such divorces will be recognised. The detail given in the report is sparse. There was no indication whether the parties were domiciled in Italy at the time, and no discussion of whether the *get* would have been recognised as a valid divorce by Italian law.

[74] [1924] A.C. 1007.

[75] [1953] 1 All E.R. 783.

domicile, Israel, and that the husband was at all times domiciled in Israel.

In America the earliest consideration of the validity of a *get* was in 1893 in *Leshinsky v. Leshinsky*.[76] The wife, who had previously obtained a *get* from the rabbinical authorities in Russia, remarried in the United States after emigration. The validity of the *get* was raised when her second husband sought a divorce.[77] After hearing evidence that religious groups in Russia had legal authority to grant divorces to members of their communities, the New York court found that the divorce was valid and should be recognised on the basis of comity. The court had to consider whether the fact that the decree was awarded by ecclesiastical authorities rather than secular authorities, as required in the United States, offended American public policy. The court stated:

> "There is nothing in the mode of divorce repugnant to our institutions, or detrimental to our society. On the contrary, such matters must be considered fully as safe in the hands of the church to which the parties belong as in any judicial branch of the government."[78]

This decision was confirmed in *Miller v. Miller*[79] where the court ruled that religious divorces recognised by civil authorities in the country of domicile must be deemed valid by the United States courts.

While Jewish divorces between Jewish foreign domiciliaries were regarded as acceptable, public policy objections were raised, particularly in England, to Muslim *talaq* divorces. The problems with such divorces were essentially two-fold. The first of these related to the nature of the *talaq* divorce itself, which the courts found in breach of natural justice and thus offensive on public policy grounds. A bare *talaq* under classical Koranic law, divorcing the spouses, requires only the unilateral repudiation of the wife by the husband. In many Muslim societies where a bare *talaq* is recognised, there is no need for the wife to consent nor does it render the *talaq* invalid if the wife is not present at the time, and does not

---

[76] 5 Misc. 495, 25 N.Y.S. 841 (Sup.Ct. 1893).

[77] In fact the validity of the *get* was questioned by the second husband with the purpose of showing that the wife had never divorced her husband and, therefore, was never married to him, thus obviating the need for him to obtain a divorce at all.

[78] *ibid.* at 496, 25 N.Y.S. at 842.

[79] 70 Misc. 368, 128 N.Y.S. 787 (Sup.Ct. 1911). See also in *re Estate of Rubenstein* 143 Misc 917, 257 N.Y.S. 637 (Sup.Ct. 1932).

know until some time after the event that she has been divorced. In addition, the wife may have no opportunity to respond, to make any representations against divorce, or to prevent divorce, even in the absence of fault, a package that English law regarded as according the wife insufficient protection.[80]

The second problem with *talaq* divorces arose because of the common law rule that an English woman took her husband's domicile on marriage.[81] By this rule, a woman marrying an Egyptian domiciled man in England in a civil marriage, was regarded as domiciled in Egypt even if she never left the English shore. If the husband chose to return to Egypt and divorce his wife there, according to Muslim law, this was, technically, by English law, a divorce obtained abroad by foreign domiciliaries. The reality of such a fiction was that the English wife married to a foreign domiciliary, but resident in England, received less protection and possibly financial provision than a woman married to an Englishman, a concept offensive to public policy. The public policy objection was expressed not in terms that such a wife was provided with inadequate protection, but that marriage in a Christian sense, which was how civil marriage was regarded,[82] should not be dissolved by methods appropriate to polygamous unions. This is a view clearly stated in *R. v. Hammersmith Superintendent Registrar of Marriages ex parte Mir-Anwaruddin*[83] where the Indian domiciled Muslim husband sought a declaration from the High Court in London that his *talaq* divorce pronounced in India, following a civil marriage to an English girl in England, was valid.[84-85] The Court of Appeal held

---

[80] Some Muslim states have sought to provide more rights to women and have added statutory requirements to be complied with before the divorce can take effect. These are generally notice periods, and the chance of reconciliation by making the pronouncement of the *talaq* revocable for a period rather than irrevocable as under classic Koranic law. The Family Law Act 1986 continues to distinguish between administrative and bare *talaq* divorces.

[81] A woman did not have the right to retain her own domicile on marriage until the Domicile and Matrimonial Proceedings Act 1973, s.1.

[82] This did not mean that the marriage was Christian in the sense that the ceremony and rites were those of the Christian religion. The ceremony was a secular ceremony of marriage, but English marriage law is based on Christian notions of marriage. In particular, at the time of the *Hammersmith* case in 1917, divorce was only obtainable on the basis of fault.

[83] [1917] K.B. 634.

[84-85] Even though the marriage was not a Muslim ceremony it was regarded as a valid ceremony in India and under Muslim law.

that although the decree was recognised as a valid divorce in India, it could not be recognised as valid in England.

In essence the court declared that when the husband entered a monogamous marriage, which he did by undergoing a civil marriage in England, a *talaq* is not a suitable way of ending the marriage. The only alternative for this husband, as he had no access to the State system of divorce in India, not being a Christian, would be to return to England and obtain a civil divorce. It is unclear from the judgment whether the Court would have reached the same decision and denied recognition of a *talaq* obtained abroad if both parties had been Muslims marrying in a civil, essentially "Christian" marriage ceremony. While the difference of religion between the two parties was obviously of importance, the Court of Appeal in A.T. Lawrence J.'s judgment makes clear their dislike of this particular form of religious divorce also rests on a perceived breach of natural justice.

"Here, it is not suggested that there was any consent on the part of the woman, but it is the man seeking to be, or purporting to be, a judge in his own cause, and dissolving his marriage without any communication with the woman, or any consent on her part, affecting her rights as well as his own. I think it contrary to natural justice that a man should be judge in his own cause and determine his marriage at his own will and pleasure."

The same ambivalence, bordering on dislike, of Muslim divorces for English residents was expressed in the 1950's in the case of *Maher v. Maher.*[86] The case, once more, involved a foreign domiciled Muslim who married an English girl in a civil ceremony. However, unlike Dr. Mir-Anwarrudin, the husband deserted his wife two months after the marriage, returning home to Egypt. Six months after her marriage, the wife was informed by the Egyptian Embassy that she had been divorced in the Court of Personal Status in Cairo in front of two witnesses. The English court[87] held that a civil marriage entered into in England pursuant to the Marriage Acts could not be dissolved by a method of divorce appropriate to a

---

[86] [1951] 2 All E.R. 37.
[87] The case reached the English court when the wife eventually sought dissolution of the marriage on the basis of her husband's desertion. The question of the validity of the *talaq* divorce then arose. If the *talaq* was recognised there would be no need to obtain a divorce from the English court.

polygamous union. Muslim divorce was not appropriate for an essentially Christian marriage. The judge found that to hold otherwise would be to encourage and sanction the purely temporary unions of Englishwomen and foreigners professing the Muslim religion during their limited residence in England. While in this case one feels some sympathy with the court's decision, as the evidence indicated that the husband had tricked the wife and only intended to remain married to her until he finished studying in England, the rationale for the decision does not hold up to close scrutiny. In Egypt, the husband was bound by his personal law, Islamic law. In refusing to recognise the validity of the *talaq* divorce, the English court left the husband with a limping marriage,[88] divorced in Egyptian law, but married in English law, with no remedy, other than that offered by the Hammersmith case, which was to return to England and obtain a divorce from the English court.[89]

Development of Recognition

Following the Hague Convention on the Recognition of Divorces and Legal Separations in 1970[90] the English Parliament enacted the Recognition of Divorces and Legal Separations Act 1971[91] and the later Domicile and Matrimonial Proceedings Act 1973. Even before these Acts put recognition of foreign divorces on a statutory basis, however, there were the beginnings of a change in the attitude of the English courts.[92]

This more flexible approach to recognition was reflected in *Qureshi v. Qureshi*[93] where the validity of a *talaq* divorce obtained by a Pakistani domiciliary was recognised:

"In my view, therefore, the fact that there has been no judicial intervention or even presence is irrelevant if the purported divorce is effective by

---

[88] A marriage where the parties are regarded as married to one another in one State and as legal strangers in another.

[89] See, however, *Nahbub v. Nahbub* (1964) 108 S.J. 337 where the court was, unusually willing to recognise a *talaq* divorce.

[90] To which the U.K., but not the U.S., are signatories.

[91] This Act brought into effect the Hague Convention.

[92] See *Russ v. Russ* [1962] 3 All E.R. 193 where the court were willing to recognise the validity of a *talaq* divorce pronounced in Egypt, the country of domicile, in the presence of the wife.

[93] [1971] 1 All E.R. 325.

the law of the domicile to terminate the marriage in question, and it should be recognised as such, unless the result would be offensive to the conscience of the English court . . . The *talaq* was valid according to the law of the domicile and . . . there is no rule in English law which precludes its recognition by means of its non-forensic character."[94]

The 1971 Recognition of Divorces and Legal Separations Act[95] introduced a "jurisdictional code", the aim of which was to prevent limping marriages, such as were created by the *Hammersmith* and *Maher* cases. It provided, in section 2, that a divorce obtained outside the British Isles by means of "judicial or other proceedings" would be regarded as valid if obtained in a country where either spouse is habitually resident, or where either spouse is domiciled within the meaning of that term in foreign law.[96] In addition the old common law rules on recognition were retained.[97] The Act further added a new restriction: notwithstanding the survival of the common law rules of recognition in s.6, a non-judicial divorce obtained "abroad"[98] would not be regarded as dissolving the marriage if *both* parties were habitually resident in the United Kingdom for the year preceding the institution of proceedings.[99]

One result of the Act was recognition of what are referred to as

---

[94] *Per* Simon P. See also *Peters v. Peters* (1968) 112 S.J. 311 where a divorce granted by the Ecclesiastical Court of the Archbishop of Cyprus after an English civil marriage, was regarded as valid.

[95] The Act incorporates a number of the rules contained in the Hague Convention on the Recognition of Divorces and Legal Separations 1970. The provisions of the 1971 Act are, however, more liberal than those of the Hague Convention.

[96] The divorce also had to be effective in the country where it was obtained. So, for instance a *talaq* obtained in Canada while valid under Islamic law, would be invalid for these purposes as not being a recognised form of divorce in Canadian law. This is a re-enactment of a common law rule.

[97] In s.6 (as amended). Under the old common law rules, a divorce obtained "abroad" would be recognised if it was obtained in the country of common domicile, or in the country of domicile of the other spouse, or in a third country when recognised in the country of common domicile.

[98] Other than a divorce where recognition would be required by the jurisdictional code.

[99] While the Act prevented a husband living with his wife in England, but domiciled abroad, returning to his country of domicile and pronouncing a *talaq*, the Act did not address the *Maher* case, see n. 86 where the husband was both domiciled and habitually resident abroad and divorced his wife through the medium of a bare *talaq*, which, while recognised in the country of domicile was not recognised in England. The Act also retained the common law rule that recognition could be withheld, although only on the basis that it would be "manifestly" contrary to public policy.

"procedural" *talaq* divorces. In a number of Islamic countries, *talaq* divorces are regulated by statute and require administrative procedures, not required by the classical Koranic form of *talaq* (the bare *talaq*). The courts, including the House of Lords in *Quazi v. Quazi*,[1] were willing to find that such divorces constituted "other proceedings" within the meaning of section 2.

> "Specifically 'other proceedings' will include an act or sequence of acts other than a proceeding instituted in a court of law, . . . The talaq is the institution of proceedings officially recognised as leading to divorce and becomes an effective divorce only after the completion of the proceedings and the expiry of the period laid down by statute. The proceedings in this case, were therefore, officially recognised and led to a divorce legally effective in Pakistan."[2]

Lord Scarman was referring in *Quazi* to the pronouncement of a *talaq* in Pakistan under the Family Laws Ordinance 1961, but what of a bare *talaq*? The difficulty with recognising this form of *talaq*, apart from public policy considerations was one of definition. Did such an act constitute a "proceeding"? Lord Fraser in *Quazi* placed a restricted meaning on the interpretation of proceedings.

> "the state or some official organisation recognised by the state must play some part in the divorce process, at least to the extent that, in proper cases, it can prevent the wishes of the parties, or one of them, as the case may be, from dissolving the marriage tie as of right."

However, Lord Fraser explicitly stated that he expressed no opinion as to whether a bare *talaq* pronounced in some country where, unlike Pakistan, it would be effective without further procedure, should be recognised under the Recognition Act of 1971 as a valid divorce.

This question was finally resolved in *Chaudary v. Chaudary*.[3] The husband, who was habitually resident in England, sought to divorce his wife in Pakistan by pronouncing *talaq* in a London mosque before two witnesses. He pronounced a further *talaq* in Kashmir

---

[1] [1980] A.C. 744. [1979] 3 All E.R. 897.
[2] *Per* Lord Scarman in *Quazi v. Quazi, ibid.*
[3] [1985] 2 W.L.R. 350, [1984] 3 All E.R. 1017.

before two witnesses, some months after his wife had left Pakistan to live in London. When the wife sought a divorce from the English courts, the husband cross-petitioned for a declaration that the marriage had already been dissolved by *talaq*. The Court of Appeal held that in order for a foreign divorce to be recognised under other "proceedings" by section 2 of the 1971 Act, it had to be obtained by means which entailed more than a mere unilateral or consensual act of either or both of the parties to the marriage, regardless of how formal or solemn the act was, or what ritual or ceremony accompanied it. What was required was a degree of formality and, at least, the involvement of a lay or religious agency of the foreign state, or an agency recognised by the state, which had some function in the proceedings and was more than merely probative. Accordingly, a bare *talaq* was not obtained by other proceedings and was not to be regarded as valid. Cumming-Bruce L. J.:

> "Such a divorce is not at first sight obtained by means of 'any proceeding'. It is pronounced. Pronouncement of talaq three times finally terminates the marriage in Kashmir, Dubai and probably in other unsophisticated peasant, desert or jungle communities which respect classical Muslim religious tradition. Certainly by that tradition the pronouncement is a solemn religious act. It might doubtfully be described as a ceremony, although the absence of any formality of any kind renders the ceremony singularly unceremonious. It can fairly be described as a 'procedure' laid down by the divine authority in the inspired text of the Koran. But neither respect for the divine origin of the procedure nor respect for the long enduring tradition which over the centuries had rendered the bare talaq effective as terminating marriage by the law of Muslim countries necessarily or sensibly should convert the procedure into a proceeding with the intent of s.2 of the 1971 Act. So I conclude that, at the date of the royal assent to the 1971 Act, a divorce obtained by a bare *talaq* would not be construed as 'obtained by means of judicial or other proceedings' within the intendment of s.2 of that Act."

All three Court of Appeal judges were of the opinion that recognition should, even apart from the definitional problems, be refused on the ground that it would be manifestly contrary to public policy. By the time the *talaq* was pronounced in Kashmir, both parties were domiciled in England. The husband's attempt to divorce in Kashmir was made with the clear motive of depriving his wife of the rights that accrued to her pursuant to the personal law of the domicile of choice, and the court would not support such an approach.[4]

The Present Position

At the time of the decision in *Chaudary*, the Law Commissions had already submitted their report on Recognition of Foreign Nullity Decrees and Related Matters which led to the Family Law Act 1986.[5] The Law Commission regarded the 1971 Act as not "altogether a happy piece of drafting". They recommended that the phrase "judicial or other proceeding" should include any acts by which a divorce may be obtained in the country concerned, provided that those acts complied with the procedures required by the law of that country. A bare *talaq* would thus be capable of being recognised as a divorce which was obtained by a "proceeding".[6] The Law Commission's proposal was, however, rejected by the Lord Chancellor in the House of Lords for policy reasons; that recognition would be against the precepts of natural justice and offer insufficient protection for women. Lord Hailsham explained his reasons for supporting a more restrictive approach:

> "But clause 46(2) adopts a more restrictive approach than that recommended by the Law Commission in relating to overseas decrees granted otherwise than by proceedings. Such divorces include, for example the bare Moslem *talaq*, and certain Hindu and Japanese consent divorces. The Law Commission recommended that informal divorces should be recognised on the same basis as those divorces obtained by judicial or other proceedings. We cannot accept this wide recommendation. There are public policy elements here. Such divorces are informal, arbitrary and usually unilateral. More importantly, there is often no available proof that what is alleged to have taken place has taken place at all. In addition, these divorces are almost exclusively obtained by men and therefore discriminate against women. Finally, particularly where the wife is resident abroad, such divorce provides little or no financial protection."[7]

---

[4] See as a contrast the American case of *Seth v. Seth* 649 S.W.2d 459 (1985) Ct. of Appeals, Texas.

[5] The Joint Report of the Law Commission and the Scottish Law Commission, Law Com. Rep. No. 137, Cmnd. 9341 (1984).

[6] See para. 6.11. The Law Commission recommended the retention of the discretion to refuse recognition on the ground that this would be manifestly contrary to public policy. So, it would be quite possible for the court hearing a *Chaudary* type case to reach the same result on a different basis.

[7] Lord Hailsham, Hansard, H.L. Vol. 473, cols. 1081–1082.

The Family Law Act 1986 thus makes a distinction between divorces obtained overseas by means of proceedings,[7a] which include
gets and administrative *talaq* divorces, such as those obtained under
Pakistan's Family Laws Ordinance, recognition of which falls
under section 46(1), and overseas divorces obtained otherwise than
by means of proceedings, which fall under section 46(2). This latter
section governs bare *talaqs* and certain Hindu divorces. Such divorces need to meet stricter criteria if recognition is to be assured.
Thus, those divorces falling under section 46(1) will be recognised
if, at the commencement of the proceedings, either party was
habitually resident, domiciled or a national of the country in which
the divorce was obtained, and the divorce was effective under the
law of the country in which it was obtained. Informal divorces,
obtained otherwise than through proceedings will only be recognised however, if, on the date the divorce was obtained.

(a) the divorce . . . is effective under the law of the country in
which it was obtained,
(b) at the relevant date—[8]
 (i) each party to the marriage was domiciled in that country or
 (ii) either party was domiciled in that country and the other
party was domiciled in a country under whose law the divorce . . . is recognised as valid and
(c) neither party to the marriage was habitually resident in the
United Kingdom throughout the period of one year
immediately preceding that date.[9]

Under the 1986 Act if either party is habitually resident in the
United Kingdom a spouse will have to obtain a divorce by means
of proceedings (including for these purposes a full *talaq*).[10]
The courts are still granted the right to refuse recognition, but
this is now put on a statutory basis.[11] In the case of a divorce

---

[7a] Divorce proceedings must be instituted and completed in the same overseas
country for recognition of an "overseas" divorce to be granted. See *Berkovits v.
Grinberg* [1995] 1 FLR 477.
[8] The date on which the divorce was obtained.
[9] Note the change from the 1971 Act, which only denied recognition if *both* parties
were resident in the U.K. for the year preceding an application. It could be argued
that this gives English resident wives sufficient protection from informal divorce
by a foreign domiciled husband. The important issue is, of course, not the prevention of divorce itself, but ensuring the right of the wife to seek ancillary relief.
[10] It is not possible for an extrajudicial divorce obtained in a country in which neither
party was domiciled to be recognised after P. II of the 1986 Act came into force.
[11] See Family Law Act 1986 s.51.

obtained by means of proceedings, recognition may be refused where there are breaches of natural justice. In the case of divorces obtained otherwise than by means of proceedings, the court may refuse recognition in the absence of official certification. In both cases a court may still refuse recognition if the divorce is manifestly contrary to public policy.[12]

It is to be regretted that the Family Law Act 1986 continued to distinguish between different forms of religious divorce and ignored the recommendations of the Law Commission. The public policy justification for continuing the distinction seems weak. The complaint of Lord Hailsham that bare *talaq* divorces are arbitrary and usually unilateral can also be applied to divorces obtained through proceedings. Procedural *talaqs* share the same characteristics, but do not receive the same opprobrium. It is true that bare *talaq* divorces are almost exclusively obtained by men and, therefore, discriminate against women. The same comment could be made, however, of procedural *talaq* divorces and also of Jewish *gets*, but the latter have been accorded recognition back to the eighteenth century. While it is alleged that a bare *talaq* leaves a wife in a very poor financial situation, it is unclear that there is any discernible difference, especially now that it is possible for a spouse divorced overseas to make a financial application in the place of habitual residence.[13] If financial protection is no longer an issue, it is difficult to ascertain what interest England and the Unied States have in maintaining different rules of recognition for non-judicial divorces. As both jurisdictions recognise unilateral divorce the only justification would appear to be the notion of certainty. However, English courts can already refuse recognition where there is insufficient proof that divorce has taken place. In the present day, neither financial protection nor the need for certainty seem sufficient justification for the much stricter rules of recognition.

England and the United States, with their state monopoly of

---

[12] *Kendall v. Kendall* [1977] 3 All E.R. 471. See also Parry, "Denying Recognition to Foreign Divorces" (1978) 8 Fam. Law 29.

[13] Under the Matrimonial and Family Proceedings Act 1984 s.12. (England). Each State in the U.S. is free to decide whether a spouse, usually the wife, can make a claim for alimony when divorce occurs in another State or another country. Most States have held that the wife's alimony claim survives the husband's *ex parte* divorce, even if the wife receives actual notice of the divorce action. See *Hudson v. Hudson* 52 Cal.2d 735, 344 P.2d 295 (1959), and Restatement (second) of Judgments s.31 (1982). For a more general discussion of this point, see Clark, *The Law of Domestic Relations in the United States*, (2nd ed., 1988), Chap. 16.3, p. 637.

secular jurisdiction over divorce, find an unregulated, purely religious system of divorce difficult to tolerate and totally alien to their historical development. Such divorces also conflicted in the past with the "Christian" concept of marriage, and in the present with notions of "fairness" and equality. However, there is little value in refusing recognition to such non-judicial divorces obtained abroad, as this seems to be productive of nothing more than the perennial problem of "limping" marriages. England has gone some way to alleviating the problems by permitting spouses to make an application for financial relief even though the divorce occurred overseas.[14-15] Little further protection can or should be provided. The parties in such a situation are unlikely to reconcile, and should be permitted to bury the dead shells of their marriage and rebuild their lives.

Obtaining A Religious Divorce: Religious Necessity and State Policy

For those couples domiciled in England and the United States a civil divorce is, as we have seen, a necessity, if either spouse wishes to contract a legally valid second marriage. However, secular divorce is not regarded as sufficient to dissolve a marriage in the eyes of many religious groups, who require their adherents to obtain a religious divorce[16] before remarrying in a religious ceremony. The obtaining of a religious divorce causes particular problems in Islamic and Jewish law. In both of these religions, women have to rely

---

[14-15] A party wishing to seek financial relief must seek the leave of the court. (Matrimonial and Family Proceedings Act. 1984, s.13.) The court has jurisdiction to make an order for financial relief if either of the parties to the marriage was domiciled in England or Wales on the date of the application for leave under s.13, or was so domiciled on the date on which the divorce obtained in the overseas country took effect in that country; or either of the parties to the marriage was habitually resident in England throughout the period of one year ending with the date on which the application took effect in that country; or either or both of the parties had, at the date of application for leave, a beneficial interest in possession in a dwelling-house in England or Wales which was, at some time during the marriage, a matrimonial home. (s.15.)

[16] In the case of Jews, this only applies where the marriage was celebrated in a synagogue. Civil marriage is not regarded as marriage any more than civil divorce is regarded as effective to end a marriage.

on their estranged husbands to initiate the divorce process,[17] having no, or little power, to do so themselves. In Islamic law the husband must repudiate the wife by *talaq*.[18] In Jewish law, although
divorce is consensual, the process must be initiated by the husband
who delivers a *get*[19] to the wife, thus ending the marriage. Without
a religious divorce, a Muslim woman cannot remarry. A Jewish
woman is in an even worse position. She cannot contract a second
Jewish marriage, without a *get*. If she chooses to marry under the
secular law, or cohabit with a new partner, she will be regarded as
an adulteress. Any children of the new family will be regarded as
illegitimate,[20] or *mamzerim*, because Jewish law still treats her as
married to her first husband. This will still be the case even if the
first husband has remarried under secular law, or formed a new
family, and has children of his own with the new partner.[21] Should
the first husband finally agree to give a *get* at some point after the
former spouse has entered into a new relationship, the wife may
not marry her new partner under Jewish law, or legitimise the children, because she is regarded as having lived in an adulterous
union. Marriage to a partner in adultery is forbidden. The same
restrictions do not apply to husbands who contract a second civil
marriage. The husband is not considered as guilty of adultery and
his marriage, though rabbinically prohibited, is legally valid.
Unlike the first wife he may remain married to the second wife
after he finally gives the first wife a *get*. This distinction is due to the
fact that in biblical times men were permitted to practice poly-

---

[17] Muslim women can divorce their husbands, but in very limited circumstances,
and usually suffer a financial penalty.
[18] This takes a number of forms, the major difference between them being the
length of time before the *talaq* takes effect. This ranges from immediately after
announcement to approximately three and a half months after pronouncement. It
is possible for the wife to initiate a divorce in limited circumstances, but this right
has to be included in the marriage contract, and is rarely found. A wife may also
obtain a divorce through mutual agreement, but must usually pay a certain sum
in return for the agreement of the husband to release her. See generally Pearl, *A
Textbook on Muslim Personal Law* (1987), Chap. 7.
[19] A bill of divorcement under Jewish law.
[20] The concept of illegitimacy in Jewish law is quite different from Anglo-American
concepts of illegitimacy. The only illegitimate child in Jewish law is the product
of an adulterous union. Such children are under severe religious disadvantages,
and may not themselves be married under Jewish law unless the other spouse is
also a *mamzer* or a convert to Judaism. A *mamzer's* children are also *mamzerim*.
[21] The husband's children are not regarded as illegitimate provided the second wife,
whom he has married under secular law, is not already married under Jewish law.

gamy. Although the practice was ended in the eleventh century no sanctions were attached to breach by the man.[22]

Muslim and Jewish women who wish to conduct their family relationships within the framework of their religious beliefs, have virtually no power to compel a reluctant husband to obtain a talaq[23] or a get.[24] While the powerlessness of women is undoubtedly due to inequalities of religious practice, there has been pressure from both Muslims and Jews for legislation or legal action to encourage, if not ensure, that a religious divorce is obtained along with a secular divorce.

Although it is occasionally argued that the state is under a duty to aid such religious divorces,[25] the real issue is whether the state, through the courts and the legislature, ought, on policy grounds, to encourage and assist couples to obtain a religious divorce. There are a number of cogent reasons for adopting an affirmative policy. Firstly, such a policy would promote remarriage. It is recognised in Article 16(3) of the Universal Declaration of Human Rights that the "family is the natural and fundamental group unit of society and is entitled to protection by society and the State". It has been suggested that the State should have the power to intervene into what is essentially a private contract (i.e. marriage) between parties, so as to ensure that its dissolution does as little harm as possible to the framework of society.[26] The inability of the wife to remarry in the absence of a religious divorce harms the possible creation of a new family, and, particularly in Judaism, potentially excludes future children of a new relationship from full standing within their religious community.

Secondly, Article 23(2) of the Covenant on Civil and Political Rights, to which both the United States and England are parties, provides that the right of men and women of marriageable age to marry and found a family shall be recognised. There is no

---

[22] Polygamy was ended by an Edict of Rabbi Gershom Ben Juda for Eastern European Jews, although Sephardic Jewry continued the practice rather longer.
[23] A divorce under Islamic law.
[24] Husbands may also be affected under Jewish law, as there is a requirement that divorce be consensual. If a husband seeks to deliver a get, but the wife refuses to accept it, he too is left in the position of being unable to contact a second Jewish marriage. However, the consequences of this disability are not so grave for a man.
[25] See Bleich (1984) Vol. 16 Connecticut Law Review 201 at p. 280.
[26] Response of the Board of Deputies of British Jews to Facing the Future, Law Commission Discussion Paper No. 170. (1988).

suggestion that the State is under any duty to suppress religious practices which prevent divorced couples from remarrying. But, on grounds of public policy, the courts and the legislature should seek to encourage the realisation of remarriage by assisting the obtaining of religious divorces. Indeed, Governor Cuomo of New York in his statement issued when signing an amendment into New York's Domestic Relations Law, known as the "*get* statute" accepted that the State has an interest in fostering a public policy that favours remarriage.[27] The importance of the right to marry was also explained in the United States case of *Stern v. Stern*[28] where the judge remarked:

> "The United States Supreme court has stated that the right to marry and raise a family are among the most fundamental civil rights guaranteed to members of a free and democratic society."

Thirdly, it is argued that fairness and equity require that the courts and legislature intervene where a religious divorce is withheld. Various expressions of the unfairness and injustice caused when an antagonistic spouse refuses, out of spite, or for reasons of revenge, to provide a religious divorce, can be found in the cases.

> "Parenthetically, the court notes that the plaintiff has remarried and that his second wife is now pregnant. In other words, the Plaintiff has taken advantage of the provisions of a secular judgment of divorce which gave him the opportunity to reorganize his life and another chance to achieve a happy life. He has denied this to his former wife by his refusal to release her from the religious consequences of his marriage to her. Unfortunately, this court has no jurisdiction over the plaintiff's conscience or over the powers granted to him because of his status as a Jewish male.[29]
> He has reaped the fruits of the secular divorce and has carved out a new life for himself. He refuses to make it possible for the Plaintiff to do the same. He has thus condemned her to a dismal future of never being able to remarry. The situation outrages the conscience of this court."[30]

---

[27] A new s.253 entitled "Removal of Barriers to Remarriage" was added to the Domestic Relations Law Act of August 8, 1983, 1983 N.Y. Laws Chap. 79 codified at N.Y. Dom. Rel. Law para. 253 (McKinney supp. 1983).

[28] (1979) 5 F.L.R. (BNA) 2810 (N.Y. Sup.Ct. 1979).

[29] *Pal v. Pal* N.Y.L.J. July 25, 1973 rev'd 45 A.D.2d 738, 356 N.Y.S. 2d 672 (1974).

[30] *B v. B* (1978) N.Y.L.J. (May 4) quoted by Meislin in (1981) 4 Jewish Law Annual 270.

Those seeking the aid of the court argue that it is clearly inequitable for one party to a marriage to obtain freedom to remarry, while denying similar freedom to the other party. It has also been asserted by Freeman[31] that the English law creates injustice, which Parliament could easily remove. Until 1971[32] an "innocent" spouse could prevent a "guilty" spouse from ever divorcing him or her. This prevented the guilty spouse from remarrying and founding a new, legitimate, family. The Divorce Reform Act 1969 and the subsequent Matrimonial Causes Act 1973, rejected the notion of "fault" divorce only, and made unilateral divorce a possibility. Under the Matrimonial Causes Act 1973[33] a divorce may be obtained after the spouses have lived separately for five years, regardless of whether the respondent spouse consents or not. This allows both spouses to remarry. However, in cases where parties, due to their religious beliefs, require a religious divorce in order to remarry, the present law continues to create injustice. It does not ensure, when a decree of divorce is granted, that both parties are able to remarry in this country, according to the dictates of their religious faith.[34] This, it is contended, is a mischief which stands in need of a remedy, and one for which Parliament could easily provide the remedy.

A similar argument is made by Bleich[35] in relation to the law of the United States:

"When the husband presents a petition for divorce without making provision for a religious divorce, the court becomes a party to the creation of a state of affairs that may result in interference with free exercise of religion or lead to a gross inequity to the wife. A divorce decree is designed to enable both parties to remarry. A woman who for reasons of religious conscience is not free to remarry is deprived, by virtue of judicial decree, of the potential for consortium, the ability to establish a home and raise a family, and often of ongoing support and maintenance.

---

[31] Freeman, "Divorce and Religious Barriers to Marriage" a Working Paper. See also M.D.A. Freeman, "Jews and the Law of Divorce in England" (1981) The Jewish Law Annual 276.

[32] When the Divorce Reform Act 1969 came into force.

[33] s. 1(2)(e).

[34] The inability of the wife to obtain a religious divorce also creates limping marriages, a status greatly disliked by international private lawyers. The wife is still married according to Jewish law and may not marry another, but is single according to civil law and is free to marry again.

[35] Bleich, (1984) Vol. 16 Connecticut Law Review 201 at p. 280.

The court, in issuing a decree of divorce, establishes this inequity and in effect, tells the divorced wife that she may herself remedy the inequity by abandoning religious scruples."

Both writers point out the inevitable truth that a secular divorce will affect the financial and social position of the parties. It is also the case that, in the absence of a religious divorce, the spouses, usually the wife, will have little chance of abating the consequences of divorce. However, the problems experienced do not arise as a consequence of any secular legal requirements but as a result of religious requirements. Neither the Islamic nor Jewish religions are prepared, or regard themselves as having the ability, to change what are regarded as immutable laws, to give women the right to unilaterally divorce their husbands. It has been suggested that "if the Jewish law produces unfairness, the Jewish law must be changed".[36] Also

"Judaism must find its own solution . . . The sad fact is that Orthodox Jewish law in this area has stagnated . . . Orthodox Judaism feels powerless to effectuate a solution within Judaism, turning instead, somewhat ironically, to the civil authorities."[37]

The State, while rejecting any implication that they are under a duty to offer more than a system of secular divorce open to all on equal grounds, are nevertheless alive to the difficulties. As will be seen below, one American State, New York, has legislated in an attempt to resolve such problems,[38] while various judicial stratagems have been developed to persuade the reluctant spouse of the wisdom of obtaining a religious divorce.

A fourth reason for State intervention is the practice of some unscrupulous husbands who,[39] knowing the value placed on a religious divorce by their wives, have used their power to grant or

---

[36] Professor June Sinclair, Member of the Project Committee. South African Law Commission Working Paper No. 45, *Jewish Divorces.* (Project 76) p. 128.

[37] Loewenstein, *Judaism* (1990).

[38] The New York *get* law provides for the delaying of a civil decree of divorce until the plaintiff has removed any barriers to the defendants remarriage and may take account of the husband's failure to do so in determining equitable distribution of marital property and award of maintenance. See pp. 129–31.

[39] In the case of Jewish divorces a wife can also hold up the obtaining of a religious divorce by refusing to receive a *get* (in effect refusing to consent to divorce). Although rare in the past, refusals on the part of wives have increased over the last decade.

withhold divorce to negotiate favourable settlements on issues of finance, property or relating to children. Allegations of extortion and inequitable settlements are to be found in a number of United States cases.[40] An example of such extortion is provided by the recent New York case of *Perl v. Perl*.[41] The wife reached a settlement with her husband, the prerequisite for which was that the husband was to furnish her with a *get* within 10 days. The husband duly served the *get*, and the settlement came into force. Under the settlement, the wife agreed to deliver to her husband all remaining securities jointly owned by the parties, a payment of $35,000 to compensate the husband for jointly owned securities which she had previously sold; an additional payment of $30,000, a deed conveying her half-share in the matrimonial home, title to her car, her engagement ring and other personal jewellery. The only economic consideration that the wife was to receive was her husband's residual claim in two companies. One of these was allegedly defunct and valueless[42] and the other was in any event owned by her as separate property after the separation of the parties. When the wife failed to deliver all that was promised, the husband sought to enforce the settlement. The wife pleaded that the settlement had been reached through coercion and duress. Desperate to obtain a *get* she had submitted to his extortionate demands. Although the Court initially upheld the husband's claim, the Supreme Court of New York reversed this decision. The Supreme Court, in coming to their decision, noted that it was articulated public policy to aid those seeking a religious divorce. Also, unlike commercial contracts, separation agreements were to be strictly

---

[40] See *Avitzur v. Avitzur* 58 N.Y. 2d 108, *Rubin v. Rubin* 75 Misc 2d 776 and *Chambers v. Chambers* 122 Misc. 2d 671. The courts have consistently held that a separation agreement may be subject to review for duress or overreaching. This review will include the question of whether the control over the *get* was used by the husband to coerce a wife to yield to a settlement which is more beneficial to the husband.

[41] 126 A.D.2d 91; 512 N.Y.S.2d 372 (1987). Such a situation should not now arise in New York after the *get* statute see n.130. However, the divorce occurred before the *get* statute came into force. Similar cases could occur in other states, as New York is the only American state with a *get* statute. For details of the working of the statute see below at pp. 131–133.

[42] The wife alleged that the husband had embezzled $170,000 in cash and gold from the company.

scrutinised, to ensure that they were arrived at fairly, equitably and free from the taint of fraud and duress.

Allegations of similar extortion by Muslim husbands were referred to in the House of Commons during a debate on the Matrimonial and Family Proceedings Bill in 1984.[43] Practices included demands for lump sums, the return of wedding jewellery, threats to deport and agreements not to claim maintenance.[44] Such extortion was seen as a very valid reason for legislative intervention to assist in the obtaining of a religious divorce.

A last possible reason put forward for state intervention in the procuring of religious divorce is that, in multicultural societies, such as England and the United States, it is difficult to impose one standard of family law for all. This is particularly the case when that family law has developed historically from Anglican ecclesiastical law. The State, it has been argued, ought to acknowledge the existence of ethnic minorities and tolerate differences in personal laws where these affect no-one but the spouses themselves. In practical terms this would mean legislating either to encourage religious divorce, or withholding benefits, such as the civil divorce itself, until a religious divorce is obtained. Should spouses who married according to religious rites be forced by the State to obtain a religious divorce? The husband might well argue that he was never a practising member of his faith, but went through a religious ceremony of marriage merely to please his wife, or he may have converted to another religion. As far as the United States is concerned, such an approach is arguably in breach of the right to free exercise of religion, as well as a breach of the Establishment Clause. However, the New York *get* law provides that no party to a marriage, where that marriage was solemnised by a religious ceremony, may obtain a civil decree of divorce unless they certify that they have taken all "steps solely within his or her power to remove any barrier to the defendant's remarriage following the annulment or divorce". In passing such a statute it has been recognised that the appropriate remedy is not to hand over divorce jurisdiction to

---

[43] *Hansard* June 13, 1984, 926–932. The information on extortion was revealed during the course of debate on an amendment to the Bill which sought to introduce a new clause to remove religious barriers to remarriage. The amendment was withdrawn for reasons explained later in this chapter. See pp. 134–135.

[44] All cases referred to by Mr Peter Thurnham M.P. for Bolton North-East had occurred within his constituency. *Hansard* June 13, 1984, 926,7.

religious courts, which would be contrary to the Establishment Clause, but to encourage the spouses to fulfil a duty, taken on when they participated in a religious ceremony of marriage.[45]

In England pressure from the State to obtain a religious divorce might be seen as conflicting with the right to freedom of religion in the European Convention on Human Rights. It can also be argued that it is inappropriate that the civil law should place express pressure upon people to comply with a particular requirement of their present or former religious faith, whatever that might be. However, it has long been recognised on the Indian sub-continent that if a party marries within a religious faith, that religion continues to be the personal law of the spouses unless they both convert.[46] If only one spouse converts, he cannot choose to be guided by the new personal law to the detriment of the other spouse.[47] Equally, it can be argued that, where a spouse has undergone a religious marriage, he should be estopped from claiming lack of faith as the reason for refusing to go through a religious divorce, whether or not the religion now offends his moral tenets.

Encouraging and Assisting Religious Divorce

It has been largely accepted in both England and the United States that refusal to provide a wife with a religious divorce causes hardship to the wife, and the potential for great bitterness between the spouses. Encouraging religious divorce has, however, been difficult, partly due to religious laws themselves and partly to national, legal restrictions and attitudes. A considerable number of different approaches have been tried, particularly by courts in the United States.

In Jewish law a *get* must be granted voluntarily. A husband cannot be compelled to grant a *get*, and consent induced by fear, threat or penalty will render the *get* invalid. Thus an order by the court to grant a *get*, reinforced by the threat of imprisonment or a financial

---

[45] It is worth noting here that it has been argued strenuously that the serving of a *get* is not a religious act, but merely the fulfilment of a contractual obligation.

[46] See *Farooq Leivers v. Adelaide Bridget Mary* 1958 P.L.D. (WP) Lah. 431 and *Syed Ali Nawaz Gardezi v. Lt. Col. Muhammed Yusif* 1963 PLD SC 51. See generally, Pearl, *A Textbook on Muslim Personal Law* (1987), Chap. 10.

[47] See *Seth v. Seth* 694 S.W.2d 459 (1985). Court of Appeals, Texas.

penalty in the event of default, would probably render the *get* invalid in the eyes of Jewish law. Even apart from such religious difficulties, courts in the United States face constitutional problems. The First Amendment prohibits establishment and provides for free exercise of religion. Actions before the civil courts in which one party seeks an order of the court in relation to the obtaining of a religious divorce, runs the possibility of violating both parts of the Establishment Clause.

THE AMERICAN APPROACH: ENFORCING THE CONTRACT

(i) Express Terms. Faced with the restrictions of the First Amendment, courts in the United States have adopted a number of different innovative approaches to assist a party to obtain a religious divorce. One of these approaches has been to apply general contract principles. Where there is an express agreement between the parties to obtain a religious divorce, such an agreement may be enforced as a matter of contract, rather than as a matter of religious law. The courts, in treating the matter purely as one of contract law hope, by so doing, to avoid establishment and free exercise challenges.

A Jewish marriage contract or *ketubah*, may contain an express agreement that the couples will submit themselves to the *Beth Din* if one of the parties so requires.[48] Alternatively, an agreement to obtain a religious divorce may be part of a prenuptial agreement, or part of an agreement made in contemplation of civil divorce and a financial settlement. There has been some debate as to whether it is constitutional for courts in the United States to order specific enforcement of what appear, on their face, to be requirements to carry out a religious act. Bleich asks:

"May the assistance of the court be invoked in order to enforce a con-

---

[48] Known as the Lieberman proposal. Such a clause is commonly found in "Conservative" Jewish ketubahs. The enforceability of such a clause was at issue in *Avitzur v. Avitzur* 58 N.Y.2d 10, 446 N.E.2d 136, 459 N.Y.S.2d 572 (1983). The Chief Rabbi of the U.K. has also introduced mandatory pre-nuptial contracts for all United Synagogue (the governing body of orthodox Judaism) members. See Jewish Chronicle 22.10.93. It is envisaged by the Chief Rabbi that this will commit the husband to supporting his wife, even after a civil divorce, until such time as he grants her a *get*. It will also require that both parties co-operate with the *Beth Din* (the religious court) in all matters relating to a *get*. It is not at all clear that English courts would be willing to enforce such a contract.

tract when the contract is designed to accomplish a religious objective? The issue raised by the question is whether the First Amendment creates a barrier between Church and State so strong that the courts may never involve themselves in matters that are essentially religious in nature, or whether such matters may be litigated before the courts because the issue at stake is a civil one, namely enforcement of a contractual right, with the subject matter of the contract being merely a collateral aspect. Indeed, it may be argued that failure to enforce such a contract constitutes a violation of the free exercise clause of the First Amendment. Freedom to enter into such a contract with another party is a civil right; to exclude from contractual agreement areas that impinge upon religious practice is to interfere with free exercise of religion."[49]

In relation to agreements made in anticipation of separation or divorce, or as settlement of outstanding issues on divorce, the willingness of the courts to order specific performance of the terms of the contract has indeed depended largely on the extent to which the court regards this as a purely civil issue. Thus in *Steinberg v. Steinberg*[50] the Ohio court, interpreting a clause to obtain a *get* as a religious act, held that it would not sanction direct enforcement of the clause because such an order violated the First Amendment.[51] However, the New York Supreme Court in *Koeppel v. Koeppel*[52] denied that enforcement of such a provision amounted to violation of the husband's First Amendment freedoms, as the obtaining of a *get* did not require any involvement in a religious ceremony, but was merely enforcing an agreement freely made.[53] The court was at pains to emphasise the civil nature of the obligation:

"Defendant has also contended that a decree of specific performance would interfere with his freedom of religion under the Constitution. Complying with his agreement would not compel the defendant to practice any religion, not even the Jewish faith to which he still admits adherence . . . His appearance before the Rabbinate to answer questions and

---

[49] Bleich, Vol. 16 (1984) Connecticut Law Review 201 at 227,228.

[50] No. 44125; 1982 WL 2446 (Ohio Ct.App. June 24, 1982).

[51] See also *Margulies v. Margulies* 344 N.Y.S.2d 482, (N.Y. App. Div.) appeal dismissed, 307 N.E.2d 562 (N.Y. 1973).

[52] 138 N.Y.S.2d 366 (Sup.Ct. 1954) aff'd 3 A.D.2d 853, 161 N.Y.S.2d 694(1957).

[53] While it appears that the court can order specific performance of an agreement to obtain a *get*, the court may not enforce the order of specific performance by means of imprisonment nor may the court order the convening of a rabbinical tribunal. See Margulies 344 N.Y.S. 2d 482, (N.Y.App.Div.) appeal dismissed 307 N.E.2d 562 (N.Y. 1973) and Bleich *ibid.* at p. 241.

give evidence needed by them to make a decision is not a profession of faith. Specific performance herein would merely require the defendant to do what he voluntarily agreed to do."[54]

The courts appear particularly willing to order specific performance where the express agreement forms part of a divorce settlement. Where one spouse is holding up implementation of the settlement through refusal to fulfil the obligation to obtain or receive a *get*, the courts have treated this as a purely secular issue, requiring enforcement as a matter not only of contract, but also of equity. Thus, in *Waxstein v. Waxstein*[55] the court was willing to uphold a provision in the couple's separation agreement that required the husband to execute a *get*, noting the inherent unfairness of permitting the husband to receive the benefits of the agreement without complying with its relatively light burdens. Similarly, in *Rubin v. Rubin*,[56] the court would not enforce an agreement to pay alimony and support where the plaintiff wife had refused to fulfil the condition precedent to the payments and accept a *get*. The judge found that the court's involvement was not with religious practice but with the obligations made contingent thereon. This was not a matter of enforcing religious discipline, but a civil issue. The wife was faced with fulfilling her side of the bargain and receiving a *get* or the proceedings would be dismissed on their merits.[57]

---

[54] The nature of Jewish marriage and divorce is often confused with that of Christianity. Jewish marriage is a contract, and does not confer any status on the spouse. The couple may terminate their contract by mutual agreement. The only role for the *Beth Din* is to ensure that the document is correctly drawn up. The actual divorce is effected by the couple themselves without any religious involvement. The husband's appeal against compliance with the contract was, in fact, upheld by the Appeal Court but for reasons that had nothing to do with the validity of the order of specific performance.

[55] 395 N.Y.S.2d 877(N.Y. Sup.Ct. 1976), affirmed 394 N.Y.S.2d 253 (N.Y.App.-Div.), appeal denied, 367 N.E.2d 660 (N.Y. 1977).

[56] 75 Misc.2d 776; 348 N.Y.S.2d 61 (1973).

[57] This case contrasts with that of *Margulies* 344 N.Y.S.2d 482, (N.Y. App. Div.) appeal dismissed, 307 N.E.2d 562 (N.Y. 1973) where the court was called upon to command specific performance and to enforce a religious discipline upon a recalcitrant party, albeit as a result of a prior undertaking on the part of that party. In Rubin the court was not asked to directly enforce the obtaining of a *get*, rather to enforce alimony payments. The two cases are distinguishable. *Margulies* required "excessive entanglement", whereas Rubin involved no such entanglement in an act of a religious nature. See Bleich (1984), Vol. 16 Connecticut Law Review 201 at 239. Breitowitz in his article "The Plight of the Agunah: A Study in Halacha, Contract and the First Amendment" (1992) 51 Md.L.Rev. 312 suggests that *Margulies* was wrongly decided.

While most of the "express agreement" cases deal with clauses contained in divorce settlements, the court has also been willing to enforce an express term in the *ketubah* or marriage contract, requiring the parties to recognise the authority of the *Beth Din*, as well as its right to summon one party to appear before it at the request of the other. In *Avitzur v. Avitzur*[58] the wife, after obtaining a civil divorce, commenced an action for specific performance of the clause, to bring her husband before the *Beth Din* and thus cause him to grant her a *get*. The husband, in opposing the action, sought dismissal of the suit on the basis that the dispute was essentially religious, and that any assumption of jurisdiction by the court would involve an unconstitutional entanglement of Church and State. The Appellate Court of New York, in a judgment echoed in the implied term cases, stated that the parties had entered into a contract when they signed the *ketubah*, and thus:

"The case can be decided solely upon the application of neutral principles of contract law, without reference to any religious principle . . . In short, the religious relief sought by plaintiff in this action is simply to compel defendant to perform a secular obligation to which he contractually bound himself. In this regard, no doctrinal issue need be passed upon, no implementation of a religious duty is contemplated, and no interference with religious authority will result."

It is submitted that the approach taken by the Appellate Court of New York in this case is correct. The issue should be one of contract, and the nature of the agreement ought to be irrelevant. However, it seems quite clear that a court could not order specific performance of an agreement by the parties to attend church every week, or to pray every day, or to maintain a level of religious observance. Thus the court must find a distinction between such acts and appearing before the *Beth Din* and obtaining a religious divorce. It can be argued that no act of overt worship is required. But, undoubtedly, reference to a religious tribunal must involve an element of religion, and in the case of *Avitzur*, pressure to comply with religious requirements.

While the courts regard the giving of a *get* as a secular act, it is difficult to regard it as anything other than an act of religious sig-

[58] 58 N.Y.2d 10, 446 N.E.2d 136, 459 N.Y.S.2d 572 (1983).

nificance. It has, after all, no civil significance, and involves co-operation and compliance with religious authority.

(ii) Implied Agreement. Whatever misgivings might exist where the courts enforce express agreements to obtain a *get*, these are even greater when the courts are dealing with implied contractual terms. It is, of course, a truism to point out that those entering in marriage do not usually have divorce in mind. Jewish couples only have their attention brought to the most general obligations of marriage under Jewish law in the *ketubah*,[59] or marriage contract, which accompanies every Jewish wedding, and without which a Jewish marriage is invalid. The *ketubah* states that the marriage shall be in "accordance with the laws of Moses and Israel".[60] But can one infer from this an undertaking that the parties will agree to give or receive a *get*, under Jewish law, when they divorce civilly? It was held in *Stern v. Stern*[61] that such a term could be implied, and the court ordered the husband to give the wife a *get*.[62] The court rejected any idea that such a decision was a breach of the Establishment Clause, and found no First Amendment barrier in imposing such an obligation. The Court found, rather astonishingly, that the rules which govern the relationship of human beings to one another are secular in nature rather than religious. Again, in *Minkin v. Minkin*[63] the court held that compelling issuance of a *get* is not prohibited establishment of religion because such an order has a "clear secular purpose", that of completing the process of dissolution.[64] Moreover, because the *get* does not involve a profession of faith and the court is simply requiring the husband to do what he had voluntarily agreed to do, there was no infringement of free exercise rights.

Both *Stern* and *Minkin* were cases where the wife had committed

---

[59] A *ketubah* is a document setting out the obligations of a husband towards his wife.
[60] It is pointed out by some commentators that the ketubah is in Aramaic and can rarely be read by the parties. However, an English translation is normally provided, either on the document or orally. How much the couple understand depends partly on their level of religious education.
[61] 5 Fam. L. Rep. (BNA) 2810 (N.Y. Sup.Ct.Aug.7 1979).
[62] The wife in this case had committed adultery, and the court found, on the basis of expert testimony, that a husband is bound to divorce his wife in Jewish law under such circumstances.
[63] 434 A.2d 665 (N.J. Super.Ct.Ch.Div. 1981).
[64] A process only required, of course, by particular religions. It is not required in order to remarry under civil law.

adultery and divorce was mandatory under Jewish law. However, a willingness to enforce implied terms has not been limited to such cases. In *Burns* v. *Burns*[65] the court found, rather surprisingly, that in every case of civil dissolution, the *ketubah* imposes an affirmative obligation on the parties to dissolve the bonds of matrimony in a religiously appropriate manner. Again, in reaching their decision the court found that no religious freedoms were infringed.[66] The court did not, however, order the husband directly to execute a *get*, but ordered him to submit to the jurisdiction of a rabbinical court and initiate the procedure. This was a fundamentally different approach to that taken by the court in *Minkin* where a direct order to obtain a *get* was made on the basis that the giving of a *get* was not a religious act.

In *Re Marriage of Goldman*[67] the enforceability of the implied terms of the *ketubah* were finally considered by an appellate court. On the husband's petition for divorce, the wife counterclaimed *inter alia* for specific performance of the *ketubah* as a premarital contact that required the husband to obtain a *get* upon dissolution of their marriage.[68] The trial court found "that the *ketubah* clearly and unequivocally obligates the husband to proceed with the *get* procedure", and ordered that the husband comply with such requirement. On appeal the husband argued that, first, the *ketubah* was not a legally enforceable contract; second, that its terms were too vague to support a decree of specific performance; and third, that the order violated the Establishment and Free Exercise Clauses. The Illinois Appellate Court rejected all of these contentions. The Court found that the trial court order did not violate the Establishment Clause as the order had the secular purpose of enforcing the contract between the parties. The court order also furthered two secular purposes; it promoted the amicable settlement of a dispute between parties to a marriage, and it mitigated the potential harm to the spouses and their children caused by the process of legal dis-

---

[65] 538 A.2d 438 (N.J. Super Ct.Ch.Div. (1987).

[66] The court rejected Mr Burn's free exercise claim. This was largely due to uncontroverted evidence that he was willing to give a *get* in exchange for a $25,000 payment. The court found the offer akin to extortion and beyond the pale of the First Amendment.

[67] 554 N.E.2d 1016 (Ill.App.Ct.) appeal denied, 555 N.E. 2d 376 (Ill. 1990).

[68] The couple had married under a "reconstructionist" ceremony, *i.e.* not orthodox, but had utilised an orthodox *ketubah*.

solution of marriage.[69] It was the opinion of the Appeal Court that the primary effect of the order to obtain a *get* was to further secular purposes and did not inhibit or advance religion. Confirming *Minkin*, the court regarded the obtaining of a *get* as a secular act. The husband was not required to engage in any act of worship or profess any religious belief. There was equally no breach of free exercise, because the husband was doing nothing more than he agreed to do when he signed the *ketubah*.

It can be vigorously argued that the State has a secular interest in such cases. Apart from policy and human rights considerations relating to the encouragement of marriage, removing the barriers to remarriage, stabilising family life and the protection of children, the State can also argue an interest in assuring adherence to contracts and in affording remedies to those aggrieved by the breach. The courts appear to have adopted *Bleich's* view that an agreement between the couple to be guided by Jewish law in relation to their marriage, will, in the absence of public policy restraints, be upheld as a valid contract, the subject matter being merely a collateral aspect. The courts have refused to support the argument that enforcing such a contract would be a breach of the free exercise rights of the objecting party. Instead, the courts have taken the view that failure to enforce such a contract itself constitutes a violation of the Free Exercise Clause, in that the courts should not prevent the couple from making agreements about their marital relationship according to their religious values and beliefs.

Such decisions, while extremely effective both in avoiding First Amendment complications and in assisting a party to obtain a religious divorce, are rather dubious. It is extremely difficult to see how such vague terms as "be thou my wife in accordance with the laws of Moses and Israel" implies an agreement to obtain a religious divorce. There is no express reference to the obtaining of a divorce in an orthodox *ketubah*. Neither does it seem that the court would be willing to provide a remedy for any other infringement of the laws of Moses and Israel. If a husband refused to attend religious services in conformity with his religious duties, thus reducing the wife's standing in the religious community, or the wife failed to keep a kosher home, it is extremely unlikely that the court would be willing to find such obligations were enforceable in

---

[69] Ill. Rev. Stat. (1987) Chap. 40, paras. 102(3), 102(4)

a court of law, on the basis of an implied term in the contract of marriage. The court would undoubtedly declare that it had no jurisdiction in such an essentially religious matter. What lies behind the willingness of courts in the United States, in both implied term and express term cases, to grant specific enforcement of the contract? The answer to this lies not in the fiction of contract, but in notions of equity and estoppel. It has been suggested by *Breitowitz*[70] that by agreeing to a religious ceremony the spouse agrees to certain disabilities and restrictions on remarriage. It would be inequitable to invoke free exercise as a protective, exonerating shield against the very harms that the party has previously created.

> "The Free Exercise Clause does not exempt a party from undoing the harms caused to another party by the very religious restrictions that the party himself invoked but now repudiates."[71]

Put another way, having agreed to enter marriage under religious jurisdiction, thus raising a need for the wife to obtain a religious divorce, the court sees no free exercise constraint in ordering a party to the marriage to exit under the same jurisdiction. Having been willing to marry in religious form, an argument that the party no longer subscribes to that religious belief is insufficient as a basis for a free exercise claim.

THE AMERICAN APPROACH: LEGISLATIVE REMEDIES

Although the contractual approach may serve as an ideal solution to the need of Jewish couples to obtain a *get* before remarriage, it does not necessarily answer for other religions where a religious divorce is necessary. It has also been recognised that the "contract" decisions are vulnerable to challenge. The fiction that obtaining a *get* is a purely secular act cannot be sustained when subjected to analysis. Indeed, in recognition of the vulnerability of the "contract" decisions, the New York legislature passed the "*get*" stat-

---

[70] "The Plight of the Agunah: A Study in Halacha, Contract and the First Amendment" (1992) 51 Md. L.Rev. 312 at 359.
[71] *ibid.*

ute.[72] An amendment to the Domestic Relations Law, paragraph 253 provides:

"(2) Any party to a marriage . . . who commences a proceeding to annul the marriage or for a divorce must allege, in his or her verified complaint that he or she has taken or will take, prior to the entry of final judgment, all steps solely within his or her power to remove any barrier to the defendant's remarriage following the annulment or divorce; or that the defendant has waived in writing the requirements of this subdivision.
(3) No final judgment of annulment or divorce shall thereafter be entered unless the plaintiff shall have filed and served a sworn statement that he or she has, prior to the entry of such final judgment, taken all steps solely within his or her power to remove all barriers to the defendants remarriage following the annulment or divorce . . .
(4) In any action for divorce . . . in which the defendant enters a general appearance and does not contest the requested relief, no final judgment of annulment or divorce shall be entered unless both parties shall have filed and served sworn statements that each has taken all steps solely within his or her power to remove all barriers to the other party's remarriage following the annulment or divorce . . .
(5) As used in the verified statements prescribed by this section 'barriers to remarriage' includes, any religious or conscientious restraint or inhibition imposed on a party to a marriage, under the principles of the denomination of the clergyman or minister who has solemnized the marriage, by reason of the other party's commission or withholding of any voluntary act. It shall not be deemed a 'barrier to remarriage' within the meaning of this section if the restraint or inhibition cannot be removed by the party's voluntary act.[73] Nor shall it be deemed a 'barrier to remarriage' if the party must incur expenses in connection with removal of the restraint or inhibition and the other party refuses

---

[72] Since 1983 model *get* bills have been introduced in the legislatures of California, Connecticut, New Jersey and Pennsylvania, but have been voted down. Preliminary drafting of bills was also carried out in Maryland and Michigan but the bills were never formally introduced before the legislature. The only other state with similar legislation is Ontario, Canada. The 1983 *get* law was amended in 1992 at which time some of the features of the Ontario statute were incorporated into the New York statute. See p. 133.
[73] The Act does not apply to restraints or inhibitions that cannot be removed by the plaintiff's voluntary act. Thus if a Catholic husband files for divorce he will be entitled to civil relief even though his spouse is unable to remarry since the barrier is not one that can be removed by the parties.

to provide reasonable reimbursement for such expenses. "All steps solely within his or her power" shall not be construed to include application to a marriage tribunal[74] or other similar organization or agency of a religious denomination which has authority to annul or dissolve a marriage under the rules of such denomination."

The effect of this statute is limited. First, the court cannot directly order the plaintiff husband to obtain a divorce, rather it may prevent him from obtaining a civil divorce until he complies, or at least alleges under oath, that he complies. The obligation to provide an affidavit when a petition for divorce is lodged, lies on both the plaintiff and the acquiescing defendant. The defendant who is contesting the divorce is not under an obligation to file an affidavit. Such a statute will provide protection to the wife whose husband, the plaintiff, wants a civil divorce but is not prepared to give a *get*. However, it will not aid the wife where she is the petitioner and the husband does not care whether or not he receives a divorce. The plaintiff wife may file an affidavit that she has removed all barriers to remarriage, but the defendant husband may fail to file and serve a statement to that effect. The only sanction that the court may impose for this refusal, and the refusal to initiate the *get* procedure, is to withhold the granting of a civil divorce. Even if the wife agrees to waive the requirement that a sworn statement be filed and obtain a civil divorce, she is no further towards obtaining a religious divorce, and the court has no means of persuasion.

Secondly, and it is submitted quite correctly, the provisions only apply to spouses who celebrated their marriage through a religious ceremony. Those who married in a civil ceremony are not covered whatever their later religious persuasion.

Thirdly, Section 6 limits the statute to:

"any religious or conscientious restraint or inhibition, of which the party required to make the verified statement is aware, that is imposed on a party to a marriage, under the principles held by the clergyman or minister who solemnized the marriage."

Thus where a marriage is celebrated under the auspices of reform or reconstructionist Judaism where a *get* is not required, a divorce

---

[74] Presumably the *Beth Din* is not a marriage tribunal within the definition of this Act. The *Beth Din's* role is only supervisory rather than judicial.

would not attract the attentions of this statute. A woman who married in a reform Jewish ceremony and later became orthodox, such as happened in *Avitzur*[75] would not be covered and would still be left without a remedy.

The promoters of the *get* law were aware that the statute posed constitutional problems both in relation to free exercise and establishment. Most commentators agree, however, that free exercise is not really impaired, even though the receipt of a civil remedy, in this case, divorce, is dependent for some on performance of an act prescribed exclusively by religious law.[76] First, by the terms of the statute the court does not directly order the plaintiff to do anything; it simply conditions the obtaining of relief on the removal of barriers to remarriage. Non-compliance with religious law imposes no burdens but simply leaves the parties where they were by continuing the *status quo*. Secondly, the statute only applies to cases where the parties married in a religious ceremony. It is arguable that when parties agree to celebrate their marriage by a religious ceremony, this carries with it an implied understanding that the parties will comply with any religious requirements relating to dissolution of the marriage.[77] Even if the court were unwilling to enforce such an implied term, the fact that the parties consented and chose religious marriage makes coercion to obtain a religious divorce less objectionable.[78]

Even if objections could be shown on the alternative ground that the statute offended the Establishment Clause, and this is doubtful, such a breach may well be overridden by compelling state interests in this field. The State has an interest in ending dead marriages and letting the parties build their lives anew. Indeed, the right to marry and found a family is a fundamental constitutional right recognised

---

[75] 58 N.Y.2d 10, 446 N.E.2d 136, 459 N.Y.S.2d 572 (1983).

[76] Not all commentators agree. Warmflash in his article, "The New York Approach to Enforcing Religious Marriage Contracts: From Avitzur to the *Get* Statute" (1984) Vol.50 Brooklyn Law Review 229, states that the statute will ultimately be held unconstitutional.

[77] This was certainly the view of the American courts in *Minkin* 434 A.2d 665 (N.J. Super Ct.Ch.Div. 1981), *Stern* 5 Fam.L.Rep. (BNA) 2810 (N.Y. Sup.Ct. Aug.7, 1979.) and *Re the Marriage of Goldman* 554 N.E.2d 1016 (Ill.App.Ct.) appeal denied, 555 N.E.2d 376 (Ill. 1990).

[78] See Breitowitz, "The plight of the Agunah: A Study in Halacha, Contract and the First Amendment" (1992) 51 Md. L. Rev. 312 and Breitowitz, *Between Civil and Religious Law* (1993).

by *Roe v. Wade*,[79] which covers remarriage after divorce as well as first marriages.

Although the *get* statute was welcomed by most,[80] its usefulness, it became apparent, was limited. To this end there was a further amendment to the Domestic Relations Law in 1992.[81] Paragraph 236B allows the court to consider, where appropriate, the refusal or failure of a husband to remove barriers to remarriage in determining equitable distribution of marital property and the award of maintenance.[82] The section finally provides the court with a sanction with teeth, when the husband refuses to provide the wife with a religious divorce. Section 253 only allows the court to withhold the civil divorce, which may be a matter of indifference to the husband. Section 236, however, allows the court to take account of the disadvantage to the wife if she does not obtain a *get*, and reflect this in the financial settlement. By requiring a plaintiff to remove any barriers to remarriage and by enforcing this with the possibility of financial sanctions, the legislation manages to provide an equality to women denied by the religious law. It can be argued that it is not appropriate for the law to single out one particular hardship caused to one particular religious group. However, although termed the *get* statute, such legislative provisions can apply to any religious group with similar problems, and such an approach should be welcomed.

THE ENGLISH APPROACH

Interestingly, the approach of the 1992 amendment to the New York *get* statute reflects that taken in the English case of *Brett v. Brett*.[83] The Court of Appeal was asked to decide whether the con-

---

[79] 410 U.S.113 (1973). The state also has an interest in protecting its citizens from being victimised by unfair and coercive practices.

[80] See, *e.g.* Marshall, "Comment: The religion clauses and compelled religious divorces: a study in marital and constitutional separations" (1985) North Western University Law Review 204.

[81] 1992 New York Laws ch.415 amending New York Domestic Relations Law para. 236(b).

[82] The statute still only applies to those barriers to remarriage that exist under the principles of a clergyman who solemnised the marriage. Thus Jews marrying under a reform or reconstructionist service would not be covered as these branches of Judaism do not require a *get* before remarriage, regarding the civil divorce as sufficient for dissolution.

[83] [1969] 1 All E.R. 1007. It also reflects the *get* statute passed in Ontario, Canada.

duct of the husband in refusing or failing to grant a *get*, thereby precluding the possibility of the wife remarrying and finding some other man to support her, in the event of her wishing to do so, was relevant in assessing the amount of maintenance due to the wife.[84] The Court thought it right to make provision in the award for the possibility of the husband persisting in his refusal to grant the *get*. The husband was, therefore, ordered to pay a lump sum of £30,000 payable in two instalments, £25,000 within 14 days and the balance of £5,000 three months later if, by that time, the husband had not granted a *get*. The Court of Appeal had no doubt that the husband was using the *get* as a weapon to seek an advantage in bargaining with the wife.[85]

While the decision was effective in persuading the husband to provide a *get*, such an approach is limited to those cases where a husband has reasonably substantial financial assets, and can be threatened. Jewish and Muslim organisations would prefer a rather firmer footing from which the courts could encourage and assist parties to obtain a religious divorce. Initially, reform activity was centred on the introduction of a Remarriage (religious barriers) Clause which was considered by the House of Commons in 1984 as an amendment to the Matrimonial and Family Proceedings Bill. The clause was based on the New York *get* statute, allowing either party to oppose the grant of a decree absolute of divorce, on the ground that a barrier to religious remarriage existed which was within the power of the other party to remove. The court would have had the power to refuse a decree absolute until the barrier was removed, or the parties had taken all steps within their power to remove any barrier.[86]

The Bill was introduced to aid both Muslims and Jews in obtaining a religious divorce, but was withdrawn when the Lord Chancellor announced through the Solicitor-General that the clause was

---

[84] The wife here divorced her husband after five and a half months marriage on the ground of his cruelty. 14 months after the civil divorce, the husband had still not granted her a *get*, a fact the court took into account when the husband appealed against the financial provision ordered by the court.

[85] There was no consideration at all of the *ketubah* as a contract as happens in American cases. There has been some doubt expressed as to whether a *get* given under such circumstances of coercion would be valid under Jewish law. See M.D.A. Freeman, "Divorce and Religious Barriers to Remarriage", a paper submitted to the Law Commission. However, such an approach has been accepted by the *Beth Din* in New York.

[86] Or, alternatively, until the application was withdrawn by the applicant.

not suitably drafted for inclusion in the Matrimonial and Family Proceedings Bill. He pointed out that he had not had a chance to consult with all relevant religious bodies, but that the issue would be reviewed by him for future action.

Since the clause was debated, attitudes towards reform have changed. The New York *get* statute before 1992 was not, on its own, that effective in providing a remedy, because it only protected a wife whose husband wanted a civil divorce. Where the husband was indifferent as to whether a civil divorce was obtained, there was no sanction or leverage that could be used against him to encourage him to comply and grant a religious divorce. A statute based on the 1992 New York amendment has not been proposed for England, but the courts could, on the precedent of *Brett*,[87] exercise discretion and take into account the inability of the wife to remarry when making orders under sections 23 and 24 of the Matrimonial Causes Act 1973.[88]

The Law Commission, in its reports "Facing the Future"[89] and the "Grounds of Divorce",[90] recommended that divorce become a "process over time". This would result in a system of divorce after a period of consideration and reflection.[90a] The Ground of Divorce report proposed that once a statement of marital breakdown was lodged with the court there would be a minimum period of eleven months before applying for a divorce. During that time the parties would seek to resolve arrangements in relation to their children, property and finances. The Board of Deputies of British Jews recommended[91] that during this time the parties should file a statement setting out their proposals for terminating their marriage religiously. Under the recommendations, the court would hold a preliminary assessment to monitor progress. This would take place no later than 12 weeks after the lodging of the statement of marital breakdown. In particular, the court would have a duty to identify issues in dispute and to consider how best these might amicably be

---

[87] [1969] 1 All E.R. 1007.
[88] In relation to financial provision and property settlement.
[89] Law Commission Discussion Paper No. 170.
[90] Law Commission No. 192 (1990).
[90a] The Lord Chancellor's Department issued a White Paper on Divorces *Looking to the Future, Mediation and the ground for divorce*, Cm.2799 (1995), which substantially supports the Law Commission's recommendations. The fact that the White Paper was released so close to publication date precludes discussion of this document in detail.
[91] In their response to "Facing the Future".

resolved. Again, the Board of Deputies proposed that this be followed in relation to the *get* procedure. Where one of the parties had not attempted to participate in obtaining a *get* this would be treated as a specific issue to be resolved. What though of those cases where this issue is not resolved? The Law Commission recognised in its proposals that there may be instances when the divorce decree may have to be delayed. Such a delay would be permitted where this was desirable in order to enable proper arrangements for the couples children or their finances or property to be made. Under the present legislation, where a petitioner relies on the fact of five years separation to obtain a divorce under the Matrimonial Causes Act 1973,[92] section 5 of the Act permits the respondent to oppose the grant of a *decree nisi*. This may be done on the ground that "the dissolution of the marriage will result in grave financial or other hardship to him *and* that it would, in all the circumstances, be wrong to dissolve the marriage".[93] The Law Commission have recommended[94] that the hardship bar be retained and applied to the new system of proposed divorce. This would enable the court to deny a divorce to a spouse who was refusing to give the other a *get*, if it could be shown that hardship and injustice would be caused. The Board of Deputies support this proposal, although on its face, it would appear to suffer from the same problems as the New York *get* procedure. In other words, there is no real incentive for the disinterested husband or wife to consent. However, if such a proposal were implemented, this would allow the courts to encourage religious divorce and free people to remarry within their own community.

No legislative action has, as yet, resulted from the Law Commissions proposals for the reform of divorce law. Thus, the problems of religious divorce remain. The Chief Rabbi's office have recently, however, pursued another avenue to encourage spouses to consent to the giving of a *get*. In October 1993[95] the Chief Rabbi

---

[92] Rather than two years separation with consent. The five year ground is used where the other party does not consent to divorce.

[93] Up until now it has been predominantly wives that have used this section; some on the ground that divorce is unacceptable to their religion and that their standing in the community would be so gravely affected that this would amount to social ostracism and thus constitute hardship. Such a plea has never been successful and the court have never found hardship to exist purely on religious grounds. See *Banik v. Banik* [1973] 1 W.L.R. 860, *Rukat v. Rukat* [1975] Fam. 63, *Balraj v. Balraj* (1981) 11 Fam. Law 110.

[94] In "Grounds for Divorce" paras. 5.72—5.76.

[95] See *Jewish Chronicle*, October 22, 1993.

introduced mandatory pre-nuptial contracts for orthodox Jewish marriages.[96] Such contracts or agreements will commit the husband to support his wife,[97] even after civil divorce, until such time as he grants the wife a *get*. It will also require both parties to co-operate with the *Beth Din*, the religious court, in all matters relating to obtaining a *get*. This agreement, by imposing a duty of support until the giving of a *get*, goes someway towards removing the hardship to the wife whose husband refuses to remove barriers to her remarriage. However, it is unclear to what extent any such agreement would be enforced by the English courts. Only a test case will provide an answer. Whatever the outcome of such a case, it would still be open to a judge to take into account the husband's failure to comply with the terms of the agreement in assessing financial provision and property division. It is also possible that the court could treat the husband's refusal as conduct which "it would be inequitable to disregard",[98] once more leading to a financial settlement in favour of the wife.[99]

Whatever financial pressure the courts are willing to place on a husband refusing to obtain a *get* after signing such an agreement, self-regulation, with a little help from the courts, is a more realistic way of dealing with the problem of *gets* in the present climate. It also meets the objections of those who argue that it is not the role of the English court to coerce a spouse to obtain a religious divorce. Where the husband has voluntarily entered into an agreement with his wife to co-operate with the *Beth Din* in the event of marriage breakdown, encouragement from the court to meet such obligations can hardly be regarded as undue coercion.

It has been argued,[1] both as a matter of policy and as a matter of equity and individual justice, that matrimonial legislation should not become a vehicle for unconscionable religious manipulation . In encouraging and assisting the obtaining of religious divorces, the courts in both England and the United States have recognised the

---

[96] This will apply to all those marrying under the auspices of the United Synagogue, the governing body of English orthodox Judaism. A similar requirement was imposed by American orthodox rabbis in the U.S. a few months earlier.

[97] The pre-nuptial contract only places sanctions on the husband who refuses to give a *get*. It does not impose any sanctions on a wife who refuses to receive a *get*.

[98] Matrimonial Causes Act 1973, s.12(2)(g).

[99] These are the suggestions of Judge Myrella Cohen and Judge Dawn Freedman, *Jewish Chronicle*, "Letters", October 29, 1993.

[1] Berkovits, "*Get* and *Talaq* in English Law: Reflections on Law and Policy" in *Islamic Family Law* (Mallet & Connors (eds.) 1990).

validity of this claim, as well as the inequity of non-intervention. They have gone a considerable, and ingenious, way towards remedying the refusal of parties to grant religious divorce.

Conclusion

Unlike marriage, where civil law has made very little difference to pre-existing religious law and religious marriage, the introduction of a civil divorce system has had quite a different effect. The introduction of civil divorce was not compatible with pre-existing religious divorce laws in either England or the United States, as divorce did not exist in the Anglican Established Church or in the Roman Catholic Church. In both England and the United States, civil divorce allowed parties to obtain a decree that was not obtainable under their religious law[2] and was directly contradictory to religious teachings. Its introduction resulted, in time, in the diminution of the influence of religious laws, and undermined the control of religions over the family.

People are free to live in accordance with their religious beliefs and values, and may choose to treat their marriage as a life-long union. However, they are also free to obtain a civil divorce and remarry. The only sanction the Christian churches have been able to impose on members who take advantage of the civil divorce law, is one of non-recognition of the divorce, and exclusion of the divorcee from certain sacraments of the church. The very availability of divorce in civil law, though, has forced some churches, particularly the Protestant churches, to change their outlook on divorce, to drop their objections to divorce and to recognise and accept civil divorce.[3]

For minority religions, such as Judaism and Islam, where religious divorce has always been a possibility, religious divorce has been overtaken by civil divorce. At the same time, the encouragement of religious divorce has become a matter of recent concern. One would expect that a society with a written constitution, prohibiting the establishment of religion and guaranteeing free exercise of religion, would have little truck with the encouragement of

---

[2] Jews and Muslims were able to obtain a divorce, but, as we have seen, the validity of such divorces was dubious.

[3] See, *e.g.* the current attitude of the church of England, discussed at p. 88.

religious divorces. In fact, the opposite is true. While both England and the United States have, through the courts, legislatures and law reform bodies, encouraged parties to obtain a religious divorce where this is a necessary precondition to religious remarriage, the United States have been far more active in this field. Establishment thus appears to have little effect on the willingness to encourage religious divorce.

The issue arises as to whether the imposition of a secular, civil divorce system is in conflict with the right to religious freedom. It is difficult to sustain an argument that civil divorce violates religious freedom. A failure to obtain a civil divorce may have an effect on a party's civil rights, such as rights to social benefits or succession rights, but it does not prevent people living in accordance with their religious values and beliefs. Further, obtaining a civil divorce in addition to a religious divorce, before remarrying, cannot be regarded as a great infringement of civil liberty, or as an attack on religious freedom, particularly as a civil divorce may be obtained unilaterally.

One may conclude that the level of tolerance for religious laws on divorce is very low in both England and the United States. Although the courts have been willing to lend their aid to encourage religious divorces,[4] there is no question of religious divorces being recognised for any purposes. Civil divorce alone, can provide a valid divorce allowing the parties to remarry.

[4] For members of minority religions who are divorcing within England or the U.S. This does not apply to overseas divorces.

Chapter Four

The Upbringing of Children

One of the most important means of transmitting religious beliefs and values, and of sustaining a religious culture, is through the family. Through religious practices in the home, and by the family joining with a community of fellow-believers, a religion is bequeathed from one generation to the next. To ensure continuity of the religion, parents must be free to teach their children its tenets, doctrines and practices. The right of parents to control their child's religious upbringing is not, however, absolute. In both England and the United States there is a duty under common law (under the *parens patriae* jurisdiction) and under legislation[1] to protect children and to act in their best interests. A similar duty exists under Article 3 of the United Nations Convention on the Rights of the Child[2]:

"In all actions concerning children, whether undertaken by public or private social welfare institutions, courts of law, administrative authorities or legislative bodies, the best interests of the child shall be a primary consideration."

A further limitation on parental action is the right of children to make their own decisions as they become mature and able to do so. Such a right can be seen in both English and United States case

---

[1] Under the Children Act 1989, s.1 in England.
[2] The U.K. ratified this Convention in October 1991, although the U.S. has still to ratify it. Art. 3 provides that in all actions concerning children, whether undertaken by public or social private social welfare institutions, courts of law or administrative authorities or legislative bodies, the best interests of the child shall be a primary consideration.

law.[3] It is reinforced by Article 12 of the United Nations Convention on the Rights of the Child:

> "States Parties shall assure to the child who is capable of forming his or her own views the right to express those views freely in all matters affecting the child, the views of the child being given due weight in accordance with the age and maturity of the child."

In the light of these potentially competing rights, the aim of this chapter will be to consider how the right of parents to determine their children's upbringing according to their religious beliefs is balanced against the right and duty of the State to protect children, to act in their best interests, and to give consideration to their wishes. The chapter will also explore whether having an Established Church in England affects the balancing of these rights, and the extent to which the best interests of the child are a primary consideration.

It is accepted in both England and the United States that individuals have a right to practice the religion of their choice.[4] It has been further accepted that a parent has the right to pass on their religion to their child. This right of a parent exists in domestic law in England, in the Constitution of the United States and in international instruments.

The right to transmit parental or in early times, paternal, religious values has long been an accepted part of common law and common understanding. Under English common law, the father was the legal head of the family. One of the rights that flowed from this position was the right to choose the religion of any legitimate children. The father retained this power throughout the child's minority.[5] The English courts were extremely reluctant to interfere with this right of the father. Indeed, as late as the 1870s the Court of Chancery held that the father was taken by the law to be the sole and proper judge of the child's temporal and spiritual welfare, and the judges of the land had no right to sit in appeal from his

---

[3] See, e.g. Bellotti v. Baird 443 US 662 (1979) and Gillick v. West Norfolk and Wisbech Area Health Authority [1986] 1 A.C. 112.

[4] This is a result of the First Amendment to the U.S. Constitution. In England a right to freedom of religion exists both at common law and under Art. 9 of the European Convention on Human Rights. See Chap. 1.

[5] A good explanation of the father's right is contained in Hawkesworth v. Hawkesworth (1871) Law Rep. 6 Chap. 539.

decision.[6] The child's welfare or wishes as to choice of religion were deemed irrelevant and not a matter for the consideration of the court, any more than were the mother's wishes regarding the religion of the child. Modifications of the father's extensive rights came at the end of the nineteenth century with a series of statutes which gave increasing, and eventually equal, rights to the mother.[7] The rights of both parents, however, were restricted generally as a result of increased invocation by the court of its *parens patriae* jurisdiction.[8] With the passing of the Guardianship Act 1925,[9] there was a further move away from parental autonomy as the child's welfare became the paramount, albeit not the only, concern of the court in making a decision relating to the upbringing of the child. The right of the parent to choose a child's religion has nevertheless remained strong throughout the twentieth century. Even when a child is to be adopted and cared for outside the family, adoption agencies and local social services are obliged to take into account the child's religious needs.[10]

In the United States, the rights of parents to determine the religious upbringing of their children followed the same route, from a rule of *patria potestas* which invested virtually absolute control over upbringing of the child in the father, to equal control by the parents, to a best interests doctrine, which allows the state to take into account the importance of the child's welfare in proceedings relating to upbringing. There is, however, an important difference between the two jurisdictions. In addition to common law and legislation, the United States have also to take into account constitutional considerations and constraints in making their decisions. The Constitution, when drafted, did not have children particularly in mind as a group whose rights needed to be specifically determined. None of the Constitutional clauses relate unequivocally or exclusively to children. The Constitution, while

---

[6] *Re Agar-Ellis* (1878) 10. Ch. Div 49.
[7] The change began with an Act to Amend the Law Relating to the Custody of Infants Act 1839, and continued with the Guardianship of Infants Act 1925, and a number of later Acts. The current provisions are contained in the Children Act 1989, s.2 which provides that mother and father have equal responsibility for their children.
[8] After the fusion of law and equity under the Judicature Act 1873.
[9] Replaced by the Guardianship of Infants Act 1971, and now contained in the Children Act 1989, s.1.
[10] Adoption Act 1976, s.7.

extending certain of its protections to children,[11] focuses on the rights of adults. In accord with this approach, the United States Supreme Court has held that the Free Exercise Clause of the First Amendment protects the rights of parents to control the religious upbringing of their children.[12] While children, according to the Supreme Court, have a right to exercise their religion,[13] it is unlikely that a court would uphold a child's right to choose its religious upbringing in the face of opposition from the parents. One may speculate that the effect of constitutional free exercise of religion may be to reduce the rights of children to make choices about their religious upbringing, and make it more difficult for courts to intervene and overrule a parent's choice of religious upbringing in the best interests of the child.

Internationally, the strongest and most explicit support for the parents' right to bring up children according to their religious beliefs is contained in Article 5 of the Declaration on the Elimination of All forms of Intolerance and of Discrimination Based on Religion or Belief, adopted by the General Assembly of the United Nations in 1981.[14]

> "the parents . . . of the child have the right to organize the life within the family in accordance with their religion or belief and bearing in mind the moral education in which they believe the child should be brought up."

Other instruments give a right to families within the context of the right to privacy and family life. Thus Article 8(1) of the European Convention for the Protection of Human Rights and Fundamental Freedoms[15] provides that "everyone has the right to respect for his private and family life . . . "

---

[11] See, *e.g. Re Gault* 387 U.S. 1 (1967).

[12] See *Prince v Massachusetts* 321 U.S. 158 (1944). In fact the case spoke of the right of children to free exercise of their religion, but it was really the religious liberty of the parents that was at issue. For further discussion see Pfeffer, *Church, State and Freedom* (2nd ed. 1967).

[13] *Prince v. Massachusetts* 321 U.S. 158 (1944). See also *West Virginia Board of Education v. Barnette* 319 U.S. 624 (1943).

[14] Declarations adopted by the UN General Assembly, being resolutions of that body, have only the formal force of recommendations. They may, however, grow to have considerable influence. In any event they serve as particularly influential yardsticks.

[15] This Convention was ratified by the U.K. in 1951, with some reservations. It will be referred to in the later text as the European Convention on Human Rights.

The International Covenant on Civil and Political Rights[16] also contains a similar provision. Implicit in the right to respect for private and family life is the right to bring up a family free from State intervention. None of the international instruments expressly give the child the right to choose and follow a religion: the right to religious choice is seen as very much a parental right. Even the United Nations Convention on the Rights of the Child follows this orthodoxy. Article 14, while providing that the States Parties shall respect the right of the child to freedom of thought, conscience and religion, qualifies this by stating:

> "States Parties shall respect the rights and duties of the parents and, when applicable, the legal guardians, to provide direction to the child in the exercise of his or her right in a manner consistent with the evolving capacities of the child."

This approach is reflected in the domestic law of both England and the United States. There is little in the way of case law that indicates willingness to allow children to make major decisions about their religious life before they reach the age of majority.[17]

Notwithstanding the freedom given to parents to bring up their children in accordance with their religion or belief, the right to transmit religious beliefs and practices is not unfettered. Restrictions exist in the domestic law of both England and the United States and in the relevant international instruments. Common law placed limits on religious practices (as opposed to religious beliefs). The powers of the father were not absolute, and in certain, very limited, circumstances the court would intervene. Intervention

---

[16] The Covenant was ratified by the U.K. in 1976 with some reservations. Art. 17 provides that no one shall be subject to arbitrary or unlawful interference with his privacy, family home or correspondence.

[17] In both *Lough v. Ward* [1945] 2 All E.R. 338, 173 L.T. 181 and *Prieto v. St Alphonsus Convent of Mercy* 52 La. Ann. 631; 27 So. 153 (1900) (U.S.) it was agreed by the courts that a parent could remove a child who had entered a convent with the expressed intention of taking vows, and remaining in the convent as a member of the order. In both cases the girls were over the age of 16, and adamant that they wished to remain in their religious orders. This was held insufficient to override the parents' right to control their children until the age of majority. It was held in both cases that the child could return to the convent on majority if they wished, but could not take vows before they reached that age. In cases where parents dispute the religious upbringing of a child, the courts have, on occasions, allowed a child to make a decision as to which parent's religion he or she wishes to follow. See *Hehman v. Hehman* 13 Misc. 2d 318; 178 N.Y.S.2d 328 (1958) (US). See also *Jacobs v. Jacobs* 25 Ill. App. 3d 175; 323 N.E.2d 21 (1974).

might be thought justified if it were shown that there was an abandonment of parental duty, for instance where the father brought up the child irreligiously,[18] or there was immoral conduct on the part of the father.[19] In such cases the courts were willing to consider the merits of the issue. The authority for this intervention was explained in the eighteenth century case of *Blisset*:

> "The paternal authority as to its civil force was founded in nature, and the care presumed which he would take for the education of the child: but if he would not provide for its support, he abandoned his right to the custody of the child's person, or if he would educate it in a manner forbidden by the laws of the state, the public right of the community to superintend the education of its members, and disallow what for its own security and welfare it should see good to disallow, went beyond the right and authority of the father."[20]

In the United States, the courts never applied the paternal preference rule on religious upbringing for children as strictly. Justice Story[21] explained the father's right to custody in terms of trust. The father was not seen as the owner of his children, but as the person to whom society entrusted their care because he was the most likely candidate to rear them properly. When, and if, it became clear that the father had breached this trust, and was not treating his children in a proper parental manner, then the court or the State was justified in revoking the trust and appointing an alternative guardian.[22]

The United States Supreme Court has since held, in *Prince v. Massachusetts*,[23] that rights of religion and parenthood may be limited to guard the State's interest in the child's well-being. The State as *parens patriae* may restrict the parents' control by requiring school attendance, regulating or prohibiting child labour, and in many other ways. The State's authority is not nullified merely

---

[18] See, *e.g. Shelley v. Westbrooke* Jac. 266n and *Re Besant* (1914) 30 T.L.R.; 28 Digest 258, 1130.

[19] *Wellesley v. Beaufort* 2 Bli.(NS) 124.

[20] 98 E.R. 899 (1773).

[21] Story (Justice), *Commentary's on Equity Jurisprudence* (14th ed., 1918), para. 1742–84.

[22] For a further explanation of this approach and a greater history of the development of common law see Mangrum, "Exclusive Reliance on Best Interest may be Unconstitutional: Religion as a Factor in Child Custody Cases" (1981–2), Vol. 15, Creighton Law Review 25.

[23] 321 U.S. 158 (1944).

because the parent grounds his claim to control the child's course of conduct in religion or conscience. The right to practice religion freely does not include the liberty to expose the community or the child to communicable disease, or the latter to ill health or death. The State has a wide range of power for limiting freedom and authority in matters affecting the child's welfare; even at the expense of matters of conscience and religious conviction.

This right of the State to intervene in upbringing and the practice of religion in the family, is recognised by the international human rights documents as being valid, but only in certain circumstances. The European Convention[24] on Human Rights provides in Article 9(2):

> "Freedom to manifest one's religion or beliefs shall be subject only to such limitations as are prescribed by law and are necessary in a democratic society in the interests of public safety, for the protection of public order, health or morals, or for the protection of the rights and freedoms of others."[25]

The International Covenant on Civil and Political Rights[26] and the Declaration on the Elimination of All Forms of Intolerance and of Discrimination Based on Religion or Belief[27] and the United Nations Conventions on the Rights of the Child[28] also contain essentially similar provisions.

While a State has the right to restrict the free exercise of religion,[29] the circumstances in which a state may intervene in the religious upbringing of a child are not capable of exact definition.

---

[24] The Convention on the Rights of the Child has a slightly different limitation clause: "such limitations as are prescribed by law and are necessary to protect public safety, order, health and morals". The U.K. has ratified the Convention, but the U.S. has not.

[25] The right to family life under Art. 8 of the European Convention on Human Rights is also restricted. Art. 8(2) provides:
"there shall be no interference by a public authority with the exercise of this right except such as in accordance with the law and is necessary in a democratic society in the interests of national security, public safety or the economic well-being of the country, for the prevention of disorder or crime, for the protection of health or morals, or for the protection of the rights and freedoms of others."
See Chap. 1, pp. 14–17.

[26] Art. 18(3).

[27] Art. 1(3).

[28] Art. 14(3).

[29] See Chap. 1, for the circumstances in which the state is allowed to restrict the free exercise of religion, both under domestic law and international law.

Simple dislike or disapproval of a religious practice or belief is not, of itself, a sufficient reason to justify intervention; but the protection of health, or the rights and freedoms of others, does provide a valid basis for potential intervention. Both jurisdictions justify restricting parental rights in relation to religious upbringing where this is necessary for the protection of the child from present or potential harm, and increasingly, where the best interests of the child require such a restriction. Neither jurisdiction provide an unequivocal definition of "harm" such that intervention in upbringing could be automatically ordered. Neither is there a uniform response by States to harm inflicted by parental upbringing. Certain forms of harm or potential harm may amount to a breach of the criminal law of the State, while other forms only render a parent liable in tort. Alternatively, the harm may justify intervention by State agencies and removal of the child from the family, or official interference in the upbringing of a child.

Harm has many disguises. It is not limited in this context to physical abuse or sexual abuse, but encompasses future physical damage, psychological damage or emotional damage, and can be further extended to cover harm to the community caused by the religious upbringing of children by their parents.

Where religious practices could result in harm to the child

ACTS WHICH BREACH THE CRIMINAL LAW

Both England and the United States have shown themselves willing, on occasion, to legislate specifically against certain religious practices which they regard as harmful. In the United States the most notable of these are statutes prohibiting snake handling, a practice central to the tenets of the "Holiness" Church among others.[30] Challenges have been made to the validity of such

---

[30] The sect believes as a tenet of their religion that they are commanded by Jesus' words to handle poisonous snakes. They also believe that, if their faith is strong enough, they will not get bitten, or if they do, that they will not be harmed. A number of followers were bitten and died, including the founder of the religion. This led States to legislate against such practices on the basis of it being a danger to public health and safety.

laws, aimed as they are at the practices of a particular religious sect. In all such cases, the validity of the legislation has been upheld on the grounds that it falls within the proper exercise of the State's power to prevent harm to its citizens. *A fortiori*, exposure of children to such practices would be equally subject to proscription.[31]

The same willingness to make quasi-religious acts unlawful can be seen in England with legislation against female circumcision. There is some doubt as to whether female circumcision is a religious custom[32] or purely a cultural custom.[33] It is, however, a widespread African custom. Circumcision of women may be carried out at any time from shortly after birth, until after the woman has reached adulthood and given birth to her first child.[34] Commonly though, the operation is carried out on girls aged between three and eight. The Prohibition of Female Circumcision Act 1985 makes it an offence to perform circumcision on a female whatever her age.[35] The prohibition arose from the desire to protect women and female children from a practice known to cause severe health problems to women, with no discernible benefits to them.[36] The practice of circumcision is regarded as customary or traditional rather than religious, and is a practice wholly alien to western,

---

[31] See, *e.g. Harden v. The State* 216 S.W.2d 880 (Tenn. 1956), *Hill v. State* 88 So. 2d 880 (Ala. Ct.App. 1956) and *State v. Massey* 51 S.E.2d 179 1949 (N.C.), *Lawson v. Commonwealth* 164 S.W.2d 972 (Ky.Ct.App. 1942).

[32] The Minority Rights Group Report No. 47 held that there was no religious basis for female circumcision, unlike male circumcision.

[33] The reasons for female circumcision are various. It has been argued that the operation initiates the girl into womanhood, increases fertility and live births, curbs women's sexual desires and maintains the moral fibre of society. Claims are also made that circumcision improves hygiene or aesthetic conditions, conforms to Muslim customs, enhances male sexual pleasure, prevents venereal disease and maintains tradition. See Boulware-Miller (1985), 8 Harvard Women's Law Journal 155.

[34] See Abdalla, *Sisters in Affliction* (1982).

[35] For a deeper explanation of this practice and its legal implications see Hayter, "Female Circumcision—Is There a Legal Solution?" [1984] J.S.W.L. 323. It should also be noted that there is no specific human rights instrument which prohibits the practice, although it has been argued that the practice falls foul of the Declaration on the Elimination of Discrimination Against Women and the Declaration on the Protection of All Persons From Torture. See Brigman, "Female Circumcision: Challenges to the Practice as a Human Rights Violation" (1985), 8 Harvard Women's Journal 155.

[36] It is arguable that female circumcision was already criminal by virtue of the Children and Young Persons Act 1933, s.1(1). However, this legislation could not positively prohibit the carrying out of female circumcision by doctors, applying as it did only to parents.

Christian culture. Thus, the introduction of legislation was not regarded as presenting an ethical problem. It is not, however, altogether clear that legislation would have been passed if such circumcision was regarded as a wholly religious act. The practice of male circumcision soon after birth is required for Jews as showing their Covenant with God, is practised by Muslims, is not uncommon in England or the United States[37] and is not prohibited. There is little evidence that shows this operation to be medically necessary or beneficial to most children. There is equally little evidence showing that such an operation is harmful in the long term, although it is believed to cause short term distress. The acceptability of male circumcision and the unacceptability of female circumcision undoubtedly relies partly on the harm factor, but partly on the fact that male circumcision is a well known practice in the west, and is accepted as a necessary, and wholly religious practice, for certain religious groups.

Apart from specific criminal legislation prohibiting certain religious practices, parents may find that their religious practices infringe the general criminal law of the State. Where this occurs, both England and the United States have had to consider the extent to which religious belief or practice is regarded as an excuse or as mitigation. As a general rule, parents are not allowed, in the name of religion, to claim exemption from acts which would otherwise amount to criminal behaviour. Thus, parents who belong to a religion which relies on charitable donations for day-to-day survival, and solicits donations on the streets, may infringe the criminal law if they allow their children to ask for money. In England, the Children and Young Persons Act 1933, section 4[38] makes it an offence for anyone to cause or procure a juvenile under sixteen to be in a street, premises or place for the purpose of begging.[39] When a parent is charged with this offence, the onus is on the defendant to

---

[37] Brigman in his article "Circumcision as Child Abuse: the Legal and Constitutional Issues" (1984–85) 23 Journal of Family Law 337 estimates that 80 per cent of American males are circumcised.

[38] As amended by the Children and Young Persons Act 1963, s.64(1) and Sched.III, para.3.

[39] The offence is also committed by anyone who, having custody, charge or care of the juvenile, allows him to be in such places, and it is proved that the juvenile was there for the purpose of begging. The onus is on the defendant to prove that he did not allow the juvenile to be there for the purpose of begging. While a criminal prosecution of the responsible adult will occur, it is also likely that care proceedings in relation to the child will commence.

show that the child was not there for the purpose of begging. A conviction of a parent or carer under this section could also lead to proceedings to remove the child from the family.[40]

In the United States, early cases established the principle that although the State may not interfere with religious beliefs or opinions, it can punish religious practices that constitute criminal offences. To do otherwise, said the United States Supreme Court, "would be to make the professed doctrines of religious belief superior to the law of the land".[41]

In the seminal case of *Prince v. Massachusetts*,[42] the United States Supreme Court upheld the validity of a conviction under a State child labour law of a member of the Jehovah's Witnesses. The defendant in the case had allowed her two young children and her nine year old ward to accompany her on the streets and help to sell or distribute Jehovah's Witness literature. A State statute prohibited boys under twelve and girls under eighteen from selling newspapers, magazines or periodicals on any street or public place, and made the adult who furnished the child with the publications subject to criminal punishment. At the trial, Mrs Prince argued that the child was not engaged in a commercial exercise, and that both she and the children believed it was their religious duty to evangelise and preach the gospel in this form, and thus she should not be regarded as having committed a criminal offence.

The Supreme Court acknowledged the child's right to exercise her religion, and the parent's right to provide religious training to the child, but it also recognised that the family was not beyond regulation in the public interest, as against a claim of religious liberty. The Court held that neither the rights of religion nor the rights of parenthood were beyond limitation, and that Mrs Prince was liable under the criminal law.[43] While conceding that it would be unconstitutional to make the selling by adults of Jehovah's Wit-

---

[40] On the basis that a conviction would go to show that the child was suffering significant harm under the Children Act 1989, s.31 justifying the removal of the child into the care of the local authority.

[41] *Reynolds v. U.S.* 98 U.S. (Otto 8) 145 (1878) and *Davies v. Beason* 133 U.S. 333 (1890).

[42] 321 U.S. 158 (1944).

[43] The court held that the state as *parens patriae* could restrict the parental freedom and authority in matters affecting the child's welfare and this included to some extent matters of conscience and religious conviction. In other words, the State could restrict religious practices where such practices were regarded by the State as harmful to the child.

ness material in the street illegal, the Court found that the State's authority over children's activities was greater than that over the same actions by adults.[44] While this case has to be seen within the context of unfavourable judicial attitudes towards Jehovah's Witnesses at the time,[45] the limitations on parental freedom remain valid and have been applied to later cases.

The examples given above both involve the active commission of an offence, for which excuse was sought on the basis of religious belief. The cases which have caused the courts far more concern, however, are those where a parent fails to act through deeply held religious belief. Each year, a number of children die, particularly in the United States, because parents rely on faith healing techniques, prescribed by their religion, rather than on orthodox medical care for readily treatable conditions. When a child dies as a result of a failure by the parents to obtain orthodox medical treatment, the State must decide whether criminal charges should be brought against the parents for manslaughter or neglect. This is often a difficult decision, especially where parents were following their religious beliefs and treating the child by spiritual means, with prayer. In most cases the parents are already extremely distressed at the child's death.

The numbers of children who are treated only by faith healing are difficult to assess, many coming to the attention of the authorities only after death occurs. One sect in the United States, the Faith Assembly Church, was the subject of an enquiry by the Indiana State Board of Health. In 1984 the sect, based in Northern Indiana, with around 2,000 members, shunned all forms of medical treatment and relied solely on faith healing. Followers were taught that to trust in the inventions of man was to question the power of God. The use of medicine, vaccinations, the taking of life insurance policies, and even the wearing of seat-belts was rejected by the Church. It was estimated that in 11 years, 88 deaths were attributable to the failure to provide medical care for treatable illnesses, with children accounting for two thirds of the fatalities.[46] The sect attributed the deaths to "God's discipline" in some cases and "a

---

[44] The court found that propagandising religion on the streets could create situations difficult enough for adults to deal with and wholly inappropriate for children; a finding that they were likely to come to harm through such activities.

[45] See *Minersville School District v. Gobitis* 310 U.S. 586 (1940) and Chap.1, pp. 23–25.

[46] Ostling, "Matters of Faith and Death", *Time*, April 16, 1984 at p.42. For more detail see Malecha, "Faith Healing Exemptions to Child Protection Laws: Keeping the Faith versus Medical Care" (1985) 12 J.Legis. 243.

complete lack of faith" in others. The Indiana Board of Health found that the perinatal mortality rate for sect members was three times higher than for non-members (Faith Assembly mothers gave birth at home with no medical assistance) and that the maternal mortality rate was one hundred times greater than for the rest of the population in the State. Despite the perinatal rate of death and the death of numerous children from treatable illnesses, the Indiana prosecutors chose not to bring charges. The reason for this was that Indiana's child protection laws contained a defence to anyone who, "in the legitimate practice of his religious belief, provided treatment by spiritual means through prayer in lieu of medical care, to his dependent".

The notion of a defence of genuine religious belief to the offence of manslaughter, and recognition that parents should be able to treat a child according to their religious beliefs, can be traced back to the English case of *R v. Wagstaffe*.[47] The case represents the common law rule that parents cannot be convicted of manslaughter solely because they unsuccessfully treated their child's illness with prayer.

Within six months of the decision in *Wagstaffe*, Parliament amended the laws which made child neglect a punishable offence, by adding failure to provide medical treatment.[48] After this, English courts rejected defences to manslaughter that were based on religious beliefs. In *R v. Senior*[49] a father, who belonged to a sect called the Peculiar People, was found guilty of manslaughter in failing to call a doctor to his seriously ill child. The question for the jury was whether the father had "wilfully neglected" the child in a manner likely to cause the child unnecessary suffering or injury to his or her health. If the jury found that the father had caused the death of the child by an unlawful course of conduct he would be guilty of manslaughter.

The jury convicted, and the appeal was dismissed. The court found that the father had wilfully neglected the child: he had deliberately failed to call a doctor knowing that the child was seriously

---

[47] 19 Cox C.C.530.
[48] The Poor Law Amendment Act 1868, s.37 provided that "when any parent shall wilfully neglect to provide adequate food, clothing, medical aid, or lodging, for his child being in his custody, under the age of 14 years, whereby the health of such child shall have been, or shall be likely to be, seriously injured, he shall be guilty of an offence punishable on summary conviction".
[49] [1899] 1 Q.B. 283, CCCR.

ill and would benefit from medical treatment. Yet he deliberately refrained from obtaining it, because he thought to do so would be sinful and would show an unwillingness to accept God's will in relation to the child. Whether his religious beliefs justified his actions was, according to the court, simply not an issue to be put before the jury. It was neither a justification nor an excuse for the father's actions; it was a non-issue.[50]

Senior is authority for the proposition that parents who follow the tenets of their religion in failing to summon medical aid for their child, will not be immune from criminal charges if the child dies or is seriously injured as a result. In *Senior*, however, the father realised that medical treatment would be of benefit to the child. What if the parent fervently and genuinely believes that prayer will cure the child, and as a result the thought that a doctor may be needed to help the child never crosses his or her mind?

In *R v. Sheppard*,[51] a case that did not raise religious issues but is nevertheless relevant, it was held that for a parent to be found guilty of the wilful neglect of his child in a manner likely to cause him unnecessary suffering or injury to health,[52] it had to be shown that the child needed medical aid at the time of the alleged failure to provide it, *and* that either the defendant was aware at the time that the child's health might be at risk if medical aid was not provided, *or* that his unawareness of that fact was due to his not caring whether the child's health was at risk. In *Senior*[53] there was no question of the father being unaware of the risk to the child that might be involved in the failure to obtain medical aid. He did not obtain medical aid because he sincerely believed that to do so would be sinful and against the child's spiritual welfare.

R v. Sheppard[54] holds that wilfully neglecting a child is not an offence of strict liability, but one which requires the Crown to prove *mens rea*. The implication is that where a parent appreciates

---

[50] A recent case, that of *Harris*, resulted in the conviction of Harris, a Rastafarian and his wife for manslaughter, on the basis that they had refused, for religious reasons to give their diabetic daughter insulin, relying instead on homoeopathic remedies. Harris was given a sentence of two and a half years imprisonment. Harris appealed against his sentence but no information was found on the outcome of the appeal.

[51] [1980] 3 All E.R. 899.

[52] Under the Children and Young Persons Act 1933, s.1(1).

[53] [1899] 1 Q.B. 283 CCCR.

[54] [1980] 3 All E.R. 899.

that an ordinary parent would call in a doctor but believes that is in the child's best interests for prayer to be used instead, the offence is committed. But, if the parent fails to appreciate the need, not out of indifference to the child's state, but through his genuine religious belief that no help is needed because God will cure the child, no offence is committed.[55]

In the United States prosecutions of parents for manslaughter, for failure to provide medical treatment for their children, have had a chequered history. Before the mid-70s some courts recognised that prayer treatments were not sufficient child care to exempt parents from manslaughter liability if the child died.[56] After the passage by Congress of the Child Abuse Prevention and Treatment Act of 1974, States were virtually compelled to enact religious exemption clauses, granting an exemption from child neglect liability for those parents who treated their children by faith healing. The compulsion arose from the fact that the Department of Health, Education and Welfare (HEW) required a State to adopt such an exemption before it could receive federal funding for State protection programmes. The Department of Health and Human Services, the successor to HEW, removed this requirement and in 1983 new regulations defined child neglect to include denial of medical care.[57] Even prior to the 1983 Regulation, however, some State courts had held that the statutory religious exemptions violated both the State and the federal constitutions.[58]

As a practical matter, prosecutors have been disinclined to bring

---

[55] Whether a jury would accept that a parent genuinely believed that faith alone would cure the child, when the child was demonstrably seriously ill and suffering, is questionable.

[56] See *Craig v. State* 220 Md. 590, 155 A. 2d 684 (1959), *Reynolds v. United States* 98 U.S. 145 (1978); *People v. Pierson* 176 N.Y. 201, 68 NE 243 (1903); *Beck v. State* 29 Okla. Crim 240, 233 P. 495 (App 1925); *Owens v. State* 6 Okla. Crim 110, 116 P. 345 (App 1911). But *cf. Bradley v. State*, 79 Fla. 651, 84 So. 677 (1920) (holding that the states definition of manslaughter did not include death by denial of medical treatment).

[57] The new Regulations as codified today, provide that the Regulations are not to be:

  "construed as ... prohibiting a finding of negligent treatment or maltreatment when a parent practicing his or her religious beliefs does not, for that reason alone, provide medical treatment for a child".

("Child Abuse and Neglect Prevention and Treatment" 45 C.F.R. para. 1340.2(d)(2)(ii) (1987)).

[58] The Ohio Supreme Court found such a provision unconstitutional in *State v. Miskimens* 22 Ohio Misc. 2d 43, 490 N.E. 2d 931, as did the Supreme Court of Delaware in *Newmark v. Williams* 588 A. 2d 1108 (1990).

criminal charges against parents. Courts have also strained to overturn convictions for manslaughter in the few cases which have been
prosecuted.[59] The recent California case of *Walker v. Superior Court
of Sacramento County*,[60] however, may herald a change of approach.

In *Walker*, the Christian Scientist mother of a child suffering
from flu-like symptoms denied her child medical treatment.
Recognising that the child was ill she followed her religious precepts, and treated the child by faith healing. During the seventeen
days that she was ill, the child lost weight and grew disoriented,
eventually dying of acute purulent meningitis. The State charged
the mother with involuntary manslaughter and felony child endangerment. The prosecution's case was that the mother's criminal
negligence proximately caused the child's death. The mother
argued that the religious exemption contained in the child neglect
statute[61] meant that she was not under a duty to provide the child
with medical care and, therefore, protected her from criminal liability. The mother was convicted.

On appeal the California Supreme Court found that the statutory
exemption did not extend to involuntary manslaughter and felony
child neglect statutes. Interpreting the statute, the court stated that
prayer treatment would be accommodated as an acceptable means
of attending to the needs of a child only in so far as serious physical
harm or illness was not at risk. When a child's life was placed in
danger, the court could discern no legislative purpose to shield
parents from the chastening prospect of felony liability.

The attitude taken by the California Supreme Court in upholding a manslaughter conviction is in opposition to earlier case law,

---

[59] Catherine Laughran, "Religious Beliefs and the Criminal Justice System: Some
Problems of the Faith Healer" (1975), Vol. 8, Loyola Law Review 396, states that
in an exhaustive search she failed to find a single appellate case upholding a
parent's or guardian's conviction on homicide charges, where religion was presented as a defence.

[60] 194 Cal.App. 3d 1090, 222 Cal.Rptr. 87 (1986). The petitioners application for a
rehearing was denied. 47 Cal.3d 112; 763 P.2d 852; 253 Cal.Rptr.1 (1988). Petition for writ of certiorari was denied by the U.S. Supreme Court 491 U.S. 905;
109 Sup.Ct. 3186 (1989). See also, for interest, *Brown v. Laitner* 432 Mich. 861,
435 N.W. 2d 1 (1989) in which the estate of a child sued Christian Science Prac-
titioners for negligence.

[61] The California Penal Code, s.270 provides "if a parent of a minor child wilfully
omits, without lawful excuse, to furnish necessary clothing, food, shelter or
medical attendance, or other remedial care for his or her child, he or she is guilty
of a misdemeanour". Faith healing constitutes "other remedial care".

but on all fours with the sentiment expressed in *Prince*[62] that while the parent may choose to make a martyr of himself, he is not entitled to make a martyr of his child. Indeed, one can only express amazement at the ease with which the Supreme Court in *Prince* was willing to impose criminal liability on a parent, compared with the reluctance of courts to impose liability where the refusal of parents to seek medical care on the basis of religious belief and practice, has resulted in the death of a child. While the decision of the court in *Prince* may have been affected by their attitude to the particular religion involved, *Walker* undoubtedly reflects the greater attention now given to the best interests of the child and the court's duty to protect vulnerable children. It remains to be seen whether future cases will follow the reasoning and judgment of *Walker*. The greater emphasis on the best interests of the child, and the corresponding lesser weight given to the parents' right of free exercise, in addition to the fact that other State courts often look to the California Supreme Court in resolving troublesome legal questions makes this a hopeful possibility.

ACTS WHICH JUSTIFY INTERVENTION AND INTERFERENCE IN UPBRINGING

Even in the absence of prohibitory legislation, courts in England and the United States have the power, under their *parens patriae* jurisdiction, and acting with the welfare of the child in mind, to circumscribe religious practices which have the potential to be harmful. Where religious practices are seen as causing harm, or as having the potential to cause harm, or a parent fails to act due to religious beliefs to prevent harm, the court may intervene to bring about the result it deems to be in the best interests of the child. Many cases have arisen within the context of medical treatment for the child. As we have seen above, a number of religions do not accept the need for medical treatment, or professional health care, for a child. Nor do they permit the use of drugs or blood transfusions. Followers of these particular religions believe in the curative

---

[62] 321 U.S. 158 (1944).

powers of spiritual healing: that sickness is cured by prayer rather than by medicine. A follower who seeks the aid of a doctor is seen by fellow members to demonstrate a lack of faith in the church.[63]

A variety of issues arise where the parents have a religious objection to medical treatment. First, whether parents are under a duty to provide their child with medical care irrespective of their own religious beliefs. One would expect a legal system which gives the best interests of the child primary consideration, to return a positive answer to this issue. Secondly, whether the State has the power to override parental religious beliefs and practices and order medical treatment for a child. If so, in what situations should a court exercise this power? And, as a practical matter, how does a court enforce treatment? Thirdly, while one might argue that the State has the right to intervene in the best interests of the child, and order treatment, should a parent be prosecuted for following their religious beliefs and practices?

(i) Life threatening medical situations. Courts tend to distinguish between two different types of medical treatment cases, those in which treatment is necessary to save the life of the child, and those in which treatment is not medically essential to save life, but which, if not performed, will result in some form of physical or mental damage to the child. When a life saving operation is required for a child, and the parent refuses consent on the basis of religious beliefs, the courts, in both England and the United States, free exercise notwithstanding, have not hesitated to intervene.

While parents could be liable to prosecution in England for refusing to consent to medical attention,[64] saving the child's life is far more important at this juncture. Parents are rarely prosecuted in such cases, and action, if any, is civil rather than criminal.

In England, a doctor may choose to proceed with life saving treatment in the face of parental religious opposition, without any form of legal intervention. A circular from the Department of

---

[63] *e.g.* Jehovah's Witnesses do not permit blood transfusions, and Christian Scientists do not believe in professional medical care, believing that illness comes from within the individual. See also the doctrines of such churches as the General Assembly and the Church of the First Born.

[64] See the Children and Young Persons Act 1933, s.1(1).

Health[65] advising doctors on procedure, points out that where a parent refuses consent to a life saving blood transfusion or operation, a hospital does not need to take the child before a court, but should rely instead on the clinical judgment of the consultant concerned. The recommended procedure in such a case is for the consultant to obtain a written supporting opinion from a colleague that the patient's life is in danger if the operation or transfusion is withheld, and an acknowledgment (preferably in writing) from the parent or guardian that, despite the explanation of the danger, he or she refuses consent. If the consultant then acts with due professional competence and according to his own professional conscience, and operates on the child or gives the child a transfusion, he would run little risk that his actions would be censured in a court of law.

If the local authority or a concerned individual takes the issue of treatment before the court, the court has two possible routes by which it may, if it so chooses, override the parents' religious objections to treatment. It can order, on the application of the local authority, that the child be placed in the care of the local authority on the basis that the child is likely otherwise to suffer significant harm, thereby placing parental responsibility and decision making power in the hands of the local authority as well as the parent.[66] However, in *Re O*[67] the Family Division of the High Court expressed the view that the appropriate action in such cases was to make the child Court.[68] Johnson J. in emphasising the advantage of the inherent jurisdiction over care proceedings in *Re O*, pointed out that even when a local authority has obtained parental responsibility and may act alone and independently of the parents in exercising that

---

[65] Ministry of Health Circular F/P9/1B *Refusal of Parental Consent to Blood*, dated April 14, 1967. There is also an agreement between the Department of Health and the Medical Defence Union under which doctors can operate when there is an urgent need for a blood transfusion and there is an objection on religious grounds in the case of a minor.

[66] The Court must also be satisfied under s.31(2)(b) of the Children Act that the harm was due to the child not receiving the care from the parent that it would be reasonable to expect or that the child was beyond parental control. The local authority may limit the exercise of the parents' parental responsibility under s.33(3)(b) of the Act.

[67] [1993] 2 FLRa ward of court or invoke the inherent jurisdiction of the High 149.

[68] These two actions are in essence the same, but which form of action is taken depends on the applicant. The local authority may not seek to have a child made a ward of court, but may invoke the inherent jurisdiction of the High Court under the Children Act 1989, s.100. In both forms of action the court will decide the particular form of treatment that the child should receive.

responsibility, the doctor may have considerable doubts about the ethics of acting in reliance on the consent of only one, of say, three persons who hold parental responsibility, and in opposition to the wishes of the other two. Where the issue of medical treatment is the only matter to be resolved and the court does not otherwise need to intervene to safeguard the welfare of the child, it has been held that the local authority need not invoke the inherent jurisdiction, but may seek a specific issues order under the Children Act 1989, section 8 instead. Because the decision of the court may run counter to the most profound and sincerely held beliefs of the parents, strenuous efforts should be made to ensure that the parents are present at the hearing, and their views heard and considered by the court.[69]

In making its decision whether to intervene and order medical treatment, the court should give respect and great weight to the religious principles underlying the family's decision, consider alternative treatments, and then act as the judicial reasonable parent.[70] When acting in such a way, the court should bear in mind the words of Cumming-Bruce L.J. in *Jane v. Jane*:

> "If there is a conflict between honouring the mother's religious belief and the interest of the child in continuing life, it is perfectly plain that in such a conflict the interests of the child and its welfare are paramount and the mother's religious beliefs have to be overridden in order to save the child."[71]

One of the functions of the court under its *parens patriae* jurisdiction has been defined as ensuring, as far as possible, that children

---

[69] See *Re R*. [1993] 2 FLR 757. Booth J. was of the opinion that, if it was not possible to ensure an *inter partes* hearing, that the Act could be interpreted sufficiently flexibly to grant an *ex parte* order. If this was not possible, the power to invoke the inherent jurisdiction of the court would be immediately available and appropriate. The order in this case gave permission to administer blood products to the child, who was suffering from leukaemia, whenever her condition was life threatening. In situations which were less than imminently life threatening, the doctors were to consult the parents as to alternative forms of management.

[70] See *Re O*. [1993] 2 FLR 149.

[71] (1983) 4 FLR 712, 13 Fam. Law 209. See also *Re S*. [1993] 1 FLR 376 where it was held that the test, even in the face of religious objection was the welfare of the child as the paramount consideration. Here, where the choice was between a 50 per cent chance of survival with a blood transfusion, or none without, there was little argument as to what the child's welfare required. The judge, in response to counsel's concern that the child would suffer being brought up by parents who considered that his life was prolonged as a result of an ungodly act, pointed out that the judicial act of ordering a blood transfusion would absolve their conscience of responsibility.

survive until the age of majority.[72] However, the court will not order medical intervention if to do so would not be in the best interests of the child. While there is a strong presumption in favour of life, if the prognosis for the child is extremely poor, and treatment can only prolong life for a time rather than effect a cure, the court will weigh the pain of treatment and the likely suffering of the child against the benefits of treatment.[73] In all such cases in England, the welfare of the child is paramount.

While the need to safeguard the child's welfare is also the paramount consideration in the United States' courts, operating under their *parens patriae* jurisdiction, constitutional rights have also to be considered. The United States Supreme Court in the case of *Prince v. Massachusetts*[74] stated that the parent's right to practise religion did not include the liberty to expose the child to ill health or death. The result of this approach has been that the courts have, generally, been willing to order that children should receive medical treatment, against their parent's religious beliefs and wishes, where the child's life is in danger.[75] However, that willingness has not been absolute. In *Newmark v. Williams*[76] the Supreme Court of Delaware, in deciding whether a 3 year old boy should receive chemotherapy against life threatening cancer, in opposition to the wishes of his Christian Science parents, held that the balancing test began with parental interest. The Court recognised that the basic principle underlying the *parens patriae* doctrine was the State's interest in preserving life, but this interest must be weighed against the constitutionally protected interests of the

---

[72] See *Re W.* [1992] 4 All E.R. 627, *per* Nolan L.J.
[73] See *Re J.* [1992] 2 FLR 165.
[74] 321 U.S. 158 (1944).
[75] See *Jehovah's Witnesses v. King County Hospital* 278 F.Supp.488 (W.D. Wash. 1967) affirmed *per curiam* 390 U.S. 598, rehearing denied 391 U.S. 961 (1968) where a three judge court upheld legislation authorising the courts to order blood transfusions necessary to save the lives of children, over the religious objections of parents and guardians; *People v. Labrenz* 411 Ill. 618, 104 N.E. 2d 769 (1952), where the court ordered a blood transfusion for an infant suffering from an RH condition who needed the blood transfusion to avoid death or substantial mental impairment; *Custody of Minor-Mass.* 379 N.E.2d 1053(1978), where a court order of chemotherapy treatment for a three year old leukaemia victim was upheld. See also *Raleigh Fitkin-Paul Morgan Memorial Hospital v. Anderson* 42 N.J. 421, 201 A.2d 537 cert. denied 377 U.S. 985 (1964), where a pregnant Jehovah's Witness was ordered to submit to a blood transfusion, if necessary, during childbirth since evidence established that a blood transfusion would probably be necessary to save the life of the child.
[76] 588 A 2d. 1108 (1991).

individual.[77] The individual interests at stake here were the parents' right to decide what was best for the child, and the child's own right to life. It was necessary to conduct two basic enquiries. First, the effectiveness of the treatment. In this instance, the doctors estimated that the child had a 40 per cent chance of survival and cure with chemotherapy, and none without. Secondly, the court must consider the nature of the treatment and the effect on the child. Medical treatment would be ordered over the religious objections of the parents where the treatment was relatively innocuous in comparison to the dangers of withholding care. The linchpin, according to the Court in all cases discussing best interests, is an evaluation of the risk of the procedure in comparison to the potential success. Such an analysis is seen as consistent with the principle that State intervention is only justifiable under compelling conditions. The State's interest in forcing a minor to undergo medical treatment diminishes as the risk of treatment increases and the benefits decrease.[78] Parental objection must also be taken more seriously when the medical treatment proposed is inherently dangerous and invasive.[79] In this instance, the Court decided that they had no power to intervene. Given the invasive nature of the treatment, the temporary and potentially permanent side-effects of the treatment,[80] and the unacceptably low chance of success, the State's authority did not outweigh the parent's prerogative.[81]

It is difficult to say whether an English court would have reached a different conclusion on the same facts.[81a] However, the decision would have been reached by a different route, concentrating on the best interests of the child, with little, if any, consideration of parental prerogative, and no need to prove compelling interest on the

---

[77] See *Cruzan v. Director of Missouri Dept. of Health* U.S. 110 S. Ct. 2841, 111 L. Ed 2d 224 (1990).

[78] The New Jersey Supreme Court recognised this principle in *Re Quinlan* 70 N.J. 10, 355 A 2d. 647 (N.J.) cert. denied 429 U.S. 922, 97 S. Ct. 319, 50 L. Ed. 2d 289 (1976). However, it should be noted that Karen Quinlan was in a persistent vegetative state, when permission was granted to cease treatment. The child in this case, while facing unpleasant treatment which could have resulted in his death, could also have recovered and lived a normal life.

[79] See *In Re Cabrera* 381 Pa. Super. 100 (1988).

[80] The child was likely to be sterile as a result of the treatment.

[81] The child died six months after the hearing, treatment having been discontinued.

[81a] But see *R. v. Cambridge Health Authority ex p. B.* [1995] 2 All E.R. 129. It is unlikely that an English Court would order treatment against the clinical advice of the doctors treating the patient.

part of the State.[82] The constitutional right to free exercise of religion is in conflict with the *parens patriae* jurisdiction and requires
that the United States courts give great weight to parental wishes.
Establishment does not give the same power to English parents,
and arguably protects children to a greater extent, by allowing the
court to concentrate purely on the best interests of the child. The
approach of the Delaware Court is unlikely to violate international
provisions, however. The United Nations Convention only provides that the "best interests of the child shall be a primary consideration"[83] and not the paramount consideration of the court.

(ii) Non life-threatening Medical Situations.   While the willingness of
the courts to intervene against a parent's religious objections, and
order a life saving operation, is easily sustainable from both a legal
and philosophical perspective, what of the situation where the condition of the child is not life-threatening? These cases pose more of
a dilemma to the courts. They involve children who have a serious
medical condition for which treatment is needed, but where the
lack of an operation will not cause the death of the child. Nonetheless, the failure to provide treatment may result in serious physical
or medical damage to the child. Cases in the United States show
that there are a number of factors to be weighed before coming to a
decision as to whether or not to order treatment. In such cases, the
courts have to perform a delicate balancing act between the parents'
right to bring up their child according to their religious beliefs, and
the court's *parens patriae* duty to protect the child.

The English courts have not been faced with the same dilemmas.
In the absence of a written constitutional right of free exercise of
religion,[84] the *parens patriae* jurisdiction is more highly developed,
through the medium of wardship and the inherent jurisdiction.[85]

---

[82] A situation could be envisaged, however, where doctors were willing to continue
treating a child, even though the prognosis was extremely poor and the child was
unlikely to ever recover to anything approaching normal life. In such an instance
it is likely that doctors would respect parental wishes that further treatment, particularly invasive treatment, should not be pursued.
[83] Art. 3.
[84] It could be argued that England has a written Bill of Rights in the European Convention on Human Rights, which it has ratified. Art. 9 provides for religious freedom. See Chap.1, p. 25. However, for the purposes of this book, it is assumed
that England does not have a written constitution.
[85] Invoked under the Children Act 1989, s.100 where the application is brought by
the local authority who may not use the wardship jurisdiction.

Further, parents are under a responsibility to provide adequate medical treatment for their child, a responsibility backed up by statute. The Children and Young Persons Act 1933, section 1(1) makes it an offence to neglect or ill-treat a child in a manner likely to cause unnecessary suffering or injury to health. Neglect is defined as including failure to provide medical aid. Such a failure may thus render a parent liable to criminal prosecution, proceedings to remove the child from the home,[86] and possible judicial interference, ordering that the child receive treatment. The guiding principle for the court is the best interests of the child. Decisions show that the court will not permit a child to be physically or mentally damaged where this is avoidable.[87]

Decisions in the United States courts have not been so uniform in this area. In *In Re Green*,[88] the doctors, in an attempt to prevent the child becoming bedridden from poliomyelitis, wished to operate. The mother consented to the surgery but, being a Jehovah's Witness, would not consent to a blood transfusion being administered. The doctors' view was that the operation could not be safely carried out without the possibility of a blood transfusion. The Supreme Court of Pennsylvania held that they would not overrule the religious objections of the parents to the medical procedure where there was no immediate threat to life. The Court, however, recognised that the child's rights were also at stake and that if the child wanted to have the operation, then his wish would prevail over the religious objections of the mother. Similarly, if the child expressed opposition to a medical procedure on the ground that it offended his or her religious views, the court would place great weight on this, particularly where the child had reached an age where he or she was capable of exercising mature, independent judgment. Indeed, in some medical situations, where the co-operation of the patient is essential to the success of the treatment,[89] the imposition

---

[86] Under the Children Act 1989, s.31.

[87] In a non-religious context, the wardship court has shown its willingness to intervene and prevent sterilisation operations against a parent's wishes where it has found it to be not in the child's best interests for the operation to occur. See *Re D*. [1976] 2 W.L.R. 279 [1976] 1 All E.R. 326. Given these sterilisation decisions it is unlikely that the court would not intervene and order an operation if it is in the child's best interests. It is difficult to contemplate the court finding that it is in the child's best interests to risk physical or mental handicap because of religious belief. See also the comments of Nolan L.J. in *Re W*. [1992] 4 All E.R. 627.

[88] 448 Pa. 338, 292 A.2d 387; 52 A.L.R. 3d 1106 (1972).

[89] See, *e.g.* In The Matter of Martin Seiferth Jr. 309 N.Y. 80; 127 N.E.2d 820.

of treatment in the face of the child-patient's objection may be counterproductive.[90]

The appropriateness of consulting the child is, however, questionable, and not all courts do so. The problem lies in determining what constitutes truly voluntary consent under the circumstances. Some courts take the view that asking the child whether he wants the operation puts the child in an invidious position. He is asked to make a decision which, if it differs from that of the parent, will put him in opposition to the primary carer upon whom, given his age and state of health, it is likely that he relies heavily. It is also likely that the child is an adherent of the same religion as the parent, and may be aware of the prohibition that the religion imposes on medical treatment. It is expecting a great deal from a child who is dependent on the family and the religious community, to make a truly voluntary decision as to whether to have an operation to make life physically or mentally better in the future. This is especially so if the child knows he may face parental and church disapproval, and even possible rejection. When the court makes the decision, the burden of opposing the parent's religious beliefs is lifted from the shoulders of the child and placed, where it arguably belongs, on the court and the State. Deferring to the child's wishes, without a consideration of the wider circumstances may provide inadequate protection to the child, and may not be in his best interests. The child's preferences should certainly be taken into account, as well as the possible psychological trauma that may arise if the child is forced to transgress the tenets of his faith, but such considerations should be balanced along with all the other factors in the best interests equation. It is worth bearing in mind in this context that most sects expect their followers to be law abiding. Therefore, if a court orders that a child should have medical treatment, submission to such an order is less likely to be seen as a breach of the religion's code, either by the child or by the parent, but as adherence to the law.

The distinction between life-threatening and non life-threatening medical treatment is often a difficult concept to sustain either medi-

---

[90] This view is supported by Nolan L.J. in *Re W.* [1992] 4 All E.R. 627. See also *Re E.* [1993] 1 FLR 386 where Ward J. held that the court should be very slow to interfere in a decision which a mature child had taken, as the freedom of choice was a fundamental human right in adults. However, in *Re S.* [1994] 2 FLR 1065 the court held that, while the mature child's wishes should be given effect, her wishes could be overridden if she did not appear to understand the full implications of her decision, and where her capacity was not commersurate with the gravity of the decision (for instance, where she was sick and weak and subject to external pressure).

cally or legally, as is vividly illustrated by the case of *People in the Interest of DLE.*[91] DLE suffered from recurrent epileptic seizures. The mother, who belonged to the Church of the Living Born, refused to comply with a medical treatment programme for her son.[92] In an action before the juvenile court, neither the mother nor DLE (who was 12 years old), agreed with the need for medical treatment, and, in a hearing before the Supreme Court of Colorado, both asserted their right to religious freedom.

For the Supreme Court of Colorado the critical issue was the proper interpretation of the religious exemption in the State's Children's Code, which recognised the parent's right to refuse medical treatment for their child on religious grounds. The court emphasised, in upholding the parent's refusal, that this was not a case where DLE's life was in danger. The medical evidence showed that while DLE suffered from periodic seizures, these seizures were not life-endangering.

Two years later the matter returned to the Colorado Supreme Court[93] due to DLE's worsening condition. Because of the frequency of his seizures, the right side of his brain was not functioning 40 per cent of the time. In addition, a stroke had caused permanent paralysis of his left arm and leg, and a nerve injury had caused restricted movement in his right arm and a dislocated jaw. The Supreme Court, reviewing its decision in the light of the child's degenerating condition, found that the religious exemption did not apply when faith healing practices threatened the child's life. The court rejected the contention of DLE and his mother that such a decision violated their First Amendment rights to free exercise of religion, and held that neither religious freedoms nor parental rights are beyond limitation. Once the child's life is threatened, the state's interest in protecting the well-being of the child requires that spiritual healing yield to medical treatment.

The case raises an interesting problem. In *DLE I*, after the decision was made that the parental religious beliefs should prevail, the child was withdrawn from any form of medication. Although at that moment in time the boy's condition was not life-threatening,

---

[91] 614 P.2d 873 (Colo. 1980).
[92] It was a tenet of her sect that if a member became ill, he should seek out church elders who would pray over the sick person, anoint him with oil, and ask that God intervene.
[93] 645 P.2d 271 (Colo. 1982).

the court appeared to pay little attention to the effect on the boy's long term health of receiving no form of medical treatment at all in the future. How much responsibility does the court bear when the child's condition deteriorates in the totally avoidable and very predictable way that occurred in *DLE*? Such an approach neglects and abdicates the court's child protection role. The distinction between life-threatening and non life-threatening is artificial. If any distinction is to be made, it should be made, at the very least, on the risk of harm to the child if the medical treatment is not given. One might, however, argue that this is unduly conservative. Instead, once the issue of medical treatment comes before the court, a decision should be made, not on the basis of possible harm, but taking into account the best interests of the child. Such an approach was taken in the 1970 case of *Sampson*.[94]

The child in this case had a large growth on the side of his head, causing severe facial deformity. Because of the deformity he had not attended school for a number of years. Doctors felt they could improve the situation, but a lengthy and potentially dangerous operation would be necessary, and would possibly require a blood transfusion. The mother, who was a Jehovah's Witness, would not agree to the blood transfusion. The Family Court found Kevin Sampson to be a "neglected" child, a decision upheld by the Appellate Division and the Court of Appeals. The boy's condition was not in any way life threatening, although it was unsightly. Indeed, what was potentially life threatening was the operation itself. Nonetheless, the Court held that the parent's religious beliefs could not stand in the way of whatever chance the boy had for a normal, happy existence. The Family Court acknowledged the fact that the case appeared inconsistent with prior authority, but stated that earlier decisions reflected outdated views on children's rights and family independence from State action. The result of the case was that the court decided that its authority to act was not limited to cases where the child's condition was life threatening, or even harmful, but extended to cases where, in the court's judgment, the child's health, safety or welfare required it. In other words the court could apply a test of the child's best interests.

This new, more child centred approach, was reflected in the

---

[94] In *Re Sampson* 65 Misc. 2d 658, 317 N.Y.S. 2d 641 (1970).

Oregon Court of Appeal in *In Re Jensen*.[95] Again, the parents refused to consent to surgical treatment for their daughter because of religious objections. The 15 month old child suffered from hydrocephalus. The child's life was in no immediate danger but, if the condition was not treated, retardation could develop, affecting the child's ability to lead a normal life. The Court ordered that the child be placed in the custody of a State agency for medical treatment. In affirming the decision the Oregon Court of Appeal held that the burden imposed on the child, in the interest of faith, exceeded the limits of parental and religious freedoms as enunciated in *Prince*. Although the child's life was not in imminent danger, the Court concluded that her parent's faith healing practices posed a risk sufficiently serious to justify State intervention: "the facts as we find them are that the most basic quality of the child's life is endangered by the course the parents wish to follow. Their right must yield".

In reaching their decisions in these medical cases, the courts in the United States have had to determine whether the State has an interest of sufficient magnitude to override a parent's right freely to practise his or her religion. While willing to find such an interest in the case of life-threatening conditions, the courts have been more reluctant to intervene where the child is suffering from a non life-threatening condition. The court may not, as in England, simply invoke the *parens patriae* jurisdiction and disregard all other competing rights. A refusal to consider the need to override religious objections of the parents at the non life-threatening stage provides inadequate protection for children. It can result in a child receiving no treatment until either the child is at the point of death, or has already suffered irreversible damage. There is a need for the courts to act at an early stage for the protection of children. By refusing to order medical treatment where there is a serious non life-threatening condition, the court also leaves medical staff and the social agencies in a quandary as to their future role in relation to the child. Such decisions imply that they must allow the child's condition to deteriorate considerably before taking any further action.

It can be concluded that, where there is a conflict between the parent's religious views and those of the State, on the need for a child to have a necessary, though not life-saving operation, the

---

[95] 54 Or.App. 1, 633 P.2d 1302 (1981).

courts, both in England and the United States, increasingly base their decisions on the best interests of the child. This approach has been more easily developed in England, where courts are not constrained by a constitutional guarantee of free exercise of religion. It is, however, an approach that is, very slowly, gaining favour in the United States as well.[96] The best interests test provides greater uniformity and certainty in decision making in medical matters. It also enables the court, while bearing a parent's religious objections in mind, to make a decision based purely on a child's welfare, and thus does not necessitate any finding against the religion or religious practice itself.

(iii) Psychological or Emotional Damage. Parents may involve children in the practice of their professed religion, provided that this practice does not adversely affect the actual day to day care of the child. If the court finds a religious practice leads to an unacceptable level of child care, the court may require an undertaking from the parent to desist from such a practice. A refusal to provide such an undertaking can result in the removal of the child from the family.

An early example of this approach is to be found in the United States case of *Ball v. Hand.*[97] The father, who had become a member of the community of Shakers, sought custody of his two daughters after the death of his wife. The children had been living with a relative. His avowed purpose was to integrate the children into the community of the Shakers where (since Shakers allegedly abjured all natural affection and denounced the parent-child relationship) their care and education would be turned over to female "care takers". The court did not look sympathetically on the father's claim and denied him custody. It pointedly commented that the father had a "morbid state of the amative and philoprogenitive faculties, bordering on insanity, and totally inconsistent with a rational discharge of parental duty". The court held that, where a parent's religious commitment interfered with his capacity to provide the proper temporal care for a child, he could be denied custody. The court did not purport to be judging the parent's religious beliefs, but only their secular effect on the child's upbringing,

---

[96] It is also the approach taken in Art. 3 of the UN Convention on the Rights of the Child to which the U.K. is a signatory.
[97] 1 Ohio Dec. Reprint 238 (1848).

which they found to be potentially psychologically harmful to the children.

The ability of the courts in the United States to intervene in what may seem unusual or undesirable religious teaching is limited to cases where harm, including psychological or emotional damage, can be shown. In *Lindsay v. Lindsay*[98] the mother had become a fanatic member of the Mazdaznan religion and a close acquaintance of its leader. The uncle of the child wanted the mother removed as one of the guardians of the child. The court held that it would intervene if the child was being exposed to immorality and vice,[99] but not where there was merely a difference of opinion as to the best course to pursue in rearing the child. There was no evidence in this case that the Mazdaznan religion was immoral or that the leader was an immoral man.

This inevitable approach was followed in the later case of *Sisson v. Sisson*.[1] The mother sought sole custody of the child after the father had become an enthusiastic follower of the Megiddo cult, and was teaching the child its precepts. The court held that it could intervene "only when moral, mental and physical conditions are so bad as to seriously affect the health or morals of the children".

The courts in England have also shown a marked reluctance to interfere in a family merely because they disapprove of the religious practices of the parents. Indeed, few such cases actually come to the attention of the courts. The situation would be different of course, if the practices were shown to be physically or psychologically harmful to the child.[2] In the difficult in-between cases, the court may demand an undertaking from the parents not to expose the child to the disapproved practice.

---

[98] 257 Ill. 328, 100 N.E. 892 (1913).

[99] This would constitute psychological damage if it could be shown. The common law always permitted interference in the parental upbringing of a child if gross immorality could be shown. See p. 145, above.

[1] 246 App. Div. 151, 285 N.Y.S. 41 (1936) rev'd 271 N.Y. 285, 2 N.E. 2d 660 (1936).

[2] This is a very difficult concept. The English courts have, on occasions, been extremely critical of Scientology practices. See pp. 187–188. However, there have been no attempts to remove children from Scientology families. Indeed, to do so, would probably be a violation of Art. 9 of the European Convention on Human Rights.

Where Religious Practices could result in Harm to the Community

In some instances, the religious beliefs and practices of the parents, while not causing any present harm to their own child, may threaten harm to the community at large. This is an issue that has arisen within the context of compulsory vaccination programmes for children, particularly in the United States. In England, vaccination for smallpox was first made compulsory by statute in 1853,[3] and the Vaccination Act of 1898 required that a child be vaccinated before she reached the age of six months. The only children who were exempted from this requirement were those whose parents could satisfy two justices[4] that they conscientiously believed that vaccination would be prejudicial to the child's health. There was no mention in the statute of exemption for religious reasons.

Vaccination ceased to be compulsory in England in 1946, but in a number of States in the United States it has remained compulsory for a wide range of infectious childhood diseases. Plaintiffs opposed to vaccination on religious grounds have argued that such a requirement infringes their constitutional right to free exercise of religion. In *Prince v. Massachusetts*[5] the United States Supreme Court stated that the freedom to practise one's religion does not include the right to expose the community or the child to communicable diseases.

The mode of enforcing vaccination laws in many States of the United States is to exclude children from public schools unless they have had the required vaccinations. Most States allow exemption for medical reasons, and some provide exemption on the ground that the religion, of which the parents are adherents, does not permit vaccination. Such an exemption has been held to apply only to those parents who are members of a church actually forbidding vaccination: private religious objections to vaccination are not enough. Thus a Catholic whose children were excluded from school because

---

[3] Vaccination was first made compulsory by statute in 1853, 16 & 17 Vict. c.100, gratuitous vaccination having been provided for in various enactments dating from 1840, all of which were repealed by the Vaccination Act 1867. The Act was amended by the Vaccinations Act 1871, 1874, 1898 and 1907. They were repealed by the NHS Act 1946, s.26, under which every health authority is to make arrangements for vaccination against smallpox and immunisation against diphtheria and, if so directed, against any other disease.

[4] Or a stipendiary or metropolitan police magistrate.

[5] 321 U.S. 158(1944).

of lack of vaccination, was held not to be able to claim that her children should be exempted on the basis of religion, because the Catholic Church recognised and agreed with the policy of vaccination. The plaintiff's own private belief was not sufficient.[6]

It has been argued, successfully, that such religious exemption clauses to compulsory vaccination statutes may be unconstitutional. In *Charles Brown v. Houston Municipal Separate School District*[7] the Court held that a religious exemption clause to a Bill requiring school children to be vaccinated against a range of childhood diseases was unconstitutional, because it would expose vaccinated children to the hazard of associating in school with children who had not been immunised. There is always a percentage risk that a vaccinated child will still catch the disease from an unvaccinated child. In the case of measles, this risk is estimated at between three and five per cent. The rationale of the Court was that the State had an overriding interest in protecting children from diseases for which known and successful means of immunisation existed.[8] Even if a parent can place her child's health in jeopardy in deference to a religious belief, there is no justification for exposing the children of parents who do not share the same religious beliefs to the risk.

Where the Child's views are in conflict with those of the Parent

When the parent and child disagree about the religious practices and faith that should be followed by the child, the parents' right to bring up a child without outside interference is in potential conflict

---

[6] See *Syska v. Montgomery County Board of Education et al* 45 Md. App. 626 (1979).

[7] 378 So. 2d 218 (1979) following *Zucht v. King* 260 U.S. 174, 43 S.Ct 24, 67 L. Ed 194 (1922). Such exemption clauses are likely to be found unconstitutional on another ground. The exemption clauses require that a court determine when an objection to vaccination is based on religious belief rather than personal belief. Such a determination would, it is submitted, involve excessive entanglement of Church and State.

[8] Also in *Sadlock v. Board of Education of Carlstadt* 137 NJL 85, 58 A. 2d 218 (1948) it was held that "the constitutional guarantee of religious freedom was not intended to prohibit legislation with respect to the general public welfare".

with the child's right to free exercise of religion. Whose right shall prevail? If the parents insist on adherence to their own religion and the child refuses, then the issue may be placed before the court. A judicial decision on the merits, however, begs the question whether the State should interfere in religious disputes between parent and child in an otherwise stable family. If a court does attempt to resolve the conflict, it must address substantive issues such as the age at which a child can choose and maintain a religion of his choice, and the stage at which the right of the parent to control the child's religious upbringing must give way to the right of the child to take up and follow a religion of his choice.[9]

At common law the father had the right to choose the child's religion. The courts, however, would not force a child to abide by the father's religious wishes if the child was already deeply impressed by a different religion in which he had been brought up. In *Stourton v. Stourton*[10] the religious preferences of a nine year old boy were considered by the court. The boy had been born one week after the death of his father and his mother had brought him up as a Protestant. When the child was almost 10 years old, the paternal relatives sought an order to ensure his upbringing as a Catholic. The Court stated that, had the relatives applied at the time of the father's death, it would undoubtedly have appointed a guardian to raise him as a Catholic. But the court found that the boys mind had become "religiously influenced and biased", and that under the circumstances of the case the relatives' petition would be denied. The court said that "the child's tranquillity and health, his temporal happiness and . . . his spiritual welfare" had to be given priority.

Conflicts between parents and child may arise in the context of the child wishing to pursue a course of action which is contrary to the parents' religious beliefs. The decision of the House of Lords in

---

[9] The Convention on the Rights of the Child provides in Art. 7 that the parents shall provide direction to the child in the exercise of his right to have or adopt a religion, in a manner consistent with the evolving capacities of the child. This does not provide a solution to the courts in disputes between parent and child, but does support the Gillick approach. See n. 3.

[10] 8 DM &G 760, 44 E.R. 583 (1857). In *Re W.* [1907] 2 Ch. 557, a 13-year-old son was permitted to be raised as a Christian rather than as a Jew, the faith of his father, even though the 11-year-old daughter who had expressed no preference was to continue to be raised in the Jewish faith. See also *Re Grimes* 11 Ir.R.Eq. 465 (1877).

Gillick,[11] although not concerned with religious conflict, is pertinent here. The Lords held that a doctor could prescribe contraceptives to a girl under sixteen against parental wishes. They found that there was no rule of absolute parental authority until the child reached the age of majority. Parental rights over a child dwindled as the child increased in age. A child had the right to make her own decisions when she reached a sufficient understanding and intelligence to be capable of making up her own mind. Therefore, a girl under the age of 16 did not lack the legal capacity, simply because of her age, to consent to contraceptive advice and treatment.

The reasoning of the House of Lords is equally applicable to cases where a child desires to make a decision in life contrary to the religious wishes of the parents, or to join a different religion against the parent's wishes. The implication of *Gillick* is that the parents' right to control religion must give way to the right of the child as she becomes mature enough to make her own decision.

A parent's religion may positively forbid an action which the child contemplates. The most common situation involves the pregnant teenager who seeks an abortion which is opposed by her parents on religious grounds. In both England and the United States, the courts have had to decide whether the parents can impose their religious views on their pregnant child, or whether the child's desire to have an abortion should prevail. In England, if a court is asked to decide whether the child should be permitted to have a termination, this will be done through invocation of the wardship or inherent jurisdiction, where the child's best interests are the paramount consideration.

In the case of *Re P*,[12] the parents of a 15 year old pregnant girl, who were practising Seventh Day Adventists, expressed their view that their daughter, who was in the care of the Local Authority, should not have an abortion because of their religious and moral beliefs that it was a crime to take human life. The Local Authority instituted wardship proceedings requiring the court to decide whether the girl's decision to have an abortion or the parent's religious based objections should prevail.[13] Having interviewed the

---

[11] [1984] Q.B. 581, [1984] 1 All E.R. 365.
[12] [1986] 1 FLR 272.
[13] The girl, who already had a one-year-old son, felt that she could not cope with another child, and wanted an abortion.

girl, the Court was satisfied that she truly wanted an abortion and was aware of the consequences. The Court recognised that, in deciding the best interests of the child, they must take into account and give weight to the feelings of the parents, but in the end their religious objections could not weigh in the balance against the needs of this girl so as to prevent a termination of the pregnancy.[14]

Courts in the United States have been faced with the same issue.[15] The decision in *Roe v. Wade*[16] recognised the woman's constitutional right to have an abortion. In *Planned Parenthood v. Danforth*[17] the Supreme Court held that minors also have constitutionally protected rights distinct from those of their parents, and that a statute which gave parents an absolute veto right over a minor's abortion decision violated her constitutionally protected right to have an abortion. The Supreme Court went further in the case of *Bellotti v. Baird*.[18] In reviewing a statutory requirement that a minor was required to notify both parents, or obtain judicial approval, before having an abortion, the Court found that the provision in no way furthered the State's interest in protecting pregnant minors or assuring family integrity, and was unconstitutional.

The decisions of the courts in the United States have given the mature, pregnant minor the right to make her own decision to have an abortion. English legislation has not gone this far in relation to a mature minor under the age of 16.[19] Following *Gillick*, though, there is no reason why a mature minor should not make such a decision. However, it is possible for a child to be made a ward of court up until the age of 18.[20] The use of wardship or the inherent jurisdiction, takes away the right of the child to make a decision, and places decision making power firmly in the hands of the court,

---

[14] See also *Re B.* [1991] FCR 889.

[15] For a wider discussion of the child's right to emancipation from the parent in religious matters see Tribe, "Childhood, Suspect Classifications and Conclusive Presumptions: Three Linked Riddles" (1975) 39 L. & Contemp.Prob. 8. Also Burt "Developing Constitutional Rights of, in and for Children" (1975) 39 L. & Contemp.Prob. 118.

[16] 410 U.S. 113 (1973).

[17] 428 U.S. 52 (1976).

[18] 443 U.S 622 (1979).

[19] Family Law Reform Act 1969, s.8 gives the child a right to make her own medical decisions. See *Re W.* [1992] 4 All E.R. 627.

[20] See *Re W.* [1992] 4 All E.R. 627.

who will decide in the child's best interests, rather than according to the child's wishes. It is, however, unlikely that a court would seek to enforce an abortion against a child's wishes, or enforce continuation of the pregnancy.[21]

Conclusion

Families have a right to follow the religion of their choice. The state is not free to intervene and prohibit a particular religion, even if a religion is unpopular or disliked, or includes elements of racial or sexual discrimination which offend the principles of democracy upon which the government of the United States and England are based. The rights of parents to transmit their religion to their children and to bring up their children according to their religious beliefs, values and traditions, is also recognised, but this right is limited. The state can intervene, either through the criminal or civil law, where religious practices are seen to cause "harm" to the child.

In defining harm, and in deciding whether to intervene, the court has to balance the rights of the parent to religious freedom with the right of the child to protection and autonomy. The underlying principle on which the balance lies, is the best interests of the child; but best interests are interpreted taking into account good practice and common values within the society. Such values may differ considerably from those held by certain of the "new Christian sects" and the "new religious movements".[22] While such an approach may seem intolerant to those whose religious practices are in conflict with such ideals, the approach of the courts is in accord with the relevant international instruments in this field. These do not require absolute toleration of all religious practices, or grant complete religious freedom, but recognise that the State must be allowed to limit religious practices. Limitations are permitted

---

[21] When two doctors have certified that the child satisfies the conditions of the Abortion Act 1967 and that the pregnancy should be terminated, it is difficult to foresee a court finding that it is in the child's best interests to continue the pregnancy.

[22] See the definition of these two groups given in Chap. 1, pp. 21–22.

where practices threaten the health, morals, rights or freedoms of children or others in the community.

The right of a child to protection against the harmful acts of parents is well recognised in the twentieth century. The right of a child to autonomy in religious practice has been slower in developing, and such development as there has been, has come largely through the interpretation of "best interests" rather than through recognition that children have separate, enforceable rights.

One of the aims of this chapter was to assess the impact of establishment on upbringing. In particular, whether establishment impairs or advances the protection of children, and the extent to which the interpretation of "best interests" is affected by establishment in England as against free exercise and non-establishment in the United States. From the cases, one can conclude that establishment has had no appreciable effect on the interpretation of "best interests", and is irrelevant to decisions in this area. This has allowed the English courts, through the well developed *parens patriae* jurisdiction, to take a child centred approach in reaching decisions relating to religious upbringing. The courts have been able to cast a wide net of protection as a result. The level of tolerance for parental, religious practices has, though, as a consequence, dropped in cases where "harm" is a likely outcome.

Constitutional free exercise of religion in the United States has had the result of impeding the courts from making decisions purely on the basis of the best interests of the child. Up until the 1980s, constitutional interpretations in the United States gave precedence to parent's rights over children's rights, notwithstanding the courts' *parens patriae* jurisdiction. Since the beginning of the 1980s, however, the United States courts have shown a greater willingness to consider the best interests of the child at the expense of the parent's rights.[23] This is partly due to an increasing judicial recognition of children's constitutional rights and partly due to a greater judicial willingness to hold that parental religious rights can be outweighed by the State's interest in the welfare of children. These

---

[23] This can only be seen as a general trend. See *Newmark v. Williams* 588 A. 2d 1108 (1991) which appears to go against this trend. However, the Newmark case is a difficult example as the court found that the treatment was so dangerous and painful and the chance of survival so low, that parents should be allowed to make their own choice for their child.

developments have been the subject of criticism by some commentators in the United States,[24] but they have been welcomed by those who believe that the interests of children have in the past been given too short shrift by the courts.

---

[24] As representative of this view see Mangrum, "Exclusive Reliance on Best Interests may be Unconstitutional: Religion as a Factor in Child Custody Cases" (1981–82), Vol.15, Creighton Law Review 25, and Colby, "When the Family Does not Pray Together: Religious Rights Within the Family" (1982), Vol.5, Harvard Journal of Law and Public Policy 39.

Chapter Five

Custody and Contact with Children

When the relationship between parents of a child breaks down and the parents decide to live separately, a number of decisions have to be taken. The parents will have to decide with whom the child shall have his or her main residence and the amount of contact the child will have with the non-residential, or non-custodial parent. Parents are encouraged to resolve such questions themselves, perhaps with the aid of a neutral third party. Where these issues cannot be settled by the parents, the court may impose a decision through court orders. In reaching any decision on custody (or residence)[1] or contact,[2] the court has as its guiding principle, the best interests of the child.

When disputes relating to the religious upbringing of children come before the courts, the court is normally required to balance the parent's right to freedom of religion against the right of the state to intervene in the best interests of the child. However, when disputes as to religious upbringing arise within the context of custody proceedings, the court has a rather different balancing act to perform: it must decide between the competing religious beliefs and practices of those, normally the parents, contesting custody. This chapter will examine how the court decides between compet-

---

[1] The term custodial parent is used to denote the parent with whom the child ordinarily resides. While this term is not the legal term used in all jurisdictions, the term is employed here to prevent confusion, and to reflect that used in the majority of cases referred to. Similarly "contact" is used to describe the contact time, access or visitation that the non-custodial parent has with his or her child. It is used in relation to the non-custodial parent. In the U.S. this contact is termed visitation.

[2] The term "contact" with a child covers "access" and "visitation".

ing religious beliefs and the impact of establishment and free exercise on such decisions.

It is often the case that by finding for one parent rather than the other, the court will also be making a decision about the religious upbringing of a child. This chapter will seek to explore the circumstances, if any, in which the court, in custody or contact proceedings, is prepared to curtail a parent's right to religious freedom, and find that it is against a child's best interests to be brought up within the traditions and practices of the parent's religion or belief.

Custody Proceedings

In common law the father had the right to choose the religion of the child, and this right held even after the death of the father, or after his withdrawal from the family. Thus the court found unexceptionally in the 1871 case of *Hawkesworth v. Hawkesworth*,[3] where the deceased father's Catholic relatives instituted an action to have the child brought up as a Catholic, even though the mother had brought the child up as a Protestant for the previous eight years, that:

> "the rule of law is that the religion of the father is to prevail over the religion of the mother, even in such a case, and that rule of course, we cannot alter".

This common law view prevailed unless the father could be shown to have abandoned or forfeited his right.[4] The prevalence of the father's right to determine religious upbringing still persisted in England in the first quarter of the twentieth century, although by this time it was tempered by the need to consider the welfare of the

---

[3] (1871) Law Rep. 6 Ch. 539.
[4] An ante-nuptial agreement to bring up the children in their mother's faith, while not binding at law or equity, could be treated as weighty evidence of abandonment or forfeiture of the father's right to determine the child's religious upbringing. Interestingly, the court did not think that in such a case where the father had forfeited his right to determine their religious upbringing, the children should be bound to be brought up in the mother's religion. In such an instance the court would instead consider the needs of the child. See Law Rep. 8 Ch. 622

child.[5] Paternal prevalence has been superseded by statutory change in both England and the United States, giving equal rights to both parents and by the growth of the welfare approach, or best interests test. The welfare approach,[6] finds its latest expression in England in the Children Act 1989. Section 1(1) of this Act provides that when the court determines any question with respect to the upbringing of a child, the child's welfare shall be the paramount consideration. In deciding with whom the child shall reside, or have contact, the court should take into account a number of factors to help them determine where the child's welfare lies, including the ascertainable wishes and feelings of the child, his physical, emotional and educational needs, and the likely effect of a change of residence.[7]

THE NEUTRALITY OF THE LAW

The English Courts have held that they do not prefer one religion to another. In *Re Caroll*,[8] Scrutton L.J. in the Court of Appeal stated that:

> "It is, I hope, unnecessary to say that the court is perfectly impartial in
> matters of religion; for the reason that it has as a court no evidence, no
> knowledge, no view as to the respective merits of the religious views of
> various denominations."

Indeed, to favour one religion over another would arguably be in breach of the European Convention on Human Rights and the Universal Declaration of Human Rights.[9] In the United States, as in England, the courts are prohibited from choosing between

---

[5] See, as an example of the enduring right of the father and his successors, the case of *Ward v. Laverty* [1925] A.C. 101, where paternal relatives who had not seen the children for four years attempted to gain custody of them so that they could be brought up as Catholics, either in their home or in a Roman Catholic institution.

[6] Put in statutory form in the Guardianship of Infants Act 1925, later in the Guardianship of Minors Act 1971, and restated in the Children Act 1989, s.1(1) in England.

[7] For the relevant legislation in the United States, see Clark, *The Law of Domestic Relations in the United States* (1988), Chap. 19.4.

[8] [1931] 1 K.B. 317.

[9] See the discussion on free exercise of religion and the right to transmit religious belief in Chap. One, pp. 12–17.

parents purely on the basis of their religious beliefs.[10] This flows from the provisions of the First Amendment to the Constitution which provide that Congress shall make no law respecting an establishment of religion or prohibiting the free exercise of religion. There have been numerous pronouncements by the Supreme Court on how this is to be interpreted, all of which stress the neutrality of the State:

"Our cases require the state to maintain an attitude of 'neutrality', neither 'advancing' nor 'prohibiting' religion."[11]

"Government must be neutral in matters of religious theory, doctrine and practice. It may not be hostile to any religion, or to the advocacy of no religion, and it may not aid, foster or promote one religion ... against another."[12]

As a result of this conscious policy of neutrality, United States courts may not question the authenticity of an individual's beliefs or doctrines, or weigh the relative merits of religions in child custody cases.[13] A pragmatic justification for this approach was given in the case of *Quiner v. Quiner*:

"If a court has the right to weigh the religious beliefs or lack of them of one parent against those of the other, for the purpose of making the precise conclusion as to which one is in the best interests of the child, we open a Pandora's box which can never be closed. By their very nature religious evaluations are subject to disbelief and difference of opinion. The First Amendment in conjunction with the Fourteenth solves the problem; it legally prohibits such religious evaluations."[14]

These statements of principle do not always seem to be reflected

---

[10] Even the most cautious application of the Establishment Clause would require application of this principle. See *Wallace v. Jaffree*, 472 U.S.38 (1985) 105 Sup. Ct. 2479 (1984/5) where it was stated that the Establishment Clause is designed to prevent government preference of one religious denomination or sect over another.

[11] *Committee for Public Education v. Nyquist* 413 U.S. 756 (1973).

[12] *Epperson v. Arkansas* 393 U.S 97 103–104 (1968).

[13] *cf.* the English case of *Re R.* [1993] 2 FLR 163 where it was held to be no part of the judicial function of the judge to comment upon the beliefs, tenets, doctrines or rules of any particular section of society, provided they were legally and socially acceptable and sincerely held.

[14] 59 Cal. Rptr. 503 (Cal. App. 1967).

in the case law. In the hard custody case, courts will look at the religiosity of the respective would-be custodians, as well as at the nature of their religious beliefs and practices. They do so, however, not to pass judgment on the merits or demerits of religion in general or a particular religion, but to determine the impact and effect of the religious practices on the well-being of the child, and to attempt to ascertain whether such practices would entail harm or endangerment to the child's health or welfare.[15] The key to unlocking any apparent contradiction between judicial pronouncements of religious neutrality and the actual examination of religious practices by the courts lies in an understanding of the nature of the custody decision. It is the paramount responsibility of the court in a child custody case to determine what is in the best interests of the children. It has been correctly said:

> "To hold that a court may not consider religious factors under any circumstances would blind courts to important elements bearing on the best interests of the child."[16]

Does the Law Prefer a Religious Parent to a Non-religious Parent?

It was certainly the case in nineteenth century England that religion was deemed to be a positive factor and a valuable attribute in one seeking custody of a child, or perhaps, to put it more accurately, the lack of a religion was deemed to be a negative factor. This attitude of the courts is well illustrated in the classic case of *Shelley v. Westbrook*,[17] involving the poet Shelley a man of well known atheist views. When he sought custody of his children, the Lord Chancellor of the day found Shelley's principles to be

---

[15] Such an approach is permissible according to the international instruments. See *Hoffman v. Austria* 15/1992/360/434, decided under the provisions of the European Convention for the Protection of Human Rights and Fundamental Freedoms. (Hereinafter referred to as the European Convention on Human Rights.)

[16] *Bonjour v. Bonjour* 592 P.2d 1233 Alaska (1979) See also *Osier v. Osier* 410 A.2d 1027 (Me 1980) and *Battaglia v. Battaglia* 9 Misc. 2d 1067, 172 N.Y.S.2d 361 (Sup. Ct.1958).

[17] (1817)Jac. 266n.

immoral and vicious, and such as to lose him the right to custody.[18]

Shelley's case was decided in the nineteenth century. It is unlikely that the decision would be followed today. The basis of the Court's opinion was its view that the practice of religion showed a person to be of good moral character, whereas, conversely, refusal to acknowledge and practice religion indicated immorality and, more significantly, unsuitability to care for children. To subscribe to such a view today would be a breach of the provisions of the European Convention on Human Rights, and other international instruments which protect both freedom of religion and freedom of belief.[19] Belief has been interpreted as encompassing theistic, non-theistic, and atheistic beliefs.[20] Thus, today, Shelley would have had an equal right with a religious parent to transmit his beliefs.

Interestingly, there is little in the way of case law after the nineteenth century as to whether the courts prefer a religious parent to a non-religious parent. One of the exceptions is *Roughley v. Roughley*,[21] where the judge ordered that custody of a girl be given to the father, even though the child had lived with her mother for the last three years. Both the parents were Roman Catholics. The father was a practising Roman Catholic who went to church regularly, while the mother was a lapsed Catholic. The mother did not give the child any religious instruction and did not take the child to church. The judge hearing the custody proceedings was outraged by this failure on her part.[22] On appeal, the Court of Appeal con-

---

[18] See also the case of *Wellesley v. Beaufort* (1827) 2 Russ 1, 5 LJOS 85, affd sub nom *Wellesley v. Wellesley* (1828) 2 Bli. NS 124, [1824–1834] All E.R. 189, 1 Dow & Cl 152, H.L.

[19] See Chap. One, pp. 14–17.

[20] It was stated in the UN publication, *Study of discrimination in the matter of religious rights and practices*, prepared by Arcot Krishnaswami, Special Rapporteur of the Sub-Commission on Prevention of Discrimination and Protection of Minorities (UN Publication, Sales No. E.60.XIV.2) that the term "religion or belief" was used there to include, in addition to various theistic creeds, such other beliefs as agnosticism, free thought, atheism and rationalism. As a result of lengthy discussions in various international bodies, the report on *Elimination of all forms of intolerance and discrimination based on religion or belief*, prepared by Elizabeth Odio-Benito as special Rapporteur of the same Sub-Commission (UN 1989) stated that it is now generally accepted that "religion or belief" includes theistic, non-theistic, and atheistic beliefs.

[21] [1973] Fam. Law 91.

[22] This omission reinforced his adverse view of the mother for being the cause of the break up of the marriage.

cluded that there was not the slightest doubt that the proper place for the girl was with her mother, and that the judge at first instance had taken such a strong position on the religious issue that he had misdirected himself.

Cases in the United States established early on that whether or not a parent practises or professes a religion should not be a factor in child custody cases.[23] Indeed, the First Amendment prohibits State action favouring the tenets or adherents of any religion over non-religion.[24] For a court to favour one would-be custodian over another because of their religiosity would constitute such prohibited State action. These principles notwithstanding, the issue of a parent's religiosity has crept into judicial decision-making. It has done so because a number of States permit the court to consider a child's spiritual welfare when reaching a decision on custody, and there is nothing to stop the court from looking at the moral environment in the respective homes of those contesting custody.

There are a large number of cases where the fact that one of the parents is religiously observant is cited as a positive factor, showing that that parent is able to provide a superior moral environment for the child. The reasoning of the courts is similar to the reasoning of the judges in nineteenth century England. They equate religiosity with good moral character. In *McNamara v. McNamara*[25] the court, in awarding custody of the child to the father, emphasised the importance of its finding that "he conscientiously adheres to religious teachings and would apparently rear his children in the same manner". Similarly, courts have commented favourably on regular church attendance by a parent with a child[26] and on parental participation in church related activities.[27] They have equated devoted attention to the church with excellent moral reputation[28] and a parent's ability to care for a child.

---

[23] See *Hewitt v. Lon* 76 Ill. Rep. 399 (1875); *Fuller v. Fuller* 249 Mich. 19, 227 N.W. 541 (1929); *Baker v. Bird* 162 S.W. 119 (Mo.1913); *Rone v. Rone* 20 S.W. 2d 545 Mo. Ct. App. (1929); *Kendall v. Williamson* 233 S.W. 296 (Tex. Civ. App. 1921).

[24] See *McDaniel v. Paty* (1978) 435 U.S. 618, 98 Sup. Ct. 1322.

[25] 181 N.W. 2d 206 (Iowa 1970).

[26] See *Strickland v. Strickland* 6 Div. 688, 285 Ala. 693, 235 So.2d 833. (1970) See also *Lewis v. Lewis* 217 Kan. 366, 537 P. 2d 204 (1975). The father's church membership and the fact that he took the children to church indicated that the children were well cared for.

[27] *Meyer v. Hackler* 219 La. 750, 54 So. 2d 7 (1951).

[28] In *Re Custody of King* 11 N.C. App. 418, 181 S.E. 2d 221 (1971).

There have also been cases in the United States where the failure of the parent to give the child any form of religious education and training has been regarded as a negative factor. In *Allison v. Ovens*[29] the court held that while it could not choose between religions, it could consider "the church and Sunday school habits of the children and their respective parents". In *Dean v. Dean*[30] the court stated that a judge could not prefer one faith to another, but he could consider a mother's failure to take the child to church. While refusing to evaluate or weigh the intrinsic truth of different religious beliefs, the Pennsylvania courts have consistently considered "spiritual well-being" to be part of the best interests equation.[31] In *Anhalt v. Fesler*[32] the court held that religion and church attendance are "not alone sufficient to determine the best interests of minor children" but are "factors to be considered".

DOES THE LAW DISCRIMINATE BETWEEN RELIGIONS IN CUSTODY CASES?

In the United States, as in England, the courts are prohibited from deciding with which parent the child shall make his or her home purely on the basis of the comparative merits of the parent's religious beliefs. This is the case regardless of the religion involved, whether a popular majority religion or an unpopular minority religion. In most cases where custody is disputed, the court is true to its expressed view of neutrality and does not favour one religion over another, or a religious parent to a non-religious parent. Rather, it bases its decision on the welfare or best interests of the child.[33] This is not to say, however, that the non-discrimination principle is absolute and overrides all other considerations. In the United States, the State is said to have a significant if not compelling interest in safeguarding the physical and psychological well-being of a minor. The First Amendment does not prevent a court from examining the religious or associational practices of prospective custodians in order to determine whether such practices entail harm of endangerment to

---

[29] 4 Ariz. App. 406, 421 P. 2d 929 vacated in part on other grounds, 102 Ariz. 520, 433 P.2d 968 (1967) cert. denied 390 U.S. 988 (1968).

[30] 32 N.C. App. 482, 232 S.E. 2d 470 (1977).

[31] See, *e.g. In Re Custody* of *J.S.S.*, 298 Pa. Super 428, 444 A.2d 1251 (1982).

[32] 6 Kan. App. 2d 921, 636 P. 2d. 224 (1981).

[33] See, *e.g.* the English case of *Re R.* [1993] 2 FLR 163.

the child's health or welfare. Similarly, in England, the court may discriminate against a parent on the basis of religion if this is necessary for the welfare of the child, which is the paramount consideration for the court.[34] The court would not be entitled to hold simply that one religion is preferable to another, but they may find that it is not in the best interests of the child to follow a particular religion. The court in reaching such a decision may need to assess the religious practices of a particular religion, the possible effect on the child if left with the parent of that religion, and the effects on the child if drawn into those religious practices. If there is a chance of danger to the child's welfare, then the court is justified in choosing a parent who does not follow what are seen to be harmful religious practices. If the court takes such a view, however, it must take care not do so out of mere apprehension of a perhaps little known or understood religion; there must be evidence to support the view of potential harm to the particular child concerned.

OBJECTIONS TO RELIGIOUS PRACTICES

In custody decisions, a party may plead that it is not in the best interests of the child to follow the religious practices of the party contesting custody. Such allegations usually fall into two categories. The first of these is that the practices of the religion as a totality are not in the best interests of the child. The second category is where it is alleged that a particular practice of a religion has undesirable consequences for the child.

(i) The totality of practices.

Where the court finds the religion per se undesirable. The First Amendment to the United States Constitution would render any decision that a religion was *per se* undesirable unconstitutional, as it would breach the Establishment and Free Exercise Clauses. Neither could the English courts reach such a decision without infringing the freedom to manifest religious belief contained in the European Convention on Human Rights and other instruments to which the United Kingdom is a signatory.[35]

---

[34] See the Children Act 1989, s.1.
[35] Although it should be remembered that the various international instruments do allow restrictions on the practice or religion in certain circumstances. See Chap. One.

However, the English courts do not appear to labour under the same restraints in relation to "beliefs". In the case of *Re B and G*[36] the judge had no difficulty in finding that it would not be in the child's best interests to be brought up within Scientology. Scientology, one of the new religious movements, had earlier been declared by the English High Court,[37] not to fall within the definition of a religion. The first instance judge in *Re B and G* declared Scientology to be immoral, obnoxious, corrupt, sinister and dangerous.

On appeal, it was submitted that it was a breach of natural justice to pass a definitive judgment about the merits or demerits of a religious sect, cult or any other body adhering to a code of behaviour or beliefs, without giving a right of audience to that group. The Court of Appeal side-stepped this contentious issue by finding that whatever force such an argument might have in normal cases, it had none where the court was exercising its powers in relation to children. In these cases the paramount importance of ensuring the welfare of the child overrode any right of audience or reply even where a parent was concerned, let alone a person or persons outside the immediate controversy. It was necessary in this case, in deciding whether exposure to Scientology was inherently dangerous to these children, to make definitive findings about the religion.[38]

Even if it is accepted, and it is debateable, that Scientology is not a religion, it must at the very least be regarded as a belief. Belief has been defined as including theistic, non-theistic and atheistic beliefs,[39] and under international instruments is regarded as subject to equal treatment and the same protection accorded to religion.[39a] It is highly unlikely that the court would make such a finding in relation to an old estblished religion. Such wholesale disapproval of

---

[36] [1985] FLR 493.
[37] *R v. Registrar General ex p. Segerdal* [1970] 2 Q.B. 697. See also *Schmidt v. Sec. of State for Home Affairs* [1969] 2 Ch. 149.
[38] The judge was able to do this according to the Court of Appeal, even though the church was not joined as a party to the action.
[39] See n. 20, above.
[39a] See, for instance, Art. 18 of the Universal Declaration of Human Rights, Art. 18 of the International Covenant on Civil and Political Rights and Art. 9 of the European Convention on Human Rights.

a belief is likely to be confined to the newer religious movements and break-away Christian sects[40] which do not command the same respect.

Where a mature child does not wish to follow the religion of the custodial parent. In England, it has been held that the following of a particular religion is against the best interests of a mature child where the child does not wish to follow that religion or its practices, and this is causing conflict to the child, and tension in the household. In *Robertson v. Robertson*[41] both mother and father had been Jehovah's Witnesses, but the father had ceased to follow the church after he left the family. The mother remained a devout follower of the religion. The oldest child, a boy of 14, made it very clear in custody proceedings, that he wanted to live with his father. When questioned about his religious commitment he stated that he went to Witness meetings, but that he did not like going, and that he did not understand the purpose of the meetings. His distinct lack of religious attachment in such a religious family and his desire to move homes, partly flowing from his reluctance to follow the religious practices in the mother's home, justified a decision to allow him to live with the father. Although this would mean splitting the boy from his two brothers, the judge found it to be in the child's best interests.

The age and maturity of the child was arguably critical to the decision in *Robertson*. The boy had reached the age where he would look for entertainment outside the home. The religious practices of the mother would forbid this, and the boy's unwillingness to follow and obey these dictates would inevitably cause conflict. Had the boy been younger, his objections would have carried less weight.[42]

---

[40] The American courts have certainly been prepared to distinguish between old and new religions; see *Wisconsin v. Yoder* 406 U.S. 205, 92 Sup. Ct. 1526, 32 L. Ed 2d 15 (1972).

[41] (1980), C.A.

[42] In *Re R.* [1993] 2 FLR 163, the religious views of a 9-year-old boy were only one factor in deciding the best interests of the child. Even though deep and sincerely held such views were not allowed to dominate, the court finding the child too young and too inexperienced to make such a decision.

In the United States, authorities also suggest that a court should give attention to the religious preferences of a mature child in assessing which parent should have custody. In *Vardinakis* the court found:

"In choosing a religion of one parent rather than the other the child is frequently either consciously or unconsciously also choosing one parent rather than the other and is indicating to the court in the clearest way possible with which parent he has the most sympathy and the greatest sense of security. The positive choice of a religion by an intelligent child of 13 or 14 years must, therefore, be seriously considered in determining what is best for his own welfare."[43]

It is possible, following *Vardinakis*, that a court in the United States would reach the same conclusion as an English court: that once the child is mature enough to have made a choice regarding religion, and has identified with a particular religion,[44] forcing the child to change and follow a different religion and its practices would be against the child's best interests. In the United States, however, there is a further dimension to these cases, that of the constitutional right to free exercise of religion. Imposing the religion of the custodial parent on an unwilling mature minor would, arguably, infringe the mature minor's right to free exercise of religion. However, it is debatable whether the child has a constitutional right to free exercise of religion.[45] The Superior Court of Pennsylvania has recently suggested that it is unclear whether a child has a constitutional right to be protected from attempts by either parent, exercising their own constitutional free exercise rights, to inculcate religious beliefs in their children, prior to the age of legal emancipation.

---

[43] See *Vardinakis v. Vardinakis* 160 Misc. 13, 289 N.Y. Supp. 355 (1936) and *Martin v. Martin* 308 N.Y. 136, 123 N.E. 2d 812 (1954).

[44] It has been suggested that a child needs to be at least 12 years-old in order to identify with a particular religion. See *Zummo v. Zummo* 394 Pa. Super 30; 574 A. 2d 1130 (1990).

[45] For further discussion of this issue, see Pfeffer, "Religion in the Upbringing of Children" (1955) 35 B.U.L. Rev. 333. Also *Bonjour v. Bonjour* 592 P. 2d 1233 (Alaska) 1979.

Where a religion advocates illegal practices or practices which contravene a valid statute.   The practices of a religion may be restricted by the need to comply with a state's legislation. Occasionally it has been found that an illegal practice, such as the taking of peyote, forms a fundamental part of a legitimate religion. In such a case, a California Court held that the right to practise one's religion was a valid defence to a criminal prosecution.[46] Such decisions are the exception, however, and as far back as 1878 the United States Supreme Court held that freedom of religion would not, for instance, constitute a bar to the prosecution of a Mormon for bigamy if he followed the dictates of his religion and married polygamously.[47]

In custody cases courts will be naturally reluctant to award custody to a parent who adheres to a religion which requires the parent or the child to break the law. It is obviously not in a child's interest, (nor in society's interest), for the child to be brought up as a law breaker. The court's objections in such a case would doubtless be multiplied if the illegal practice would also be physically harmful to the child. Thus, if the parent was a keen member of the Holiness Church and intended that both she and the child should become involved in snake-handling, an essential religious practice of this sect, and a practice which has been made a criminal offence in many States of the United States,[48] it is extremely likely that the court would find it against the child's best interest to be raised by this parent.

Where the court finds that the religious practices taken as a whole are harmful to the child or not in the child's best interests.   In both England and the United States, courts have expressed disapproval of certain religious lifestyles and their effect on children. In England this has occurred in particular in relation to the Exclusive Brethren. The

---

[46] *People v. Woody*, 61 Cal. 2d 716, 394 P.2d 813, 40 Cal. Rptr. 69 (1964). However, such an argument did not succeed in the snake-handling cases, see Chap. 4.
[47] *Reynolds v. United States*, 98 U.S. 145 (1878).
[48] See Chap. 4, p. 147.

religion and practices espoused by the Exclusive Brethren have been characterised as extremely harsh and restrictive on a child, and courts have found it undesirable to leave a child in that milieu if there is an alternative possibility of custody with a non-Brethren parent.[49]

In *Re C*[50] the High Court found the separationist practices of the Exclusive Brethren intolerable and that the child's best interests lay in life with a non-Brethren parent. Disapproval of the practices of the Exclusive Brethren was expressed again in *Hewison v. Hewison*.[51] The Court of Appeal agreed with the assessment by the judge at first instance who found that the mode of life and code of behaviour enforced by the sect upon its members and their children was harsh and restrictive. He found that the children were greatly deprived of normal social contacts, and handicapped in respect of further education, professional qualifications, opportunities for academic life and technical skills, as education after sixteen was actively discouraged.[52] The sanctions for disobeying any of the rules of the sect were severe and could, as they did in this case, result in the children being "shut up", and being denied any contact or communication with other sect members.

The judge at first instance had to ask himself whether, given these facts, it would be in the interests of the children that they should be brought up in the Exclusive Brethren tradition. Even though the children had lived with their father for six years, the judge found that the children's best interests would be served if they were free from the harsh doctrines and way of life of the

---

[49] Although See *Re R*. [1993] 2 FLR 163 where it was held that the practices of the sect were only relevant in so far as they affected the child concerned.

[50] *The Times*, August 1, 1964.

[51] [1977] Fam. Law 207.

[52] Although the children in this case were allowed to attend a normal school, they did not attend any religious instruction period, or assembly, did not share any school meals and did not join in any team games.

Exclusive Brethren. While the judge was careful to state that this was only one of many factors to be taken into account, the religious factor was, undoubtedly, the determining factor. None of the other factors cited would have justified moving children who had lived with their father for six years and found to be happy and healthy. The Court of Appeal upheld the judgment, agreeing that it would be in the children's best interest to have greater educational freedom and social opportunities, and to be free from the harsh limitations of life in the fellowship of the Exclusive Brethren.

The courts in the United States have been faced with the same issue as the English courts: What custody disposition should be made, and where does the child's best interest lie, when one of the parents would compel the child to follow a "harsh and restrictive" religious regime. The resolution of this issue has depended largely on the way the courts have balanced the concept of the child's best interests with the parental right to free exercise of religion and, implicit in that, the parental right to transmit religious values to the child. The approach of the courts in the different States where the issue has arisen has varied, from one which is predominantly parental rights orientated, to one where the child's best interests take clear precedence, to virtually everything in-between.

A parental rights approach is reflected in the case of *Quiner v. Quiner*,[53] where the mother was bringing up her son as a member of the Plymouth Brethren, a separatist sect with practices virtually identical to those in *Hewison*.[54] The trial court initially awarded the custody of the two and a half year old boy to the father, using language very similar to that of the court in *Hewison*—that the child's mental welfare and opportunity for personality growth would be furthered best with the father. On appeal, this judgment was reversed, on the basis that there was no evidence that the principles of separation had had any effect on the child or had impaired

---

[53] 59 Cal. Rptr. 503 (Cal. App. 1967). The terms Plymouth Brethren and Exclusive Brethren are used to denote the same sect for convenience, although it is recognised that in England these are two different groups, the Exclusive Brethren having broken away from the Plymouth Brethren.

[54] [1977] Fam. Law 207.

the physical, emotional or mental health and well-being of the child. The Court of Appeals concluded that the courts had:

"no power to tell parents who teach nothing secularly immoral, unlawful or against public policy, how to shape the minds of their children,
particularly on the subject of accepted religious belief . . . The fact that
judged by the common norm, it may be logically concluded that custody in the father is for the child's best interests, does not warrant us in
taking custody away from the mother when such an order must be bot-
tomed on our opinion that the mother's religious beliefs and teachings,
in their effect on the child are, and will continue to be contrary to the
child's best interests."

However, as a proviso, the Court agreed that if, in the future, the mother was found to be teaching the child not to care for or respect his father, then such indirect indoctrination would undoubtedly warrant judicial review. Also, if as a consequence of teaching the principle of separation the child's well-being was shown to be affected or jeopardised, or if the mother was found to be disobey-ing a court order in relation to the child, then, even regardless of the fact that the mother's actions were mandated by her religion, the Court could act.[55]

The California Court of Appeals in *Quiner* required actual evi-dence of impairment before it could act in the child's best interests. Without that evidence, the parental right to free exercise of religion and the right to transmit religious values and beliefs to the child took precedence over the child's welfare. The trial court was not allowed to intervene simply because it disapproved of the practices and tenets of the religion. The dissent in this case characterised the decision, correctly it is submitted, as one that sacrificed the child's best interests at the expense of parental rights.

The *Quiner* standards were critically examined by the Wash-ington State court in *In the Marriage of Hadeen*.[56] Here the court held that religious practices could be considered in a custody decision but only to the extent that these practices would jeopardise the tem-

---

[55] The California Supreme Court granted a hearing on this case that had the effect of nullifying the reported opinion. However, the parties reached a settlement that makes this case moot. For a similar approach see *Johnson v. Johnson* 564 P. 2d 71 (Alaska 1977).

[56] 27 Wash. App. 566; 619 P 2d 374.

poral mental health or physical safety of the child.[57] The court found that the *Quiner* requirement of actual impairment was improvident, and stated that before a court could intervene there only had to be a showing of reasonable and substantial likelihood of immediate or future impairment. Such a test was held to best accommodate the general welfare of the child and the parent's right to free exercise of religion.

However, the court in *Hadeen* took a rather narrow view of what types of harm and impairment it was appropriate to consider. The case concerned another exclusive, new religious movement (the First Community Churches of America) which church required its members total loyalty. Again, children were heavily discouraged from contact with anyone outside the religious membership on a social basis. The trial judge hearing the case awarded custody of four of the five children to the father. The basis for his decision was the children's need to maintain a relationship with their father for their emotional well-being. If the children stayed with their mother the judge feared that the father would be totally excluded from their lives.

The Appeal Court, finding that the children wished to stay with their mother, ordered a rehearing. At no point did the majority give attention, consideration or weight to the practices of the religion, other than those which might have adversely affected the relationship between the children and their father. For instance, the court took no account of the fact that the mother believed that children overriding parents was tantamount to witchcraft, or the fact that the Church believed that a parent should hit a child until its will was broken, a practice that the mother not only agreed with but implemented.[58] Furthermore, the children were taught to use foul language to anyone who was not a member of the movement. If a child disobeyed the parent or a Church rule, that child was to be sent to her room without food until she repented. Lastly the mother had already rejected one of the children who was disturbed and exhibiting a range of behavioural difficulties, and it was likely

---

[57] Interestingly the possibility of alienation was not regarded as an issue which of itself could be a reason for intervening in this case.

[58] There was evidence that the mother had hit one of the children with a table tennis bat for two hours, having got the other children to hold her down.

that the child would be rejected again if she was unable to conform to the strict rules of the movement.

It is difficult to see why these issues were not considered. As pointed out by the dissenting judge, the behaviour of the mother when carrying out the practices of her religion bordered on child abuse. The majority apparently felt that the practices of the mother were part of the doctrine of her religion and, therefore, not a proper matter for review by the court. It is certainly arguable that, although the court paid lip service to the standard of the best interests of the child, its approach undercut that standard. If *Hadeen* is representative, it would seem that although the courts of both England and the United States purport to apply a best interests standard, the constraints put upon certain States of the United States by free exercise considerations result in a judicial approach which is less flexible than that employed by the courts in England.

There are States, however, in which the best interests of the child are much more evenly balanced with the free exercise of religion, or even made paramount to it. In *Burnham v. Burnham*,[59] the court pointed out that in a custody dispute, the parents begin with an equal right to have custody, with no preferences based on the sex of a parent nor any presumptions that one parent is inherently more fit than the other. From this base, the trial judge must consider the evidence and decide with which parent it would be in the best interests of the child to remain. The court preserved an attitude of impartiality between religions and stated, following authority,[60] that it would not disqualify a parent because of his or her religious belief. However, unlike the cases of *Quiner* and *Hadeen*, the Court recognised that it was under a duty to consider whether beliefs held and practised by a parent threatened the welfare and well-being of the child. The primary consideration for the trial judge was the welfare of the child, and to this end the trial judge was to consider not only the spiritual and temporal welfare of the child, but also the child's further training, education, and morals, as well as the ability of the proposed guardian to best take care of the child.

In what way can a court consider religion as a factor in the best interests equation? According to the court in *Burnham*, the auth-

[59] 208 Neb. 498; 304 N.W.2d 58.
[60] *Goodman v. Goodman* 180 Neb. 83 141, N.W. 2d 445 (1966).

orities support the view that it is legitimate to examine the impact of the parent's beliefs on the child. In this case the court found that the mother, who had become a member of the Tridentine Church,[61] held a number of beliefs which could have an adverse impact on the child: first, the belief that her child was illegitimate because the parents were not married in the Tridentine Church; secondly, the willingness of the mother to cut the child out of her life if she disobeyed the rules of the Church; and thirdly, the racist views held by the mother and the Church (the mother believed the Jews and Communists were involved in a plot to take over the world). A further complicating factor was that the mother intended to send the child to a Tridentine school out of the State, and this would interfere with the father's visitation rights.[62] The court concluded that for the child to stay with the mother would not only have a deleterious effect on her relationship with her father, but more importantly, it would have a deleterious effect on the well-being of the child. For this reason the court placed the child in the custody of the father.

There was no requirement in *Burnham* that the non-custodial parent show that the mental or physical health of the child was substantially impaired or even that there was a reasonable likelihood of substantial impairment in the future. The judge had to make a decision on the basis of the child's best interests taking all the circumstances into account.[63] In considering the practices of the Tridentine church as they affected the child, the court found it was not in her best interests to stay with her mother.

This seemingly pure best interests case has not escaped critical comment. The not surprising basis for criticism is that the court deprived the mother of her child because of the mother's religious beliefs, and in breach of her constitutional right to free exercise of

---

[61] The sect were otherwise known as the Fatima Crusaders, an extreme Catholic sect.

[62] It is clear from the report that the court was dubious about the proposed school. Unless the child went to a Tridentine school, the mother would be excommunicated. On entry of the child to the school, the mother had to sign a release giving full permission for the use of corporal punishment and strict discipline. It also relieved the Academy, all teachers, etc., of all responsibility for the child in case of accident, or unforeseen mishap.

[63] There are of course, a whole range of factors to be taken into account in a custody decision, but the factor of religion weighs very heavily in these cases.

religion.[64] It is fair to say that in many of these cases the practices of the religion are realistically inseparable from the religion itself, and that a finding that the child's best interests lie in transferring her away from the "harmful" religious practices is tantamount to a disapproval of the religion. But there is a difference. The court is not denying the mother the right to follow her chosen religion or to manifest her religious beliefs. The court's only concern is with the well-being of the child, and the cause of the danger to the child is less important than the fact of danger.

It is hard to see how a court committed to the best interests of the child could do otherwise. The alternative would be not to consider the religious factor at all, but to wait until the child had suffered or was on the verge of suffering actual harm stemming from the religious practices. It is difficult to argue, when the harm is clearly foreseeable, that such delay is in the best interests of the child. The court is not, after all, depriving the parent of the right to practise his or her religion freely. As was pointed out by the court in *Battaglia*:

"The parent, of course, enjoys her Constitutional right to freedom of religion and may practice the religious faith of her choice without interference. She has not, however, the right to impose upon an innocent child the hazards flowing from her own religious convictions. The welfare of the child is paramount. The child has a right to survival and a chance to live and the court has a duty to extend its protecting arm to the child. It is of no concern to the court what religious preferences the parent may elect. The best interests of the child are the primary concern in all custody conflicts and not the desires of the mother or the father."[65]

(ii) Particular practices.

The discussion to this point has dealt with instances where the court has found that, looked at in their totality, the practices of a religion are against the child's best interests. There are also instances where the court finds that while the religion and its prac-

---

[64] For detailed criticism of this case see Mangrum, "Exclusive Reliance on Best Interest May Be Unconstitutional: Religion as a Factor in Child Custody Cases" (1981–82) Creighton Law Review, Vol.15, p. 25. The author sees *Burnham* as representing an unconstitutional subjection of the parental rights of the mother to the prejudices of the Supreme Court Justices justified vaguely by the best interests standard. See also *Hoffman v. Austria* 15/1992/360/434 before the ECHR where a similar allegation was made.

[65] 9 Misc. 2d 1067, 172, N.Y.S. 2d 361 (1958).

tices are not *per se* harmful, nevertheless as a consequence of a particular practice of the religion, an individual child suffers from undesirable consequences which result in either emotional or educational disadvantage to the child.

In one sense the difference between the totality of practice cases and the particular practice cases is a matter of degree. Rarely does one find a religion or belief, all of whose practices are totally unacceptable to a court. It is when a court comes to fashioning remedies, however, that the difference between the totality cases and the particular practice cases becomes evident. In the totality cases the court's only option is to choose between the competing parties as to whom to award custody. In the particular practice cases, the court has a second option: to allow the child to remain in the custody of the parent adhering to the religion which has the objected-to feature, but on the condition that the parent give an undertaking not to engage in the practice in question. This option makes little sense in the totality cases for it is unrealistic to expect a parent to abstain from practising all aspects of his religion, and, indeed, an undertaking to this effect would be unlikely to be believed.[66]

Both the totality and particular practice cases raise the vexing question of what is meant by best interests. What is an ideal life for a child? Some authorities seem to assume that it is a western, largely secular life with all the opportunities that a modern society can provide. But in a multi-ethnic society which subscribes to religious tolerance, less traditional life styles may have to be accepted, at least where the child does not suffer significant harm. It has thus been held in England that mere restriction of a child's activities, and a rather narrower way of life are not of themselves reasons for denying a Jehovah's Witness parent custody of a child.[67] However, where social isolation is allied with a contempt for non-members of the sect, and a refusal to communicate, where this could lead to alienation from the other parent and the child's wider family, the court is willing to find the practices not in the best interests of the child.

Alienation: The possibility of alienation from the non-custodial parent, particularly where that parent has ceased to be a member of

---

[66] See, *e.g. Re B. & G.* [1985] FLR 493.
[67] See, *e.g. Robertson v. Robertson* (1980, C.A.; unreported). See also *Re R.* [1993] 2 FLR 163.

the religion practised by the custodial parent and the child, is a matter of concern to the courts. This was an important factor in the English case of *Re B and G*[68] where the custodial father was a Scientologist. The judge found that to allow the children to remain with the father and the stepmother would result in alienation from their mother, and that this would be nothing short of disastrous for the children. Furthermore, as the mother had renounced Scientology, the father was likely to be under pressure from the Church to "disconnect" from her, and disconnect the children from her as well.

As illustrated in *Re B and G*, the problem is particularly acute where the non-custodial parent was previously a member of a separatist, new religious movement to which the custodial parent still belongs. Thus, in *Re R*,[69] despite the strong religious beliefs held by the boy, aged nine, who was a member of the Exclusive Brethren, the court found that the alienation of the boy from his father, which would be an inevitable result as the father was an outcast from the movement, was not in the immediate, medium or long-term interest of the child. In *Townsend v. Townsend*[70] the same issue arose in relation to a mother who had left the Jehovah Witnesses and was seeking custody from their father who remained a member. The Court of Appeal held that it was not a question of deciding whether the religion espoused by the Jehovah's Witnesses was a bad religion; clearly it was not. What the judge had to decide was whether it was in the children's best interests that they should have their feelings of security and love for their mother imperiled, and whether there was any danger that they might come to the view that, by leaving the group, their mother had betrayed the standards of the religion they were learning in their home. The Court of Appeal found that it would not be in the children's best interests to be cut off from their mother, and transferred custody of the two younger children to her.[71] While no criticism was made of the religion as such, the consequences that would flow from leaving the children with their father were regarded as undesirable and

---

[68] [1985] FLR 493.
[69] [1993] 2 FLR 163.
[70] (1984, C.A.; unreported).
[71] The oldest child was already alienated from the mother by the time of the proceedings.

likely to lead the children to regard the mother with disapproval and contempt.

Emotional Disadvantage: On the whole the courts are unwilling to look at which religion might be the most emotionally advantageous to the child, or which religion would make the child happier. Such considerations would require a court to evaluate the merits of the religion and would breach the concept of the court's neutrality. In the United States, such an evaluation would also breach the First Amendment to the Constitution. But the courts, in both England and the United States have been willing to consider the child's emotional needs and whether the practices of a particular religion meets them.

In the unusual English case of *Kaasikmae v. Fabian*[72] the contest for custody was between the grandparents of the child and the mother and step-father. The mother and stepfather both belonged to a new, evangelical religious movement[73] which held as a central tenet that the husband had total authority over the family. The child had expressed a wish to return to live with the grandparents or at least to have increased contact with them. This was unacceptable to the step-father who, after consultation with the elders, had decided that contact with the grandparents should cease. The court found that the rules and way of life of the step-father's religion meant that the boy's emotional needs were simply not adequately considered or met. Given the mother's subservience to the step-father, it was very unlikely that she would be willing to intervene on the boy's behalf, or act in his best interests. The religion was insufficiently sensitive to the needs of this individual child and emotional deprivation was likely to result. Given the father's intransigence to contact, the court found that the child's emotional development would be better served by his living with his grandparents.

The courts stress in these cases that it is the consequences of the religion, rather than the religion itself, which is not in the best interests of the child. Although many of the "undesirable consequences" cases have involved Jehovah's Witnesses, a judge will not automatically conclude that following the beliefs and practices of

---

[72] *Kaasikmae v. Kaasikmae; Kaasikmae v. Fabian* (1985, C.A.; Unreported).
[73] The Fellowship of the Kings.

the Jehovah's Witnesses is inimical to the best interests of the child. Where both parents are Jehovah's Witnesses, the President of the Family Division[74] has stated that "no court could possibly say, or would think of beginning to say, that the children should not be brought up as Jehovah's Witnesses."

Where the parents are of different religions, however, the court will often require undertakings on the part of the Witness parent to refrain from certain religious practices before it will agree to leave the child in that parent's care. In effect, therefore, as long as the Jehovah's Witness parent, or a parent from another "separatist" religious group, promises to be "reasonable" in their religious practices, the court will not interfere. However, if the parent is an "orthodox" member of the religious group and follows all practices to the full, and where these practices will inevitably lead to alienation from the other parent, or too great a degree of social and emotional isolation for the child, the court will not hesitate to find that this is not in the child's best interests.

UNDERLYING ISSUES

In cases involving State intervention, it is normal to require some showing of harm to a child before the State is given the right to intervene and prevent a parent carrying out certain religious practices in relation to the child. Custody decisions are, however, made on a different basis, that of the best interests of the child. This is a standard that cannot be concretely defined, including as it does the consideration of a whole range of factors. It is also a relative concept, confined by the alternative forms of care offered by the parents.

Given that both England and the United States have ratified instruments providing for free exercise of religion, is the State ever justified in finding that certain religious practices are against the best interests of the child, and thus refusing custody to the parent following that religion? It is clearly acceptable in English law and the laws of the various States of the United States and under the European Convention on Human Rights and other international

---

[74] *T. v. T.* [1974] Fam. Law. 191.

instruments, to place limits on the free exercise of religion and respect for family life. These limitations may apply where restriction is necessary in a democratic society for the protection of health or morals or for the protection of the rights and freedoms of others.[75] However, where religious practices, or the religion itself, do not fall within these limitations, the court should not find in favour of the non-religious partner purely because they do not approve of the religion, or believe that the upbringing offered to children by that religion is not ideal. In other words, a distinction based on difference in religion alone is not acceptable, and would be likely to be in breach of Articles 8 and 9 of the European Convention on Human Rights, and a breach of the Free Exercise and Establishment Clauses. But the practical consequences of membership of a particular religion, such as a very restricted social life for children, separation for non-believers and a rejection of blood transfusions may be taken into account when considering the best interests of the child and may, in themselves, be capable of tipping the scales in favour of one parent or another.[76]

There are rare instances where a court has found that the religion or belief itself is inimical to the child's best interests, and falls within the limitations imposed on free exercise of religion and the right of respect for family life. This is particularly pertinent in the case of Scientology. In *Re B and G*[77] the judge found the practice of Scientology inimical to the child's best interests, and not only because of the possibility of isolation from the non-custodial parent. Such a finding raises an important question. Ought the social welfare agencies to at least investigate the welfare of any children born to practising Scientologists? Further, ought there to be intervention, as a matter of course, both through the welfare agencies and the courts to protect such children? Such an approach would be likely to infringe the European Convention on Human Rights and other international instruments concerning freedom of

---

[75] See Articles 8 and 9 of the European Convention on Human Rights. The exception provisions in the International Covenant on Civil and Political Rights (Art. 18(3) and the Declaration on the Elimination of All Forms of Intolerance and Discrimination Based on Religion or Belief Art. 1(3) are slightly different). See Chap. One, n. 17 for a further discussion of this point.

[76] See *Hoffman v. Austria* 15/1992/360/434.

[77] [1985] FLR 493.

religion.[78] However, the question still remains: are these children adequately protected?

There are no easy answers to these questions. By western secular ideas of child rearing, the narrow restrictive lifestyle imposed by many religions is less than ideal. Some religious practices, such as those that affect the child's education, may severely restrict the child's opportunities in later life. Moreover, the critical decisions, such as those relating to education, may be made before the child is old enough to decide whether he or she wishes to continue in the ways of the religion. Intervention is arguably necessary to preserve future options for the child. On the other hand, in England and the United States the State is under a duty to tolerate other religious ideals, and not to impose their own western, Christian standards. The fact that majority opinion might support the imposition of such standards is irrelevant, for minority rights need to be protected. This consideration argues for non-intervention until such time as it is shown that the effects of the religious life-style, or the practices of the religion, threaten to cause physical or psychological harm to the child, or at the very least are depriving children of their basic rights as a member of a democratic society.

FOLLOWING A CUSTODY DISPUTE, WHICH PARENT CHOOSES THE CHILD'S RELIGION?

Flowing from the need to treat the welfare of the child as the paramount consideration, the present approach of the courts in England is similar to that taken in the United States: the parent with whom the child resides normally has the right to determine the religion of the child. There are a number of reasons why this approach is seen as being in the child's best interests. One is that it will avoid the conflict which is likely to occur if the custodial parent and the child were to belong to different religions and adhere to different

---

[78] Art. 5 of the Declaration on the Elimination of All Forms of Intolerance and Discrimination Based on Religion or Belief provides that the parents have the right to organise life within the family in accordance with their religion or belief and bearing in mind the moral education in which they believe the child should be brought up. The State could only restrict this right if they could show that Art. 1(3) applied, and that it was necessary to limit the practice of the religion because of need to protect public safety, order, health or morals or the fundamental rights and freedoms of others. See also the provisions in the European Convention on Human Rights and the International Covenant on Civil and Political Rights. Chap. 1, p. 17.

religious practices. Also important is the desire not to confuse the child or otherwise create conflict in the child's mind. The potential for this is particularly great where the religion of the non-custodial parent is a minority religion, or not easily known to the custodial parent.

The general rule also makes sense in light of the fact that religious observance often involves elements of "culture". So, for instance, it would be difficult to ask a Catholic to bring up a child as a Moslem or as an orthodox Jew, because these religions depend on practices in the home as well as community worship. It would be reasonable for the court to require that the child be *acquainted* with the religion of the non-custodial parent, but unrealistic to expect the hypothetical Catholic parent to bring the child up in another religion. With the best will in the world the Catholic parent would find it an awesome task, and it would in effect require the custodial parent to change her religious practices to suit the child. Unless the Catholic parent was willing to do this, and on the whole we must assume that this is not the case, or the issue would not be before the court, it is likely to lead to tension and resentment, as well as a very ineffectual religious education for the child.

This reluctance to order that the child be brought up in a religion other than that of the custodial parent is particularly strong in the United States, and appears to apply even where the custodial parent decides to change her religion and that of the child. The only remedy for the non-custodial parent who wishes to prevent a change in the child's religious adherence is to present evidence to the court that this change would cause harm to the child and that custody should be transferred to him.

The problem is very clearly illustrated in the case of *Schwarzman v. Schwarzman*.[79] The four children of the family were born to a Jewish father and a mother who was originally Roman Catholic,

---

[79] This is a very strange case. The judge decided that the children were not born Jewish because although the wife converted, her heart wasn't in it, thereby making it a false conversion and invalid under Jewish law. Also, the orthodox Jewish law did not recognise her conversion as she was converted by the Reform Jewish movement, and therefore, concluded the judge, she had never been Jewish at all, and as Judaism flowed from the mother, neither had the children. This is an amazing finding for a United States court given the duty to maintain strict neutrality under the First Amendment. It was certainly beyond the capacities of the court to determine whether a Reform conversion was a valid conversion to Judaism. Under Reform Judaism this was a wholly recognised conversion.

but who converted to Judaism before the birth of the first child. On divorce, custody of the children was awarded to the mother who shortly afterwards remarried, and reverted to Catholicism. She then proceeded to bring up the children as Catholics. The father sought an order that the children should continue to be brought up as Jews, and in evidence he produced an ante-nuptial agreement in which the parties had stated that any children should be brought up Jewish. The court held that the ante-nuptial agreement would not suffice because it did not contemplate divorce but only marriage, and that the custodian was the proper and appropriate party for determining the religious education and orientation of minor children.

The decision in *Schwarzman* notwithstanding, the courts have generally upheld the validity of agreements between parents as to the religious and moral training of a child. A parent seeking to avoid the effect of such an agreement would have to show that it is not in the best interests of the child for the agreement to be enforced. The general rule is illustrated in *Spring v. Glawon*,[80] where an agreement was made between the parents that the child should have no religious upbringing without express written agreement between the parties. The father in this case was Jewish and the mother Roman Catholic. The mother, after obtaining custody of the child, enroled him in a Catholic school. The Court ordered the mother to remove the child from the Catholic school and place him in a public school or non-sectarian private school. Where an agreement existed between the parents, and the child was not of sufficient age and intelligence to make his own decision, the agreement should be honoured. If no such agreement exists, the custodial parent is allowed to choose the child's religion.

In England the choice of the child's religion is a by-product of the custody decision. A court must first determine with which parent it would be in the best interests of the child to reside. It then follows, to avoid conflict in that family, as well as confusion to the child, that the custodial parent will be allowed to choose the religion of the child. When applying the best interests test, religion should not be given inordinate weight, except perhaps in the exceptional case where the child already has specific religious needs.

---

[80] 89 A. D. 2d 980; 454 N.Y.S. 2d 140 (1982).

In *H v. H*[81] the father, an Egyptian Muslim, and his English Christian wife were contesting the custody of two boys aged one and five. The judge awarded custody of the five year old to the father on the ground that the provision of a religious and cultural education by the father outweighed the other considerations which, in the normal circumstances, would have resulted in both children being placed in the custody of the mother. On appeal, the Court of Appeal held that having settled in England and entered into a mixed marriage, the father must have faced the difficulty of maintaining his cultural roots. The court had to consider the boy's best interests. The child was half Egyptian and half English, and would grow up and go to school in England. There was no overriding need for a close connection with the boys Arabic and Muslim background given this situation, and no reason why this factor should be treated as being of overriding importance. Treating the religious issue as just one more factor to put in the best interests balance, the Court of Appeal concluded that the child should be with his mother, even though she was unable to instruct him or bring him up as a Muslim.[82]

EXCEPTIONS

On occasion, a non-custodial parent who disapproves of the religious practices of the custodial parent has been successful in imposing restrictions on those practices in relation to the child. Sometimes a custodial parent is willing to give an undertaking to refrain from including a child in his or her religious practices. Usually this is done to avoid losing custody of the child. Such cases generally involve minority, new religious movements. It is not uncommon in England, for example, for a Jehovah's Witness parent to give an undertaking to agree to a blood transfusion for the child if the need arises.[83] A Jehovah's Witness parent may also give an undertaking not to take the child to meetings, or to take the child witnessing, and to allow the child to participate fully in school

---

[81] 119 Sol. J. 590.

[82] See *Re O.* [1962] 2 All E.R. 10, [1962] 1 W.L.R. 724 for the converse view. See also *Re C.(M.A.)* [1966] 1 All E.R. 839.

[83] In *Re H.* (1981) 2 FLR 257 the mother agreed that she should be supplied by the father with a certificate indicating his consent to medical treatment on the child if necessary, and that she would present this certificate to the doctor should it be necessary.

activities. The purpose of such undertakings is to leave the child free to choose a religion when he or she is of an age to make such a decision. Such undertakings are particularly likely to be required by a court where the custodial parent has changed religions, and the non-custodial parent has not agreed to the child being brought up in the custodial parent's new religion.

Undertakings will not always satisfy the court. There must be evidence that the undertakings are sincerely made and likely to be complied with. In *Re B and G*,[84] the Scientology case, the father offered to give several undertakings to the court. First, he promised to transfer the children from their school, which was under the control of Scientologists, to a conventional local school; secondly, he agreed not to involve them in Scientology until they were old enough to decide for themselves; and thirdly, he and the step-mother said that they would stand back from Scientology while the children were growing up. The judge, however, refused to accept that the father would fulfil those assurances. The judge feared that the influence of the church would still be ever present, and he doubted that the father could withstand this pressure. In the court's view, there was a distinct possibility that the children would remain gravely at risk.

The ability to control a custodial parent's religious activities is extremely limited in the United States due to the constitutional right of free exercise of religion. An attempt was made in the case of *Hilley v. Hilley*.[85] The father obtained an order that while the children were in the custody of the mother, she would curtail all activities that required her to be away from the children, or required the children to travel from the home during the week, except for one church function of reasonable duration and normal school and social functions. The court found this an impermissible infringement of the mother's right of free exercise of religion. The judge was certainly free to consider the impact of the mother's religious activities on the children, and was free to determine who was the most appropriate custodian given her level of religious involvement, but he could not prevent the mother from attending church and participating in religious activities.

---

[84] [1985] FLR 493.
[85] 405 So. 2d 708 (Sup. Ct. of Alabama 1981).

Rights of the non-custodial parent

While the parent with whom the child resides usually chooses the child's religion, the non-custodial parent may continue to teach the child the precepts and practices of his own religion. In many cases, it is the view of the court that where parents are from a different religious and cultural background, a child will gain by learning about more than one religion. Thus, a child who lives with an English Anglican mother may be enriched by learning from his father about his Muslim background and culture. Indeed, the court often encourages such education.[86]

On occasion, however, the custodial parent objects to the religious activities of the other parent. These objections fall largely into two categories. First, the custodial parent may object to the particular religious practices *per se* on the basis that they have an undesirable emotional and mental effect on the child, or that they are being used as a means of frustrating or undermining the relationship between the child and the custodial parent. Secondly, the parent may object to religious practices which conflict with the religious upbringing being given to the child by the custodial parent.

The English courts have been willing to restrict religious teaching by the non-custodial parent and, indeed, if necessary, any contact with that parent if it thinks that the non-custodial parent will use such occasions to try and indoctrinate the child, and that this would cause conflict, either to the child, or between the custodial parent and the child. Any decision taken to restrict the religious activities of the non-custodial parent is based on the best interests of the child.[87]

In the United States, it has been held that the non-custodial parent has a constitutional right, under the First Amendment, to impart his religious beliefs to the child during visitation, and to involve the child in religious activities.[88] Just as in England, how-

---

[86] See, *e.g. Al-Okaidi v. Al-Okaidi* (1983, C.A.; unreported).

[87] See *Wright v. Wright* (1980) 2 FLR 276.

[88] See *Ledoux v. Ledoux* 234 Neb. 479, 452 N.W.2d 1 (1990), *Khalsa v. Khalsa* 107 N.M. 31, 751 P.2d 715 (App. 1988), *Petition of Deierling* 421 N.W.2d 168 (Iowa App. 1988) In *Re Marriage of Mentry* 142 Cal.App. 3d 260, 190 Cal.Reptr. 843 (1983) *Sandborn v. Sandborn* 123 N.H. 740, 465 A.2d 888 (1983), In *Re Marriage of Hadeen* 27 Wash.App. 566, 619 P. 2d 374 (1980).

ever, the custodial parent may object to the religious activities of the non–custodial parent. The court is not free, as it is in England, to resolve such disputes purely by reference to the best interests of the child, but must also take into account the non–custodial parent's constitutional right to free exercise of religion.

The question facing the court in such cases, is how much weight should be given to the constitutional right of free exercise and how much to the best interests of the child. In *Morris v. Morris*,[89] a case where the mother objected to the father involving the child in his Jehovah's Witness activities, the Superior Court of Pennsylvania were willing to order that the father be precluded from "dragging his daughter with him during his door-to-door proselytization efforts". In giving great weight to the best interests of the child, the Court found that a parent could not flaunt the banner of religious freedom and family sanctity when he has abrogated the unity by inviting the court into the family to cause its dissolution. This justification for restricting a parent's free exercise of religion was, however, specifically disapproved of in *Zummo v. Zummo*.[90] The suggestion that parental authority is diminished as the result of the dissolution of the parents' spousal relationship was held to be inconsistent with constitutional recognition of parental authority where the parties were never married.[91] The court further condemned the tone of moral disapproval and implicit penalisation of divorce which, they found, was inconsistent with the enactment of "no-fault" divorce. Parents who "abrogate the unity of marriage" were not to be punished for their decision to divorce with denial of custody or the imposition of burdensome restrictions on contact with their child.[92]

The court in *Zummo* were asked to determine whether an order prohibiting the father from taking his children to Roman Catholic services, violated the father's constitutional rights. The father and mother had agreed that the children should be brought up in the

---

[89] 271 Pa. Super 19, 412 A 2d 139 (1979).

[90] 394 Pa. Super 30, 574 A.2d 1130 (1990).

[91] See *Caban v. Mohammed* 441 U.S. 360, 99 S. Ct. 1769, 60 L. Ed 2d 511 (1972). See also Mangrum, "Exclusive Reliance on Best Interests May be Unconstitutional: Religion as a factor in Child Custody Cases" (1981–82) Creighton Law Review, Vol. 15 pp. 25, 52.

[92] See *Santosky v. Kramer* 455 U.S. 745, 102 S.Ct. 1388 (1988). The fundamental liberty interests of natural parents in the care, custody and management of their children does not evaporate simply because they have not been model parents.

Jewish faith, and the whole family had participated actively in the Jewish community until the time of the divorce. The court held that a prior agreement on religious upbringing did not bind the father. While the court recognised that a parent's religious freedom might yield to other compelling interests, it could not be bargained away.[93] The mother argued that the children, the oldest of whom was eight, already had a religious identity, and that it was in the best interests of the child not to be confused in that identity. The court, placing great emphasis on constitutional rights, was not able to accept this argument, holding that it would only recognise a religious identity when it was asserted by the child him or herself.[94] But, even if a child expressed a personal religious identity it was not clear that the child would have any constitutional right to resist, or be protected from, attempts by either parent to exercise their constitutional rights to inculcate religious beliefs, prior to the child's legal emancipation.[95]

The mother in this case further asserted that, as Catholicism was irreconcilable with Judaism, attendance at Mass would confuse the children, causing conflict and possible distress, and should not be permitted. Cases have varied in their findings as to whether being brought up in two religions is harmful. In *Munoz*,[96] the Supreme Court of Washington found that the children suffered no adverse effects from attending both the Catholic church and the Mormon church, and were not convinced that duality of religious belief necessarily created conflict *per se*. Similarly, the Californian Court of Appeals has found that "a diversity of religious experiences is itself a sound stimulant for the child".[97] Other courts have disagreed. They fear that significant inconsistency in religious teaching can create conflict and confusion in the child and lead to the child disregarding the teaching of all religion. The danger of con-

---

[93] This is in direct contrast to the case of *Spring v. Glawon* 89 A.D.2d 980; 454 N.Y.S. 2d 140 (1982).

[94] The court thought that the minimum age for asserting a religious identity would be at 12. In this case the oldest child was only eight.

[95] In *Wisconsin v. Yoder* 406 U.S. 205, 92 S.Ct. 1526, 32 L.Ed. 2d 15 (1972) the majority declined to decide the issue of whether children had constitutional rights pertaining to religious education which could be asserted by their parents, although the majority expressed concerns suggesting that they were not predisposed to favour a claim to such rights.

[96] *Munoz v. Munoz* 79 Wash. 2d 810; 489 P.2d 1133 (Sup.Ct. of Washington 1971).

[97] See *In Re Mentry* 192 Cal.App. 3d 260, 190 Cal. Rptr. 843 (1985).

flict is particularly great where the religions of the parents are very different and require different life-styles.[98]

Even if exposure to more than one religion does cause conflict in the child, is this a sufficient reason to prevent the religious activities of the non-custodial parent? The Superior Court of Pennsylvania in *Morris*,[99] concentrating on a best interests test, found that inconsistent teachings would probably result in some mental disorientation and that this alone was a sufficient basis on which to restrict the non-custodial parent's religious activities. Some 10 years later, in the case of *Zummo*, the same Court expressly disagreed with its earlier findings in *Morris*. The court in *Zummo*, relying on authorities both before and after *Morris*, concluded that each parent must be free to provide religious exposure and instruction without restriction. Granting primacy to constitutional rights, the court found that the challenged beliefs or conduct of the parent could only be restricted where they posed a substantial threat of present or future physical or emotional harm to the child.[1] Applying this standard, speculation by parents and by experts that such exposure would cause potential future emotional harm would be insufficient.[2] "Substantial threat" rather than "some probability" must be shown. Disquietitude, disorientation or confusion arising from exposure to "contradictory" religions would be patently insufficient "emotional harm" to justify encroachment by the government upon constitutional parental and religious rights of parents, even in the context of divorce.

Even where the court restricts religious activities as a result of a finding that these would cause substantial harm, the court cannot restrain the non-custodial parent from talking about his religion with the child as this would be a violation of the First Amendment right of free exercise of religion. Neither can a court prevent the non-custodial parent from following his religious lifestyle at home

---

[98] See *Morris v. Morris* 271 Pa. Super 19, 412 A 2d 139 (1979).

[99] ibid.

[1] See, *e.g. Ledoux v. Ledoux* 234 Neb. 479, 452 N.W.2d 1 (1990) *Khalsa v. Khalsa* 107 N.M. 31, 751 P. 2d 715 (App. 1988). *Petition of Deierling* 421 N.W. 2d 618 (Iowa App. 1988).

[2] See *Kelly v. Kelly*, 217 N. J. Super. 147, 524 A. 2d 1330 (1986), *Fisher v. Fisher* 118 Mich. App. 227, 324 N.W. 2d 582 (1982), *Robertson v. Robertson* 19 Wash. App. 425, 575 P. 2d 1092 (1978) and *Munoz v. Munoz* 79 Wash. 2d 810, 489 P. 2d 1133 (1971).

when the child visits.[3] Only in the most exceptional case would the court order contact to cease. Unlike England, where contact with the non-custodial parent is seen as the right of the child, there is a view in the United States that contact with a child is a constitutionally protected right of the non-custodial parent.[4]

Conclusion

When parents of a child separate, the question arises whether either or both retain the right to pass on their religious beliefs and traditions to the child. Where the parties concerned share the same religion or belief, this is not an issue. However, where the parents follow different religions, or have different beliefs, this may become an issue to be resolved by the courts, frequently within the context of a custody proceeding. Where the religious upbringing that a parent has in mind is nothing more than "acquainting" the child with the traditions, beliefs and culture of that parent's religion of belief, the situation is relatively uncontroversial. The courts in both England and the United States have acknowledged the right of both parents to continue such "acquainting". Where one or both parents are, however, devout followers of their respective religions or beliefs, the English courts have been willing, in certain instances, to curtail the religious freedom of the non-custodial parent,[5] to pass on his or her religious beliefs. The justification for such curtailment is that it is not in the best interests of the child to be brought up in two different religions. Courts in the United States, faced with the claim of free exercise of religion, have found themselves unable to prevent a non-custodial parent involving a child in his religious

---

[3] *e.g.* A court could order that a parent should not take a child to Jewish services over the custodial parent's objection, but refuse the application of a custodial parent to phone her children on Saturday during a contact period when such a phone call would violate the father's orthodox Jewish principles.

[4] See Novinson; "Post-Divorce Visitation: Untying the Triangular Knot" (1983) U.Ill. L.Rev.121.

[5] Limitations are also occasionally placed on the custodial parent. The parent is prohibited from involving the child in religious practices. Such limitations are normally imposed on custodial parents who have become a member of a new religious movement or a break-away Christian sect after the marriage. The justification for such limitations is that the child should not be socially or educationally limited as a result of the custodial parent's change of religion, and should be left free to decide at a later age which religion or belief he or she wishes to adopt.

beliefs and practices unless it is shown that this would cause a substantial threat of present or future physical or emotional harm to the child.

It must be questioned whether submitting a child to the full range of religious observances and teachings of two religions is in the child's best interests. Some have gone so far as to suggest that this may verge on emotional abuse of the child,[6] especially where the beliefs of the two religions are conflictual, and the pressure by the parents to conform is strong. While the English courts have the power to prevent this conflict by simply finding it not in the best interest of the child that the religious activities, or contact, be continued, courts in the United States are constrained by constitutional free exercise principles.

The second issue that arises is the weight to be given to competing religious beliefs in determining questions of custody. The English courts have, on occasion, been willing to treat religious belief as a determining factor in custody cases. Thus, where the religion followed by a parent would unduly isolate or alienate the child from the non-custodial parent, or be an emotional disadvantage to the child, the court has found that to remain in the custody of that parent would not be in the best interests of the child. Courts in the United States are only willing to consider the relevance of religion when the particular practices of the religion would cause substantial present or future harm to the child. It should be noted that in virtually all cases where religion has been a critical factor in a custody case, the religion involved was one of the new religious movements, or a break-away Christian sect, such as the Jehovah's Witnesses or the Plymouth or Exclusive Brethren.

While the tolerance of English courts for the practices of Jehovah's Witnesses and Plymouth Brethren has increased over the last 20 years, the courts are still prepared to find the practices of some of the new religious movements antithetical to a child's best interests. The United States courts, constrained by the constitutional right of free exercise, have been more "tolerant".

It can be concluded that the establishment of the Church of England has had little impact on custody cases. The English courts continue to make decisions in the best interests of the child. A parent's

---

[6] For a greater discussion of relevant cases and the tensions between constitutional rights and the child's best interests see White, 38 Oklahoma Law Review 284 (1985).

religious freedom to pass on their religious beliefs to their children receives greater protection in the United States as a result of the constitutional right to free exercise of religion. It is unclear, however, that children, whose rights were not specifically addressed in the Constitution, have sufficient attention paid to their interests. The parental right to free exercise of religion constrains the child's own right to religious freedom. Further, in certain instances, it constrains the courts from reaching decisions based on the child's best interests. While a balance between tolerance and a child's best interests is a delicate one, a requirement that substantial harm exist or be threatened is, it is argued, too high a threshold, and unduly emphasises parental religious rights at the expense of children's best interests.

Chapter Six

Adoption

In Roman law, and earlier codes of law[1] the primary purpose of adoption was the continuity of the adopters family. Such adoption had a deep religious significance[2] and the adoptee was admitted not only into a new family but also into a new religion. Indeed Kocourek and Wigmore postulate that the "duty of perpetuating the domestic worship was the foundation of the law of adoption among the ancients."[3] Adoption was a well known concept although, unlike adoption in modern societies, there was no visible concern for the best interests of the child, and welfare was not a relevant consideration.

The attitude to adoption of children in Anglo-American jurisprudence has been very different. It was a principle of common law, emanating from the natural law stance of the Catholic church, that the rights of a parent over a child could never be alienated. Changes to this principle only came through legislation, starting in the 1850s in the United States.[4] In England, however,

---

[1] In the Hindu Laws of Manu dated between 200 B.C. and 100 A.D. and Hebrew and Egyptian law as well as in the Code of Hammurabi. See 1 Kocourek and Wigmore, *Evolution of Law, Sources of Ancient and Primitive law* 387 (1915). See also Huard, "The Laws of Adoption: Ancient and Modern" (1956) 9 Vand.L.Rev 743.

[2] II Kocourek and Wigmore, *Evolution of Law, Primitive and Ancient Legal Institutions* 344 (1915) at 345.

[3] *ibid.*

[4] In its earliest form, adoption legislation in the U.S. authorised the transfer of children by deed from one set of parents to another, without legal proceedings, rather like transfer of a chattel. However, statutes after 1850 required a court order to effect a legal adoption. Adoption is regarded now as effecting a complete transfer of all parental rights, duties and responsibilities from the natural parents to the adoptive parents.

adoption[5] was not legally recognised until the passing of the Adoption of Children Act 1926. Until this time, the rights of parents of a legitimate child, or the mother of an illegitimate child, could not be transferred to another person, even if all parties agreed.[6]

The purpose of this chapter is not to examine the process or development of adoption in the two jurisdictions, but to determine the extent to which religion is a consideration in the placement, adoption and future upbringing of children. In both the United States and England, regardless of their constitutional differences, there has, at various times, been a concern both to preserve the religious ties of the natural parent and the child, and to ensure that children are not lost to the faith of the birth family, even after adoption. This chapter will examine the extent to which domestic legislation and judicial decisions in England and the United States, allow parents or adoption agencies to determine the future religion of the child, and the impact of establishment as compared to free exercise on such rights.

Right up until the end of the nineteenth century, the religion of a legitimate child was that of the father. The father had the right to determine the child's religion and to insist that the child received an appropriate religious upbringing. This right to religious inheritance prevailed throughout the child's minority, whether the father was alive or dead.[7] In the case of an illegitimate child the mother had the same rights as the father of a legitimate child.[8] The remnants of this principle, it can be argued, are to be found today in England in the Adoption Act 1976, section 7. The section provides that an agency shall, in placing a child, have regard (so far as is practicable) to any wishes of a child's parents or guardians as to the religious upbringing of the child.[9]

Similarly, in a number of the States of the United States there is

---

[5] Adoption, according to the Houghton Committee, reporting in England in 1972, is "the complete severance of the legal relationship between the parents and child and the establishment of a new one between the child and the adoptive parent". Cmnd. 5107 (1972) at para. 14.

[6] *Brooks v. Blount* [1923] 1 K.B. 257, *Humphrys v. Polak* [1901] 2 K.B. 385.

[7] See *Re Agar-Ellis* (1878) 10 Ch. D. 49 for a good explanation of the father's right. Only in exceptional circumstance would the court make a ruling contrary to this principle. For more detail on this common law right see Chap. Four, pp. 141–142.

[8] See *Re Carroll* [1931] 1 K.B. 317.

[9] Prior to the Children Act 1975 consent to adoption could be given subject to a condition with respect to the religious persuasion in which the child was to be brought up.

an express recognition of the right of the natural parent to determine the religion of the child at birth and for the future, even though there may be a subsequent loss of parental rights. Statutes granting such rights are known as religious protection or religious matching statutes, and have been the subject of much debate and a number of constitutional challenges. Approximately one third of States in the United States continue to have some form of religious matching provision for adoptions.

Although the right to determine the religion of a child flows from common law in England and the United States, it is also recognised in more recently promulgated international instruments, albeit primarily as a means of protecting minority religious and cultural rights. Thus, the Declaration on the Elimination of All Forms of Intolerance and Discrimination Based on Religion or Belief,[10] Article 5 (4) provides:

> "that in the case of a child who is not under the care either of his parents or of legal guardians, due account shall be taken of their expressed wishes or of any proof of their wishes in the matter of religion or belief, the best interests of the child being the guiding principle".

Article 20 of the United Nations Convention on the Rights of the Child dealing with protection of children without families states:

> "(3) . . . when considering solutions, due regard shall be paid to the desirability of continuity in a child's upbringing and to the child's ethnic, religious, cultural and linguistic background".

This right of the natural parent to determine a child's religion after that child has passed out of the parent's care and after parental rights over the child have ceased, is remarkable in itself. No other right of the natural parent continues after adoption. The process is, after all, one which is designed to transfer completely all responsibilities, rights and duties in relation to a child. No natural parent could expect to determine the child's school or place of residence after parental rights cease, so why should the right to determine religion continue? The original justification for this approach in

---

[10] Proclaimed by General Assembly Resolution 36/55 of November 25, 1981.

England was undoubtedly the Catholic natural law doctrine adopted by the common law, of the prevailing right of the father or the unmarried mother to determine a child's upbringing until the child's majority, even though that parent might not be looking after the child.[11] The reasons for preserving this right however, have changed. The modern day justification is reflected in the international instruments previously cited, the preservation of minority religious rights, and the importance to children of a cultural heritage.

In the United States, while the minority rights argument is recognised in relation to Indian tribes,[12] the predominant argument for extending such a right to parents was founded on the free exercise of religion[13]; and on the parents' right to follow the religion of their choice,[14] which is taken as extending to their child.[15] More recently, however, courts in the United States have expressed concern as to the constitutionality of the religious matching statutes on the basis that such requirements are detrimental to the life chances of the child, and may reduce the chance of a child finding an appropriate adoptive placement.[16]

---

[11] Contained within this right is the view of many religions that children are, in effect, born into a religion, and that that religion should be preserved and not changed thereafter. This is reflected in many of the early "Catholic" cases in the U.S., even though many commentators have pointed out that children are not members of most Christian sects, including the Catholic Church, until they have been baptised. See Ramsey, "The Legal Imputation of Religion to an Infant in Adoption Proceedings" (1959) 34 NYU.L.Rev. 649.

[12] The Indian Child Welfare Act 1978 provides that exclusive jurisdiction respecting child custody proceedings involving an Indian child who resides, or is domiciled on a tribal reservation, is vested in the Indian tribe, unless jurisdiction is otherwise vested by federal law. "Child custody proceeding" is defined to include foster care placements, proceedings for the termination of parental rights, pre-adoptive placements and adoptive placements. 25 U.S.C.A. para. 1911(b).

[13] Note, "Religious Matching Statutes and Adoption" (1976) 51 NYU.L.Rev. 262 at 281.

[14] Or the mother's choice of religion if the child was not born into a marriage.

[15] To change the child's religion without the mother's consent before the moment when she loses all her parental rights, would be tantamount to interfering with the mother's free exercise of religion, and may well run foul of the Establishment Clause by preferring one religion as against another, and unduly entangling the state in religion.

[16] The Report of the Departmental Committee on Adoption of Children (the *Houghton Report*) Cmnd. 5107 (1972) in England expressed very similar concerns.

The State and religious placement

Up until the latter part of the twentieth century courts in the United States had little concept of the religious-free child. The religion of the child was regarded as being that of the parents, or in the case of a non-marital child, that of the mother. It was inconceivable to the judges that a child could be without a religion. If the mother failed to indicate the religion of a child, the court would impute a religion to the child. This would normally be the mother's birthright religion if known, or the religion she was known to practice. In the absence of evidence as to either of these, the court would assign a religion to the child. Thus in New York, up until the 1950s, abandoned children were assigned alternatively to Catholic, Protestant and Jewish agencies.[17]

Natural parents did not, however, always adhere as closely to religious matching requirements as the statutes governing adoption required. Where the parent had consented to placement of the child with a couple or an agency of a different religion, the court had then to decide whether such cross-religious adoption could be permitted. Many States in the United States, had religious matching or religious protection statutes which provided that children should be placed with adoptive parents of the same faith, although such a requirement was generally qualified with the proviso, "wherever practicable or whenever possible".[18] The early Massachusetts case of *Purinton v. Jamrock*[19] provided that religious difference did not constitute an absolute bar to adoption.[20] However, up until the 1960s the courts were reluctant to permit cross-religious adoption, regardless of the consent of the mother.

---

[17] See Wicklein, "Religion as a Factor in Adoption Administration" (October 11, 1959) *N.Y. Times.*

[18] Many statutes required that the child be brought up by adoptive parents of the same faith where this was "practicable". However, what constituted "when practicable" varied. Sometimes it was very strictly interpreted to mean that if there were potential adopters in the community of the child's faith it was practicable for the child to be brought up in that religion, even though a parent had not been found. Other States have interpreted "when practicable" to mean not contrary to the child's welfare. See generally, Comment, "Matching for Adoption: A Study of Current Trends" (1976) 22 Cath. Law 70 and Comment, "Religion and Adoption—Constitutionality of Religious Matching Practices" (1971) 17 Wayne L.Rev. 1509.

[19] 109 Mass. 187 (1907).

[20] See also *Dickens v. Ernesto* 30 N.Y. 2d 61, 281 N.E. 2d 153, 330 N.Y.S. 2d 346 (1972) appeal dismissed 401 U.S. 917 (1972) and *In Re Walker* 159 Cal. App. 2d 463, 324 P. 2d 321 (1958).

The judicial attitude is well evidenced by such cases as *Goldman*[21] where two week old twins were placed with a Jewish couple by their mother. The mother was a lapsed Roman Catholic who no longer practised her religion. When the twins were eight months old, the Goldmans sought to adopt them. The mother consented in writing to the adoption petition, and stated that she knew that the Goldmans were Jewish and was quite satisfied that the children should be brought up in the Jewish faith. The judge hearing the petition treated the children as still being of the Catholic faith even though they had not been baptised.[22] He went on to find that there were a number of Catholic couples who had applied to adopt with the Catholic Charities Bureau, and that although none of them knew about the twins, it was "practicable" for the twins to be adopted by a Catholic couple. He concluded that "it would not be in the best interests of the twins to decree adoption" and that the twins should therefore be returned to a Catholic agency for placement.[23] The Jewish adoptive parents argued that the children should not be regarded as Roman Catholic children because their mother had abandoned her religion before they were born. She had committed adultery, obtained a civil divorce (both mortal sins under Church doctrine), failed to have her children baptised and placed them with Jewish parents in the knowledge that the children would be brought up Jewish.[24] The court rejected this argument:

"the mother did not cease to be a Catholic, even if she failed to live up to the ideals of her religion. If that were the test of belonging to a religious faith it is feared that few would qualify for any faith."

The Court also ignored evidence that the mother did not in any

---

[21] *In Petitions of Goldman* 331 Mass. 647, 121 NE. 2d 843 (1954) cert. denied, 348 U.S. 942 (1955).

[22] Under Catholic theology the children were not Roman Catholic until they had been baptised. There may have been an expectation that the once Catholic mother would baptise them, but at the moment the children were handed over to the Goldmans they formally belonged to no religion. By handing the children to Jewish adoptive parents one could argue that was the mother's choice of religion for the child.

[23] The judge did not consider whether there was a real possibility that other adoptive parents would be found, particularly in view of the fact that one of the twins was retarded.

[24] This was a necessary argument as the consent of the mother was obviously, due to the interpretation of the religious matching statute, insufficient to permit cross-religious adoption.

way follow the tenets of the faith and had not chosen Catholicism for her children. The decision reflects very clearly the practice of the courts, but not necessarily of the relevant religion, of imputing religion to a child at the moment of birth. Dismissing an appeal by the Goldmans, the Supreme Judicial Court of Massachusetts agreed with the lower court's finding.[25] They rejected any suggestion that the statute as interpreted in *Goldman* was unconstitutional either as a law respecting an establishment of religion or a prohibition of free exercise of religion.[26]

It can be argued that the decision in *Goldman* was unconstitutional. While a court would be acting constitutionally in upholding a mother's wishes as to the religious upbringing of her child, there is no basis for imputing a religion to a child where the mother has not chosen that religion for the child. Such a choice by the State infringes the First Amendment. It also, in the *Goldman* case, imposed a burden on the Goldmans. They were unable to adopt these children because, quite simply, they were Jewish and not Roman Catholic. The *Goldman* Court paid scant attention to the future welfare of the children, the effect that removal from the Goldmans would have on them, or the probability of an immediate suitable placement with a Catholic family. The possibility that the twins might have to spend an extended period of time in an institution before a suitable adoptive placement could be made was not considered. Any court following the *Goldman* decision today, and failing to recognise that the mother has a right to change her religion and that of her children, would find itself in breach of international law. The Universal Declaration of Human Rights not only declares freedom of religion as a basic freedom, but includes within

---

[25] The State Department of Public Welfare began proceedings to take the twins from the Goldmans and place them in a Catholic institution, but before these were completed, the Goldmans abandoned their home and their business and moved to another state with the children.

[26] The Supreme Court declined to review Goldman. Paulsen in, *The Wall Between Church and State* (1963) suggests that the Church-State issue in Goldman was to some extent blunted by the fact that the trial judge had been unable to satisfy himself concerning the manner in which the twins had come into the home of the petitioners. The appellate court's opinion found that "the judge may well have doubted whether all the circumstances had been revealed and whether the requirements of the law . . . had been fully observed". While this may be the case, it does not explain or justify the lack of concern over the children's future welfare.

that the freedom to change religion. Even the Covenant on Civil and Political Rights, which has been ratified by the United States, gives individuals the right to have *or adopt* a religion of choice. This power to change religion or adopt a different religion can also be extended to an individual's minor children.

Later cases involving religious matching statutes have moved away from the approach of the *Goldman* case and have placed far greater emphasis on the phrase "where practicable", contained in nearly all religious matching statutes. The aim is to balance the importance of religious matching against the need to find an appropriate placement for the child whose parents cannot look after her. Fifteen years after the *Goldman* decision, in 1970, the Family Court of New York in *Efrain C*[27] took a very different approach to the right of the state to impute a religion to a child, the extent of the right of the parent to determine the child's religious upbringing when adoption was intended, and the power of agencies acting on behalf of the state to regulate placement according to religious affiliation.

The decision in *Efrain C*[28] represents a break with the thinking of the nineteenth and first half of the twentieth centuries as represented by *Goldman*. The right of the parent to determine the child's future religious upbringing, and the State's custom of imputation of religion, gave way to an emphasis on the best interests of the child. The two year old child, who was the subject of the case, was deemed to be Roman Catholic as the mother identified herself as a Catholic and had expressed no contrary wish as to the child's religion. The Catholic agency with whom the child was placed were unable to find adoptive parents. However, a non-sectarian agency offered to place the child immediately with a Protestant husband[29] and Jewish wife. The relevant statute required that adoptions

[27] At one time New York had the strictest religious matching statutes, only permitting departures from matching in the most exceptional circumstances. See, *e.g. Starr v. De Rocco* 29 App.Div. 2d 662, 286 N.Y.S.2d 313 (2d Dep't 1968) aff'd mem., 24 N.Y. 2d 1011, 250 N.E.2d 240, 302 N.Y.S.2d 835 (1969).

[28] In *The Matter of Efrain C*, 63 Misc. 2d 1019; 314 N.Y.S. 2d 255, (1970) Family Court of New York, New York County.

[29] The husband and the child were both Puerto Ricans although of different religious background; the child was Catholic. Because of the child's background and age (two), it was always going to be difficult to find a family.

should be granted "when practicable" only to persons of the same religion as the child, but the "when practicable" requirement should be ignored if a duly authorised society or institution under the control of persons of the same religious faith or persuasion as that of the child, was available and willing to assume the responsibility for any such child. The court found that, if applied literally, this would require the child to remain with the Catholic agency even if they were unable to find a placement, and even if his welfare required that he be placed with a family. Such a result was unacceptable to the court:

"[T]he biological parent's constitutional rights would seem to entitle him to express his religious or non-religious preference as a condition of his surrender of the child for adoption. Other than this limited parental right, there appears to be no other ground, consistent with the constitution for attributing a religious preference to an adoptive child who is below the age for actual religious training. Certainly it would be unconstitutional to stamp an adoptive child with his progenitor's religion on the basis of any theological doctrine of a congenital transmission of faith, contrary to temporal concepts and laws on the status of adopted children. Adoption being a creature of State power and secular law, it would violate the constitutional principle of State neutrality on religion for the state in its adoption practice to promote church interests, or to force a religious identification upon a child.

Accordingly, . . . the biological parent's right to express a religious preference in connection with his voluntary surrender of his child, appears to be the only right that can constitutionally weigh on the side of religious conformity. However, even in the case of such a voluntary surrender, the State cannot constitutionally enforce the parental religious preference at the expense of the welfare of the child. For, the state's power with respect to the custody and adoption of children stems from its duty as *parens patriae* to safeguard the welfare of the helpless and dependent. Even parents with custody of their child cannot for the sake of his religious upbringing obstruct his temporal welfare. Certainly this principle is all the more true when the parent's right is attenuated by the fact that he is surrendering his responsibility for the child.

It is clear that the State unconstitutionally denies to a child the equal protection of the laws—specifically his right to equal protection of his welfare—if it deprives him of the opportunity for a beneficial adoption because of his birth to a parent of a particular religion or religious preference. The State is obliged as *parens patriae* for its children to regulate its adoption practice to secure for them the best available adoptions; and it is constitutionally prohibited from sacrificing this paramount objective to religious interest . . . "[30]

Efrain C is, of course, only a state case and at Family Court level. It does, however, represent a new approach to religious matching requirements. Up until the time of the decision, there is very little evidence that the courts were prepared to examine the constitutionality of such statutes, or the practice of imputing religion to a child too young to have any views. Indeed, such statutes have never been the subject of a Supreme Court decision.

The imputation of a religion to a child also came under constitutional attack in the California Court in *Scott v. Family Ministries*.[31] The court stated that it was not unconstitutional to allow parents to express a religious preference and for the State to uphold this. However, the court continued, if the State is permitted to specify the religious affiliation of the adoptive home without reference to the natural parentage or parental preference, the State then invades the area proscribed to it by the Establishment Clause.[32] A religious requirement imposed upon adoptive parents by the State is thus unconstitutional unless it is limited to religious matching with the religion of the natural parent or matching with parental preference. In this case, Family Ministries were seeking to limit adoption of Cambodian children of unknown religious heritage to evangelical Protestant parents, an action which was held to amount to a breach of the Establishment Clause.[33] The Utah court in *Easton v. Angus*[34] nearly a decade later, hammered a further nail into the coffin of religious matching by finding that religious matching between children and adoptive parents, where this was not specifically requested by the natural parents, was unconstitutional as a violation of the Establishment Clause.

---

[30] *Per* Nanette Dembitz J. at pp. 264–265. The explanation of the role of the court under its *parens patriae* jurisdiction is extremely interesting. In adoption cases in England, the welfare of the child is not the paramount consideration but the "first consideration". See Adoption Act 1976 s.6.

[31] 65 Cal.App. 3d 492; 135 Cal.Rptr. 430 (1976) Second Dist.Div. One.

[32] This is because the State is no longer in a position of neutrality.

[33] The State government is inextricably entangled with the activity of licensed adoption agencies, and is, therefore, inextricably entangled with any religious restriction beyond matching imposed by the agency upon prospective adoptive parents. The agencies are delegated governmental case work functions in adoption cases. In essence, if a private licensed adoption agency imposes a religious restriction in exercising its delegated power and responsibility, it is acting for, and on behalf of, the State when it does so.

[34] No. C–84–0261 W (D. Utah June 13 1985). See Note, "Religious Matching and Parental Preference" (1986) 3 Utah L.Rev. 559.

The *Scott* case was concerned with whether an adoption agency could impute a religion to a child and then place religious requirements on couples seeking to adopt. The burden of these requirements falls both on the children, whose pool of potential adoptive parents is reduced, and also on the would-be adoptive parents, whose attempts to adopt are frustrated by the requirement of necessary religious affiliation. In the New Jersey case of *Burke*,[35] one of the few adoption cases at appellate level, the issue concerned only the parents; was it constitutional for the State to impose any form of religious requirements as a precondition to adoption.

Mr and Mrs Burke were initially refused a final decree of adoption in relation to a baby girl, E, owing to their admitted lack of any religious affiliation. The court found that they did not believe in a Supreme Being and that this rendered them unfit to be adoptive parents.[36] The Supreme Court of New Jersey reversed this decision finding that lack of religious affiliation or of a religious faith should not be a bar to consideration of any applicants for adoption.[37] However, the court did not go so far as to require that the religious factor be eliminated altogether. It stated that it could be viewed as a relevant factor to be weighed in determining whether to grant an adoption, but it could not be controlling.

The court also rejected the suggestion of the court-appointed *amicus curiae* that a prospective ruling should be made allowing an agency to require membership in an established religion as a prerequisite for adoption, "if there is an abundant supply of adopting parents". The court rejected this suggestion[38] finding not only that it was contrary to New Jersey's case law and statutory scheme, but

---

[35] In *The Matter of the Adoption of E., a Child*, by John Burke and Cynthia Burke. 59 N.J. 36; 279 A. 2d 785; 48 A.L.R. 3d 366. (1971) Supreme Court of New Jersey.

[36] There was nothing in the opinion to indicate that the Burkes were in any other way unfit or that E's "best interests" would be impaired by some other factor. The agency found them to be morally fit.

[37] Other *amici curiae*, the N.J. Bureau of Children's Services, the Council on Adoptable Children, the New Jersey Council of Churches, the Department of Church in Society, Division of Homeland Ministries of the Christian Church (Disciples of Christ) in the United States and Canada, the Division of Human Relations, Board of Christian Social Concerns and the United Methodist Church all urged the appellate Court to reverse the trial court's decision and to make it clear that, in the future, courts may not deny persons the right to adopt a child solely because of their religious beliefs or non-beliefs.

[38] Unlike many other States, New Jersey adoption statutes do not impute religion to a child, nor do they insist on same religion placement "where practicable". However N.J.S.AA. 9:3–23S(4)(b) provides that an agency should be appointed "with due regard for the religious background of the child".

also that it would constitute a breach of the First Amendment. The court in its judgment, while focusing on those would-be adoptive parents who followed no religion, once more sounded the death-knell of religious matching requirements by the State rather than by the parent:

> "The issue is . . . whether the government has the power to impose a religion or to place a burden on one's beliefs regarding religion. Burdening the opportunity to adopt with religious requirements does both and if, as we believe, the government lacks such a power, religious requirements violate the Establishment Clause and the Free Exercise Clause of the First Amendment. The courts are an arm of the State, and, as such, they are required to maintain a neutral posture on the issue of belief and non-belief."

While it is difficult to anticipate the outcome of constitutional challenges to religious matching in all of the states of the United States, the cases indicate a great shift in judicial attitudes over the last 30 years. It is likely, that a court presented with a religious matching case today, would find that a State has no right to impute a religion to a child, except where a parent expressly requests that the child be placed with adoptive parents of a particular religious affiliation. The notion that children belong to a particular faith on birth and should not be lost to that faith has disappeared. The state may not now impose on would-be adoptive parents a requirement that they be of a particular religion, or indeed any religion, before they may be considered as adoptive parents. Even where the parent has expressed a preference for adoptive parents of a particular religious affiliation, the State should only be prepared to uphold this where such a requirement is not against the child's best interests.[39] Thus, parental rights have given way to a child's best interests.

The State and the presentation of cultural heritage

The English courts have not in the past expressed any particular concern at cross-religious placements in the absence of an objection

---

[39] Such decisions will inevitably have an effect on voluntary religious bodies bringing children into the United States for adoption. No longer will they be able to insist that the children only go to persons sharing their religious beliefs.

by the parents. However, where a parent did wish to ensure a
child's religious upbringing it was possible, up until 1975, for consent to adoption to be given subject to a condition that the child be
brought up in a particular religion.[40] Since the beginning of the
1980s, however, there has been a discernible trend towards preserving a minority child's "cultural identity". This manifests itself in an
attempt to match the child, when placing for adoption, with
parents of the same cultural identity. Such an approach can be seen
as consistent with the United Kingdom's obligations under the
various international instruments which it has ratified.[41] However,
the principle is not always underpinned by a clear and coherent
policy. There has been no definition of cultural identity and what is
included within the meaning of the term. Neither has there been a
reasoned justification for its preservation. It has also led, on
occasions, back to the practice of imputing a religion and in
addition, a culture, to a child. This is very clearly illustrated by the
case of *Re JK*.[42] The child, who was illegitimate and born to a Sikh
mother, was placed with short term foster parents at the age of six
days, and had remained with them. At the time of the hearing she
was three years old, well integrated with the foster family, secure
and well settled. The intention of social services was that the child
would remain with the foster family until such time as a suitably
matched family of similar background could be found. This however, proved to be a problem,[43] and an appropriate placement had
still not been found by the time of the hearing. When the foster

---

[40] Such conditional consent was abolished by the Children Act 1975. However, the
court did, on occasion, require an undertaking from adoptive parents as to
religious upbringing, normally to bring up the child in the religion of the natural
parent, even though this was not the religion of the adoptive parent. The recent
case of *Re S*. [1994] 2 FLR 416 in the Court of Appeal held that it should be rare to
impose conditions on adoptive parents against their will. The best thing for a
child going through the process of adoption, was that he or she should become, as
near as possible, the lawful child of the adopting parents, Thus, a condition to
bring up an adopted child in a religion different to that of the adopted parent
should not now be imposed.
[41] See Art. 20(3) of the UN Convention on the Rights of the Child, above.
[42] [1991] 2 FLR 340. See also *Re B*. (1984; unreported; Lexis transcript). For a more
robust judicial approach to cultural heritage *vis-à-vis* welfare see *Re M*. (1983;
unreported; Lexis transcript).
[43] Adoption is rare within the Sikh community, and the adoption of an illegitimate
child even rarer. The stigma of illegitimacy makes such a child an unattractive
proposition for adoption. Social services approached 63 agencies in the hope of
finding a suitable placement, but were unsuccessful.

parents informed social services that they would like to adopt the child, it was resolved that the child would be moved to a bridging family until suitable adoptive parents were found.[44] Three possible families were being investigated, two Hindu families and one Catholic but all Asian or mixed marriages with one Asian partner.

The central question for the court[45] was the value of matching cultural identity. Should three years settled attachment, or racial and cultural aspects, determine where the child was to live. The issue was not whether the policies of social services on racial matching were acceptable,[46] but whether this child should be moved from foster parents with whom she was well settled, purely to preserve cultural heritage. The judge reviewed the evidence given by the child psychiatrist appointed by the Official Solicitor[47]:

> "He has expressed the firm and considered opinion that to move the child from the only home that she has known during her life, would be very likely to cause irreparable psychological damage. She would probably never trust anyone again. She might well feel that she was not good enough to stay in the foster home and would feel a sense of despair and rejection. She would almost inevitably reject any substitute parents with whom she was placed. He has also said that from the depths of her being she understands that the foster parents have been her parents all her life."

The psychiatrist's report was bolstered by the natural mother's expressed wish that the child should remain with the foster parents. Against these considerations the court weighed the local authority's view that the foster mother, although a "splendid lady" who had given love and affection to the child, was not capable of undertaking the difficult and sensitive task of helping this child become aware of, and come to terms with, her Sikh traditions and Sikh culture. The local authority complained that the foster mother had in

---

[44] The purpose of such a move would have been to weaken the bond between the foster parents and the child, and enabling the child to move to appropriate adoptive parents if any were found.

[45] The foster parents brought wardship proceedings, asking the court to give them care and control, while the local authority asked the court for a care order and leave to place the child with long-term foster parents with a view to adoption.

[46] The Chief Inspector of Social Services wrote a letter to directors of Social Services entitled Issues of Race and Culture in January 1990, to which this particular local authority adhered.

[47] The child was represented by the Official Solicitor, who appointed a child psychiatrist to assess and examine the child and report to the court.

fact taken no steps to that end, although it appeared that no-one had requested her to do so.

The judge accepted, without comment, the local authority's assertion that this child was a Sikh, although, just as in the *Goldman* case, this could only be through imputation, and through an acceptance that the child was born into, and inherited, her mother's culture and religion. The resolution of this case was that the overwhelming welfare needs of the child required that she be left with the foster parents. But, in response to the local authority's concerns, the judge pointed out that he had every reason to believe that the foster parents would keep the child in touch with her background. Indeed, the foster parent had begun to take the child to the Sikh temple every week.[48] In this instance, the value to the child of remaining with the foster parents outweighed the need to cultural heritage. It is not wholly clear that the same result would have been reached if suitable Sikh adoptive parents had been available and willing to take the child, or even if, at the time of the hearing, one of the other potential adoptive couples had been found appropriate for the child.

The decision merits closer consideration. What constitutes a cultural heritage in this instance? In considering potential adoptive parents who were Hindu or Catholic, the adoption agency were clearly not seeking to match religious heritage. The common denominator amongst the potential adoptive parents was their ethnicity: all were Asian, or mixed marriages with one Asian partner. While it can be argued that white parents are not as well equipped to help a minority child deal with problems of racism and alienation in later life, is racial matching the preservation of cultural heritage?[49] If the aim of removing the child from her then foster parents was to preserve her cultural heritage, and this was the expressed aim in *Re JK*, different considerations should have applied. For most of those termed minority groups in England, cultural heritage is inextrica-

---

[48] Interestingly, the President said nothing as to what was to happen to this child's religious affiliation post-adoption, and no requirement was placed on the family to bring her up as a Sikh. Since the case of *Re S.* [1994] 2 FLR 416, it has been held that conditions as to religious upbringing should not be contained in an adoption order. See n. 40 above.

[49] The Interdepartmental Report on Adoption, *The Future*, Cm. 2288 (HMSO, 1993) points out that there is no conclusive research which supports the proposition that children adopted by people of a different ethnic group will necessarily encounter problems of identity or prejudice later in life (para.4.33).

bly linked with religious observance and identity.[50] Thus the cultural heritage of an Indian Hindu child is quite different from that of an Indian Sikh child, although the ethnic background may be the same. Preservation of cultural heritage would thus require that a Sikh child be placed with a Sikh family.

In imputing a culture to a new born or very young child, it is not wholly clear that the court is acting in the best interests of the child. Such an approach can be discriminatory, as the United States courts have recognised,[51] because the pool of potential adoptive parents is reduced to the possible detriment of the child. The child may have to spend longer periods of time in institutional placement or with a series of short-term foster parents. It is also difficult to argue that in either the short-term or the long-term a child's best interests will be demonstrably better served by being brought up as a Sikh rather than as a Hindu or Muslim. There has been no research evidence to the effect that same-culture placements of a baby or young child are any more successful than cross-cultural placements.[52] It is also not clear, on occasions, which cultural heritage parents should be identified with. If parents who were brought up as Sikhs convert, and become Jehovah's Witnesses a year before the child's birth, which cultural heritage attaches to them? Would the court impute a Jehovah's Witness cultural heritage to the child? Similarly, if Caucasian parents converted to the Sikh religion immediately before the child's birth, would the court impute a Sikh cultural heritage to the child? Cultural heritage is not used by adoption agencies or the courts in its pure sense, but as a code for a mixture of culture, religion and race. The issue of a child's cultural heritage only arises where the parents' religion, race and culture are all different from that of the majority.

The imputation of a cultural heritage is logically unsustainable, and the reasoning for the preservation of cultural heritage is little developed from the reasons given for religious imputation. Indeed, the imputation of cultural heritage is an unnecessary fiction. The

---

[50] This may be a significant difference from the U.S. where minority groups are defined far more by race than by culture or religion.

[51] The discrimination argument was successful in *Scott v. Family Ministries* .5265 Cal.App. 3d 492; 135 Cal.Rptr. 430 (1976) Second Dist.Div.One. It has also been argued with great success in relation to religious matching in foster placement. See *Wilder v. Bernstein* 848 F. 2f 1338 (2d Cir 1988) and Note, "Child Foster Placement" (1989/90) 28 Journal of Family Law 152.

[52] See *Adoption: The Future*, Cm. 2288, para.4.33 (1993).

only justification for preserving what we inaccurately term cultural heritage, is the preservation of minority rights. In a confused way, that is what the court seeks to do in *Re JK*. The preservation of minority rights requires the adoption agency, or the court, to try and place the child within the community of his or her birth family. The reason for such a placement is not just that it benefits the child, but because the minority should have the right to keep children within their community, if at all possible, to ensure the survival of the minority into the next generation. There is nothing wrong in declaring this to be the aim of preservation of cultural heritage, except that it carries with it an implication that the concept of the best interests of the child will be interpreted differently in the case of a child belonging to a minority culture, than one belonging to a majority culture. Such an approach obliges the court to accept that, although the care that can be offered by the child's community may not be as good as the care that can be offered outside, provided the care is adequate, the community should be given the chance to retain the child.

In the latest White Paper, "Adoption: The Future",[53] it is recommended that there be a statutory requirement that ethnicity and culture be taken into account in placing a child for adoption.[54] However, these factors should not be given an unjustifiably decisive influence but should be considered along with all other relevant factors when assessing adoptive parents' suitability. This new requirement is unlikely to solve the confusion as to what is meant by cultural heritage or to give clear guidance to the adoption agencies and the courts.

If the preservation of minority rights is the primary justification for the preservation of cultural, as against ethnic, heritage, the court needs to stop being disingenuous and define with more certainty the parameters of such preservation. It is quite clear in these cases that communitarian interests are taken into account. This being so there is a need for greater consideration as to how the child's best interests are to be balanced with community rights.

---

[53] Cm. 2288 (1993).
[54] The relevant provisions would be along the lines of what is now in the Children Act 1989. Ss.64(3)(c) and 61(3)(c) require that due consideration be given to the child's religious persuasion, racial origin, and cultural or linguistic heritage. A new Adoption Act would presumably have a similar requirement in relation to placement of a child.

While these are difficult questions to answer, the adoption agencies and the courts need to face up to them in an increasingly multi-cultural society.

Parental right to choice of religion and placement of children

As has been seen above, adoption laws in both England and the United States recognise the right of parents to express a preference as to the religious upbringing of their child, and adoption agencies in both jurisdictions are required, either by statute or practice, to pay heed to such expressed preferences in placing a child. A parent wishing a child to follow a particular religion after adoption may place a child with a religious adoption agency operating within the State adoption system,[55] or with a non-sectarian adoption agency, stipulating that the child be brought up by adoptive parents of a particular religion.

The courts have differed over time in the extent to which this right to choose the child's religion should be enforced. Enforcement of parental preference has been particularly troublesome where parents have changed their mind as to the religion of the child post-placement. Early cases, in both England and the United States, indicate a willingness to uphold parental desires, based on the common law principle that a parent[56] had a right to determine the child's religion throughout the minority years, even where this appeared to be detrimental to the welfare of the child. The most extreme examples of enforcement of a parent's right to determine the child's religion, and thus her placement, can be seen in the United States case of *Re Santos*[57] and the English case of *Re Carroll*.[58] In both cases the mother agreed to cross-religious placement and later changed her mind.

In *Santos*, a Roman Catholic mother placed her two children

---

[55] Provided that such agencies are approved under the relevant State regulations. Much early adoption work was done through religious adoption agencies, and they continue to provide adoption services in both jurisdictions.

[56] This was a right, initially of the father, although in the 20th century it was regarded as the right of both parents. In the case of the illegitimate child the right was that of the mother alone.

[57] 278 App.Div. 373, 105 N.Y.S. 2d 716 (1st Dep't 1951).

[58] [1931] 1 K.B. 317.

aged seven and eight, in a Jewish home. The foster mother informed the natural mother that she kept a kosher home, and would give the children intensive training in the Jewish religion. The natural mother agreed to this. Some four years after their initial placement with the foster mother and over a year after they had lived with their Jewish adoptive parents, the mother re-appeared and opposed the adoption on the ground that she now wished the children to be brought up as Catholics. The court initially ordered that the children should stay with the adoptive parents, finding that the mother was an unfit guardian. The court also found that the children were happy in their adoptive home and considered themselves Jewish, although the court took notice that the children had been baptised as Catholics by their mother.[59] To move them, the court found, would be a tragic disregard for their welfare.

On appeal, the appellate court took quite a different view, concentrating not on the welfare of the children, but on the children's initial religious designation and the natural mother's wishes. As the mother and the children had been baptised Roman Catholics, the children remained Catholics.[60] The court in interpreting the applicable religious statute held that:

"on the facts presented herein ... the legislative mandate leaves no area of judicial discretion ... children have a natural and legal right [to their religious faith] of which they cannot be deprived by their temporary exposure to the culture of another religion prior to the age of reason".

This approach, upholding the mother's right to choose a child's religion long after she had ceased to care for the children, and after she had agreed to their religious upbringing as Jewish, was justified on the basis of "natural" law. The idea that the mother might have irrevocably committed the children to another religion was not given serious consideration. Neither was the fact that, psychologically, the children, by the time of the hearing, considered them-

---

[59] Against their Protestant father's wish.

[60] This assumption was criticised by some commentators who saw the mother's act in placing the child in a Jewish household as changing the child's religion. See Pfeffer, *Church, State and Freedom* (2nd Ed., 1967), p. 590, Ramsey, "The Legal Imputation of Religion to an Infant in Adoption Proceedings" (1959) 34 NYU. L.Rev. 649 and (1952) 65 Harv. L. Rev. 694.

selves to be Jewish. The wishes of the children, the oldest of whom was twelve, were not considered, and neither was their welfare. The court found that it was practicable for them to be adopted by a Catholic family, regardless of what had gone on in their lives. The tragedy wrought by the decision can be seen in the fact that the children remained in institutional care or temporary foster homes long after the case closed and never found another adoptive family.

A very similar decision was handed down by the English court in the earlier case of *Re Carroll*.[61] The mother of an illegitimate child placed her child with a Protestant adoption agency, although the mother and the child were baptised Catholics. The mother signed an agreement consenting to the child being adopted, and the child was placed with a Protestant family. Some days later she changed her mind and asked that the child be placed with Catholic adopters. After vacillating for a period of time, she eventually asked that the child be returned to her. By this time the child was settled with the would-be adoptive parents, and the adoption society was unwilling to hand the child back. The intention of the mother on reclaiming the child was to place her with a Catholic adoption society. The issue for the court was whether the mother could enforce her right to determine the child's religion, reclaim custody of the child and place her in the care of the Catholic society, or whether the welfare of the child required that she stay with the adoptive parents. The majority of the Court of Appeal found that the mother had the right to determine the child's future religious upbringing, and that it was right that the child should be placed with the Catholic society and be brought up as a Catholic.

Scrutton L.J. found the welfare factor to be of little weight. He held that there was an insufficiently substantial difference between being with a family and being housed in an institution to overrule the right of a parent to control the religion of a child too young to have wishes of her own. In conclusion, he stated:

> "I may add that it is not universally accepted that a [family] 'home' with no external [boarding] education is the best thing for a child. Many home-brought-up children are spoilt and deprived of independent initiative."

---

[61] [1931] 1 K.B. 317.

He also added, when referring to the role of the court;

> "But, in my opinion it has this duty, where the character of the parent is not attacked, to give effect as to religious education of the parent of a child too young to have intelligent views of its own. The responsibility for religious views is that of the parents, not of the Court. The Court should not sanction any proposal excellent in itself which does not give effect to the parent's views on education religious and secular."

The fact that the mother had initially consented to prospective adopters or the agency's plans for the religious upbringing of the child did not prevent the mother from withdrawing her initial consent. Neither were considerations of welfare sufficient to overcome the natural law right to have the child follow a particular religion under the care of similarly religious adoptive parents.

Parental rights and the child's welfare

The emphasis on parental rights and the scant attention given to the child's needs and welfare could not, one would think, survive the post-second world war change of attitude both in England and the United States, towards the "welfare" of children. The courts have indeed been forced to effect compromises between parental rights and welfare, although these were slow in coming. The compromises reached have differed in the two jurisdictions. In England, parents, or the mother in the case of the illegitimate child, had the right, up until 1975, to give consent to adoption subject to a condition on religious upbringing. Thus, where there was a cross-religion placement, adoptive families could find themselves bound to bring up the child in a religion completely different to that followed in their own home. The Houghton Committee,[62] reporting in 1972 found the arguments against the retention of such a parental right persuasive and recommended its abolition. Various arguments were advanced against continuance of such a right, many of which are reflected in adoption cases in the United States.[63] It was pointed

---

[62] *The Report of the Departmental Committee on the Adoption of Children*, Cmnd. 5107, (HMSO, 1972).
[63] See *Scott v. Family Ministries* 5 Cal.App. 3d 492; 135 Cal.Rptr. 430 (1976) Second Dist.Div.One. Also, *Wilder v. Bernstein* 848 F. 2f 1338 (2d Cir. 1988).

out that the definition of adoption is the complete severance of the legal relationship between the parent and the child and it was, therefore, anomalous that a parent should appear to retain control over this one aspect of the child's future. Such a condition was also unenforceable post-adoption, and widespread non-adherence could bring the law into disrepute. Further, such a condition could be against the child's best interests in that the pool of adopters willing to bring up the child in the religion named by the parents might be small, and could lead to a considerable delay in placement of the child.

The report recommended that while the parent should no longer have the right to stipulate a child's religious upbringing when consenting to adoption, he or she should still have the right to make his or her wishes on religious upbringing known to the adoption agency. The agency should have regard to such wishes, where practicable, in placing the child. If, however, it was impracticable to comply with the wishes expressed, or where to do so might be harmful to the child's welfare because, for example, it would cause undue delay, the report recommended that the agency should be free to make whatever placement appeared in the best interests of the child. Such recommendations recognised the need for an increasingly professional adoption service whose primary task was to provide for the needs of those children who could not be looked after by their natural parents. The Houghton Report accepted that parents should still retain the choice to place the child for adoption with one of the recognised voluntary adoption agencies which serve specific religions, in the expectation that the child would be adopted by those of the same faith.[64] These recommendations were implemented in the Children Act 1975, and are now contained in the Adoption Act 1976. They are also reflected in the latest White Paper on Adoption.[65]

Courts in the United States had also to re-examine the balance between parental rights and the welfare needs of the child after the watershed decision of *Santos*.[66] A total disregard of welfare became

---

[64] The majority of witnesses supported the recommendations of the Houghton Report, but some, although not all, Roman Catholic witnesses opposed the abolition of the parental right to determine religious upbringing after adoption.

[65] *Adoption: Facing the Future*, Cm. 2288 (1993).

[66] 278 App.Div. 373, 105 N.Y. Supp. 2d 716 (1st Dep't 1951) (per curiam), appeal dismissed for want of jurisdiction, 304 N.Y. 483, 109 N.E.2d 71 (1952).

increasingly unacceptable. In the case of *Maxwell*[67] a balance was achieved by a re-interpretation of the religious matching statutes. Once more, the case involved a mother who placed her child for adoption declaring in an affidavit that "she did not at the present time embrace any religious faith". The child was placed with Protestant adoptive parents, although the mother was by upbringing a Catholic. When the adoptive parents petitioned to adopt the child, the mother withdrew her consent, asking that the child be returned to her, or, failing this, that the child be brought up as a Catholic. In a rigorous judgment, the New York Court found that the mother had voluntarily signed the affidavit, and knew what it contained. The court refused to look behind the document. The statute, while requiring the court to give custody to parents of the same religious faith as that of the child "when practicable" could not be employed as a means of wiping out the relationship between foster parents and a child which had originated in good faith and continued for four and a half years of the child's life.

The court held that to tear the child from the love and care of the foster parents and send him to an institution until other adoptive parents were found, would be inordinately cruel and harsh, and that no law required a consequence so distressing.[68] The decision, while representing a radical change in the balance between parental rights and child welfare from that found in the cases of *Goldman* and *Santos*, reflects the modern concern in adoption and fostering cases. Apart from the trauma that the child would have suffered were he removed from the parents, finding Catholic parents for the child might not have been easy, and may well have necessitated a lengthy stay in an institution or with short-term foster parents. The prospect of upheaval and uncertainty, and the difficulty in finding alternative, matching, adoptive parents led to the court's conclusion that religious matching of the child and the adoptive parents could not be deemed "practicable" within the meaning of the statute. Given the emphasis placed by child care experts on a stable environment in early infancy, a delay of more than a month or two

---

[67] 4 N.Y. 2d 429; 151 N.E.2d 848; 176 N.Y.S.2d 281 (1958). See for a general comment on this case, Ramsey, "The Legal Imputation of Religion to an Infant in an Adoption Case" (1959) 34 NYU. L. Rev. 649.

[68] In fact, the parents in *Maxwell* agreed to have the child baptised and brought up a Catholic. This apparently played no part in the court's decision, was not taken up, and would, in any event, have been extremely difficult to enforce post-adoption.

in the child's placement with adoptive parents, even in order to
secure religious conformity must be deemed detrimental. This is a
problem that has been recognised by the religious bodies themselves. In 1968 the National Conference of Catholic Charities[69]
recognised that religious matching may be precluded by the
unavailability of adoptive parents of the relevant religion.[70]

Conclusion

At the beginning of the twentieth century, courts expressed great
concern that children, even those not cared for by their parents,
should be brought up in the religious faith of their parents, whether
the parents requested it or not. Indeed, if the parent did not indicate
a choice of religion for the child, courts in the United States would
impute a religion. This concern to maintain the religious faith of
the natural parent has largely disappeared. The only visible rem-
nant in the United States is a willingness to try and place a child
with parents of a particular faith if this is specifically requested by
the natural parent. It is curious that a State with a constitutional
prohibition of establishment and a constitutional guarantee of free
exercise should have been so concerned about religious matching in
the absence of parental request for such. While the reasons for such
practices are not clear, they might well have reflected the anxiety of
different religious groups to keep children within their religious
community, and not to lose them to another religion.

England, with its established Church was not as concerned with
religious matching. Unless a parent specifically requested that the
child be placed with parents of a particular religious denomination,
cross-religious placement was acceptable. However, recently, the
courts in England have turned their attention to the need to preserve a child's cultural heritage. At the behest, normally of the local
authority, courts have been prepared, when children of minority
parents are placed for adoption, to impute a culture, and generally
this includes a religion, to a child, and to promote religious and cultural matching. The English courts could argue that their approach

---

[69] Child Welfare League of America in their report, *Standards for Adoption Services*
(1968).
[70] See also Katz, "Judicial and Statutory Trends in the Law of Adoption" (1962) 51
Georgetown L.J. 64.

is supported by Article 20(3) of the United Nations Convention on the Rights of the Child, and they are merely paying due regard to the child's ethnic, religious and cultural background. In reality, though, most of the children involved have had no knowledge of their parent's cultural background or religion. Imputation of culture, therefore, has little to do with religious freedom or tolerance, but is concerned instead with the preservation of minority rights. While imputation of culture and religion is a clumsy tool, it is necessary to bear in mind the sensitivity of minority groups to "loss" of their children. Such losses have, historically, been of very real concern to minority groups, such as the American Indians, the Australian aborigines, Afro-Americans[71] and also to Jews in the aftermath of the Second World War.[72] The assimilation of children into a majority culture and the resulting diminution of minority cultures is still seen as a threat, particularly in England, amongst the more recent immigrant communities. One cannot simply dismiss these concerns, or a parent's wish that their child should not lose their cultural heritage. But, the need to keep children within their cultural communities has to be balanced with the need to assure the child's welfare. Preservation of cultural identity cannot take precedence over the need to preserve and act in the child's best interests. Real and positive efforts have to be made both by placement agencies and by the minority communities to recruit adoptive parents, so that children from these communities do not have to spend long periods of time in children's homes or short-term foster placements awaiting an appropriate placement.

Where matching adoptive parents cannot be found within a reasonable period of time, the best interests of the child require that adoptive parents from a different religious group are to be preferred to no family at all. The courts should not resolve the lack of minority religious placements by imposing a requirement that adoptive parents bring up their child in a religion different from their own. This not only hinders integration of the child into his or her new family, but is likely to be half-hearted and ultimately unsuccessful.

---

[71] See Howard, "Transracial Adoption: Analysis of the Best Interests Standard" (1984) 59 Notre Dame L.Rev. 503, Hollinger, "Beyond the Best Interests of the Tribe: the Indian Child Welfare Act and the Adoption of Indian Children" (1989) 66 U.Det. L. Rev. 451. See Schwartz, "Religious Matching for Adoption: Unravelling the 'Best Interests' Standard" (Summer 1991) XXV Family Law Quarterly 171. No. 2.

[72] See 12 Encyclopaedia Judaica 354 (1971) and 14 Encyclopaedia 137 (1991).

The English requirement that adoptive parents acquaint their children with the religious and cultural background of their natural parents appears to be an acceptable compromise, and should continue. It allows the child security and stability, a knowledge of his or her roots, is in line with international requirements, and ensures that the child is not totally lost to the natural parent's cultural community.

Chapter Seven

Religious Education

In the late twentieth century, every State in the world recognises the importance of educating its children.[1] In England and the United States, the twentieth century has been a time of rapid expansion in State education and increasing government concern and control over the nature and form of a child's education. This is reflected in the establishment of minimum standards for schools and increasing control, particularly in England, over the taught curriculum. At the same time, both England and the United States recognise the right of parents to educate children according to their religious values and beliefs. The duty on the State to educate children and the right of the parent to have the child educated in accordance with the family's religious values and beliefs, on occasions, causes conflict. One of the aims of this chapter will be to examine the extent of the parent's right to control a child's education, and how the State balances this right with an individual child's best interests.

One means of ensuring that children are educated in accordance with their religious beliefs and values is by keeping children out of the State schooling system and educating them in private schools run by the parents' religious community. This chapter will explore the legal acceptability of private schools, the extent to which they are tolerated by the State, and the extent to which they may be regulated and their curriculum controlled.

For those parents who send children to State schools, ensuring

---

[1] All but a handful of States are signatories to this Convention. Even those who have not ratified the Convention (and this includes the U.S.), recognise the need and right of children to be educated.

that a child is taught in accordance with the religious values and beliefs espoused by the parents can be difficult. While schools in the United States are, as a result of constitutional interpretation, "neutral" towards religion and secular in nature, historical accident and political will have resulted in religion maintaining a firm presence in English schools. The majority of English schools receiving State funding are required by statute to hold an act of collective worship each day and to include religious education within the curriculum.[2] This chapter will examine the impact of a written constitution guaranteeing free exercise of religion and non-establishment of religion, as compared to establishment of the Church in England, on the parents' right to ensure that education of their children is in conformity with their religious values and beliefs.

Historical Development

ENGLAND

In England the first schools for children were provided by churches. Well into the nineteenth century[3] the education of children was seen as a matter falling within the particular remit of religious bodies, and as such, jealously guarded by them. Indeed, the established Church of England saw the State as playing no part in the provision of education, a view also held by a large number of politicians. Within church-run schools, religious doctrine and thinking permeated the entire curriculum. Even such seemingly secular subjects as reading, mathematics and writing were taught from a religious perspective. As long as England remained religiously homogeneous, with a largely rural population, there was little tension between Church and State. However, a number of factors combined in the nineteenth century which led to a struggle between Church and State for the control of schools. These factors included the movement of a substantial proportion of the population from rural areas into urban areas, the growth of a sizeable non-

---

[2] This provision does not apply to maintained special schools, which are schools specially organised to make special educational provision for pupils with special needs; c/f the Education Reform Act 1988, s.6(7) and the Education Act 1944, s.9.

[3] Other than in New England where the hold of the churches over education of children ceased in the 18th century.

Anglican population, animosity between the various religious groups, as well as concern by minority populations as to the religious education provided by schools. These factors together led to two major problems in the middle of the nineteenth century. First, those who were not members of the Church of England (or Anglican) Church began to object to their children being taught within Anglican schools,[4] permeated as they were with Anglican doctrine. The second problem was the inability of the Anglican Church to provide sufficient school places to enable every child to receive an education. This was a particular problem in relation to children of the urban poor in areas of rapid population increase. This latter problem was exacerbated by the need, not only to provide more school places, but to provide a higher quality of education.[5] The industrial revolution and the need to compete with other trading countries required a more sophisticated education than hitherto-fore. The State was confronted with a dilemma. Either it had to finance religious groups to enable them to provide higher quality education for all children, or it had to provide those schools itself.

In England, the answer to the two problems of sufficiency of school places and religious control was solved by the implementation of a dual system of schooling, allowing for both church and State schools. The churches were free to provide and run "voluntary" schools under their sole control, offering denominational education. At the same time, the government started to provide funds to the voluntary (i.e. religious) schools in return for control over the secular education of the school. Model trust deeds were to be adopted by schools built with State assistance, and lay managers were to be included on the boards of management. The intent of the government when it passed the Elementary Education Act in 1870[6] was to provide elementary education for all children. Where there was an insufficiency of school places the government would finance the building and running of schools, to be known as board schools.

In the 1870 Act, the government declared that henceforth it

---

[4] Although the Church of England accepted Roman Catholic pupils, Roman Catholic children were forbidden to attend such schools by their parish priests. Methodist and Non-conformists also objected to their children attending Church of England schools.

[5] This would obviously have required a greater input of resources and would have increased the cost for each school place.

[6] Elementary Education did not become compulsory until 1880.

would only be providing funds to schools run by religious bodies in respect of provision of secular education. The State formally declared in the Act that no grant would be made "in respect of any instruction in religious subjects"[7] and that there would be no requirement "that the school shall be in connection with a religious denomination, or that religious instruction shall be given in the school".[8] The move towards secularisation of schools was further emphasised by the "conscience clause". A parent would be allowed to withdraw a child from religious instruction in any school that received a grant from public funds.[9] The key-note of the 1870 Act was the requirement that secular and religious subjects be separated in the new publicly funded State schools. A religious ethos should not permeate the entirety of a school's teaching as the denominationalists practised in their own "voluntary" schools. As far as religious education in these new board schools was concerned, it was agreed that the school boards might, if they wished, exclude all religious instruction. If religious instruction was given then "no religious catechism or religious formulary which is distinctive of any particular denomination should be taught".[10] This form of teaching was referred to as "unsectarian" or "undenominational" teaching. The teachers were free to introduce Christian precepts but not to teach the dogma or doctrines of any particular church.[11]

Control of the board schools passed to local education authorities under the Education Act of 1902. Under the provisions of this Act the cost of running schools, and of providing instruction, both secular and religious, was to be met by government grants and

---

[7] Elementary Education Act 1870, s.97(1).

[8] Elementary Education Act 1870, s.97.

[9] Elementary Education Act 1870, s.74(2). This included those schools run by religious bodies that took any form of government funding.

[10] Elementary Education Act 1870, s.14(2). Known as the Cowper-Temple clause.

[11] This was not always adhered to. In 1888, 34 rural board schools admitted using the Anglican catechism and when nine of these schools were slow to mend their ways, the Education Dept. warned them that their recognition, and therefore grant, would be removed. The board schools were only allowed to teach the Lord's Prayer, the Ten commandments and the Apostles Creed. It was decided by the Secretary of State that the Apostles Creed was not a distinctive formulary. The Protestant Alliance complained in 1872 that Roman Catholic schools were using readers in ordinary lessons which contained doctrinal teaching and contained unfavourable references to the Reformation. Cardinal Manning ordered their withdrawal. (See Murphy, *Church, State and Schools. In Britain 1800–1970* (1971)).

local rates. This covered both council (previously board) schools and voluntary schools.[12] This strengthened the hold of the local authorities over secular education in the voluntary schools, but resulted, contrary to the 1870 Act, in the local authority paying for religious instruction. Non-provided schools (previously known as voluntary schools) were to continue to provide religious instruction in accordance with their trust deed. As far as provided or council schools were concerned, the Cowper-Temple clause was to remain and although religious instruction was to be given, no catechism or religious formulary which was distinctive of any particular religious denomination was to be taught.[13]

Where a school received a grant or was maintained by the council, no child attending could be required to attend or abstain from attending any Sunday school, place of religious worship, religious observance or instruction in school or elsewhere.[14] Further, the time of religious worship or for any lesson on a religious subject was to be conveniently arranged for the purpose of allowing the withdrawal of any child where requested.[15]

After the First World War, the voluntary church schools found it increasingly difficult to maintain the standards of schooling and buildings required by the local authorities. For many voluntary bodies the death knell was sounded when the government proposed to raise the compulsory school leaving age to 14. The Church of England authorities, in particular, felt unable to build the new schools necessary, even though grants were available. As a

---

[12] Voluntary schools had not previously been financed from the State through local rates. One of the reasons for change was that some religious bodies running the schools were finding it very difficult to continue adequate financing of their schools. At the time of the 1902 Balfour Bill, which resulted in the 1902 Education Act voluntary schools provided places for 3,729,261 children as against 2,881,155 places provided by the board schools. The early voluntary schools were provided by the National Society (Church of England) and the British and Foreign School Society (largely Non-conformist). They were joined later by the Catholics and the Wesleyans. Not all voluntary schools chose to put themselves under the control of the local authority.

[13] See Education Act 1902, s.4.

[14] Education Act 1902, s.4(2)(a).

[15] Education Act 1902 s.4(2)(b). Religious bodies could apply to set up new voluntary schools. A need for a voluntary school plus the names of parents representing 30 children in attendance, would receive equal consideration with a council school. Under the 1902 Act voluntary schools which wished to retain a degree of control over their school and continue to offer denominational religious instruction retained a greater degree of financial liability for the school.

result, many of the schools run by the Church of England were surrendered to the local authorities.[16]

The Act which formed the basis of the modern system of education was the Education Act 1944. Huge costs arising from war damage, and the generally poor state of the nation's finances, meant that the Government were unable to contemplate providing sufficient school places for every primary and secondary child without the help of the existing voluntary system funded by religious bodies.[17] After much negotiation, a series of compromises were reached with the Church of England and particularly, the Roman Catholic church. In the negotiations which led up to the passing of the 1944 Act, the Anglicans and the Catholics lobbied heavily for a daily act of corporate worship and religious instruction in all primary and secondary schools, to be paid for out of public funds. Although this had been rigorously opposed, since the middle of the nineteenth century, by the Non-conformists, it was agreed to by the government. Surprisingly, this change gave rise to very little comment, supposedly only formalising what had already occurred in many schools since the 1870 Act. Such an agreement may be explained first, by the fact that England was a nation at war and more ready to reach compromises at home; secondly, by the distinct lessening of hostility between the different Christian denominations, who expressed themselves as willing to participate in corporate worship;[18] and thirdly, by the need to draw together as a society and repair the dislocation of the war years. This is reflected in the 1943 White Paper on "Education Reconstruction" which preceded and informed the Act:

"There has been a very general wish, not confined to representatives of the Churches, that religious education should be given a more defined place in the life and work of the school springing from the desire to

---

[16] Unlike the Catholics, the Anglicans handed over a considerable number of schools to local authorities. It can be surmised that perhaps the Protestants were not so concerned as the Catholics at maintaining their denominational schools because religious education taught in the State schools was essentially Protestant in any event, and parents appeared to be happy with this level of religious instruction.

[17] The school leaving age rise had still to be implemented. Because of the outbreak of the Second World War the rise in the school leaving age had been temporarily suspended for the duration of the hostilities.

[18] However, the Roman Catholic church was still very unhappy at the idea of Catholic children participating in essentially Protestant worship.

revive the spiritual and personal values in our society and in our national tradition."

The 1944 Act contained a number of provisions relating to religious education:

1. In all primary and secondary schools assisted from public funds,[19] the right of withdrawal would be preserved,[20] and those withdrawn might be given religious instruction in accordance with parental wishes if this could be arranged.[21]

2. In secondary and primary schools wholly maintained from public funds, the provision of religious instruction and a daily act of "corporate worship" was to be compulsory. The instruction was not to "be distinctive of any particular religious denomination" and, in each locality was to be in accordance with a syllabus unanimously agreed upon by a Committee representing the local education authority, the

---

[19] The State agreed to provide financial support for three categories of primary and secondary "voluntary" denominational schools, in all of which the secular and religious educational costs would be covered by public funds. These were the voluntary aided schools, the special agreement schools and the controlled schools. Unless the governors of a voluntary school could satisfy the Secretary of State they could meet the necessary financial commitment, the school was to become a controlled school. In such a case, religious instruction was to be in accordance with an agreed syllabus. Where the parents of any pupils requested that their child receive religious instruction in accordance with the provisions of a trust deed relating to the school, or the practice observed at the school before it became a controlled school, the governors were to make such arrangements, unless there were special circumstances making it unreasonable to do so. The religious instruction given to the pupils in attendance at an aided school or at a special agreement school was under the control of the governors or managers, and was to be in accordance with the trust deed relating to the school, or where provision for such education was not made under the deed, in accordance with practice before the school became a voluntary school. However, where parents at the school wanted their children to receive religious education in accordance with the local education authority's agreed syllabus, arrangements should be made for this unless it would in the circumstances be unreasonable to do so. See the Education Act 1944, ss.27 and 28.

[20] Education Act 1944, s.25(4).

[21] Education Act 1944, s.25(5). The requirement under the Education Act 1902 that times for religious instruction should be "conveniently arranged" to facilitate withdrawal would be abolished, so that greater use be made of those teachers willing and able to give instruction.

Church of England and such other religious denominations as the authority considered appropriate.[22]

The 1944 Act remained the dominant Act, its philosophy and main aims continuing until the passing of the Education Reform Act 1988 and the later Education Act 1993.[23] While introducing considerable changes to education law, it is the provisions on collective worship and religious education contained in these recent Acts that are particularly relevant for the purposes of this book. The 1988 Act maintains[24] and expands the provisions on religious instruction contained in the 1944 Act. During the passage of the Education Reform Bill concerns were raised that the legal duties imposed on schools under the 1944 Act to provide a daily act of collective worship were not being met. Further there was unease at the development of multi-cultural religious education and a view that insufficient recognition was being given to Christianity as the main spiritual tradition of England.[25] The Act provides that religious education (rather than religious instruction) should be provided as part of the basic curriculum,[26] and "shall reflect the fact that the religious traditions in Great Britain are in the main Christian".[27] Such education is subject to the parental right of withdrawal. The duty on schools to provide a daily act of collective worship, again subject to the right of withdrawal, remains,

[22] Education Act 1944, s.26.

[23] The Education Reform Act 1988 has been amended by the Education Act 1993, but provisions relating to religious education in local education authority maintained county schools and voluntary schools are unchanged. The requirements in respect of certain grant maintained schools are changed by the 1993 Act to reflect the greater autonomy of these schools. The provision of collective worship is again slightly amended by the 1993 Act in relation to exemption from the provisions of the Education Reform Act 1988, s.7(1), but the 1988 Act is still the dominant Act.

[24] The 1988 Act refers to "maintained" schools which include county schools, (wholly funded by public funds and non-denominational) voluntary schools (which are funded denominational schools) and special schools as well as grant maintained schools. This latter group of schools are those who have opted out of local education authority control and receive their funding directly from central government.

[25] For a further discussion of the passage of the Education Bill and the introduction of amendments, see below at p.

[26] Education Reform Act 1988, s.2(1)(a). This applies to all pupils at maintained schools.

[27] Education Reform Act 1988, s.8(3). For a much more detailed discussion of these provisions see below at pp. 298–303.

but such worship in State (county) schools must be "wholly or mainly of a broadly Christian character".[28]

THE UNITED STATES

The move towards compulsory education for all children started earlier in the United States than in England, so that by the end of the eighteenth century, States were beginning the provision of elementary education for all children, financed by direct taxation, and subject to local control.

Unlike English schools, secularism was constitutionally established in schools in the United States by the middle of the nineteenth century.[29] There are a number of theories as to why this transition from Protestant religiosity within schools, to secularism, came about. It was undoubtedly the case that the dominance of Anglicanism had been drastically reduced in the eighteenth and nineteenth centuries, both by an increase in the numbers of nonconformist Protestant sects, and the large influx of Catholic immigrants. The Catholics refused to participate in any form of Protestant religious instruction. They wanted the right to run their own publicly funded schools or, alternatively, to bring Catholic religious instruction into the public schools for the teaching of Catholic children. The Protestants would not agree to either Catholic teaching in the public schools or to the public funding of Catholic schools. The acceptable compromise solution for the Protestants was to take religion out of schools rather than agree that Catholicism be brought in.[30] The end result was secularisation.

---

[28] Education Reform Act 1988, s.7(1). The underlying structure established by the Education Act 1944 largely remains. The form of religious education once more depends on the type of school. For county schools, religious education has to be in accordance with the locally agreed syllabus. In voluntary controlled schools, it is to be in accordance with the L.E.A.'s agreed syllabus, but if parents request it, arrangements must be made for religious education to be taught in accordance with the trust deed, or the practice followed by the school before it became a voluntary school. For grant-maintained schools, education is to be in accordance with their former status. Where schools are set up as grant-maintained schools under the Education Act 1993, s.49, religious education shall be in accordance with the trust deed, if any.

[29] See Pfeffer, *Church, State and Freedom* (2nd ed., 1967). In many schools secularity was only notional. A large number of schools were still permeated with a Christian ethos, teaching creationism and still maintaining school prayer.

[30] This did not satisfy the Catholics who, as in England, proceeded to provide a large number of parochial schools for their adherents.

Secondly, many of the States had written into their constitutions, provisions for religious liberty and nonestablishment comparable to that of the national constitution. The inevitable result of this was the end of State financial support for church schools.[31] Thirdly, there was an expansion of trade and commerce, and a rise of nationalism and democracy. The continuation of democracy was seen as requiring an educated citizenry. This resulted in the gradual change of the position of education as a medium for the promotion of religion, to an agency for training for economic living and civic responsibility.[32] One last reason was a pervasive change of philosophical thought in the country in the eighteenth century, brought about particularly by the rationalists and the humanists, both of whom were in favour of complete separation of Church and State.

According to Justice Frankfurter in *McCollum v. Board of Education*[33]:

> "by 1875 the separation of public teaching from Church entanglements, of the state from the teaching of religion, was firmly established in the consciousness of the nation".

However, such secularisation was not always easily imposed upon States. The United States remained an overwhelmingly Christian country and it is not at all clear that the compromises reached between the Christian denominations resulted in the total removal of Christian practices from public schools. In many States, readings from the bible and recitation of the Lord's Prayer continued. Indeed, the battle over secularism within public schools has continued well into the twentieth century, and is still a matter of contention.

THE INTERNATIONAL PICTURE

Education is no longer simply a matter of individual concern, or State concern. It is regarded as a fundamental right, and as such should be available to everyone. Article 26 of the Universal Declar-

---

[31] For a more general discussion of this issue, see Pfeffer, *Church, State and Freedom* (2nd ed., 1967), Chap. 9.
[32] For a further discussion of this point see Flowers, *Benevolent Neutrality*, p.378.
[33] 333 U.S. 203. (1948).

ation of Human Rights[34] provides that every person has a basic right to education. This right is repeated in other international instruments, such as the United Nations Convention on the Rights of the Child,[35] the International Covenant on Economic, Social and Cultural Rights[36] and the European Convention on Human Rights.[37] These instruments also indicate the appropriate form of education to be offered by a State. The Universal Declaration of Human Rights requires that education shall be directed to the full development of the human personality and to the strengthening of respect for human rights and fundamental freedoms, and shall promote understanding, tolerance and friendship among nations, racial and religious groups, and further the activities of the United Nations for the maintenance of peace.[38] The International Covenant on Economic, Social and Cultural Rights follows the aims of the Universal Declaration but, in addition, requires that such education shall enable all persons to participate effectively in a free society.[39] The Convention on the Rights of the Child is rather more specific. It provides that the education of a child shall be directed to the development of the child's personality, talents and mental and physical abilities to their fullest potential,[40] and towards the development

---

[34] Adopted and Proclaimed by General Assembly Resolution 217A (III) of December 10, 1948. All Declarations of the UN are regarded as setting standards which member states should aspire to. It has been suggested that declarations, resolutions and recommendations may be treated as evidence of customary law. See Lillich and Newman, *International Human Rights: Problems of Law and Policy* (1979) pp.65–66 and Reporters notes to s.102 of the 1986 revisions of the American Law Institute's Restatement of Foreign Relations Law.

[35] Art. 28 "States Parties recognize the right of the child to education". This Convention came into force on September 2, 1990. It was ratified by the U.K. in 1991. It has not, as yet, been ratified by the U.S.

[36] Art. 13 "The States Parties to the present Covenant recognize the right of everyone to education". The covenant came into force on January 3, 1976. It has been ratified by the U.K., but not by the U.S.

[37] Art. 2 of Protocol 1. "No-one shall be denied the right to education". The Convention for the Protection of Human Rights and Fundamental Freedoms (referred to in this chapter as the European Convention on Human Rights) came into force on September 3, 1953, and Protocol 1 on May 18, 1954. The U.K. has ratified both the Convention and the Protocol.

[38] Art. 26(2). Repeated in Art. 5(a) of the Convention against Discrimination in Education. Adopted on December 14 by the general conference of UNESCO December 14, 1960. The U.K. has ratified the Convention, but not the U.S.

[39] Art. 13(1).

[40] Art. 29 UN Convention on the Rights of the Child. England ratified the Convention in December 1991 with some reservations. The U.S. is not, as yet, a signatory to the Convention.

of respect for the child's parents, his or her own cultural identity, language and values, for the national values of the country in which the child is living, the country from which he or she may originate, and for civilisations different from his or her own.[41]

While a state is generally free to set up its own system of education, there is a qualification to this freedom. Article 2 of Protocol 1 of the European Convention on Human Rights states that in the exercise of any functions which it [the State] assumes in relation to education and to teaching, the State shall respect the right of parents to ensure such education and teaching in conformity with their own religious and philosophical convictions.[42] This right of the parents is echoed in the International Covenant on Economic, Social and Cultural Rights and the Convention against Discrimination in Education,[43] in the International Covenant on Civil and Political Rights[44] and in the Declaration on the Elimination of all Forms of Intolerance and of Discrimination Based on Religion and Belief.[45] This latter instrument which, as a Declaration of the United Nations serves as a standard to which all Member States should aspire, provides that:

"every child shall enjoy the right to have access to education in the matter of religion or belief in accordance with the wishes of his parents . . . and shall not be compelled to receive teaching on religion or belief against the wishes of his parents . . . the best wishes of the child being the guiding principle."[46]

Following from this right of the parents, the relevant Conventions and Declarations recognise the right of individuals or bodies

---

[41] The Declaration on Elimination of all Forms of Intolerance and of Discrimination Based on Religion and Belief also provides in Art. 5(3) that "the child shall be brought up in a spirit of understanding, tolerance, friendship among peoples, peace and universal brotherhood, respect for freedom of religion or belief of others". As a Declaration of the UN, this instrument does not need ratification by individual states, but is a standard setter that all states should seek to aspire to. It may also be regarded as an expression of customary law. See Chap. One, pp. 18–19, 20.

[42] The U.K., although a signatory to the European Convention on Human Rights has entered a reservation in relation to Art. 2 of Protocol 1.

[43] See Art. 5(b).

[44] Art. 18(4). This Covenant entered into force on March 23, 1976. The Covenant has been ratified both by the U.K. and the U.S., although the latter only ratified in 1992 (with reservations).

[45] Proclaimed by UN General Assembly Resolution 36/55 of November 25, 1981.

[46] Art. 5(2).

to establish and direct their own educational institutions.[47] There is, however, no inherent right to make the State pay for the establishment or running of such schools. Indeed, the United Kingdom entered a reservation to Article 2 of Protocol 1 of the European Convention on Human Rights to ensure that the State was not under an obligation to provide such schools itself,[48] while an obligation on any of the States in the United States to set up such schools would be in breach of the Constitution.[49]

The freedom to run private, religious schools is circumscribed by the requirement that the education in such establishments shall conform to minimum standards as may be laid down by the State.[50] A further limitation is laid down by Article 5(1)(c)(i) of the Convention Against Discrimination in Education which, while recognising the rights of members of national minorities to carry on their own education activities, provides that the right must not be exercised in such a manner so as to prevent the members of these minorities from understanding the culture and language of the community as a whole and from participating in its activities, or which prejudices national sovereignty. Neither must the standard of education be lower than the general standard laid down or approved by competent authorities.[51]

The right of religious groups to set up their own schools and educate their children according to their religious beliefs and traditions has caused conflict between the State and parents ever since the introduction of compulsory education. Throughout the twentieth century, in both England and the United States, the State has sought to increase its degree of control in relation to the extent and content of the curriculum, and to raise minimum educational standards. Such a move has created tension between two contrasting

---

[47] This right is recognised in Art. 13(3) of the Covenant on Economic, Social and Cultural Rights, Art. 5(1)(b) of the Convention Against Discrimination in Education and Art. 29(2) of the UN Convention on the Rights of the Child. All of these Conventions have been ratified by the U.K.

[48] The reservation entered by the U.K. stated that in view of certain provisions of the Education Acts in the U.K., the principle affirmed by the second sentence of Art. 2 is accepted by the U.K. only so far as it is compatible with the provision of efficient instruction and training, and the avoidance of unreasonable expenditure.

[49] Such an obligation would infringe the First Amendment prohibition against establishment of religion.

[50] Art. 29(2) UN Convention on the Rights of the Child, Art. 13(3),(4) the International Covenant on Economic, Social and Cultural Rights, Art. 5(b) Convention against Discrimination in Education.

[51] Art. 5(1)(c)(ii).

principles: that of equality of opportunity and pluralism. A democratic society must offer equality of opportunity—the right of a child to receive an education of equal quality to that received by the majority, while at the same time recognising the need to protect pluralism. Pluralism requires that the state respect the religious wishes of all groups, whether the majority or the minority.[52]

If the State allows a religious community total freedom over the education of their children, the child's equality of opportunity may be threatened. However, if the State restricts the freedom of a religious community to educate their children too greatly, to ensure equality of opportunity, it runs the risk of being regarded as intolerant, insufficiently pluralistic and, in the case of England, in violation of the provisions of Article 2 of Protocol 1. The tension between these two principles, that of equality of opportunity and pluralism, becomes most acute in relation to orthodox religious groups of virtually any denomination. The role of the courts and legislature when faced with a conflict between these two principles, has been to try and maintain a balance between the needs of children within their society to receive an adequate education, while at the same time respecting the parent's religious conviction. The balance has, on occasions, been a precarious one, sometimes tilting towards the State and sometimes the parents. Rather troublingly, the State does not have any established criteria for balancing these two principles and, indeed, in England, applies different balances according to whether the child is privately or publicly educated.

While international instruments provide that States must respect minority rights and the parents' religious beliefs, it is fair to ask whether parents should have any right to control their child's education where this conflicts with the child's right of equality of opportunity. It has been held by the European Commission in *H v. United Kingdom*,[53] that the State has a right to establish compulsory schooling. Thus, it is acceptable for the State to exercise a right of control over the child, by insisting that the child shall receive education for a certain number of years, and of a basic minimum form, even in the face of religious and philosophical objection from the

---

[52] See Protocol 1 Art. 2 European Convention on Human Rights and UN Convention on the Rights of the Child Art. 29 as examples of international instruments protecting pluralism.

[53] Dec 6, 31984 D & R Vol. 37 105. Application No. 10233/83.

parents. Should the right of the State to insist that the child shall receive education extend to ensure equality of opportunity?

If the parents had no right of control over their child's education, and each child within the country received the same education, one could argue that the child was at least being provided with equality of educational opportunity, allowing each child to be in a position to fulfil his or her own potential as far as this was possible within the system offered. It may well be that a child would choose never to fulfil this potential, but the choice would, at least, have been available.

This was a view taken by the American State of Ohio. Until the end of the Second World War, Ohio required all children to attend public school,[54] and recognised no other form of schooling. While such a view may be reasonable within a homogeneous society, it is very much less acceptable once a society becomes racially and religiously mixed, with cultural differences which parents wish to preserve in their children. It is also a view which is unacceptable under international law. International instruments recognise the rights of minority cultures to preserve their religious and cultural identities and accept the concept of pluralism. The right of parents to set up and send their children to private schools is recognised. Thus, neither of the two approaches to parental control over religious education, reflecting the two ends of the spectrum is acceptable. States have to find a balance between the two conflicting principles. The compromise that appears to have been reached in both jurisdictions is to permit parents to take their children out of the State system of education, into a lightly controlled private sector,[55] catering for particular religious beliefs and offering a different curriculum in keeping with traditional cultural and religious values and beliefs. Such a compromise raises, however, the spectre of discrimination. Only those who can afford to pay are to be allowed to maintain their cultural and religious identity in the way they choose, while those who are poor must take what the State offers.

---

[54] In the U.S. the term public school refers to a free school run by the state. Such schools in England are currently referred to as maintained schools. In this book such schools will be referred to in these terms, but when the two systems are described as a whole, the term state school will be used.

[55] The level of control over private schools varies between American states and between the U.S. and England. Private religious schools are, by their very nature, less subject to State control and regulation is light compared to State run schools.

Should those parents who cannot afford to send their children to private schools, be offered the same facility of education in accordance with their religious values and beliefs within the State system? Is a failure to make such provision a breach by the United Kingdom of Article 2 of Protocol 1? England has recognised the validity of such a claim in relation to some religious groups and has provided State funding for schools run by certain religious denominations.[56] This is a trend likely to increase under sections 49 and 96 of the Education Act 1993, which allows a body of persons, including a religious body, to establish a grant maintained school, or change the character of an existing grant maintained school, with the approval of the Secretary of State.[57] Such an approach would, of course, be constitutionally unacceptable in the United States as it would involve undue entanglement between Church and State and would constitute an infringement of the First Amendment.

It can be argued that such attention to parents' religious and philosophical convictions is unnecessary where the school is religiously neutral. The view in the United States is that schools should not reflect any form of religious values or belief, but should be wholly secular institutions. However, such a position does not address the question of how the State is to balance its insistence on secularism and equality of opportunity with the need to preserve cultural identity. Religious identity could, perhaps, be preserved by education outside of school hours, as was suggested by the Non-Conformists in England. But many religious groups would find

---

[56] There are 4,903 voluntary Church of England schools, 2,220 Roman Catholic schools, 22 Jewish schools and 31 Methodist schools. Out of a total school population of 6,768,081: 1,618,950 pupils are educated in Church schools. *The Independent* August 6, 1992. There are no state aided Muslim, Hindu or Sikh schools. This may be rectified by the Education Act 1993 s.49, under which it is possible to set up new grant-maintained schools.

[57] It is possible that some schools, which are predominantly of one minority religion may be able to apply for a change of character and become a religious grant maintained school under s.96 of the 1993 Act. The Secretary of State must give approval under s.98. Where an application is made to establish a new grant maintained school, the State will fund 85 per cent of the capital costs of the school and the running costs, once approval is granted. Loans will be available from the Funding Agency for Schools to enable groups to raise the 15 per cent necessary. Up to April 1994, there had been 20 groups expressing interest in obtaining such a loan. These schools would be maintained schools, and as such would be bound to apply the national curriculum. This has been put forward as a reason for the low number of applications.

this unacceptable. For them, cultural or religious identity cannot be preserved by secular schooling. Neither can substantive instruction be separated from religious ideas. Their religious identity depends upon children not being exposed to a western, secular education, conflicting with their principles. Some commentators[58] refer to religions which restrict exposure to modern western ideas as operating within an ideological enclosure. Such religious groups would not welcome education of their children which leads to the child questioning or criticising their ideology, fearing that once this occurs, adherence will cease.

To what extent should the State recognise the concerns of such parents, and what attention should be given to the child's needs for equality of opportunity in the modern State? If too much control is given to the State there is always the fear that this will lead to cultural oppression of a minority. It is the history of such oppression that led to the international instruments preserving the rights of cultural minorities, many of whom had been subjected to genocide or cultural suppression during World War Two and after. However, in a western technological, liberal society, the question posed is rather different. It is one of the degree of recognition to be given to a religious group who do not fit into the ethos of the modern State, and who are not, by current "good practice" standards seen as acting in the best interests of their children.

The next section of this chapter will look at attempts by England and the United States to resolve these tensions, giving due weight to the need to preserve both equality of opportunity and pluralism.

Religious Schooling

THE ENGLISH EXPERIENCE

In England, the Education Act 1944, section 76, in line with international instruments concerning the right to education, provides that the Secretary of State for Education and the local education authorities shall have regard to the general principle that, as far as is compatible with the provision of efficient instruction and training and the avoidance of unreasonable public expenditure,

---

[58] See, *e.g.* Hull "Religious education in the state schools of late capitalist society" (1990), Vol. 38, Pt. 4, pp.335–48.

pupils are to be educated in accordance with the wishes of their parents.

There is no obligation on a parent in England to send a child to a State school. Indeed, for some minority religious groups such an education would be against the tenets of their religion. Although a religious group may set up an independent school, they do not have complete freedom with regard to the structure of the school or its curriculum. Such schools are subject to supervision by the Secretary of State for Education. Section 70 of the Education Act 1944[59] provides that all independent schools must be registered.[60] In starting the school, the proprietor must initially register the school. This registration is only to be regarded as provisional until there has been an inspection of the school, and notice has been given to the proprietor that the registration is final.[61]

If the Inspectors are not satisfied with the school, under Part IV of the Act, the Secretary of State may serve on the school a notice which is known as a complaint.[62] This sets out a series of matters to which objection was taken and the measures necessary, in the opinion of the Secretary of State, to remedy these matters, and the time to be allowed for the remedying of these matters (not less than six months), unless the Secretary of State finds them unredeemable. The Secretary of State may object to the registration on a number of grounds, including the unsuitability of the premises or accommodation or the nature of the instruction offered to pupils, which is required to be "efficient and suitable" having regard to the ages and sex of the pupils.[63]

---

[59] As amended by the Education Act 1980.

[60] It is an offence to conduct an independent school which is not registered or provisionally registered under s.70(3). But see s.70(3)(A). The Education (Particulars of Independent Schools) Regulation 1982 specify the details of the school to be given to the Registrar.

[61] An independent school will not be registered if the proprietor or the premises are disqualified.

[62] Under the Education Act 1944, s.71. Under the Education (Schools) Act 1992, s.16(9). Regulations may make provision enabling the Secretary of State, in such circumstances as may be prescribed, to order the deletion from the Register of independent schools, of any independent school, the proprietor of which fails to comply with any of the requirements imposed under the regulations. No such regulations have, as yet, been issued.

[63] Other grounds are that the proprietor or a teacher are not fit persons to act in those roles or that there has been a failure, in relation to a child provided with accommodation by the school, to comply with the duty imposed by the Children Act 1989, s.87.

Where a complaint is served, there is a right to appeal[64] by "referring the complaint" to an Independent Schools Tribunal. The Tribunal has wide powers, including the power to order that the complaint be annulled. It may order that the school be struck off the register unless the requirements are, subject to modifications made by the Tribunal, complied with to the satisfaction of the Secretary of State. Non-compliance with the requirements of a complaint can result in the school being struck off the Register and may ultimately result in criminal sanctions.

There has been little in the way of case law on these sections. For the religious schools, the important question is whether the education they offer, while in accordance with their religious beliefs, will be regarded by the State as "efficient and suitable" instruction for the pupils attending the school. This was an issue discussed in the case of *R v. Secretary of State for Education and Science ex parte Talmud Torah Machzikei Hadass School.*[65] The school provided the traditional form of education as required by the Belz section of the orthodox Hasidic Jewish community. After inspection, a complaint was served in relation to the instruction received by the children.[66] In particular, it was alleged that the instruction at the school was not efficient and suitable having regard to the ages and sexes of the pupils.[67] After the serving of such a complaint, the school had a right of appeal to an Independent Schools Tribunal.[68] In this case, however, the school decided to seek judicial review as well, as a more appropriate procedure to have the complaint notice quashed. It was contended by the school that if they were required to comply with the part of the complaint relating to "efficient and suitable instruction", it would be quite impossible for the children at this school to be educated in accordance with the traditions of the community to which they belonged, and in accordance with the requirements of their religion. This would mean that children belonging to the Hasidic community in England would not be able to receive the same traditional education as the Hasidic communities of the United States and of Western or Eastern Europe.

---

[64] Under the Education Act 1944, s.72.

[65] *The Times* April 12, 1985 and lexis.

[66] A complaint was also served in relation to the premises, which the school did not dispute and which they had taken steps to remedy.

[67] After such a complaint the school has six months in which to remedy the deficiency of close down.

[68] Under the Education Act 1944, s.72.

The High Court had first to decide the extent of the power of the Secretary of State to interfere with the education of children which is in accordance with the traditions of a religious sect, and the wishes of their parents who are members of that sect. Woolf J., in giving his judgment, appeared to circumvent this issue. He held that the Secretary of State, in applying section 71 of the Education Act 1944, and deciding whether or not efficient and suitable instruction is being provided, must take into account the wishes of the parents. This is underlined by Article 2 of Protocol 1. When dealing with a school to which members of a minority sect are sent by their parents, the Secretary of State should bear in mind that the education which is provided is the education which the parents wanted the children to have. This is particularly so where the parents regard it as a religious requirement that the children are educated in this manner. However, the wishes of the parents, although an important consideration, are not the sole consideration, and the Secretary of State is perfectly permitted to have a policy setting down a minimum requirement which he will normally apply to all schools irrespective of the background of the children sent to that school and the wishes of their parents.

Counsel for the Secretary of State agreed that education would still be suitable if it primarily equipped a child for life within the community of which he or she is a member rather than the way of life in the country as a whole, as long as it did not foreclose the child's options in later years to adopt some other form of life if he or she wished to do so. However, what amounted to foreclosing of options was not discussed and no definition given. The judge agreed with counsel for the school that the Secretary of State was not entitled to require the school to become a mini state school,[69] but was entitled to regard a particular form of education as being too narrow. What minimum standards may the Secretary lay down for a religious school? The answer appears to be tautologous—only

[69]. This is a rather surprising statement. If religious schools should in the future be required to teach to the national curriculum, would this be a breach of Art. 2? It is presumed that the limitation on the Secretary of State referred to, relates to the level of control that may be exercised over private schools, rather than the limits imposed by Art. 2 of Protocol 1. If not, this raises some interesting questions. If new, religious, grant-maintained schools come into existence under the Education Act 1993, they will be required to teach to the National Curriculum. It is not envisaged that the Department of Education would be willing to exempt a religious school from such a requirement.

those necessary in his opinion to make the education suitable, being duly sensitive to the traditions of the minority sect and only interfering with them so far as this is necessary to make the school suitable.

The court gave little more help on the issue of "suitability". Most of the teaching in the school was conducted in Yiddish, although the children also learned Aramaic and Hebrew. Secular subjects were taught in English, for between one and one and a half hours in the afternoon, an amount of time considered insufficient by the inspectors. The Judge, however, held that it would be difficult to find a justification for a requirement that specific subjects should be taught, or that a specific number of hours be allotted to secular subjects. Nonetheless, excessive requirements by the Secretary of State did not justify granting relief by way of judicial review, as this would involve quashing the complaint. The complaint would have to be taken before the Independent School Tribunal which could, if it wished, amend the complaint.

The view of the Secretary of State that an education would be suitable if it primarily equipped a child for life within the community of which he or she is a member, rather than the way of life in the country as a whole, appears, in this case, to stand in direct contradiction to the proviso that such an education should not foreclose the child's options in later life. The school was very clear on the academic instruction that needed to be offered to its pupils to satisfy religious requirements and for the child to be equipped to fulfil his or her role within the religious community. Such instruction wold not enable a child who chose to leave the community to fit easily into British society. Indeed, it is even possible that the child would not be able to speak fluent English. The judge failed to lay down any guidelines to ensure that a child's options would not be foreclosed. Indeed, the judge expressed doubts as to whether the Secretary of State was justified in requiring a specific number of hours to be devoted to secular subjects. Without such a requirement, how could a child ever hope to have any form of equality of opportunity to an English child, limited as he or she would be by language, a complete lack of any modern technological or scientific education, and cut off from social contact with the majority community and its culture. It is doubtful that a child who chose to leave such an enclosed group could participate effectively in the economic, and perhaps more importantly, the democratic process. It is difficult to defend such a restricted education, to find that such education provides equality of opportunity, or that it meets the needs of a child competing in a western, technological society. Allowing a child to be educated within such an ideological, social and educational enclosure cannot amount to equality of opportunity, although it undoubtedly upholds the principle of pluralism. However, the concession towards pluralism and parents' religious values and beliefs is too great. Article 5 of the Convention against Discrimination in Education limits the right of parents in so far as the education received should not be exercised in such a manner as to prevent the child from understanding the culture and language of the community as a whole. It is not at all clear that the education provided to these children was in line with this requirement. Furthermore, the Declaration on the Elimination of All Forms of Intolerance and of Discrimination based on Religion or Belief, while providing that the child has the right to religious education in accordance with the wishes of the parent, states that the best interests of the child shall be the guiding principle. There appears to be no discussion in the *Talmud Torah* case of what constitutes the best interests of the child, or indeed any discussion of a child's right to education and equality of opportunity. Such a decision also sits uneasily with the fundamental principle of the Children Act 1989 that in any question relating to the child's upbringing, the welfare of the child is to be the court's paramount consideration.[70]

It has been suggested that a child at a school such as the *Talmud Torah* school is receiving a stimulating, intellectually challenging education, and that this should be the only concern of the State.[71] The argument may also be made that orthodox Jews are not often recipients of welfare benefits and are supported by members of their own group, so that the state should have no right to intervene in their law-abiding community. Such arguments fail, however, to focus on the issue of the child's best interests.

---

[70] See the Children Act 1989, s.1.
[71] Such a suggestion was made to the author by an Inspector of Jewish schools in London.

The requirement in the United Nations Convention on the Rights of the Child, that the education of a child be directed to the development of the child's personality, talents and mental and physical abilities to their fullest potential, and towards the development of respect for his or her own cultural identity, illustrates very clearly the problem of the *Talmud Torah* school, and the interpretation of international instruments in this area. The Convention sets up an impossible tension where the element of respect for religious and cultural identity requires that the child not reach his or her full potential within the modern state where he or she now lives.

In setting up a standard that an education would be acceptable if it primarily equipped children for life within their community, rather than the wider society, the High Court may have tilted too far towards the rights of parents. One can only speculate whether the High Court would reach the same decision if a religious school, following the tenets of its religion, gave its girls an inferior education to that received by its boys or by girls generally. The role of girls will, in many orthodox, enclosed communities, be ones of wives and mothers within the confines of the home, their education being directed towards enabling them to fulfil their future roles. The Convention on the Elimination of All Forms of Discrimination against Women specifically forbids this accommodation with parental wishes.[72] Indeed, it has been held that, as far as the European Convention on Human Rights is concerned, the right to education in Article 2 of Protocol 1 takes precedence over the right of the parent to have the child educated in conformity with their religious and philosophical views.[73]

The Experience of the United States

In the United States, much the same dilemmas are faced. Different States have imposed a range of requirements for approval on the

---

[72] Art. 10. "States Parties shall take all appropriate measures to eliminate discrimination against women in order to ensure them equal rights with men in the field of education".

[73] See *Campbell & Cosans v. U.K.* (1982) 4 EHRR 293, European Convention on Human Rights. The Court held that Art. 2 of Protocol 1 is dominated by its first sentence. For a much more detailed discussion, see Cullen, "Education Rights or Minority Rights" (1993) IJLF, 7 143.

private and religious schools. While some states have "deregu-
lated"[74] private schools, others have increased the amount of State
regulation, imposing standards on premises and safety, minimum
time for certain secular subjects, minimum teaching hours, and a
requirement that teachers be certified.[75] Such requirements have
been challenged on the basis that they are religiously offensive and
violate the free exercise rights under the First Amendment. The
fundamentalist Christian schools have claimed on occasion, that
they already have approval from God, and that approval from a
lesser authority is unnecessary and a burden on their free exercise of
religion. Such arguments have received short shrift, with the court
finding it not unreasonable that the State should require a school to
comply with approval regulations.[76] Other objections have focused
on the need for certified teachers.[77] On the whole, the approval
requirements have been upheld, the applicant being unable to show
a sufficient burden on his or her free exercise of religion. However,
the court has been willing to strike down such requirements where
these are such that they would eradicate the difference between the
private and the public schools, and would deprive the parents of the
right to direct their child's upbringing and control.[78]

Where a party seeks to allege that the need for approval infringes
his or her religious freedom, that party will have the burden of

---

[74] Tennessee statutes provide that "The State Board of Education and local boards
of education are prohibited from regulating the selection of faculty or textbooks
or the establishment of a curriculum in church related schools." Tenn. stat. Ann.
paras. 49–5–201–49–5–204 (1970). North Carolina only requires that private
schools keep a record of student attendance and select and administer a nationally
standardised test each year.

[75] Alabama, Iowa, Nebraska, North Dakota, Ohio, West Virginia and Wisconsin
are among the most regulatory states.

[76] See, e.g. North Dakota v. Shaver 294 N.W. 2d 883 (1980).

[77] The Supreme Court in North Dakota v. Shaver 294 N.W. 2d 883 (1980) found that
the need for certified teachers was not an undue burden for the Bible Baptist
Church. The Church required that all teachers had been saved and born again,
and opined that certified teachers were not necessary for the programme taught in
the schools. The court found that the school had no objection if teachers were
both certified and saved, and therefore, there was no basis for not meeting the
states approval requirements.

[78] See State v. Whisner 47 Ohio St. 2d 47 351 N.E. 2d 750 (1976). See also the anomalous case of Kentucky State Board v. Rudasill 589 S.W. 2d 877 (Ky. 1979) where it
was held that the state could not require non-public schools to comply with the
curriculum, teaching and textbook standards because such a requirement would
violate s.5 of the Kentucky Constitution "nor shall any man be compelled to send
his child to any school to which he may be conscientiously opposed".

proving infringement of free exercise. In the United States Supreme Court case of *Wisconsin v. Yoder*[79] guidelines were given by the court which require that a party seeking exemption from State approval or licensing requirements on religious grounds must establish certain points. First, the party's objection to complying with State laws must be truly religious in nature, not merely a personal moral preference,[80] secondly, the religious beliefs must be "truly held" and thirdly, the burden on the religion must be to a degree that is unreasonable or unnecessary for the achievement of legitimate State interest. Even where this can be shown, however, it is generally recognised that the State's interest in assuring a minimum adequate education is sufficiently "compelling" in some circumstances to override even legitimate objections of interference with free exercise of religion.[81]

The compelling interest of the State in the education of its children has not always been regarded as adequate to override the burden on free exercise of religion. Although parents cannot claim, in either England or the United States that their children should be exempted from compulsory schooling altogether,[82] the United States Supreme Court were prepared to find that the requirement of compulsory schooling up to the age of 16, infringed the free exercise rights of the Amish. In *Yoder*,[83] parents of Amish children sought to remove their children from school after the eighth grade, when they were either 14 or 15, although the State education laws provided for compulsory education for all children until the age of 16. After their removal, the children did not receive any further academic schooling, but instead received what was described as "vocational" training or "learning-by-doing", with the boys learning Amish attitudes, self-reliance and the manual tasks of farming, and the girls learning how to run an Amish household.

The parents of these children were convicted of violating the

---

[79] 406 US 205, 32 L Ed 2d 15, 92 S Ct 1526 (1972).

[80] See, *e.g. North Dakota v. Rivinius and Weikum* 328 N.W. 2d 220 (1982).

[81] One obvious exception, where the compelling interest was found not to justify requiring pupils to continue beyond eighth grade, was *Wisconsin v. Yoder* 406 US 205, 32 L Ed 2d 15, 92 S Ct 1526.

[82] In England, children may be educated at home rather than in a school, but the provisions of the Education Act 1944, s.36 must be satisfied, that while the child is of school age, he or she is receiving efficient full time education suitable to his age, ability and aptitude. Some of the states in the U.S. permit home education, but impose conditions on the content of the curriculum.

[83] 406 U.S. 205, 32 L. Ed. 2d 15, 92 S. Ct. 1526.

compulsory attendance laws. They appealed on the ground that their First Amendment right to free exercise of religion had been violated. The parents argued that during these two formative adolescent years, their children would be taught values and beliefs contrary to those held by the Amish community. Also, their physical absence from their community during this time would hinder integration into the Amish way of life, which, the court accepted, was not only a matter of preference but one of deep religious conviction shared by an organised group and intimately related to daily living. The Supreme Court saw the threat to the religious beliefs of the Amish from these extra two years as extremely serious. Chief Justice Burger accepted that for the Amish, schooling up to 16 meant either the abandonment of belief and assimilation into society at large, or a forced migration to some other more tolerant region, which would allow the children to cease their schooling at 14. This finding was based on expert evidence called by the parents, which the State did not contradict. However, the evidence only indicated a potential long-term problem of disaffection within the religious community. It could not be argued from this expert evidence that the religious faith and practices of the parents would be totally destroyed if the children attended a further two years of high school. Neither was there any indication in the expert evidence that a further two years of education would cause the children in question to abandon their religious practices or faith. Although at a later stage the Court emphasised that it was the individual rights of the parents that were at issue, because they were the ones facing prosecution, nevertheless it appears that the constitutional rights of the individuals were not at stake here so much as the constitutional rights of the Amish community as a whole. The majority of the Court[84] accepted that there was a violation of the free exercise rights under the First Amendment.

Given this finding, the question remained whether the State had an interest of sufficient magnitude to override the infringement. The Court took the initial view that the State's interest in universal compulsory education was not absolute to the exclusion or subordination of all other interests. The State of Wisconsin argued that its interest in compulsory education was so great that it took precedence over the undisputed claims of the Amish that their mode of

---

[84] Mr Justice Douglas dissenting.

preparing their youth for Amish life, after their traditional elementary education, was an essential part of their religious belief and practice.

The State advanced a number of arguments to establish the nature of its compelling interest. Their two primary arguments were first, that some degree of education was necessary to prepare citizens to participate effectively and intelligently in the open political system of the United States if freedom and independence were to be preserved. This argument was immediately dismissed. The court pointed out that the Amish had shown that they were capable of fulfilling the social and political responsibilities of citizenship over the last two hundred years without their children being educated beyond the eighth grade.

The second argument was that education prepared individuals to be self-sufficient and self-reliant participants in society. This argument was countered by the Court which held that while an extra two years or so of education might be necessary for the child being prepared for life in modern society, as the majority live, it was not necessary if the goal of education was the preparation for a child in the separated agrarian community that is the keystone of the Amish faith.

The State attacked these views of the Court as "fostering ignorance" from which the child should be protected by the State. The Court agreed that the State had a duty to protect children from ignorance, but found that this argument was inappropriate in relation to the Amish. The record showed that the Amish community has been a highly successful social unit within society, even if apart from the "mainstream". The evidence for this was to be found in the productivity of its members, the law abiding nature of the community[85] and their rejection of any form of public assistance. In addition to this, although the Amish rejected State education, they nevertheless continued to provide vocational education, in the form of agricultural experience, to their children.

The State put forward two final arguments in support of its policy of two years extra compulsory education. The first of these was based on the need to put an Amish child in the same position as any other child should he or she decide to leave the Amish com-

---

[85] See the dissenting of judgment of Douglas who holds this factor to be completely irrelevant.

munity.[86] Without the extra two years education the child would
be ill-prepared for life outside the community. The court found this
argument highly speculative, as there was no evidence of adherents
leaving the Amish community, or that they became burdens on
society if they did so.[87] In any event, as the court pointed out, the
Amish did not allow their children to grow in ignorance, but provided what experts referred to as "ideal" vocational training in their
formative adolescent years. To counter any cross-argument that
Amish children were not being provided with equal opportunity,
or that two years of agricultural manual work hardly equivalated to
two more years of education leading to the possibility of a college
education, the court pointed out that the purpose of requiring
schooling up until the age of 16 was not merely to provide education, but as an alternative to undesirable and unhealthy child
labour. However, employment on a farm between the ages of 14
and 16 was an ancient tradition, and there was no indication that the
Amish employment of children on farms was deleterious to their
health, or that the Amish exploited their children. The Court did
admit that these children would not receive any further intellectual
challenge within their "vocational training", but merely concluded
that the Amish were not purporting to be learned people, but self-
sufficient people.

The final argument of the State was that a decision exempting
Amish children from the State's requirements failed to recognise the
substantive right of the Amish child to a secondary education, and
failed to give due regard to the power of the State as *parens patriae* to
extend the benefit of secondary education to children, regardless of
the wishes of their parents. These last two arguments were both
founded on the right and the need of children to be given equality of
opportunity: to have the right to education. The response of the
court to these submissions was in terms of the constitutional rights
of the parents, and whether the State has a compelling interest
which overwhelmed the parental right to free exercise. The *parens
patriae* argument was curtly dismissed, with the Court pointing out
that the case involved a consideration of the validity of the parent's
conviction for not sending children to school, and not children's
rights. But, in any event, the child was not to be seen as the mere

---

[86] This is, of course, the equal opportunity argument.
[87] Again see Douglas' dissenting judgment. Up to 30 per cent of Amish leave the
community in some areas.

creature of the State. The State should only intervene in religious upbringing when it appeared that parental decisions would jeopardise the health or safety of the child, or have a potential for significant social burdens, none of which could be shown here.

In his dissenting judgment, Mr Justice Douglas found that if the parents were allowed a religious exemption, the inevitable effect of this was to impose the parent's notion of religious duty upon the children. Given this, the children should have been consulted as they also had constitutionally protected interests. It was the future of the child, not the future of the parent, that was at stake. If the parent was successful in removing the child from the school, the child would be barred from further education. That might, of course, be the child's wish, but the court should at least give the child the right to be heard. While this is a move towards greater recognition of the rights of children, it is unlikely to have produced a different result in such a case. It would be the brave child, brought up all his or her life within an enclosed community, obeying the principles and precepts of their shared religion, who would go against the expressed wishes of both his parents and the community. In any event, it would be likely that a child, indoctrinated as these were, would agree that they should leave school. What the Court failed to consider is the objective issue; is it in the best interests of the child, and is it acceptable to society, in the late twentieth century not to give the children of Amish parents the same level of education as other children within the wider society, and does the child have a right, separate from the wishes of his or her parents, to equality of opportunity in education? Should an exemption from the last two years of compulsory education be allowed, given that the withdrawal is aimed specifically at greater integration of these children into their enclosed community, and preventing exposure to the intellectual ideas and way of life of the wider community?

It is undoubtedly the case that withdrawal of non-Amish children from school at the age of 14 for similar agricultural training, even if it was thought to be "ideal vocational training" by their parents, would be unacceptable, even if the child were to inherit the farm. Such an act would be regarded as exploitative child labour, there being no reason why the child could not learn the same agricultural skills at 16. The same can be said of Amish children. It is not the need to learn agricultural skills that requires the Amish to remove their children from school at 14, it is the need to prevent these children being subject to a "worldly" influence; to prevent children possibly being lured away from the Amish culture and religion. By failing to address the question of the child's best interests or wishes, and by treating this as a matter of the parent's constitutional rights, the Court evaded a discussion of the right of the child to equality of opportunity.

CONCLUSION

In recognising the claims of the Amish in *Yoder*, and in finding an education suitable if it primarily equips a child for life within the enclosed community to which he or she belongs, rather than for life in the majority culture, the courts indicate their approval of these enclosed communities and their way of life. The courts also, by their decisions, recognise the claim made by these orthodox religious groups that they would lose large numbers of adherents if the children were given a "modern" education and released from the strict regulation of everyday life within their communities. The courts are prepared to forgo a consideration of equal opportunities and best interests of the child, in the interests of the continuance of, what is usually, an old, traditional form of religion.[88] It is questionable whether this tolerance would, however, be extended to all enclosed communities. For instance, it is unlikely that a Court would approve the withdrawal of children from school, or the setting up of private schools, by a sect who believed that white children should not mix with children of other races, as other races are the progeny of the devil. While such a belief may genuinely be a tenet of a particular religion, it conflicts with the accepted political view, and international standards, that racial discrimination and segregation of races is wrong and anti-social. Nor is the Court likely to approve of an enclosed group whose religious belief involved animal sacrifice, or even worse, child sacrifice. Obviously each state must make value judgments as to what their society can tolerate. Pure religious liberty is not possible in a society predicated upon western, liberal, Judaeo-Christian ideals. Those religions which do not espouse these ideals are unlikely to find approval from the courts

---

[88] Chief Justice Burger made it clear in *Yoder* that the Amish had a long history stretching back over two hundred years in the U.S. The court was not dealing with a way of life and mode of education recently discovered by some "progressive" or more enlightened process of rearing children for modern life, and that few groups could make the convincing showing of the Amish.

for their own private schools, or for teaching children according to their own values. It is highly unlikely that the State would allow a religious group freedom from State intervention in education, where the teaching impeaches the values of the State, even in the United States where parental rights are stronger. A forewarning of this approach is contained in the judgment of Chief Justice Burger in *Yoder* in which he found that the power to determine the religious upbringing of a child may be limited if it appears that parental decisions will jeopardise the health or safety of the child, or have a potential for significant social burdens, or prevent the child from discharging the duties and responsibilities of citizenship, or in any other way detract from the welfare of society.

Collective Worship and School Prayer

COLLECTIVE WORSHIP IN ENGLAND

The question of whether State schools should have a period of prayer or worship during the day, and the nature of that prayer, has been the subject of contention in England, while in the United States it has been a matter of continuous debate up until the present day. In England, the 1944 Education Act required an act of corporate worship each day, although such prayer was to be non-denominational.[89] In many schools, however, this requirement of non-denominationalism, although originally intended to ensure that prayers did not reflect any one particular Christian sect, had, by the middle of the 1970s been interpreted as requiring that prayers should not reflect any one religion, but be acceptable to all religious groups.[90] The requirement of non-denominationalism[91] was repeated in the government's Education Reform Bill.[92] This latter

---

[89] Although non-denominational, it was clear that such worship was intended to be Christian. "It is the intention of the government and of the Bill that . . . the corporate act of worship shall be an act of Christian worship". The Earl of Selborne, *Hansard*, H.L., 5th Series, Vol. 132, Col.366, June 21, 1944. The framers of the Act were not, of course, at this time having to take into account a large minority of non-Christian children.

[90] This resulted in "multi-cultural" acts of worship in many schools where children were of mixed faiths.

[91] The term religious denomination is sometimes used interchangeably with faith. See *Hansard*, H.L., Vol 496, Col. 433 May 3, 1988, the Bishop of London.

[92] In 1987/8, leading to the Education Reform Act 1988.

interpretation of non-denominationalism was seen by the government, in an earlier review of religious worship contained in the Secondary School Curriculum and Examinations Report in 1981,[93] to be acceptable:

> "The government recognises that a variety of practice has grown up in the form and content of worship. The government believes this reflects the complexity and variety of present-day society and differences in the organisation of schools. They do not believe it would be helpful to standardise practice in this respect, but they are ready to receive representations about the act of worship from the Churches and others at any time."

However, this interpretation was not acceptable to all. During the passage of the Education Reform Bill through Parliament, the House of Lords moved a number of amendments to ensure that the daily act of collective worship was to be a Christian act of worship. Lord Thorneycroft proposed an amendment to change "collective worship" to "collective Christian worship". This amendment was passed, but the House was deemed inquorate, their being only 17 members of the House at the debate. Further amendments were moved at a later date. One amendment, which called for "education which does not promote any particular religion or belief" was overwhelmingly defeated.[94] At the third reading, the Bishop of London introduced an amendment which is now section 7 of the Education Reform Act 1988, requiring that collective worship shall be wholly or mainly of a broadly Christian character. In proposing the amendment the Bishop of London explained that he was seeking to uphold a number of principles. The first of these was to maintain the contribution of collective worship as part of the process of education, giving proper place to the Christian religion. Secondly, the House did not seek to impose inappropriate forms of worship on certain groups of pupils, and thirdly, it did not aim to break up the school into communities based on the various faiths of

---

[93] *The Secondary Schools Curriculum and Examination; Initial Government Observations on the Second Report from the Education, Science and Arts Committee.* Cmnd. 8551 HMSO.

[94] Introduced by Lord Sefton (Amend. No.8) on June 21, 1988. The vote was 31 in favour and 120 against. For a more detailed account of the debate in the House of Lords see Alves, "Just a Matter of words? The Religious Education Debate in the House of Lords" British Journal of Religious Education, Vol 13, no. 3, p. 168.

the parents, and wished to avoid any group feeling that they were not really part of the community being educated in the school.[95]

Baroness Cox, who had herself moved a number of amendments seeking to strengthen the role of Christianity in schools commented, on the passing of the amendment:

"There is now explicit recognition on the face of the Bill of the expectations that . . . worship should, in the main, be Christian, thus enshrining Christianity as the main spiritual tradition of this country and providing young people with opportunities to learn about Christianity and to experience Christian worship, opportunities which have too often been denied to many of them in recent years. There is also enshrined a respect for the other major faiths and opportunities for those of other faith communities to teach and worship according to those faiths if parents request that and teachers find it feasible."[96]

The Education Reform Act, section 7(1) requires that collective worship organised by the school, must be "wholly or mainly of a broadly Christian character". Collective worship is of a broadly Christian character if it reflects the broad traditions of Christian belief without being distinctive of any particular Christian denomination. Not every act of worship need comply with section 7(1) provided that, taking any school term as a whole, most such acts which take place in the school do comply.[97] The meaning of "wholly or mainly of a broadly Christian character" was tested in the judicial review case of *R v. Secretary of State for Education ex parte Ruscoe and Dando*.[98] The parents complained to the Secretary of State that Manchester City Council and the governors of Crowcroft Park primary school had failed to discharge duties imposed upon them by sections 6 and 7 of the Education Reform Act 1988. In particular, they complained that the school did not have a daily act of collective worship wholly or mainly of a broadly Christian character. The parents did not wish their children to be exposed to non-Christian acts of worship, and contended that the multi-faith worship which was offered by the school did not, and could not

[95] It is doubtful that the amendment achieves these ends. Non-Christian children will inevitably feel alienated and such children, where they form a sizeable group, will almost certainly seek their own form of religious worship.
[96] It is questionable whether the aspirations expressed by Baroness Cox are in keeping with the proposals of the Bishop of London.
[97] See Education Reform Act 1988, s.7(3).
[98] February 26, 1993 Lexis.

ever, amount to collective worship as defined by the Act.[99] The Secretary of State considered the parents' complaint under four separate headings:

1.   that the worship practised at the school was not worship,
2.   that it was not an act of worship,
3.   that the worship was so constituted by the school as to prevent some pupils taking part,
4.   that the multi-faith worship provided at the school was illegal.

The Secretary of State found that none of these complaints was made out. He did, however, define worship for the purposes of the first head of complaint:

"to constitute worship as normally defined in common English parlance, the courts would be likely to judge that collective worship in school must in some sense reflect something special or separate from ordinary school activities; that it should be concerned with reverence or veneration paid to a being or power regarded as supernatural or divine; and that the pupil, at his or her level, should be capable of perceiving this".

The Secretary of State also defined the nature of "broadly Christian" and accepted the legality of multi-faith worship:

"For worship to be regarded by the courts as wholly or mainly of a broadly Christian character, as Section 7(1) requires, it must contain some elements which can be related specifically to the traditions of Christian belief, and which accord some special status to the person of Jesus Christ, although it must not be distinctive of any particular Christian denomination. But broadly Christian worship under the Act is clearly intended to be such that pupils of a non-Christian background can take part. Section 7(1) of the ERA is regarded as permitting some non-Christian elements in the collective worship without this depriving it of its broadly Christian character. Section 7(3) provides that not every

---

[99] The report is not altogether clear, but it appears that the parents argued that the presence of non-believers and non-Christians at the act of worship detracted from the act being "wholly or mainly of a broadly Christian character". The judge found that it was clear that Parliament contemplated that pupils who did not come from Christian families should be able to take part in the daily act of collective worship.

act of worship need comply with the broadly Christian requirement, provided that taking any term as a whole, most of such acts which take place at the school do so."[1]

In dismissing the parents' petition for judicial review, the judge held that it was necessary, in order to understand the legislation, to note the words used in section 7; "most" rather than "all", "mainly" rather than "exclusively", "reflect" rather than "conform to" or "conform with", "broad" rather than "specific" and "traditions" rather than "doctrine".

While finding multi-faith worship legal, the Secretary of State referred to a rather different definition of "multi-faith" from the meaning usually given to this term. Here it is used as permitting the introduction of some non-Christian elements or elements of worship common to more than one religion, into what is still, essentially, Christian worship. The more commonly accepted definition of multi-faith worship, and that referred to in the Swann Report[2] is non-denominational worship, where the worship reflects no one particular religion, but concentrates on themes, elements and moral issues common to all religions. It is doubtful whether this latter form of multi-faith worship would now be legal under section 7,[3] and indeed, doubtful whether such acts would constitute "worship" as defined by the Secretary of State.[4] While the Secretary of State for education propounded the view that collective worship, which must accord special status to the person of Jesus Christ, is intended for pupils from all religious backgrounds, such a view is naive. Collective worship of this nature would be unacceptable to Muslims and Jews. Furthermore, it is unclear what the required content of worship is to be when worship is not of a "mainly Christian" character. Few schools have staff with sufficient training

---

[1] This statement by the Secretary of State for Education reiterates the advice given to schools in DES Circular 3/89. This circular is now superseded by DFE circular 1/94 "Religious Education and Collective Worship".

[2] *The Report of the Committee of Inquiry into the Education of Children from Ethnic Minority Groups.* Cmnd. 9453.

[3] Unless, of course, the school had sought exemption from the "broadly Christian" requirement under the Education Reform Act 1988, s.12(1).

[4] The new DFE Circular 1/94 providing guidance on collective worship, incorporates the Secretary of States definition of "broadly Christian worship".

or experience in taking such worship, and it is unlikely that all secondary schools will be able, or indeed willing, to comply.[4a]

How collective worship is organised within a school is for the head teacher to decide after consultation with the governing body. Any departure from the broadly Christian requirement must be justified in terms of the family backgrounds, ages and aptitudes of the parties concerned.[5] These considerations should inform:

> "(i) the extent to which (if at all) any acts of collective worship in the school are not of a broadly Christian character;
> (ii) the extent to which the broad traditions of Christian belief are reflected in those acts of worship of a broadly Christian character; and
> (iii) the ways in which those traditions are reflected."[6]

Where does this leave those children who do not profess the Christian faith or indeed, any faith? The right of the parent to withdraw the child from collective worship still remains.[7] That child will not be provided with an alternative activity, and neither will the child necessarily be offered prayers appropriate to his or her faith. There are two possibilities for children and families in this situation. First, the parents of the withdrawn children, if they are members of the same religious faith, can request that denominational prayers should be provided for their children, provided this is in accordance with the law. The Secretary of State believes

---

[4a] It has been suggested that fewer than 1 in ten secondary schools fully comply with the requirements for content of worship. Indeed, many Christian religious groups are beginning to express disquiet about collective worship. This book went to press too early for a full discussion of these issues raised by the Archbishop of York in January 1995. But see *The Daily Telegraph*, January 7, 1995; *The Independent*, January 7, 1995.

[5] See Education Reform Act 1988, s.7(5) and DFE Circular 1/94 para. 66.

[6] DFE Circular 1/94 para. 66.

[7] Education Reform Act 1988, s.9(3)(a), The Swann Report, *Education For All: The Report of the Committee of the Inquiry into the Education of Children from Ethnic Minority Groups*. Cmnd. 9453 (1985) found that up until this time few ethnic minority parents in England were making use of the conscience clause and withdrawing their children. The reasons for this were thought to be twofold. First, the changing nature of the corporate worship led to less need to withdraw children and secondly, that many ethnic minority parents were simply unaware of their rights. The position appears to have changed since the introduction of the Education Reform Act 1988, particularly amongst Muslim children.

that governing bodies and head teachers should seek to respond positively to such requests from parents:

> "(i) unless the effect would be that denominational worship replaced the statutory non-denominational collective worship[8];
> (ii) provided that such arrangements can be made at no additional cost to the school."[9]

The second possibility is for the headteacher to make an application to the Standing Advisory Council on Religious Education (SACRE) under the Education Reform Act 1988, section 12(1), for a determination that it is not appropriate in the case of this school or this particular group of pupils for the daily act of Christian worship to be broadly Christian in character.

The purpose of SACRE is to "advise the authority upon such matters connected with religious worship . . . as an authority may refer to the council or as the council may see fit."[10] The SACRE is made up of five groups or committees:

(a) Christian and other religions and religious denominations, the number of whose representatives shall "so far as it is consistent with the efficient discharge of the committee's functions, reflect broadly the proportionate strength of that denomination or religion in that area".[11]

(b) The Church of England;

(c) such associations representing teachers as, in the opinion of the authority, ought to be represented, having regard to the circumstances of the area;

(d) the local education authority;

(e) under certain circumstances, the governing bodies of those

---

[8] There was evidence in some of the 1990 SACRE reports that parents were withdrawing their children from collective worship in large numbers. In one school 1,200 out of 1,300 children were withdrawn. Such action should result in an immediate application by the headmaster to his local SACRE.

[9] See DFE Circular 1/94 para. 88. There is a third requirement: provided that the alternative provision is consistent with the overall purpose of the curriculum set out in the Education Reform Act 1993, s.1, in particular that such alternative worship promoted spiritual and moral development.

[10] Education Reform Act 1988, s.11(1)(a).

[11] Education Reform Act 1988, s.4 amended by The Education Act 1993, s.147. See also Education Act 1944, Sched.5 as amended.

grant-maintained schools in the area without a religious foundation or which are former controlled schools.[12]

In considering a head teacher's request, the SACRE must take into account any relevant circumstances relating to the family background of the pupils concerned.[13] Where such a determination is granted in respect of all or some of the pupils in the school, daily collective worship must still be provided for them. Where a determination has been granted in respect of a class or description of pupils of a particular faith or religion, the alternative collective worship may be provided for those pupils as a whole. It may not be distinctive of any particular denomination of any faith or religion, but may be distinctive of a particular faith or religion. Thus where, for instance, a determination is sought in relation to a Muslim group of pupils, Islamic worship may be offered, provided that this is not distinctive of one particular Islamic denomination. Where a single determination is made for the whole school, because, normally, there are so many non-Christian children, it is not permissible for pupils to be divided into faith groups for worship. But if the school make separate applications for determinations in relation to different religious groups in the school, a single act of worship may be provided for each group of pupils covered. Thus, if the school, instead of asking for a determination to exempt the whole school from section 7(1), make separate applications in relation to its Muslim pupils, its Hindu pupils and its Sikh pupils, and all are granted, these religious groups may all be provided with their own

---

[12] A SACRE may also co-opt members. In para. 110 of the Draft Circular of October 11, 1993 which preceded Circular 1/94 it was provided that the inclusion of a humanist representative on committee A of a SACRE would be contrary to the legal provisions referred to in para. 95 of the DFE draft circular, as humanism is not regarded as a religion or a religious denomination. This is omitted in the new DFE circular 1/94. Humanism may or may not be a religion but it is certainly a belief, and therefore, falls under the provisions covering "religion or belief" and must be treated as a philosophical conviction under Art. 2 of Protocol 1. It is not clear whether a humanist may now be included in committee A.

[13] When a SACRE has made a determination on the request—which can only take the form of acceptance or rejection without modification—it must communicate this in writing to the head teacher and state the date from which it should take effect. It is then for the head teacher to decide what form the alternative worship will take, although the SACRE should be informed of the proposed arrangements.

faith worship. This would appear to be explicitly against the aim of section 7(1) as proposed by the Bishop of London.[14]

The aim of the section was not intended, according to the Bishop, to break up the school into communities based on the various faiths of the parents. Indeed, the Secretary of State has made it clear that the intention of the law is that all pupils should be able to take part in collective worship even though a pupil may not come from a Christian background. Such a view, given the interpretation of "mainly or wholly of a broadly Christian character" in *Ruscoe*[15] may be naive, however, and parents continue to have a right to withdraw their children from this collective worship.[16]

In the National Curriculum Council analysis of local SACRE Reports for 1990,[17] collective worship was, for the majority, the most time consuming single issue. Some of the reports indicated that efforts had been made by heads of schools to provide acts of worship which would be acceptable to all parents, thus avoiding a perceived need to withdraw pupils. In a number of schools, meetings were held with parents to reassure them of the school's approach to worship. A survey of 79 reports received by the National Curriculum Council[18] indicates that in 32 local education authorities there were applications to be exempt from Christian worship in that year.[19] Determinations were normally granted for whole schools. From information provided to the National Curriculum Council it appears that applications were carefully considered and were not automatically granted, with most reports listing at least one that was refused.[20]

The usual reason for an application being granted was that a large percentage of children in the school were from religious back-

---

[14] See p. 272, above.

[15] (1993; unreported; Lexis).

[16] Any determination under these arrangements must be reconsidered after five years. See Education Reform Act 1988, s.12(5) and DFE Circular 1/94 para.73.

[17] The Annual Report of the National Curriculum Council. 1990.

[18] A 78 per cent sample of all SACREs.

[19] Seven of the 79 reports did not mention requests for determinations, while in 38 LEAs there were no applications. In one authority over 60 schools applied for exemption, while in a further 28 local education authorities up to 20 schools applied for exemptions.

[20] See DFE Circular 1/94 para. 81. Under the Education Reform Act, s.12A as amended by the Education Act 1993 the Secretary of State has the power to direct the SACRE to revoke a determination if satisfied that the SACRE has acted unreasonably or has failed to discharge its duty in this respect.

grounds other than Christian.[21] Most schools, once granted exemption from the need to provide Christian worship, have provided non-denominational acts of worship, not representative of any one particular faith, but drawing from all religions represented in the school.[22] However, a small number of schools have offered different acts of worship for different faith groups. One local education authority, having taken legal advice, told schools that this was not permissible except for pupils who had been withdrawn.[23]

One can only speculate on the reasons why there was not greater protest by minority religious groups at the amendments to the Education Reform Bill and the introduction of explicitly Christian worship into what had been increasingly regarded as multi-cultural, non-denominational schools. This is especially so in view of the fact that schools have never been more mixed in terms of their religious population.[24]

There are perhaps a number of reasons for the seeming lack of reaction. First, the Church of England is the Established Church of England, and minorities may not feel themselves in a strong enough position, or even be willing, to attack such an institution.[25] Secondly, many minority religious leaders favour the introduction of more religious education in schools, provided, of course, it is that of the child's own religion. If more Christianity is provided in schools, and if the Government considers it so important that a child learns about his or her religion, then, it is reasoned, the state should allow non-Christian children the same rights, and provide them with the facilities to conduct their own religious worship. Lord Jacobovitz, the then Chief Rabbi, echoed this view in his speech in the House of Lords in replying to the proposal of the

---

[21] Applications were refused when the school's intended plans made an application unnecessary, or when the school's alternative proposals were inconsistent with the law.

[22] The Boroughs of Ealing and Brent, Birmingham and Bradford have given permission for multi-faith assemblies as there is no other acceptable community policy.

[23] See Annual National Curriculum Council Report, 1990.

[24] From the 1970s the non-denominational requirement was treated as meaning that the collective worship and religious education required by the Education Act 1944, should not be representative of any one faith, and, therefore, that religious teaching and worship should be acceptable to all faiths.

[25] Indeed, Lord Jacobovitz stated in his speech that he was skating on very thin ice when it came to religious education in schools.

Bishop of London to make collective worship broadly Christian in nature. He responded that the Jews would welcome a provision which would require non-denominational maintained schools to provide religious education for minority groups at the request of parents and where numbers warrant it. The best schools, he opined, were those that taught religion *per se*—Christianity to Christians, Judaism for Jews. In other words, Lord Jacobovitz would welcome the introduction of greater teaching in Christianity if the same rights were extended to minority religious faiths. In this way Jewish children would not be exposed to multi-cultural worship, but to more Jewish worship. Such a view reflects the dislike of religious leaders of all persuasions for multi-cultural worship, and their preference for faith teaching.[26]

A further reason for the apparent acceptance of the dominance of Christianity is that minority groups expect that such a provision will enhance their chances of obtaining voluntary maintained schools for their own belief group. After all, if a school is predominantly Christian ought not the non-Christians to be allowed separate schools? Such schools become far more necessary when children are being exposed to a more explicitly Christian ethos against parental wishes, than when the school was truly non-denominational, *i.e.* it did not favour one religion over another. The amendments of the Education Reform Act were seen, perhaps optimistically on the part of the religious minorities, as strengthening their hand when it came to the provision of separate voluntary maintained schools for their own religious denomination.[27]

The changes to the collective worship requirements brought about by the Education Reform Act 1988, and the Secretary of State's interpretation of these provisions in the *Ruscoe* case,[28] raise the question of England's compliance with the various international instruments which abound in this field, particularly whether

---

[26] Faith teaching was not, of course, permitted under the Education Act 1944 for state schools. Collective worship was not to be representative of any one Christian sect.

[27] This is more likely since the Education Act 1993. As yet no Muslim school has been awarded grant maintained status, although a decision is awaited on the Islamia school in Brent.

[28] (1993; unreported; Lexis transcript). See also DFE Circular 1/94 para. 63 which incorporates this interpretation.

England is discriminating against its non-Christian citizens. Article 2 of protocol 1 to the European Convention on Human Rights provides that:

> "in the exercise of any functions which it [the State] assumes in relation to education and teaching, the State shall respect the right of parents to ensure such education and teaching is in conformity with their own religious and philosophical convictions".

State schools in England, other than those religious schools voluntarily maintained by the State, must now, unless exempted from the requirement by SACRE, have an act of Christian collective worship each day,[29] obviously an aspect of schooling unacceptable to the majority of non-Christian parents. Whether England satisfies Article 2 would appear to depend on whether the right to withdraw children from collective worship is sufficient to constitute "respect" for the religious and philosophical convictions of parents in the education of their children. While it negatively ensures that the child is not subjected to Christian teachings, it does not positively reinforce the parents' religious convictions. Parents are free to organise alternative worship provided there are enough children to make this feasible and provided that this can be arranged at no cost to the local education authority.[30] If the parents cannot afford to make such arrangements, or there are insufficient children of one religious persuasion, no alternative activity to Christian collective worship will be arranged for the children. Such a provision appears clearly discriminatory in financial terms, in that Christian worship can be paid for by the local education authority, while non-Christian worship must be funded by the parents themselves. It is not clear, however, that this would be sufficient for the European Court of Human Rights to find a breach of Article 2. The court has been reluctant to find that a State need do more than provide a right

---

[29] This term is used to differentiate the form of worship required under the ERA 1988 as opposed to multi-cultural worship reflective of no single faith that was practiced in a number of schools before the Act. The requirement is that the worship be wholly or mainly of a broadly Christian character. While it may include some aspects of non-Christian religion, it is nevertheless Christian rather than non-denominational in nature.

[30] Or to the school where the school is grant maintained.

to withdraw. It has not, as yet found that a State should fund alternative religious education.[31]

The Declaration on the Elimination of All Forms of Intolerance and of Discrimination based on Religion or Belief[32] urges all states to take effective measures to prevent and eliminate discrimination on the grounds of religion or belief in the recognition, exercise and enjoyment of human rights and fundamental freedoms. Article 5(2) provides:

> "every child shall enjoy the right to have access to education in the matter of religion or belief in accordance with the wishes of his parents or, as the case may be, legal guardians, and shall not be compelled to receive teaching on religion or belief against the wishes of his parents or legal guardians, the best interests of the child being the guiding principle".

Thornberry, in his book International Law and the Rights of Minorities[33] suggests that where states are parties to international instruments that provide for access to religious education in accordance with parental wishes, this implies a duty on the state to remove any obstacles to this as well as to provide facilities for such education if the right is to be an effective right. Collective worship is regarded as part of a child's educational experience[34] and it is,

---

[31] Such a case has never been before the European Court, but it is unlikely that such an appeal would be successful. See Kjeldsen, Busk, Madsen and Pedersen, Judgment of December 7, 1976 A/23 (1976) 1 E.H.R.R. 711. However, the European Convention on Human Rights provides an important avenue for potential test cases, as it allows for individual petitions against State law, and the court's judgment is binding.

[32] Adopted without a vote by the General Assembly of the UN in November 1981. A Declaration has no binding legal effect, but sets a standard to which all nations should aspire.

[33] Thornberry, International Law and the Rights of Minorities (1991).

[34] See Hull, "Editorial" (Spring 1990) British Journal of Religious Education, Vol. 12, No.2. See also DFE Circular 1/94 para.50. The aims of collective worship are to provide the opportunity for pupils to worship God, to consider spiritual and moral issues and to explore their own beliefs; to encourage participation and response, whether through active involvement in the presence of worship or through listening to and joining in the worship offered; and to develop community spirit, promote a common ethos and shared values, and reinforce positive attitudes. It is extremely difficult, given these aims and given that worship must be explicitly Christian in nature, at least for the majority of the time, to foresee a common ethos resulting. Such worship, regardless of the Secretary of State's hopes is likely to be unacceptable to a significant number of children.

therefore, arguable that if Christian children are being provided
with this facility in school at the expense of the state, non–Christian
children should be provided with the same access to education in
the matter of religion, in this instance collective worship, at the
expense of the state.[35]

While no child in England is forced to attend collective worship
against the parent's wishes, the right of withdrawal often poses a
real dilemma for the child. If the child conforms to the parent's
request and withdraws from collective worship, she marks herself
out as different from other children at a time when pressure to conform to the attitudes and values of the majority is great.[36] Alternatively, if the child attends Christian collective worship so as not to
seem different from other children, she disobeys the parents'
wishes for her religious education. Such pressure on the child does
not sit well with Article 29(1)(c) of the United Nation's Convention on the Rights of the Child, which requires the development of
respect for the child's parents, his or her own cultural identity,
language and values. Indeed, it is debatable whether state funding
of Christian worship alone, the separation of children into Christian and non-Christians for the purposes of worship and the treating of Christianity as the dominant ethos within the school, in a
society with a sizeable minority population of different religions,
fully implements Article 29(d) of the Convention on the Rights of
the Child.[37]

The introduction of specifically Christian worship is to be
regarded as a retrograde step in the promotion of respect for different religious persuasions, and for equality between children in
schools, which the right to withdraw children hardly seems to rec-

---

[35] This is probably not an approach that would be supported by the European Court
of Human Rights. Art. 2 of Protocol only provides that the State should respect
the right of the parent to ensure education in accordance with their values and
beliefs, it does not impose a duty on the state to provide it. The U.K. has entered
a reservation to Art. 2 making it clear that the state will not pay for such education unless compatible with the provision of efficient instruction and the avoidance of unreasonable expenditure.

[36] For a further discussion of this point in relation to the United States decisions, see
below, pp. 290–291.

[37] "The preparation of the child for responsible life in a free society, in the spirit of
understanding, peace, tolerance, equality of sexes and friendship among all
peoples, ethnic, national and religious groups and persons of indigenous origin".

tify.[38] It seems inevitable that more children will now be withdrawn from assemblies, and this must result in a degree of alienation of non-Christian children from their peers, and the separation
of children into faith groups.[39] The Report of the Committee of
Inquiry into the Education of Children from Ethnic Minority
Groups (the Swann Report) in 1985[40] found that the requirement of
a daily act of worship could no longer continue to be justified with
the multiplicity of beliefs and non-beliefs now present in our
society, a view which was ignored by the Education Reform Act
1988. Not all Christian groups agreed with the concept of Christian
collective worship. In the debate in the House of Lords on the Education Reform Bill, Lord Houghton expressed the long held view
of the non-conformists that such an amendment amounted to an
abdication by the churches to the state educational system, of their
duties and responsibilities.[41]

BIBLE READING AND SCHOOL PRAYER IN THE UNITED STATES

The difficulties presented by collective worship in England, and
particularly the effect on children of separating them into different
groups based on religious affiliation, has also been tackled by the
courts of the United States. Although schools in the United States
were considered secular institutions from the nineteenth century, the
practice of bible reading and prayer in schools was still widespread

---

[38] Some commentators postulate that the new provisions will make little difference to schools because although Christianity has been introduced, the Act
takes away the Christian emphasis by qualifying the requirements for worship
to be Christian (*i.e.* worship need only be *mainly* of a broadly Christian character). Such worship is not to be distinctively Christian or uniquely Christian,
but just to reflect a broad Christian character. See Hull, "Editorial" (Spring
1990) British Journal of Religious Education, Vol. 12, No.2. This argument is
difficult to sustain after the case of *Ruscoe and Dando* (1993; unreported). There
must, after all, be veneration of Jesus, which makes the worship uniquely
Christian.

[39] The analysis of SACRE reports for the year 1992 (National Curriculum Council)
indicates that only small numbers of children are being withdrawn. However, it
is not by any means clear that all schools are, as yet following the guidelines on
collective worship, and there have been more "determination" exempting
schools, or certain classes or groups of children from the requirements of s.7(1).

[40] Cmnd. 9453.

[41] Lord Houghton also pointed out that the Education Reform Act 1988 requires
everyone to pay for the teaching of Christianity whether or not they are in sympathy with what is being done, when the churches should be responsible for the
provision and funding of their own education.

until the middle of the twentieth century. According to a National Education Association survey in 1946[42] only eight superintendents of schools responded negatively to the question of whether bible reading was permitted in schools.[43] However, although bible reading was permitted, the teacher was not allowed to comment on the passages read.

There are a number of possible reasons that might explain the continuance of such seemingly religious practices. One of these reasons is akin to the compromise that was reached in England. Although schools in the United States were to be regarded as secular, the meaning of the word "secular" was really "non-sectarian". All religious practices that could be seen as sectarian were to be removed from schools, but the ethos of Christianity could remain. Stemming from this, the second reason for the continuance of bible reading and recitation of the Lord's prayer in schools was that the bible was regarded as fundamental to the beliefs of the country and was not regarded as specific to any sect, and therefore acceptable. For those parents who objected to such readings, the possibility of withdrawal of their children from this activity was permitted. Any further action to prevent such readings, such as challenges to the constitutionality of such readings were largely unsuccessful[44] until the case of *Engel v. Vitale* in 1963.[45]

Before 1963, the United States Supreme Court had never determined the constitutionality of Bible reading in the public schools;

---

[42] *The State and Sectarian Education*. The conclusions of this survey were supported by a later survey carried out by Professor Dierenfeld in 1961. He found that 41.74 per cent of the respondents answered in the affirmative to the question whether bible reading was conducted in their public school systems. See for more detail on the extent and nature of the practice of bible reading, Pfeffer, *Church, State and Freedom* (2nd ed., 1967), pp.436–466.

[43] Even New York which was listed as one of the states where bible reading was not practised had a bye-law of the New York City Board of Education providing that "regular assemblies" of all schools shall be opened by reading to the pupils a portion of the bible without comment.

[44] See, *e.g. Hackett v. Brooksville Graded School District* 120 Ky. 608. See also *Spiller v. Inhabitants of Woburn* 94 Mass 127 (1866). In this case it was successfully argued that bible reading and the recitation of the Lord's prayer was not religious but merely to quieten the children and prepare them for the school day. However, a child who refused to bow her head during the recitation of the Lord's prayer was expelled. See also *Donahoe v. Richards* 38 Me. 376 (1854) and *Board of Education of Cincinatti v. Minor* 23 Ohio St. 211 (1872).

[45] 18 Misc. 2d 659 (1959).

but it had, in effect, decided that the exclusion of the Bible from schools did not violate any constitutional right. [46]

In 1962, however, the United States Supreme Court was required to consider the issue of school "prayer". In 1951 the New York State Board of Regents acting in its official capacity recommended to all schools the following prayer:

"Almighty God, we acknowledge our dependence upon Thee, and we beg Thy blessings upon us, our parents, our teachers and our country." [47]

In 1958 the New Hyde Park Board of Education directed that the prayer be said aloud by each class at the beginning of the school day. The prayer was the subject of much objection; from the Lutherans and certain other Protestant sects because there was no mention of Christ, and by the Jews who had always supported the complete secularisation of public schools. But, it was welcomed by main line Protestants and the Catholics as a step in the right direction towards the reintroduction of religious education and prayer in schools. The use of the prayer was challenged by a group of parents in one of the schools where it was used. [48] The Supreme Court held in *Engel v. Vitale* [49] that the practice was unconstitutional and violated the first Amendment ban on the establishment of religion. According to Justice Black, writing the majority opinion, the New York programme was unconstitutional because it was a clearly religious activity:

"there can of course, be no doubt that New York's daily classroom invocation of God's blessing as prescribed in the Regent's prayer is a religious activity. It is a solemn avowal of divine faith and supplication for the blessings of the almighty".

The state laws requiring or permitting use of prayer, he continued, must be struck down:

---

[46] *Clithero v. Showwalter* 284 U.S. 573 (1930). The court dismissed for lack of a substantial Federal question, an appeal from a decision of the Supreme Court of the State of Washington, that refused to direct the State Superintendent of schools to institute Bible reading in the public schools.

[47] About 10 per cent of schools in the area adopted the prayer.

[48] The objecting parents were Jewish, Ethical Culturists, Unitarians and non-believers.

[49] 18 Misc. 2d 659 (1959).

"the constitutional prohibition against laws respecting an establishment of religion must at least mean that in this country it is no part of the business of government to compose official prayers for any group of the American people to recite as part of a religious program carried out by the government".

"The fact that the prayer was non-denominational and that students were under no compulsion to participate, and could excuse themselves from prayer, was irrelevant. No element of coercion is necessary to show a breach of the establishment clause."[50]

The decision in *Engel v. Vitale* was the subject of huge media interest, most of it critical. The accusation levelled at the court was that God had been taken out of the classroom! The fact that schools were supposedly secular was not mentioned by those critical of the judgment.[51]

Hard on the heels of the decision in *Engel v. Vitale*, the Supreme Court agreed to hear two other cases: *Abington Township School District v. Schempp*[52] concerning the constitutionality of Bible reading in schools, and *Murray v. Curlett*[53] which involved not only Bible reading, but also the recitation of the Lord's prayer. The two cases were decided together, with the Supreme Court finding that required recitation of the Lord's prayer or any other prayer was a violation of the Establishment Clause, as was devotional reading of the Bible. The test as to whether there has been a breach of the establishment clause was explained as follows:

" . . . what are the purpose and the primary effect of the enactment? If either is the advancement or inhibition of religion then the enactment

---

[50] For a discussion of the Establishment Clause see Chap. 1, p.12.

[51] Some of the comment against the case was vitriolic. The Jesuit weekly "America" was highly critical of the Jewish parents who had brought the action and also the American Civil Liberties Union and the various humanist organisations. It predicted a rise in anti-semitism and warned the Jews against action to remove the Lord's prayer and Bible reading from the schools. For an interesting discussion of media reaction see Pfeffer, *Church, State and Freedom* (2nd ed., 1967), pp.466–469.

[52] 374 U.S. 203 (1963). Unitarian parents brought this case and testified that literal reading of the Bible was contrary to their religious beliefs and teachings, but that they did not seek to have the children excused, because they feared that this would adversely affect the relationship between the child and the teacher.

[53] 374 U.S. 203 (1963). Mrs Murray, an avowed atheist, challenged a State statute that required public schools to start the day with "reading, without comment, of a chapter in the Holy Bible and/or the use of the Lord's prayer". The two cases were assigned to Justice Clark, a conservative Protestant from Texas. Concurring opinions were given by Justice Brennan (Catholic) and Justice Goldberg (Jewish).

exceeds the scope of legislative power as circumscribed by the constitution. That is to say that to withstand the strictures of the Establishment Clause there must be a secular legislative purpose and a primary effect that neither advances nor inhibits religion."

The action by the legislature was clearly a breach of the Establishment Clause, and the fact that the children had a right to be excused was again insufficient to remedy the defect. As in *Engel*, the court accepted that the element of coercion was irrelevant in relation to a breach of the Establishment Clause. The fact that the reading and prayer advanced religion and did not have a secular purpose was sufficient of itself to show a breach of the Establishment Clause. But did the statutes also breach the Free Exercise Clause?

"The free exercise clause . . . withdraws from legislative power, state and federal, the exertion of any restraint on the free exercise of religion. Its purpose is to secure religious liberty in the individual by prohibiting any invasions thereof by civil authority. Hence it is necessary in a free exercise clause for one to show the coercive effect of the enactment as it operates against him in the practice of his religion. The distinction between the two clauses is apparent—a violation of the free exercise clause is predicated on coercion while the establishment clause violation need not be so attended."

While the European Convention on Human Rights and the British courts and legislature see a right of withdrawal from collective worship or prayer as sufficient to protect the child's rights and that of the parents, this is insufficient for courts in the United States. If there were no right of excusal, and children were coerced into attending prayers which were religiously objectionable, such a policy would undoubtedly be a breach of the Free Exercise Clause and, if the purpose of the prayers was the advancement of religion, the Establishment Clause as well. But what of the situation where there is a policy of excusal?[54] The courts have never looked with

---

[54] Although the Supreme Court has never explicitly held that indirect pressure constitutes a violation of the establishment clause *per se*, nevertheless the cases support this and such pressure is heavily frowned upon. See Choper (1963) Minnesota Law Rev. 329 and (1962) 9 U.C.L.A. L. Rev. 500, n.25. See also Synagogue Council of America Report of the "Conference on Religious Education and the Public School" (1944), p. 26. Although a Jewish child was excused from Bible instruction, he was kept in a closed wardrobe while his classmates took part in the lesson.

favour on the fact that the child can be excused, as mitigation of the wrong done by introducing the religious exercises initially. They have taken the view that a right of excusal is insufficient, because if there is required prayer or Bible reading, there will be a subtle compulsion to attend, exercised on impressionable school children. It is also known that in fact, most children stay in class for religious exercises regardless of their personal views on the subject of religion.[55] As Justice Douglas pointed out in *Schempp*,[56] many small children, in spite of parental instruction, will not withdraw and risk being identified by their peers as "different" or as "odd-balls". Low rates of withdrawal of non-Christian children from essentially Christian collective worship are also found in England where there is a right of withdrawal.[57] Such rates of withdrawal are partly due to ignorance: many parents do not know of their right of withdrawal, or do not wish to exercise their right and thus single out their children as different.

Courts in the United States have recognised that a policy of exclusion or withdrawal does not prevent such programmes being divisive and discriminatory. In *People ex. rel Ring v. Board of Education*[58] the court noted that:

> "the exclusion of a pupil from part of the school exercises in which the rest of the school joins, separates him from his fellows, puts him in a class by himself, deprives him of his equality with the other pupils, subjects him to religious stigma and places him at a disadvantage in the school, which the law never contemplated."[59]

A similar approach was taken by the court in Wisconsin:

> "When, . . . a small minority of the pupils in the public school is excluded, for any cause, from a stated school exercise, particularly where such cause is apparent hostility to the Bible which a majority of

---

[55] See *State ex rel. Weiss v. District Board* 76 Wis. 177, 200, 44 N.W. 967 (1890). See also *North v. Board of Trustees* 137 Ill. 296, 27 N.E. 54 (1891).

[56] 374 U.S. 203 (1963).

[57] See the "Analysis of SACRE Reports" 1992.

[58] 245 Ill. 334 (1910).

[59] The Court held that, in this case the fact that the plaintiff's children could request to be excused from participation did not make the programme voluntary or remove it from the taint of unconstitutionality. In reaching such a decision the Court was, at that time, out of step with other state decisions, only a minority of which found that such religious observances were unconstitutional.

the other pupils have been taught to revere, from that moment the excluded pupil loses caste with his fellows, and is liable to be regarded with aversion and subjected to reproach and insult."[60]

In the Engel case[61] the United States Supreme Court made the same point: "When the power, prestige and financial support of government is placed behind a particular religious belief the indirect coercive pressure upon religious minorities to conform to the prevailing officially approved religion is plain".

Justice Clark, giving the majority opinion in *Schempp*,[62] endeavoured to reassure the United States that the court was not insisting upon a religion of secularism; nor did the holding in any way mean that the bible could never be taught in public schools for its literary or historic value. He pointed out that "the place of religion in our society is an exalted one" but warned that such an exalted and secure status was best preserved by relying on home and family, the churches, and individual hearts and minds, and that only bitter experiences resulted from government intrusion into matters of religion.

Public reaction to the decision was, on the whole, negative and compliance with the finding of unconstitutionality was slow and uneven,[63] but inevitable under the threat of judicial decrees and contempt orders. Nevertheless, the problem of prayer in the public schools has not disappeared, but has evolved into a major and divisive issue in contemporary American politics. Opinion polls in the 1980s, demonstrated continued public dissatisfaction with the court's firm position. President Reagan supported two proposed constitutional amendments,[64] both of which failed to pass the Senate. Other attempts to overturn *Schempp* continued until the Republicans lost control of the Senate in 1986.[64a]

---

[60] *State ex rel. Weiss v. District Board.* 76 Wis. 177 (1890).

[61] 370 U.S. 421 (1962).

[62] 374 U.S. 203 (1963).

[63] Particularly in the south. See, *e.g. Dolbeare v. Hammond, The School Prayer Decision* (1971) and Muir, *Prayer in the Public Schools* (1967).

[64] The First Amendment proposed "that nothing in the constitution should be construed to prohibit individual or group prayer in public schools or other public institutions". The second, less radical proposal concentrated on silent prayer: "nothing in this constitution shall be construed to prohibit individual or group silent prayer or reflection in public schools".

[64a] There have been renewed attempts at constitutional change in 1995. The Republicans intended to introduce a constitutional amendment for a congressional vote on July 4. However, at the time of going to press, the proposed amendment had hit legal and political obstacles, and an agreement on wording had not been reached.

Shortly after the Senate hearings, the Supreme Court heard the case of *Wallace v. Jaffree*.[65] In 1978 the State of Alabama introduced a statute which provided that public schools should have a daily minute of silence "for meditation". In 1981 the words "voluntary prayer" were added to the law. This additional phrase was challenged for unconstitutionality. The Supreme Court declared that the 1981 revised law was invalid as it constituted a violation of the Establishment Clause. In a six to three judgment Justice Stevens concluded that the State failed to assert any secular purpose. The addition in the 1981 statute of the phrase "or voluntary prayer" amounted to an endorsement and promotion by the State of a religion, and a particular religious practice. The State's purpose in passing the 1981 legislation was deemed to be purely religious and hence the law was held unconstitutional.[66] The majority pointed out that a mere moment of silence during the school day, particularly at the start of the day, was perfectly acceptable, and that such a moment could be used for voluntary prayer should a pupil so wish.[67]

It is plausible to argue that a moment of silence, officially sponsored with a secular purpose by the public schools could, nonetheless, still advance religion in ways that could collide with the Establishment Clause. School children may have difficulty determining exactly what they are meant to do during the moment of silence; if the majority of students opt to pray, there may be a perceived approval of that activity by a teacher supervising the silence, and the problem of pressure to conform to the perceived norm may rise again. Several justices in earlier cases acknowledged the indirect or subtle pressure that works upon children—the pressure to conform. Justice Frankfurter explained this rather bluntly when he wrote "the law of imitation operates, and non-conformity is not an

---

[65] 472 U.S. 38 (1985). Initially three Alabama statutes were challenged, the 1978 and 1981 statutes mentioned above, and one which provided that teachers could lead all willing students in group oral recital of a specified prayer that was set out in the statute. The Supreme Court summarily upheld the invalidation of this statute.

[66] This decision led to a debate between Edwin Meese, President Reagan's Att.-Gen. and Justices Brennan and Stevens. Meese argued against the interpretation of the Establishment Clause, as well as the view of the Supreme Court that the First Amendment is applicable to the states. Such an attack by the Attorney-General against the Supreme Court is highly unusual.

[67] Around half of the states passed moment of silence laws in the 1980s. See Note, "Unconstitutionality of State Statutes: Authorizing Moments of Silence in the Public Schools" (1983) 96 Harv. L.R. 1874.

outstanding characteristic of children".[68] Studies have shown that students unwilling to participate in released time programmes testified about pressure upon them to participate,[69] and parents instructing their children not to participate in voluntary school prayer have expressed fear that their children would be derided as "un-American".[70] It may well be that officially sponsored moments of silence in the public schools could generate a similar coercive impact on confused or reluctant children.

CONCLUSION

The English legislature has reinforced the place of collective worship in schools, and required that such worship be "wholly or mainly of a broadly Christian character". Courts in the United States have moved in the other direction, rigorously preserving secularism in their schools. Although there has been public pressure for change, the Supreme Court has remained intransigent, keeping all prayer, of whatever religious group, out of the public schools. The reason for their insistence on secularism is well explained by Justice Frankfurter in *McCollum v. Board of Education*:

> "the public school is at once the symbol of our democracy and the most pervasive means for promoting our common destiny. In no activity of the state is it more vital to keep out divisive forces than in its schools, to avoid confusing, not to say fusing, what the Constitution sought to keep strictly apart."[71]

In the religiously pluralistic society of the United States, such an approach is seen as both necessary to promote democracy, to preserve fairness, and to ensure that no religious grouping becomes dominant, and potentially prejudicial to others. It is in this area that establishment of the Church of England has had particular impact. For England and its multi-faith community, the role of the Established Church has prevented an equality of balance between religions in the state run schools. Instead, the primacy of Christianity

---

[68] *McCollum v. Board of Education* 333 U.S. 203 at 227 (1948).
[69] See Pfeffer, *Church, State and Freedom* (2nd ed., 1967), pp.356–366 and Jesse H. Choper, "Religion in the public school; A proposed constitutional standard" (1963) 47 Minnesota Law Review 388, 396–7.
[70] *Abington School District v. Schempp* 374 U.S. at 208 n.3 (1963).
[71] 33 U.S. 203 (1948).

is enshrined in legislation. The English approach is likely to lead to greater pressure by the religious minorities for their own schools, the end result of which would be religious segregation of children. This would not be a consequence looked on favourably by those who sought the introduction of specifically Christian worship, but inevitable if parents see worship alien to their own beliefs being promoted as the norm within the school.

Religious Education

Religious education, a compulsory subject for all English school children, is totally absent from the school curriculum in the United States. While members of the House of Lords in discussing the Education Reform Bill in 1987 were disturbed by what they saw as the deliberate flouting of the requirement of religious education in many schools in England, courts in the United States have concentrated on ensuring that religious education is kept out of public schools.

Although England has been unclear about the purpose of religious education for children in the past, there appears to be little support for the American solution to religious differences: that of removing religious education from schools altogether. The Religious Education Council in response to an earlier discussion paper,[72] found a wide range of different viewpoints as to why children should receive religious education. One view was that religion should be taught because it is true and beneficial to pupils, another was that parents want their children taught Christian values and morals. A further perspective was expressed by those who felt that society should be underpinned by a specific ethos, and that this is provided by the Christian religion. A rather different, and interesting, slant on the need for religious education was provided by those who believed that such education is needed to enable pupils to live in a more open and pluralistic society.

This latter view was examined more thoroughly in the Report by the Swann Committee[73] examining the Education of Ethnic

---

[72] "What Future for the Agreed Syllabus Now?" (1977), Religious Education Council.

[73] *Report of the Committee of Inquiry into the Education of Children from Ethnic Minority Groups*, Cmnd. 9453.

Minority Children. The members were of the opinion that one of the fundamental aims of religious education should be to broaden the horizons of all pupils, so that they have a greater understanding and appreciation of the diversity of values and lifestyles now present in society.[74] The Committee viewed such education as necessary to tackle the roots of racism, which lay in regarding groups of people as strange and inferior. The report gives three reasons why religious education should continue to be a part of a child's school curriculum.

First, children need to learn and have an understanding about the nature of belief, of different belief systems and how these have affected human experience. Secondly, it is necessary for the understanding of the motivation, values and outlooks of people from a range of religious backgrounds. Thirdly, it provides moral education. It develops consideration for other people, respect for moral and legal obligations, and concern for fairness and justice in society as a whole.

Whatever the purpose of religious education, the extent to which such teaching might be acceptable to minority faith parents, depends not only on the content of the course, but also the way in which it is taught. The Schools Council Report[75] defined three main approaches in England. First, there is the "confessional" or dogmatic approach to teaching, which assumes that the aim of religious education is indoctrination. Second, there is the anti-dogmatic approach which views religious education as an academic exercise, both objective and dispassionate. The National Secular Society, for example, suggests that the study of religion on these terms should be regarded as part of the history syllabus. Last, there is the phenomenological or undogmatic approach. This sees the aim of religious education as the promotion of understanding. It uses the tools of scholarship in order to enter into an emphatic experience of the faith of individuals and groups. It does not seek to promote any one religious viewpoint, but it recognises that the study of religion must transcend the merely informative.

It would be fair to say that the approach of religious education laid down by the framers of the 1944 Education Act could be

---

[74] The vast majority of ethnic minority children are from non-Christian cultures.
[75] "Religious Education in Secondary Schools" (1971) Schools Council Working Paper 36.

largely viewed as confessionalist. While the Act did not specify that religious instruction should be explicitly Christian, it is clear from the assurance given by the Earl of Selborne in the House of Lords that this was the intention.[76]

The Education Act 1944 covering England and Wales provided that religious instruction[77] was to be given in every county and voluntary school.[78] The Education Reform Act 1988 re-enacts and reinforces this requirement.[79] Religious education is part of the curriculum which is provided to all maintained schools,[80] but is not to be regarded as part of the National Curriculum. The effect of this is that while religious education is a compulsory course, it is not subject to nationally prescribed attainment targets, programmes of study, and assessment.

For children in local education authority maintained county and voluntary schools, religious education must be in accordance with a locally agreed syllabus.[81] The syllabus is to be drafted by a confer-

---

[76] See *Hansard*, H.L., 5th Series, Vol. 132, Col 366, June 21, 1944. The present aim is to develop pupils' knowledge, understanding and awareness of Christianity, as the predominant religion in Great Britain, and the other principal religions represented in the country; to encourage respect for those holding different beliefs; and to help promote pupils' spiritual, moral, cultural and mental development. DFE Circular 1/94 on religious education and collective worship, para. 16.

[77] Although the term used was instruction, schools came to refer to the subject as religious education, and so it is termed in the Education Reform Act 1988.

[78] These county schools were formerly called board schools, then provided schools, funded by the local education authority, as opposed to schools funded by a voluntary society (nearly always a religious body.)

[79] See Education Reform Act 1988, s.2(1)(a) and Education Reform Act 1988, s.8(1), subject to the exceptions in s.9. The Education Act 1993 changes the requirements for religious education in respect of certain grant maintained schools.

[80] Essentially all those who receive any public funds.

[81] See Education Act 1944, s.26(1). Grant maintained schools equivalent to county schools, or which were formerly voluntary controlled schools, may follow the locally agreed syllabus of any LEA in England and Wales, so long as the syllabus meets the 1988 Act's requirements. For grant maintained schools that were former voluntary aided or special agreement schools, or are newly established under s.49 of the 1993 Act with provision for religious education, the religious education to be offered is that determined by the governors in accordance with the trust deed or (where such provision is not made by a trust deed) in line with practice before the school became grant maintained, or for a new school, with the approved statement. Education Act 1993, s.140(2), but see s.140(3) and (5). Those grant maintained schools which have trust deeds providing for religious education, may provide religious education in accordance with the deed. See para. 23 of the DFE Circular 1/94 for provisions relating to voluntary aided and special agreement schools.

ence[82] convened by each local authority comprising five committees each with one vote.[83]

The original syllabuses drawn up by the Church of England and the free churches were intended to define an area in which positive teaching about Christianity could be given without incurring the charge of proselytising.[84] They contained material which had been agreed by the churches as representing common Christian ground. By the provisions of the 1944 Education Act, the syllabuses did not include formulae distinctive of any particular denomination.[85] The intention of the syllabus was to nurture children in the Christian faith, an approach taken by the local authorities over the next 30 years.[86]

Such an approach became inappropriate as the numbers of non-Christian children in the schools began to grow. In 1975 Birmingham drew up a new syllabus which looked, not only at a range of other faiths, but also at other life stances, such as humanism and Marxism. The new form of syllabus was controversial, and the issue of whether its approach diverged so far from the intention of the 1944 Act so as to be in breach of the provisions was raised in Parliament in 1976. It was suggested then that the syllabus should be declared illegal, or the provisions concerning syllabuses should be repealed in order to encourage other authorities to cater for their multi-faith populations. The government took the view that since the syllabus was prepared in accordance with the procedures laid down in the Act, and since the letter, if not the spirit, of the Act did not explicitly require a syllabus to be Christian orientated, the syllabus was legal. Following this a number of other

---

[82] In order to prepare a syllabus, Sched. 5 of the 1944 Act provides the local authority should convene a conference. The DFE Circular 1/94 and annex F lays down who shall be represented on the conference, and the procedures to be followed in reaching a decision on the syllabus, which should be unanimous. In the event of failure to reach agreement, the Secretary of State for Education shall appoint a body of persons to draw up such a syllabus.

[83] Education Act 1944, Sched. 5 as amended by Sched. 1, para. 7 of the Education Reform Act 1988 and the Education Act 1993, s.147.

[84] Which was offensive to the free churches, and largely carried out by the Church of England.

[85] It is interesting to note that the Education Reform Act 1988 provides that this is not to be taken as prohibiting the study of such formulas or catechisms within the syllabus.

[86] An approach that can be described as confessionalist.

authorities adopted a similar broad syllabus, using a phenomenological teaching method.

The Education Reform Act 1988 clearly intended that religious education should become, once more, Christian education. Section 8(3) of the Act provides that religious education:

> "shall reflect the fact that the religious traditions in Great Britain are in the main Christian whilst taking account of the teaching and practices of the other principal religions represented in Great Britain".

Will multi-faith syllabuses taking a phenomenological approach satisfy the requirements of section 8(3)? There has been no legal interpretation as yet of the phrase "in the main". It is questionable whether this requires that the majority of the teaching on a religious education course should be Christian, or merely that the course should acknowledge the primacy of Christian traditions in England.[87] Local education authorities have been able to continue working to their old, multi-faith syllabus, unless the syllabus has been deemed unsatisfactory, or there has been an application for a review.[88] Where either of these situations occurs, any new syllabus drawn up by the syllabus conference must comply with the requirements of section 8(3).[89] Very few local authorities have reviewed their old syllabuses and many are still working to a syllabus which is multi-faith, five years after the passing of the Education Reform Act. Such syllabuses do not, of course, reflect, as section 8(3) requires, that the religious traditions in Great Britain

---

[87] Colin Hart in his pamphlet, *From Acts to Action* (Christian and Tyneside Schools Action Research Workers Trust, 1991) points out that in Great Britain around 79–80 per cent of people give their religious allegiance to Christianity. He argues therefore that the syllabus should be at least 79–80 per cent Christian if it is to comply with the fact that religious traditions of Great Britain are in the main Christian.

[88] There are a number of reasons why syllabuses have not been reviewed. The Gloucester SACRE report for 1989/90 stated that the agreed syllabus met the required balance between Christianity and the other religions, and thus there was no need for a review. The London Borough of Barnet in their 89/90 report also decided to leave the syllabus untouched in view of the fact that there had been no application to re-convene a syllabus conference.

[89] Education Act 1944, Sched. 5, para.13(3) as substituted by Education Reform Act 1988, Sched. 1. Under para.13(4) if the conference are unable to reach unanimous agreement, or it appears that the authority have failed to give effect to the unanimous recommendation of the conference, the Secretary of State shall proceed in accordance with paras. 10 and 11 of Sched. 5.

are in the main Christian. The 1993 Education Act[90] seeks to resolve the reluctance on the part of local education authorities to move away from their flexible, open, sometimes multi-faith syllabuses, by requiring that any local education authority that has not adopted a new syllabus since September 1988 must convene an agreed syllabus conference for that purpose by April 1, 1995.

Attempts had previously been made to change old syllabuses not in line with section 8(3) by using the complaints procedure established by section 23 of the Education Reform Act 1988. This avenue has been used to challenge what was seen as the inadequate focus on Christianity in the agreed syllabus used by schools in the London Borough of Ealing in 1990. The syllabus in question did not require the teaching of any specific aspect of Christianity. The complaint was rejected initially by the local education authority, but upheld by the Secretary of State to whom the parent subsequently appealed. The syllabus concerned was withdrawn and a conference was established to agree on another syllabus which would meet the requirements of section 8(3).[91] This approach was also used in Tyneside, again with success and resulted in a change of syllabus.[92] However, such actions should no longer be necessary since the Education Act 1993 provisions. It is possible though, that religious pressure groups will still complain to cause another review of the syllabus, or to influence the content of a locally agreed syllabus when it is being reviewed.

Section 8(3) does not, of course, indicate to the local authority exactly what proportion of the syllabus should be concerned with Christianity. Faced with the possibility of having a syllabus rejected because of the lack of specific Christian content, some conferences, have decided to leave the content of the religious education programme to the individual school, so they may have greater flex-

---

[90] Amending the Education Act 1944, Sched. 5.

[91] The complaint was reported in the *Daily Telegraph* April 26, 1990, *The Times* June 6, 1991. House of Commons Official Report (*Hansard*) June 8, 1990, Col 925, *The Times* April 4, 1991.

[92] A parent-teacher group called Christians and Tyneside Schools (CATS) conducted a campaign against the proposed religious education syllabus for Newcastle, on the basis that the draft syllabus did "not reflect mainly Christian traditions" and that there was a blurring of distinctions between faiths. Local political support was sought, coverage was given in the local media and signatures of support gathered. The result of the concerted campaign was an increase in the Christian content of the syllabus with the introduction of the Bible as the major resource at every stage.

ibility in meeting their needs. The Oldham conference[93] pointed out in their report that an agreed syllabus for religious education should not be a list of contents to be taught, but rather an agreed list of aims to be worked towards and realised through the curriculum content. Such an approach, intended to give maximum flexibility to schools with a sizeable number of minority pupils, may however, fall foul of legal advice issued to all Directors of Education in England by the Department of Education and Science[94]:

" . . . the Secretary of State is not satisfied that an agreed syllabus could fully meet the requirements of Section 8(3) unless it gives sufficient guidance to the reader, and thus the teacher, as to what Christian traditions, learning, teaching and festivals are going to be taught".

The Oldham conference approach is unlikely to satisfy the guidance in the Circular on religious education[95] which provides that the syllabus must be written so as to ensure that teaching which follows the syllabus will be in accordance with the Act.

The DFE circular on religious education points out that syllabuses must not be designed to convert pupils, or to urge a particular religion or religious belief on pupils.[96] But, Christianity should predominate. In determining the extent to which children should be taught other religions, the circular advises schools to take into account the school population in order to minimise withdrawals from religious education.[97] Where the children are from predominantly Christian backgrounds, more Christianity should be taught, although enough time should be given to other religions to enable them to be taught effectively. It appears from the circular that an essentially phenomenological or undogmatic approach is to be taken to the teaching of religion.[98] The syllabus should extend beyond the provision of information about religions and cover wider areas of morality, including the way in which people's religious beliefs and practices affect their understanding of moral

---

[93] Report of the syllabus Conference 1989 for Oldham Metropolitan Borough Council. Oldham in Lancashire has a sizeable religious minority population.
[94] Letter to the Chief Education Officers of English LEAs, DES, March 18, 1991.
[95] DFE Circular 1/94, para. 33.
[96] DFE Circular 1/94, para. 32.
[97] See DFE Circular 1/94, para. 35.
[98] For an explanation of this approach, see p.295.

issues and the consequences their behaviour has upon the family and society.[99]

Whether the changes to religious education brought about by the Education Reform Act are acceptable to religious minority parents, or to atheists, remains to be seen. Much depends on whether schools seek to revert to a more confessionalist style of teaching in relation to Christianity, or whether the focus will remain on the phenomenological approach—teaching children about different religions and the significance of their practices in order to further understanding.[1] Parents retain the right[2] to ask that the child be "wholly or partly excused" from the religious instruction provided. If the parent exercising this right wishes the child to receive religious instruction of a kind not provided at the school, and not provided at a convenient maintained school, the pupil can be withdrawn from the school to receive instruction elsewhere, provided that this does not interfere with the attendance of a child, or at the beginning or end of a school day.[3]

Parents may also request, under Education Act 1944, section 26, that a pupil receives religious education according to the tenets of their own particular religious denomination. This can only be done where the local authority is assured that the cost of such education will not fall on them. In schools where there are a sizeable number of children of one particular minority faith, it will be up to the parents to organise and fund such education. Its provision may provide the school with difficult organisational problems, but if suit-

---

[99] See DFE Circular 1/94, para. 36. Religious education is not part of the national curriculum or the subject of a nationally determined syllabus. To help syllabus conferences, the School Curriculum and Assessment Authority, at the government's behest, produced two model syllabuses in early 1994. The first is structured on the knowledge and understanding of what it means to be a member of a faith community, while the second is structured on the key beliefs of different religions.

[1] The approach of the Church of England is not always clear. Dr Graham Leonard, the Bishop of London in a worrying comment in the *Daily Telegraph* September 23, 1989 stated:

"the general attitude of the 1960s, that you presented a variety of faiths and allowed the child to make up its mind . . .. The implication was that all religions were of equal validity. This will not now be the case. Children will be taught that Christianity is our faith. That is one of the fundamental changes we have secured."

[2] Previously found in the Education Act 1944. Now s.9(3) (b) and (c).

[3] Education Reform Act 1988, s.9(4).

able personnel can be found to teach at no cost to the school it is permissible under the Act.[4]

While it was suggested by many fighting for the introduction of more specific teaching on Christianity in the syllabus, that leaders of other religions supported their fight, such support was misleading. While neither the leader of the Islamic or Jewish communities favoured multi-faith teaching,[5] neither did they favour their children being taught about Christianity. Lord Thorneycroft commented in the House of Lords[6] in a complete misunderstanding of the minority position:

> "with the West Indians clamouring for it, with the Moslems praying for it, and with the Jews urging it in this House, what case is there for not having Christian education in the schools?"

The lack of support for teaching Muslim children anything about Christianity is clearly shown by the Director of the Muslim Educational Trust,[7] who points out that withdrawal of children from religious education is the absolute minimum that a Muslim parent should do.[8] While accepting that withdrawal in schools where Muslim children are very much in the minority can be difficult, nevertheless the Muslim Trust recommends that parents should ask the headteacher or the local education authority if a parent can be sent into the school to teach the children, and that the children should be allowed to study suitable books. In a letter to the then

---

[4] Again, it could be argued that this is financially discriminatory. See Thornberry, *International law and the Rights of Minorities* (1991) p.119, and above at p.283.

[5] See the comments made by Lord Jacobovitz, the former Chief Rabbi, in the debate in the House of Lords. However, see "The Teaching of Islam in British Schools: An Agreed Statement", published by the Islamic Academy, Cambridge 1985. The statement is in favour of multi-faith teaching, provided that R.E. lessons do not alienate children from Islam, do not destroy their faith or make them sceptical about their religion. Teachers should be concerned to help the child learn what it is to have a faith, and seek to help children to understand a religion from the point of view of its adherents—the phenomenological approach.

[6] House of Lords Official Report (*Hansard*) May 3, 1988, Col.514.

[7] The E.R.A. 1988. "Compulsory Christian Collective Worship and Christian Religious Education in Schools. What can Muslims Do?", Ghulam Sarwar, Director, The Muslim Educational Trust 1989.

[8] The pamphlet provides a draft letter for parents wishing to withdraw children. The author, far from wanting Muslim children taught about Christianity points out that to allow their children to join in Christian worship and Christian religious education, praying to Jesus and learning about their Trinity, would be to allow the children to commit the awesome sin of *Shirk*, associating others with Allah. This is the worse thing a Muslim can do.

Secretary of State for Education after the introduction of the amendments relating to religious education in the House of Lords, the director of the Muslim Trust stated that, while Muslims were in favour of the primacy of Christianity in religious education for Christians, Muslims wanted explicit provisions in the then Education Reform Bill for the minority faiths to pursue their own forms of education, and a declaration of intent that Christianity would not be imposed on non-Christians. On behalf of the Muslim community, the Director asked that the Education Act 1944, section 26, be amended to allow local education authorities to facilitate and meet the cost of religious education for children of minority faiths. What is envisaged here, and amongst many of those minority religious organisations that supported the introduction of a more specific Christian content to the religious education syllabus, was that this would be for Christian children, and would add impetus to their claim for separate religious education for their children.

What the Education Reform Act 1988 may have achieved is simply more polarisation. It may cause more parents to withdraw their children from religious education, and rather than achieve its aim of teaching all children the Christian cultural nature of English society, may leave those children with no knowledge of Christian traditions at all. This is in direct contravention of the recommendations of the Swann report,[9] and sits poorly with the United Nations Convention on the Rights of the Child which requires in Article 29 that education be directed towards, *inter alia*, the development of respect for the child's cultural identity as well as respect for the national values of the country in which the child is living. The Education Reform Act 1988 may have missed the chance to provide children with a wide knowledge of the main religions in the country, and to develop tolerance and respect not only for their own religions, but also those religions different from their own, but adhered to by large numbers of their fellow citizens. The government, by its reforms, can be accused of promoting ignorance rather than tolerance.

In the United States, with its secular education, the difficulties of religious education should not be an issue, as the provision of con-

---

[9] *Report of the Committee of Inquiry into the Education of Children from Ethnic Minority Groups*, Cmnd. 9453.

fessional religious instruction would violate the Establishment Clause. But the question of whether there can be any elective religious instruction or non-confessionalist teaching about religion remains. An attempt was made in a number of states to allow children to receive religious instruction through "released time" programmes. Essentially, children would be released from their secular studies to attend religious instruction of their choice, with those who did not wish to attend any form of religious instruction being excused. In the case of *McCollum*[10] in 1948, interested members of the Jewish, Catholic and Protestant faiths had formed a voluntary association called the Champaign Council on Religious Education. The Council obtained permission from the Board of Education to offer weekly classes in religious instruction where parents had signed cards requesting that their children attend.[11] The Council employed the teachers at no expense to the school authorities, but the instructors were approved and supervised by the Superintendent of schools. The classes were carried out by Protestant teachers, Catholic priests and a Jewish rabbi, although by the time the programme was challenged there had been no Jewish classes for a number of years. Classes took place in the school building. Those students not taking part in the classes went elsewhere in the school to pursue their secular studies. An avowed atheist challenged the practice as a breach of the Establishment Clause and the Supreme Court agreed. The court found that released time programmes used the coercive power of the school compulsory attendance laws to increase attendance at religious instruction.[12] There was little for non-attenders to do while the classes went on, they were not allowed to leave the school premises, and were, therefore, more inclined to attend the classes. Justice Black found:

"The . . . facts . . . show the use of tax-supported property for religious

---

[10] *People of the State of Illinois ex rel. McCollum v. Board of Education of School District No. 71 Champaign County*, 333 U.S. 203, 68 S. Ct. 461, 92 L.Ed. 649.

[11] As Galanter points out in "Religious Freedoms in the United States: A Turning Point" (1966) Wisconsin Law Review 216, the children were not free to decide whether or not to go to the classes, or which religion's classes to attend. Not one of the Justices suggested that it was other than the parent's prerogative to make such a decision.

[12] It is not necessary, however, that there be any coercion on the part of the school for there to be a breach of the Establishment Clause. See *Abington Township School District v. Schempp* and *Murray v. Curlett* (heard together) 374 U.S. 203, 83 S.Ct. 1560, 10 L. Ed. 2d 844 (1963).

instruction and the close co-operation between the school authorities and the religious council in promoting religious education. The operation of the state's compulsory education system thus assists and is integrated with the program of religious instruction carried on by separate religious sects. Pupils compelled by law to go to school for secular education are released in part from their legal duty upon the condition that they attend the religious classes. This is beyond all question a utilization of the tax-established and tax-supported public school system to aid religious groups to spread their faith. And it falls squarely under the ban of the first Amendment. This is not separation of Church and State."

This decision, as with the school prayer decision of *Engel v. Vitale*[13], caused a great deal of protest, particularly from Protestant and Catholic organisations who once again claimed that the decision promoted secularism as the cost of Christianity. They also claimed that the decision manifested a hostility to religion, that the framers of the Constitution had never envisaged. The intention of the framers was not to bar governmental aid to religion, but only to forbid preferential treatment of one sect over another. Four years later, in *Zorach v. Clauson*[14] a different form of "released time" programme was considered by the court, known "as dismissed time". The difference in this case was that children were released from school, at the request of the parents, to attend religious classes off school premises. Those not released stayed behind in school. The churches made weekly reports to the schools, including an attendance record. The programme was challenged on the basis that there was really no difference between the programmes. It was argued that the school was lending its weight and influence to the religious instruction programme; public school teachers policed it, keeping tabs on students who were released; the classroom activities came to a halt while the released students were absent; the school was a crutch on which the churches were leaning for support in their religious training; and without the co-operation of the school, this programme, just like the one in *McCollum*, would be futile and ineffective. The Supreme Court accepted that this case did not involve any discussion of free exercise, but rested entirely on whether the programme was a breach of the Establishment Clause. They found that, unlike the *McCollum* case, there was no breach of

---

[13] 18 Misc. 2d 659 (1959).
[14] 343 U.S. 306, 72 S.Ct. 679, 96 L. Ed. 954 (1952) [Case No. 3].

the Establishment Clause. The fact that the children went outside school to receive their religious education was all important. Here the public schools did no more than accommodate their schedules to a programme of outside religious instruction.[15] Other dismissed time cases have also subsequently been upheld,[16] provided that no credits are given for participation in such programmes.

It is difficult to see a real distinction between *McCollum* and *Zorach* particularly as in both cases, a part of the school day is being used for religious education. Whether this takes place on or off the premises, it is nevertheless taking place during the school day, lending the official approval of the school to the programmes, and discriminating between different groups of children. Some writers believe that even dismissed time programmes put pressure on children to attend, a pressure specifically disapproved of in *Engel v. Vitale* and other cases.[17] It would appear that there is no reason why children could not attend religious education after school has finished. Such a compromise according to Justice Jackson, giving a dissenting judgment, was rejected by the advocates of released time, because they believed that if they made attendance totally voluntary, many students would opt not to receive any religious instruction. Accordingly, he found that the state used "its compulsory education laws to help religious sects get attendants presumably too unenthusiastic to go unless moved to do so by the pressure of this state machinery."

It is instructive to note that the need for religious education in schools grew out of the perceived failure of the Sunday schools to reach a wide enough group of children. As Justice Frankfurter noted in his concurring opinion in *McCollum*:

"Out of these inadequate efforts evolved a week-day church school, held on one or more afternoons a week after the close of the public school. But children continued to be children; they wanted to play when school

---

[15] Some political scientists and historians explain the *Zorach* decision as an aspect of the strong anti-communist and hence pro-religious stance of the nation in 1952. See Pfeffer, *Religious Freedom*, (1977) at p. 75.

[16] *State ex rel. Holt v. Thompson* 66 Wis. 2d 659, 225 N.W.2d 678 (1975) and *Smith v. Smith* 523 F 2d 121 (4th Cir. 1975). But see *Fisher v. Clackamus City School District* 507 P. 2d 839 (Ore. App. 1973).

[17] 370 U.S. 421 (1962). See also Pfeffer, *Church, State and Freedom* (2nd ed., 1967), pp. 356–366, and Jesse Choper, "Religion in Public Schools: A proposed Constitutional Standard" (1963) 47 Minnesota law Review, 388, 396–7. For earlier discussion of whether the existence of religious classes puts pressure on children to attend, see pp.290–293.

was out, particularly when other children were free to do so. Church leaders decided that if the weekday church school was to succeed, a way had to be found to give the child his religious education during what the child conceived to be his 'business hours'."

It was pointed out by Justice Clark, giving the majority opinion in *Schempp*,[18] that schools were not totally barred from offering Bible classes, providing such courses were "secular". A course could be offered on the Bible or religion, as part of a programme of education, if taught in a purely objective way. Such a course would be acceptable and would not violate the First Amendment. The requirement of "objectivity" may, however, cause difficulty. In *Hall v. School Commissioners of Conecuh County*[19] the fifth circuit Court of Appeals disapproved of a Bible literature course because of the viewpoint from which the course was taught—"essentially a Christian religious perspective and within that a fundamentalist and/or evangelical doctrine". Although the teacher was fully certificated (and an active Baptist Minister) and testified that he used a recognised secular teaching guide, the court found that his approach and examination, which stressed rote learning of the Bible, were not consistent with the guide, and violated the Establishment Clause.[20]

An earlier series of decisions, show that courts will permit courses about religion, but only if certain criteria as to form and content are satisfied to keep instruction secular, rather than sectarian.[21] Ensuring secularity is not an easy task. Thus, it is permissible to teach about the fall of Jericho for its historical value, or the Parable of the Talents to compare its story telling ability with that of Aesop's fables, or to show that a student's talents grow only as they are used. But, it is impermissible to teach about Belshazzar's Feast, Lot's wife being turned to stone, or the destruction of Sodom and Gomorrah, if the implication is that God punishes the wicked.[22] In *Crockett v. Sorenson*,[23] the court added a further requirement. While

---

[18] 374 U.S. 203 (1963).

[19] 656 F. 2d 999 (5th Cir., 1981).

[20] The course violated the Establishment Clause test as its main purpose was the promotion of fundamentalist Christian beliefs.

[21] 468 F.Supp. 133 (E.D. Tenn. 1979) (Wiley 1); 474 F. Supp. 525 (E.D. Tenn. 1980) (Wiley II); 497 F. Supp. 390 (E.D. Tenn.1980) (Wiley III).

[22] For greater detail see *Wiley v. Franklin* 497 F. Supp. 390 (1980).

[23] 568 F.Supp. 1422 (1983).

a constitutionally acceptable Bible study class might be regarded as a purely secular course, nevertheless it was still possible that there would be pupils who would find such a course offended their sincere religious beliefs, and who would claim that attendance at such a course would violate their free exercise rights. The court felt it would be oppressive and constitutionally unacceptable to require a child to enrol in a Bible teaching class when the very subject matter being taught violated religious beliefs. Therefore, to be constitutional, any such course should be optional. Children who chose not to take the course should be offered a reasonable alternative course.

It is very unlikely that these will be the last cases before the court. The line between acceptable and unacceptable Bible courses or religion courses is so very thin, and so difficult to define, that slipping over the line from constitutional to unconstitutional will be difficult to avoid.

CONCLUSION

Establishment or non-establishment appears to make little difference as far as private religious schools are concerned. Both England and the United States, in line with international instruments, are prepared to allow parents and religious communities to establish and run their own schools, subject only to light, arguably too light, regulation.

In State schools in England, however, the establishment of the Church of England has had a significant and continuing impact. The effect of establishment has not been to preserve Anglicanism *per se* in schools, but to preserve Christianity. Thus, collective worship and religious education are to be predominantly Christian in nature. While the specific reintroduction of Christian worship and education through the Education Reform Act 1988 may satisfy a number of parents, for others it will be in direct contradiction to their religious beliefs. It is difficult to justify the introduction of worship which is to be "wholly or mainly of a broadly Christian character" in State schools. While the intention of the Secretary of State is that all pupils should be able to take part in such collective worship, it is unlikely in the light of the *Ruscoe* and *Dando* case and the new Circular issued by the Department for Education, that such worship would be acceptable to non-Christians. Withdrawal of children, or resentment at having to participate in worship which does not reflect their beliefs must inevitably cause conflict and divisions in schools. It is, indeed, difficult to find any justification for daily collective worship of such a nature.

It is, however, highly debatable whether England should follow the United States and keep religious education out of schools altogether. While, denomination based, confessionalist religious education within schools causes divisions between children, religious education taught from a phenomenological approach, and covering a number of religions, has its own educational justification. Indeed, a total lack of religious education brings its own problems. Without any education on religion, children will find it difficult to learn of each other's beliefs and the need to understand and be tolerant of those who follow a different religion. The views of the Swann Committee[24] are perhaps pertinent even in another continent. The members of the Committee saw a value in phenomenological religious education, which was a greater understanding and appreciation of the diversity of values and lifestyles within society, the broadening of horizons of all pupils, and perhaps, most importantly, for the United States, they viewed such education as necessary to tackle the roots of racism. If the introduction of some form of religious education is constitutionally too difficult for the states, an acceptable compromise might be a course in human rights education. If the aim of a religious education course is tolerance and the appreciation of the rights and needs of others, then such a course might provide a very viable alternative. Such teaching has already been tried and been found useful as providing "value education and broadening horizons".[25]

---

[24] *Report of the Committee of Inquiry into the Education of Children from Ethnic Minority Groups*, Cmnd. 9453.
[25] Patricia Dye, *Active Learning for Human Rights in Intermediate and High Schools in The Challenge of Human Rights Education* (Starkey ed. 1991). Council of Europe.

Chapter Eight

Secular Education

As has been seen in the previous chapter, there is a willingness in both England and the United States to accommodate the religious beliefs and values of parents and children where their objections relate to direct religious practices in schools. However, parents belonging to some religious groups also find certain elements of the secular curriculum offensive to their religious beliefs. Parental objections fall largely into two categories. The first of these is where a secular course is alleged to have a religious content favouring one religious viewpoint, which another seeks to have expunged. The second category is where a parent or child objects, on religious grounds, to the very nature of the secular course, its contents or the teaching methods. Objections to the supposedly religious nature of a secular course, or the absence of religious teachings in secular courses, have been of particular importance in the United States, especially in relation to the teaching of evolution. It appears that, in both jurisdictions, the legislature and the courts are less willing to accommodate and to tolerate such religious objections, even though international instruments may be seen as applying equally to this form of religious objection.

A Secular Course or a Religious Course: Evolution and Creationism

For those Christian groups who believe in the literal interpretation of the Bible, and the inerrancy of the scriptures, the teaching of the Darwinian theory of evolution to children is viewed as an attack

310

both on the Bible and on their religious beliefs. It promotes, they would maintain, the undesirable growth of secularism in society. These groups, termed Fundamentalists by the courts, have taken positive actions over the course of this century to prohibit the teaching of evolution, or at least to ensure that the biblical view of creation is also taught in schools.[1]

In the famous trial of *Scopes v. State*[2] in 1927, Scopes was convicted of teaching Darwinian evolution, and in particular, that man was descended from the apes, in contravention of State law. Although the conviction was reversed on appeal, this was due to a technicality; the Tennessee Supreme Court upheld the constitutionality of the law which prohibited the teaching of evolution. It was not until 1968 that the Supreme Court finally held in *Epperson v. Arkansas*[3] that such statutes were unconstitutional. The Arkansas statute being challenged in this case made it unlawful for a teacher in any State supported school or university to teach the theory or doctrine that mankind ascended or descended from a lower order of animals, or to use a textbook that taught this theory. Violation of the statute could lead to a criminal prosecution, and dismissal of the violator from his or her teaching position. The Supreme Court found that the Act conflicted with the constitutional prohibition of State laws respecting the establishment of religion or prohibiting the free exercise thereof:

"The overriding fact is that Arkansas' law selects from the body of knowledge a particular segment which it proscribes for the sole reason that it is deemed to conflict with a particular religious doctrine: that is,

---

[1] For a history of the growth of fundamentalism and their views see *McClean v. Arkansas Board of Education*. 211 U.S. 539 (1909).

[2] 154 Tenn 105, 289 S.W. 363 (1927) The case was also known as the Monkey trial.

[3] 393 U.S. 97 (1968). It should be noted that at the time of this case only Arkansas and Mississippi continued to have such statutes. The Supreme Court held that the ban on the teaching of the theory of evolution violated the Establishment Clause because it could not "be justified by considerations of state policy other than the religious views of its citizens", *ibid.* at 107. In this case the Court found that evolution was banned because it conflicted with religious doctrine and that "The First Amendment does not permit the State to require that teaching and learning must be tailored to the principles or prohibitions of any religious sect or dogma."

with a particular interpretation of the Book of Genesis by a particular group.[4]"

Quite clearly, a ban on the teaching of evolution would now be unconstitutional. However, those parents whose religious beliefs are offended by the teaching of evolution, believing that the world was created by God in seven days, as portrayed in the bible in the book of Genesis, have since sought accommodation of their religious beliefs by seeking to balance the teaching of evolution with their religious belief in creationism. These attempts have been directed at requiring teachers or textbooks that discuss evolution, to give equal treatment to the biblical account or requiring teachers to point out that this is merely one theory about the creation of the world.[5] Alternatively, they have sought to have their children excused from such teaching. Pressure for the teaching of creationism along with evolution had a limited measure of success. A number of state legislatures introduced statutes requiring the "balanced treatment" of evolution and creation science,[6] although when challenged, such statutes have been found to be constitutionally invalid.

A rather different approach was taken by students opposed to the teaching of evolution in *Wright v. Houston Independent School District*.[7] The Plaintiffs in this case[8] maintained that by restricting the study of human origins to an uncritical examination of the theory of evolution,[9] the defendants were lending official support

---

[4] *ibid* at p. 103. For a much fuller discussion of this case, see Note, "Freedom of Religion and Science Instruction in Public Schools" (1978) 87 Yale L.J. 515 and Strossen (1986) 47 Ohio L.J. 333 at 347.

[5] *Daniels v. Waters* 515 F.2d 485 (6th Cir. 1975).

[6] Cole and Scott, "Creation Science and Scientific Research" (1982) 63 Phi Delta Kappa 557. At this time 19 State legislatures had introduced such statutes.

[7] 366 F. Supp. 1208 (S.D. Tex. 1972), affirmed *per curiam*, 486 F. 2d 137 (5th Cir. 1973), cert. denied, 417 U.S. 969 (1974).

[8] The schools were willing to excuse the students from classes teaching evolution, but the students declined this offer and proposed instead that either evolution be eliminated from the curriculum, or that the curriculum grant equal time to all theories regarding the origins of the world.

[9] *i.e.* excluding the Biblical account of the world's creation.

to a "religion of secularism",[10] and were thus "establishing" a particular religion in contravention of the First Amendment.[11]

The court rejected the arguments put forward by the Plaintiffs, finding that the teaching of evolution did not serve a religious purpose, nor did it promote religious beliefs.[12] The court, while accepting that science and religion necessarily dealt with many of the same questions, and that they frequently provided conflicting answers, did not see it as the business of government to suppress real or imagined attacks upon a particular religious doctrine.[13]

The plaintiffs, alternatively, sought an injunction directing teachers who taught evolution, to give equal time to the Biblical account of creation. The court commented that such a remedy might be feasible if the beliefs of fundamentalism were the sole alternative to Darwinian theory, but virtually every religion had its own belief in how the world was created. To give each religious view equal time would be impractical, unworkable and ineffective. The view of the court was that such an approach could open the floodgates. If equal time was given to religious views on the creation of the world, what of other areas of learning where religious views did not always accord with the secular views taught? For instance, if the school were to teach that all people are equal and all are to be treated equally, should time be given to the Mormon view of racial inequality, or to the Christian Scientist's belief that health and disease are not governed by medical science? In addition to the pragmatic objections to the plaintiff's "equal time" argument, the court also thought that such an approach would be constitutionally invalid as a breach of the First Amendment; such a requirement would fall foul of the three pronged test laid down in *Lemon v.*

---

[10] In *School District of Abington Township v. Schempp* 374 U.S. 203, 83 S.Ct. 1560, 10 L Ed.2d 844 (1963), the Supreme Court held that the State may not establish a "religion of secularism" in the sense of affirmatively opposing or showing hostility to religion and thus preferring those who believe in no religion over those who do believe. Secularism is often used interchangeably in this context with atheism.

[11] The claim that secular humanism is being promoted is a basic approach of those who make such challenges to the curriculum.

[12] There was no suggestion in this case that a student could not challenge the teacher's presentation of Darwinian theory, unlike in the case of *Epperson v. Arkansas* 393 U.S. 97 (1968) where any discussion on the subject of evolution was prohibited.

[13] See *Burstyn v. Williams* 343 U.S. 495, 505, 72 S.Ct. 777, 96 L.Ed. 1098 (1952).

Kurtzman[14] and would violate the Establishment Clause. The State Board of Education, as one of the Defendants, suggested that the Plaintiff take advantage of a provision in the Texas Education Code which permits any child to be exempted where material taught conflicts with the family's religious beliefs. The court found merit in this suggestion.

In *Mclean v. Arkansas Board of Education*[15] the court examined rather more deeply a statute that compelled equal treatment of evolution and "creation science". The development of creation science occurred as a result of the recognition by fundamentalist Christian groups that the courts would not accept the teaching of creationism as valid if it appeared to be a religious doctrine. Creation science promotes the Genesis account of creation, not as a religious tenet, but as an alternative theory to evolution, with its own scientific base.[16] However, the court in this case was unwilling to accept that creation science was a true science, lacking as it did the essential characteristics of a science.

1.   It is guided by natural law;
2.   It has to be explanatory by reference to natural law;
3.   It is testable against the empirical world;
4.   Its conclusions are tentative, *i.e.* are not necessarily the final word;
5.   It is falsifiable.

Since creation science was not science, the inescapable conclusion was that the *only* real effect of the Act was the advancement of re-

---

[14] 403 U.S. 602 (1971). For a discussion of the interpretation of the Establishment Clause see Chap. 1, p.12.

[15] 529 F. Supp. 1255 (E.D. Ark. 1982).

[16] s.4 of the Act defined creation science as the scientific evidences for creation and the inferences from those scientific evidences. Creation science includes the scientific evidences and related inferences that indicate:
1.   sudden creation of the universe and life from nothing;
2.   The insufficiency of mutation and natural selection in bringing about development of all living kinds from a single organism;
3.   Changes only within fixed limits of originally created kinds of plants and animals;
4.   Separate ancestry for man and apes;
5.   Explanation of the earth's geology by catastrophism, including the occurrence of a world-wide flood; and
6.   a relatively recent inception of the earth and living-kinds.

ligion, and to this extent was invalid under the Establishment Clause of the First Amendment.

The *McClean* court had also to confront the argument, previously raised in *Wright v. Houston*,[17] that evolution is, in effect, a religion, and that by teaching a religion which was contrary to some student's religious views, the state was infringing the students free exercise rights under the First Amendment. The argument continued that a course that taught only the Darwinian theory of evolution presented both a free exercise problem and an establishment problem, which could only be redressed by giving balanced treatment to creation science. The court reasoned that if evolution was a religion or religious tenet, the appropriate remedy was to stop the teaching of evolution, not to establish another religion in opposition to it. But, it had been clearly established in case law that evolution was not a religion and that teaching evolution did not violate the Establishment Clause.[18]

It was further argued that the public school curriculum should reflect the fact that a "significant majority" of the public thought creation science should be taught if evolution was taught. The court gave this argument short shrift, finding that the application and content of First Amendment principles were not determined by public opinion polls or by majority vote. Whether the proponents of the Act constituted the majority, or the minority, was quite irrelevant under a constitutional system of government. No group, no matter how large or small, could use the organs of government of which the public schools were the most conspicuous and influential, to foist its religious beliefs on others.[19]

Yet another approach to the teaching of creationism was challenged in *Edwards v. Aguillard*.[20] Louisiana's "Balanced Treatment for Creation Science and Evolution-Science in Public School Instruction" Act forbade the teaching of the theory of evolution

---

[17] *Wright v. Houston Independent School District* 366 F.Supp. 1208 (S.D.Tex 1972) affirmed *per curiam*, 486 F. 2d 137 (5th Cir. 1973), cert. denied 417 U.S. 969 (1974).

[18] *Epperson v. Arkansas* 393 U.S. 97 (1968) and *Wright v. Houston Independent School District* 366 F. Supp. 1208 (S.D. Tex. 1972) aff'd *per curiam* 484 F.2d 137 (5th Cir. 1973) cert. denied 417 U.S. 969 (1974).

[19] A very different view from that held in England with its established Church, where the government finds that the teaching of Christianity in schools is not only valid but desirable.

[20] 482 U.S. 578; 107 S.Ct. 2573; 96 L.Ed. 2d 510; 55 U.S.L.W. 4860. (1987).

unless accompanied by instruction on the theory of creation science. The Act did not require that either theory was taught to the children, but in the event that one theory was taught, the other had also to be taught.[21] The Act also required that both explanations of human origins were to be treated as theories only. The Supreme Court found that the legislature's actual intent was "to discredit evolution by counterbalancing its teaching at every turn with the teaching of creationism, a religious belief" and[22] that the Act was invalid as violative of the Establishment Clause because it lacked a clear secular purpose, and promoted a particular religious doctrine.

These cases show quite clearly the consistent approach by the highest level of courts in the United States. They have refused to allow religious groups to proscribe the teaching of evolution, or to insist on the teaching of creationism, finding such attempts to have a religious intent, and to offend the Establishment Clause. It is unlikely, given this approach that a further case will arise on this issue or that the courts would be willing to accommodate a religious belief in creationism within the school curriculum.[23] The teaching of Darwinian evolution is not, however, the only matter of contention. Other facets of the secular curriculum continue to be a matter of concern for many parents.

---

[21] It is interesting to note who filed *amicus curiae* briefs. In favour of the Act were the Catholic League for Religious and Civil Rights, the Christian Legal Society and Concerned Women for America. (A very small number of the groups in favour of creationism.) Against the Act; *inter alia*, the State of New York, the American Association of University Professors, the American Jewish Congress, Americans United for Separation of Church and State, National Academy of Sciences and 72 Nobel Laureates.

[22] This statement was made initially by the United States Courts of Appeals for the Fifth Circuit and confirmed by the Supreme Court. The court did not scrutinise the legitimacy of creation science as a science, as it did in *McLean* above, rather it examined the central tenet of creation science, which was that the world was created by a Supreme Being, and accepted that this incorporated religious doctrine.

[23] It is possible that the same issue might arise in England. See the *Telegraph*, "letters" Saturday April 11, 1993, in which it is clear that some Islamic groups object to the teaching of evolution.

Secular Materials and Teaching Methods

Objections by religious groups in the United States and England relate, to the substantive content of the curriculum not only such as courses in health education or computer studies,[24] but also extend to ancillary matters, such as the use of television programmes or films in teaching,[25] the use of certain text books,[26] the wearing of particular clothing in physical education lessons,[27] co-educational physical education or dancing classes[28] and the wearing of immodest school uniforms.[29]

In England these issues have not been ruled upon by the courts, but have been the object of discussion within Parliament[30] and the Department for Education. The Department and local education authorities have issued circulars to try to accommodate a limited number of religious objections.[31-32] In the United States such matters have been the subject of challenge, particularly under the Free Exercise Clause. In both jurisdictions, the essential question is whether parents have the right to withdraw their children from classes and programmes which they find religiously offensive. In England there has been a willingness to accommodate religious objections where the matter objected to is peripheral to the requirements of the national curriculum. In the United States, where the course or activity objected to violates the Free Exercise Clause of the First Amendment, the courts will excuse the student. However, where no breach is found the courts are reluctant to grant the right

---

[24] See *Davis v. Page* 385 F. Supp. 395 (1974), and *Hansard* December 20, 1990, 590–596.

[25] *Davis v. Page* 385 F.Supp. 395 (1974).

[26] *Mozert v. Hawkins* 647 F. Supp. 1194 (E.D. Tenn. 1986), rev'd, 827 F.2d 1058 (6th Cir. 1987). cert denied 108 S.Ct. 1029 (1988); *Grove v. Mead School Dist.* No. 354, 753 F.2d 1528 (9th Cir.) cert. denied 106 S. Ct. 85 (1985).

[27] *Moody v. Cronin* 484 F. Supp. 270 (C D Ill. 1979); *Mitchell v. McCall* 273 Ala. 604, 143 So. 2d 629 (1962).

[28] *Hardwicke v. Board of School Trustees* 54 Cal.App. 696, 205 P. 49 (Cal.Ct.App. 1921).

[29] See the Swann Report, *Education for all, the Report of the Committee of Inquiry into the Education of Children from Ethnic Minority Groups*, Cmnd. 9453. pp.341–2.

[30] See, *e.g. Hansard* December 20, 1990, Col. 589.

[31-32] Particularly in relation to school uniform, seen as immodest by certain groups, and to the problem of mixed physical education. The Department for Education has not been willing to accommodate the Muslim community on its desire for single sex schooling. See Cumper, "School Admissions Policies: *Choudhury v. Bishop Challoner R.C. School*" 2 J.C.L. 95.

of excusal,[33] particularly if, as in England, the course is seen as an integral part of the total educational curriculum.

While the Establishment Clause ensures that public schools in the United States remain neutral to promotion of religion or religious practices, and thus excludes overtly religious acts from schools, the Free Exercise Clause exists to allow parents and children to practise their religion freely without interference from the State. Thus, the clause prohibits acts that compel people to violate their religious beliefs, and acts that burden their religion, even though the act requested is not overtly religious in nature, unless there is a compelling State interest.[34] In *Hardwicke v. Fruitridge Board of School Trustees*[35] the court held that the plaintiff's children could not be compelled to join in dancing at school when this contravened their religious beliefs, and in *Spence v. Bailey*[36] that the school could not insist that a student take part in military exercises in order to obtain his diploma, where the student had a religious objection to any form of military activity. To take part in such activities would force the student to choose between following his religious beliefs and forfeiting his diploma, or abandoning his religious beliefs and receiving the diploma. The court held that "the state may not put its citizens to such a Hobson's choice . . . without showing a compelling state interest".[37] Courts in the United States will only find a breach of the Free Exercise Clause, however, where there is "coercion" by the school to perform an act.[38] Where there is no coercion it is likely there will be no breach. It is also quite possible that the court may find a breach, but find that the State has a compelling interest in the act taking place. So, for instance, if the parent has a religious objection to his child being educated at all, the State could show that, despite this religious objection, the State has a compell-

---

[33] See *Grove v. Mead School Dist.* No. 354, 753 F.2d 1528 (9th Cir.) cert. denied 106 S.Ct. 85 (1985) where it was allowed. But this could be said to be just a peripheral part of the case.

[34] However, a breach of the Free Exercise Clause will only result where there is coercion to do some act which is forbidden by the objector's religion. Thus, passive listening would be insufficient.

[35] 205 P. 49 (Cal. 1921).

[36] 325 F. Supp. 601 (1971) aff'd 465 F. 2d 796 (1972).

[37] For discussion of the nature of a compelling State interest, see *Wisconsin v. Yoder* 406 U.S. 205, 32 L Ed 2d 15, 92 S. Ct. 1526 (1972) and discussion in Chap. 7 at p.265.

[38] Coercion in this context is defined as an act or requirement which a schoolchild is compelled to perform or comply with under the school's rules.

ing interest in educating its children. This showing of a compelling interest would override the religious objections of the parent.

Courts in the United States have, on the whole, been reluctant to find a violation of the Free Exercise Clause where what is objected to appears to be totally neutral in religious content. In addition, both jurisdictions have appeared unwilling to grant the remedy of excusal where the activity complained of is seen as an integral part of the curriculum.

THE USE OF AUDIO-VISUAL AIDS

The use of audio-visual aids, which includes the watching of television and films, is forbidden by certain fundamentalist Christian groups, including, in England, the Plymouth Brethren. Such aids are commonly used in schools, particularly at elementary level, to teach a wide range of subjects. Religious groups have sought the right to withdraw children from classes when a television programme or film is shown. In England, the Plymouth Brethren have argued that the right to withdraw exists under Article 2 of Protocol 1 of the European Convention on Human Rights:

> "The State shall respect the right of parents to ensure such education and teaching in conformity with their own . . . religious convictions".

The Minister of State for Education in England has expressed his willingness for children to be excused from viewing television programmes where these are used as a teaching aid:[39]

> "the use of television and radio programmes and videos as a medium for teaching is not a requirement of the National Curriculum . . . DES Circular 3/90, which was issued on 6 March with the National Curriculum Order for technology made clear our hope that schools would have regard to parents' views in their choice of media for teaching purposes."

It was pointed out in a later Parliamentary debate on the National Curriculum in 1990[40] that the letter had produced a range of responses. Some schools and local education authorities had been

---

[39] Stated in a letter dated August 29, 1992. See *Hansard* December 20, 1990, 589.
[40] *Hansard* December 20, 1990, 589. The issue was raised by Mr Robert Hughes, MP for Harrow, West,

supportive,[41] but others actively hostile,[42] threatening disciplinary procedures if pupils were excluded from any lesson, or part of a lesson, or any procedure used by the teaching staff to deliver the curriculum.[43] Responding to these different approaches, the Minister of State for Education again reiterated that the National Curriculum did not require the use of television, videos or radios in school.

However, the Minister accepted that the guidance contained in the circular was not legally binding. The final decision on teaching methods rested with the schools, and the Government had no power to direct them to have regard to parents' views. Nevertheless the Minister expressed his expectation that local authorities and schools would be sensitive to the beliefs of families in considering teaching methods and materials, and that schools should adopt a friendly and helpful approach to members of the Brethren to help their children remain within maintained schools.

In the United States, courts have taken a less sympathetic approach when faced with a similar objection, regarding the use of television as non-sectarian in both purpose and manner. In *Davis v. Page*,[44] the parents, Apostolic Lutherans, sought an order from the court requiring school officials to excuse their children from class whenever the television was used, claiming that the use of audiovisual aids was forbidden by their religion.[45] When the children initially attended their school, any student who voiced religious objections to classroom activities was allowed to leave the room. However, due to the sizeable number of students who objected,

---

[41] In Humberside, a school wrote to the parents saying: "your children will be allowed to leave the room whenever a video is shown, in all subjects and in each year group; you will be informed of a suitable textbook in Science, which you may wish to purchase as an alternative source of information . . . In English you will be sent a copy of texts which are to be used, so that you may decide upon their suitability. Should you feel that they are not acceptable then we will try to provide an alternative."

[42] In Stafford, a Chairman of Governors wrote; "your particular interpretation of the Bible places demands upon the school's resources that cannot be met without a very considerable amount of hard work".

[43] Letter to parents from the governors of Longfield School, Harrow, London. See *Hansard* December 20, 1990, 591.

[44] 385 F.Supp. 395 (1974). They also sought exemption from health education classes.

[45] *Davis v. Page* 385 F. Supp. 395 (1974). The parents also objected to the children engaging in play acting, singing or dancing to worldly music, studying evolution, humanist philosophy, partaking in sexually oriented programmes, openly discussing personal and family matters, or receiving the advice of secular counsellors.

and the resulting disciplinary problems of having large numbers of children leaving the classroom, the school adopted a new policy which required students, regardless of their religious objections, to remain in the classroom. The children were given the option of turning their heads or chairs away, or standing at the back of the classroom. The plaintiffs, parents of two children at the school, found this alternative unacceptable.

Although the children were asserting a constitutional right to free exercise of religion, the court recognised that, in essence what was being asserted was the right of parents to inculcate and mould their children's religious beliefs to conform to their own, without the children being subjected to methods of teaching and material which the parents deemed offensive and subversive to their beliefs.[46]

The Court, while accepting that the policy of the School Board burdened the parents' constitutional rights, also found that the State was under a duty to provide children with a proper education. The court cited the Supreme Court's admonition against restrictions on the educational process,[47] and recognised that, in a culturally pluralistic society, there is a real need for children to be exposed to a broad educational spectrum. In balancing the interests of both parent and State with regard to the use of audio-visual equipment, the court found that the balance tipped in favour of the State. If the children were allowed to leave the classroom whenever audio-visual equipment was used, this would have an adverse effect upon their education, and such excusal was not required by the First Amendment, despite the parents allegation of a violation of their religious beliefs. To find in favour of the parents would require the State to provide separate courses of instruction for such children, and this in turn, said the Court, would violate the Establishment Clause.[48] However, where television or videos were used as enter-

---

[46] The Davis' alleged that the School Board's policy violated their free exercise of religion and their fundamental right to control the upbringing of their children. It was not the content that was the subject of this particular complaint, but the use of television or film itself.

[47] See, *e.g. Epperson v. Arkansas* 393 U.S. 97, 89 S.Ct. 266, 21 L.Ed 2d 228 (1968). "The First Amendment does not mandate nor does it tolerate laws that cast a pall of orthodoxy over the classroom."

[48] There was no consideration here of the possibility of teaching without audio-visual aids. These were treated as a necessary mode of imparting information to children.

tainment rather than instruction, the parents rights became dominant again and the children could not be required to remain in the classroom.

Exemption from Secular Subjects

In the case of both *Davis v. Page* and the Plymouth Brethren in England, the parents also sought exemption from certain secular courses which offended their religious beliefs. In England, such objections have been made to courses on information technology, involving the use of computers,[49] and sex education.[50]

Where a course forms an integral part of the English national curriculum, as the course on information technology does, the Government has been unwilling to allow parents to withdraw their children on the basis of religious objection.[51] In 1989, in reply to a Parliamentary Question on the right of withdrawal under Article 2 of Protocol 1 of the European Convention on Human Rights, the Minster of State for Education stated that Article 2 did not give parents a general right to withdraw children from secular courses, and that, as a matter of policy, the government would not allow parents to withdraw children from the secular curriculum in maintained schools on the grounds of religion or conscience, but these parents remained free to make alternative arrangements.[52]

The same issue was raised again in 1990 during a Parliamentary debate. More extensive reasons were given as to why the government would not allow parents a right of withdrawal where a course was religiously offensive. The reasons given bear a remarkable resemblance to the limitations imposed on the Free Exercise Clause by the United States Court of Appeal in *Davis v. Page*[53] when

---

[49] Again, by the Plymouth Brethren, who object to the use of modern technology, and particularly to the use of television or film screens, whether used for educational or entertainment purposes.

[50] This has been resolved by the Education Act 1993 amending the Education Reform Act 1988, s.17 and giving parents the right to withdraw children from sex education. The right of withdrawal came into force September 1994.

[51] The objections of the Plymouth Brethren are based on the use of television screens, and the use of modern technology of this nature.

[52] In other words, parents are free to move their children to a private school more sympathetic to their views and where the national curriculum is not compulsory. See *Hansard* October 23, 1989, 321.

[53] 385 F.Supp. 395 (1974).

parents sought to withdraw their children from elements of the secular curriculum.

In deciding that parents should not have a right to withdraw children from secular courses that they found religiously objectionable, the Secretary of State relied on three factors. The first of these was the need for plurality: all children should receive a broad and balanced education. The second was the need to provide children with equality of opportunity: all children should be fully prepared for the opportunities, responsibilities and experiences of adult life and not be disadvantaged by receiving anything less than a full and broad curriculum.[54] The third reason was the administrative inconvenience of such a request. If the Plymouth Brethren were allowed to withdraw their children from information technology, then other parents might well expect to make similar claims on grounds of other religious, conscientious or philosophical objections to other parts of the curriculum, and this would undermine the concept of a national curriculum.

But what of the right contained in Article 2 of Protocol 1 requiring that the State shall respect the right of parents to ensure teaching is in conformity with their religious convictions?:

"The government's view is that the article [2 of protocol 1 of the European Convention on Human Rights] does not require a state to provide education in accordance with the particular religious or philosophical convictions of parents. Nor does it prevent the state from including in the school curriculum matters that do not accord with some parent's conviction, provided—this is a big proviso—that the material is presented in an objective, critical and pluralistic manner. We believe that the requirements of the national curriculum are compatible with article 2".[55]

For those parents to whom such teaching continues to be religiously objectionable, a choice exists. They can remove their chil-

---

[54] The Secretary of State found it essential that children should be prepared for the world in which they live. This is not a view the government hold in relation to private schools, who are allowed to offer a very much narrower curriculum, and need not necessarily be one which prepares them for the modern world. See *R. v. Secretary of State for Education ex p. Talmud Torah Machzikei Hadass School, The Times* April 12, 1985.

[55] *Hansard* December 20, 1990, 594, Mr Timothy Eggar, Minister of State for Education. It is difficult to know exactly what is meant by "pluralistic" in this context, but it is most likely that it is intended to mean "broad and balanced". In some cases this is exactly what the parents object to.

dren from State schools and place them in private schools or teach
them at home. When placed in a private school or taught at home,
the Secretary of State's requirement for a broad and balanced education and the need to provide children with equality of opportunity appears not to apply. In such instances, the Department for
Education will be satisfied if education is merely "efficient and
suitable".[55a]

When courts in the United States have been faced with similar
demands to withdraw children from parts of the secular curriculum, they have responded by pointing out that it is impossible for a
state to provide an educational programme which is totally acceptable to all religious faiths. The First Amendment does not provide
protection from nonsectarian views which are distasteful to them.
To allow students to pick and chose which courses they want to
attend would create a stratified school structure where division and
derision would flourish. The Supreme Court in New Hampshire
provided a further reason for refusing parents the right to withdraw
their children from objectionable courses:

> "[T]he power of each parent to decide the question what studies the
> scholars should pursue, or what exercises they should perform, would
> be a power of disorganizing the school, and practically rendering it sub-
> stantially useless. However judicious it may be to consult the wishes of
> parents, the disintegrating principle of parental authority to prevent all
> classification and destroy all system in any school, public or private, is
> unknown to the law."[56]

Sex or Health Education

Sex education, or health education, as it is sometimes referred to
in the United States, while regarded as a secular subject, has more
obvious religious overtones, and potential for offending religious
sensibilities. The objections voiced to such teaching, focus partly
on the fact that sex education is taught at all, and partly on the content of the course. Some religious groups may not object to teaching children basic sexual mechanics, but do object to discussions of
contraception, abortion, pre-marital sex, and the role of women.

Where parents have sought to prevent schools from teaching sex

---

[55a] See Chap. 7 and n. 54 above.
[56] *Kidder v. Chellis* 59 N.H. 473, 476 (1879).

education, arguing that instruction in such matters should be the exclusive right of the parents, such challenges have failed. In the United States challenges to the sex education programme were made on the basis that the programme offended the Establishment Clause, and established a religion of secular humanism: the same argument put forward in the evolution cases. In considering the issue, the courts[57] have followed the decision in *Epperson*,[58] that to prohibit public schools from offering sex education on the ground that it offended the religious or moral views of a particular group, would be tantamount to enshrining the group's view as State policy, thereby violating the Establishment Clause.

Such courses have also been subjected, unsuccessfully, to challenge under Article 2 of Protocol 1 of the European Convention on Human Rights. In the case of *Pedersen v. Denmark*,[59] it was held that obligatory sex education does not breach Article 2 of Protocol 1. The U.K. government has recognised, however, that sex education is an issue which affects religious values. The Department of Education in a Circular on sex education[60] issued to all State schools, points out that parents are key figures in helping their children with the physical and emotional aspects of growing up and preparing them for the challenges and responsibilities which sexual maturity brings. Thus teaching offered by the schools should be complementary and supportive to the role of parents, and parents should be consulted on the content of sex education.[60a] Sex education should be provided in a manner which encourages pupils to have due regard to moral considerations and the values of family life.[61]

In the great majority of the states in the United States, parents are allowed to withdraw their children from sex education, thus frus-

---

[57] *Citizens for Parental Rights v. San Mateo County Board of Education* 51 Cal.App 3d 1, 124 Cal.Rptr. 68 (1975) appeal dismissed 425 U.S. 908 (1976), *Medeiros v. Kiyosaki* 52 Haw. 436, 478 P. 2d 3124 (1970).

[58] 393 U.S.97, 89 S. Ct. 266, 21 L. Ed 2d. 228 (1986).

[59] The case was heard before the ECHR, and considered Art. 2 of Protocol 1 in relation to obligatory sex education in Danish state schools. The practice was upheld. See Application No. 5926/72 *Pedersen v. Denmark* [1973] Yearbook of the Convention on Human Rights 340 and Secretary to the Convention, Stocktaking on the European Convention on Human Rights.

[60] DFE Circular 5/94 Education Act 1993: Sex Education in Schools.

[60a] DFE Circular 5/94 *ibid.* at para. 7 & 18.

[61] Education (No. 2) Act 1986, s.46. Local authorities are prohibited from promoting homosexuality by teaching or publishing such material.

trating potential free exercise claims.[62] However, it is not at all clear that even where a sex education programme is compulsory, and there is no right to withdraw children, that a free exercise claim would be successful. In *Hopkins v. Hamden Board of Education*[63] the compulsory nature of the course was upheld, the court failing to find evidence that the secular course conflicted with religious beliefs, or that there was any coercion directed at the practice or exercise of the plaintiff's religious beliefs.[64]

It has been argued that even though a sex education programme permits excusal, this nonetheless inhibits the free exercise of religion. In *Ricci v. Smith*[65] the parent appellants maintained that requiring pupils to assert their objection to the programme in front of teachers and their peers exerted an intolerable pressure on those pupils. The pressure was such that they might be compelled to abandon their beliefs and choose not to exercise their option to be excused. They argued that such pressure was unconstitutional.[66] The court rejected this argument as misconceived. Although the court accepted that the exercise of the right to be excluded may be difficult for some, they found that the constitution did not guarantee that the exercise of religion would be without difficulty!

In England the governors of State schools are responsible for determining policy on the organisation of sex education provision. Primary school governors are not obliged to offer a sex education programme within their school, but all state secondary schools

---

[62] See *Ricci v. Smith* 89 N.J. 514; 446 A. 2d 501 (1983) where the court found that where a child is not required to participate in the programme, there is no element of compulsion and thus no infringement of the appellants' right to free exercise of religion. See also *Medeiros v. Kiyosaki* 52 Haw. 436, 478 P. 2d 3124 (1970), *Citizens for Parental Rights v. San Mateo County Board of Education* 51 Cal.App. 3d 1, 124 Cal.Rptr. 68 (Ct.App. 1975), appeal dismissed, 425 U.S. 908, 96 S.Ct. 1502, 46 L.Ed. 2d 759 (1976); *Hopkins v. Hamden Board of Education* 29 Conn.Sup. 397, 289 A 2d 914 (Ct.Com.Pls. 1970), appeal dismissed, 305 A 2d. 536 (Conn. 1973).

[63] 29 Conn.Supp. 397; 289 A.2d 914. (1971).

[64] The court also held that to permit such interference in the public school system could lead to fragmentation of the system. Following *Cantwell v. Connecticut* 310 U.S. 296 (1940), the court held this was not the intent of the guarantees under the First Amendment, and that the State's interests must also be weighed and the public protected. However, it should be noted that the court regarded this as much more in the way of health education than sex education, even though the course explicitly included reproduction and sex education.

[65] 89 N.J. 514; 446 A. 2d 501 (1983).

[66] Relying on *School District of Abington Township v. Schempp* 374 U.S. 203 83 S.Ct. 1560, 10 L. Ed. 2d 844 (1963).

must offer a sex education programme. Each school is required to publish information about the "manner and context in which education as respects sexual matters is given",[67] including the types of materials used, thus allowing parents to exercise a degree of choice when choosing a school for their child. Interestingly, in a survey by the Sex Education Forum in 1992,[68] it was discovered that 25 per cent of schools, even though under a legal obligation to state their policy on sex education, had failed to do so, while six per cent had decided against including sex education in their curriculum at all. However, as a result of amendments introduced by the Education Act 1993, all maintained secondary schools will be required to provide sex education for their pupils.[69] The Education Act 1993 has made one other significant change. It provides[70] that education about human sexual behaviour, including HIV, AIDS and other sexually transmitted diseases will no longer be part of the science curriculum, but will be taught within sex education. There is, of course, no right of excusal from parts of the national curriculum, but parents are given the right to withdraw their children from all or part of the sex education offered by the 1993 Act.[71] This right of withdrawal, which was previously discretionary, allied to the changes in the science curriculum means that those children who are withdrawn, will no longer receive vital information on AIDS, HIV, contraception or sexual safety. The removal of education on human sexual behaviour from the science curriculum is to be regretted. It amounts to an over-accommodation of parental wishes at the expense of adequate protection of children; hardly in keeping with the earlier expressed aspirations of the Department for Education that schools have a clear responsibility to ensure that pupils are adequately prepared for adult life.

---

[67] Under the Education (School Information) Regulations 1981, made under the Education Act 1980, s.80. In DFE Circular 5/94 para. 9 the Government sees sex education as a means of meeting the targets set in their "Health of the Nation" paper in 1992: a 50 per cent reduction in teenage pregnancies and the lessening of sexually transmitted diseases.

[68] See the *Independent*, April 4, 1992.

[69] Education Act 1993 amending the Education Reform Act 1988, s.2(1).

[70] Education Act 1993, s.241(4). The section orders the Secretary of State to revise the science curriculum. See also DFE Circular 5/94 paras 16, 17, 20, 23–25.

[71] See DFE Circular 5/94.

Objections to Neutrality; Reading Books, Values and Secular Humanism

Just as certain secular courses are objectionable to certain religious groups, so too are some of the texts used in schools. If a parent or child finds a reading scheme violates their religious beliefs, the school is then faced with the problem of whether the child should read from the book that is objected to, be excused from reading classes or given a different book. Where the curriculum in use does not specify the exact books that have to be read, a child who has religious objections to one particular book may normally substitute another.[72] However, not all schools in the United States have the same flexibility, nor are the courts necessarily willing to enforce such flexibility, as shown by the celebrated case of *Mozert v. Hawkins County Public Schools*.[73]

The Hawkins County School Board required all their schools to use the Holt reading series, and required every pupil to attend classes using these books. A group of fundamentalist Christian parents[74] who objected to the chosen reading scheme on the basis that it included material which offended their religious beliefs, asked the court to order the school board to provide these students with alternative texts.[75]

In their complaint the plaintiffs asserted that they had sincere religious beliefs which were contrary to the values taught or inculcated by the reading textbooks. They alleged that it was a violation of the religious beliefs and convictions of the plaintiff pupils to be required to read the books, and a violation of the religious beliefs of the parents to permit their children to read the books. In particular,

---

[72] This flexibility may, however, be coming to an end in England, as the Secretary of State for Education is attempting to lay down more specific requirements in the English course, including the books that children of different ages should be expected to read.

[73] 647 F. Supp. 1194 (E.D. Tenn. 1986), rev'd, 827 F.2d 1058 (6th Cir. 1987). cert denied 108 S.Ct. 1029 (1988). There are a large number of commentaries and articles on this case to be found in the American journals. See, for instance Kaplan, Vol. 95 Dickens Law Rev. 259 Winter 1991, Breyer, 20 Journal of Law and Education 63 (1991). Van Geel, 21 Journal of Law and Education 445 (1992), Dent, 61 S. Cal.L.Rev. 863, (1988) West, Vol. 26 Wake Forest Law Review 361 (1991), Sendor, "A Legal Guide to Religion and Public Education" (1988), Strossen, 47 Ohio St. L.J. 333 (1983).

[74] 14 parents and 17 children.

[75] Most of the children were ultimately taught at home, or attended religious schools, or were transferred to public schools outside Hawkins County. One student returned to school because the family were unable to afford alternative schooling.

the parents objected to stories involving the supernatural, occult themes, magic, telepathy, the teaching of evolution (which equated with teaching that there is no God), role reversal or role elimination and the emphasis on biographical material about women who had been recognised for their achievements outside the home, rather than their roles as wives and mothers based in the home. The plaintiffs further objected to passages which exposed their children to other forms of religion and to the feelings, attitudes and values of other students that contradicted the plaintiffs religious views without a statement that the other views were incorrect, and the plaintiff's views correct. The defendants accepted that the plaintiff's religious values were sincere, but denied that mere exposure to religiously offensive materials which did not indoctrinate, oppose or promote any particular values or religion, burdened that right of free exercise.

The question for the court was whether a governmental require-ment that a person be exposed to ideas he or she finds objectionable on religious grounds, constitutes a burden on the free exercise of that person's religion. [76] In order to prove that the right of free exer-cise of religion was burdened, it was necessary to prove an element of compulsion; either to do, or refrain from doing, an act which is forbidden or required by one's religion. [77] The court failed to find any element of compulsion here. There was no evidence that a pupil was required to express belief or disbelief in any idea or prac-tice contained in the readers. Neither was there any proof that any child was required to affirm or deny a religious belief, or engage or refrain from engaging in any act either required or forbidden by the student's religious conviction. If there had been evidence that a child had been required to participate beyond reading and discuss-ing assigned materials, or if the school had required the plaintiff children either to believe, or say they believed, that "all religions are merely different roads to God", this might well show compul-sion and be an infringement of the Free Exercise Clause, but this was not the case.

The judge did consider[78] whether a more balanced reading scheme was desirable, but concluded that balance in the treatment

---

[76] The defendants agreed that the plaintiffs' religious beliefs were sincere, and that certain passages in the book offended those beliefs, but argued that reading the Holt books did not impose a burden on the plaintiffs constitutional right to free exercise of religion.

[77] See *Abington School District v. Schempp* 374 U.S. 203 (1965).

[78] Judge Lively with Kennedy and Boggs concurring.

of religion lay in the eye of the beholder. If Hawkins County had sought to provide what the parents in this case thought was a more balanced reading scheme, this may have been the subject of objections by another group of parents. Any effort to achieve the particular balance desired by any individual or group might lead to an allegation of a forbidden entanglement of the public schools in religious matters, if the School Board had acted with the primary purpose of advancing or inhibiting religion.[79]

More interestingly, the court took the opportunity to comment on the role of public school in teaching "values". While accepting the constitutional right to free exercise of religion and the restrictions of the Establishment Clause, the court held that schools were not prevented from teaching children society's values and norms, even if these conflict with the religious beliefs and values of the parents and children. The Supreme Court in *Bethel School District No. 403 v. Fraser*[80] had previously affirmed that public schools serve the purpose of teaching fundamental values essential to a democratic society. These values include tolerance of divergent political and religious views while taking into account the considerations of the sensibilities of others. In *McCarthy v. Fletcher* the Court held:

> "what is critical . . . is that a school board does not have the power to advance or inhibit a particular religious orthodoxy as a 'community value': no matter how prevalent or unpopular the orthodox view might be in the community. This is the essence of the Establishment Clause of the First Amendment".[81]

The "tolerance of divergent . . . religious views" referred to in *Bethel* is a civil tolerance, not a religious one. It does not require a person to accept any other religion as the equal of the one to which that person adheres, it merely requires a recognition that in a pluralistic society it is necessary to "live and let live". The reading scheme chosen by the Hawkins County School Board was designed to acquaint students with a multitude of ideas and con-

---

[79] If balancing were undertaken with the express desire of making a reading scheme acceptable to one religious group, it is very likely that a court would find that this was done to accommodate the religious views of the objectors and, therefore, its primary purpose was the advancement of religion, and therefore, a breach of the Establishment Clause.

[80] 106 S.Ct. 3159, 3164 (1986).

[81] 207 Cal.App. 3d 130. 139, 254 Cal.Rptr. 714, 721 (1989).

cepts. While the reading books dealt with ethical issues, at least on the surface, the court found that they did not contain either a religious or anti-religious message. In the absence of this, no infringement of the Free Exercise Clause could be shown. Mere exposure to distasteful or offensive ideas was not, of itself, sufficient.[82] The philosophy behind this conclusion, and the hostility of the higher courts towards religious groups seeking accommodation of their religious beliefs in the public schools, was well summed up by Justice Jackson in *McCollum v. Board of Education* in his concurring opinion:

> "Authorities list 256 separate and substantial religious bodies to exist in the . . . United States . . . If we are to eliminate everything that is objectionable to any of these warring sects or inconsistent with any of their doctrines, we will leave public education in shreds. Nothing but educational confusion and a discrediting of public schools system can result from subjecting it to constant law suits".[83]

As in England, there are options for parents who have such objections and do not want their children exposed to ideas offensive to their religious beliefs, and that is to send children to church schools or private schools, or to teach them at home.

Conclusion

In both jurisdictions, the argument against accommodation of the child's or parents' religious beliefs is based on the need to ensure that, in a pluralistic society, children are exposed to a range of beliefs and values, that children receive equality of opportunity, and that the educational system is not undermined by the meeting of individual religious needs. But if these concerns are paramount, why do both the United States and England allow them to be so easily circumvented? While both countries espouse plurality and equality of opportunity for children educated in State schools, they are quite willing to accept private schools which provide neither, and for children to receive, on occasion, a very limited education. The administrative inconvenience argument also seems weak,

---

[82] *Burstyn v. Williams* 343 US 495, 72 S.Ct. 777, 96 L.Ed. 1098 (1952).
[83] 333 U.S. 204, 235 (1948).

when such difficulties have been brushed aside where statute requires it, for instance in the imposition of the national curriculum in England or busing to achieve racial integration in schools in the United States.

The real issue at stake here is the limit of tolerance. What religious beliefs and practices can a pluralistic state accommodate? Within the educational sphere, there are it appears, at least three limitations on the State's ability to tolerate religious beliefs. The first of these limitations is that the act complained of needs to be recognisably religious in nature, rather than a neutral act which offends religious beliefs.[84] Thus, a parent who claims that listening to any worldly music, rather than spiritual music, is religiously offensive, is unlikely to persuade a court that his child should be excused from any class where music is played, because such a requirement is not recognisably religious and the objection not easily defined.[85] In refusing the request for Plymouth Brethren children to be excused from information technology classes, the Secretary of State made no reference to the nature of the religious objection. Although it was argued that these children needed, for the sake of equality of opportunity, to learn to use a computer and study information technology, this is a very dubious argument. If these children remained within the Plymouth Brethren, their religion would forbid them to take a job which involved the use of computers. It is difficult to argue that such children would be unduly prejudiced if they left the Plymouth Brethren and had not learnt to use a computer in school. They would still be able to function perfectly well in the labour market, and would be able to acquire any necessary computer skills they had not been taught in school with great rapidity and ease. It is more likely that the Secretary of State dismissed the objections of Plymouth Brethren parents because they were not recognisably religious objections. Such objections could be seen as cultural rather than religious, and com-

---

[84] Dent, in his article "Religious Children, Secular Schools" (1988) 61 S.Cal.L. Rev. 863, suggests that most judges, as fallible human beings, undoubtedly sympathise more with religious beliefs that they find plausible and widely shared, than with views that they consider absurd or aberrant.

[85] See *Davis v. Page* 385 F.Supp. 395 (1974). The court was told that only those who have accepted the Spirit of God can determine the difference between spiritual and worldly music. The court held there was no burden on the parent's free exercise rights as music was not *per se* religiously offensive.

puter studies as a purely neutral rather than a religiously offensive activity.

A second limitation to the State's willingness to tolerate and accommodate religious values is where the objections made are to practices which the State finds both legally and morally acceptable. In both jurisdictions, divorce is legally recognised as a mode of resolving marital disputes, and abortion is legalised. However, many religious groups find both religiously offensive and unacceptable. Can a State be expected to respect the wishes of parents that children should not, while in school, be exposed to the religiously offensive view that either is permissible or acceptable? It is submitted that such a wish, which would require children to be excused from certain courses, or parts of courses, cannot be tolerated in either jurisdiction. Schools cannot be expected to teach children that laws passed through a democratic process are wrong, unacceptable or immoral, or preserve them from exposure to such laws.

A third limitation on tolerance is where religious objections conflict with the basic philosophies and aims of the State's educational programme. Although the objection may be regarded as a valid and recognisable religious objection, the State is not prepared to accommodate such religious beliefs. An illustration of this limitation in both England and the United States is the call by some religious groups for separate schooling for boys and girls. In both jurisdictions, co-educational schools are recognised as the desirable norm. Neither England nor the United States see the provision of single sex schooling as a matter for the State. Instead, they view the remedy as lying in the hands of the religious community: communities are free to set up their own single-sex schools outside the State sector.[86] A further illustration of this limitation is the refusal to grant exemptions from secular courses which are seen by the State as an integral part of the curriculum and necessary for a broad and balanced education.

It is worth noting that, in both jurisdictions, the limit of tolerance is seen as an issue between the parent and the State. In neither country is the child's view given any great weight, or for the most

---

[86] But see the Education Act 1993, in which the U.K. government has shown a willingness to aid religious groups to set up their own schools within the state system.

part, even considered.[87] Indeed, it is unclear whether, in this context, the child has any capacity to consent or refuse, or whether choice of religious training is purely a parental right.[88]

Tolerance for religious beliefs and values, in terms of the willingness of the State school system to excuse children from classes is at present limited. It is, however, questionable, whether such tolerance should be extended, and if it is, where the limits are to be placed. One issue, in particular, poses difficulty: how much credence and respect should be given to those religious groups who claim that mere exposure to a wide range of ideas and views constitutes indoctrination of itself, and conflicts with their religious beliefs. Can a western, liberal democratic state encourage ignorance of different views and values, and support a religious view that there is only one approach to God and one right way of life? There are risks to upholding such religious values. Western States are both religiously and racially mixed, and there is a need both to expose children to different lifestyles and religions, and to develop in children a respect and tolerance for others regardless of race or creed.[89] The remedy for parents who object to such an approach should not be, as the courts and British Parliament have suggested, the choice of a private school, but an explanation to the child that their family and religion takes a different view. While such an approach may lessen the parent's control over their child's religious development, this may be an inevitable price of living in a society which supports international Conventions predicating tolerance,[90] and whose governmental systems legislate to prevent discrimination and promote tolerance. There is in fact little, if any, research evidence to show that the school is more influential in forming a child's ideas and values than a strong, religious, family background. Indeed, in cases where parents and children have challenged the school curri-

---

[87] *e.g.* in the *Hansard* debate on Plymouth Brethren the children's views were not mentioned, and it is not at all clear whether they are ever considered.

[88] For a further and much more detailed consideration of this issue in the American context, see Galanter, "Religious Freedoms in the United States: A Turning Point" (1966) Wisconsin Law Review 217.

[89] See "Spiritual and Moral Development—A Discussion paper", National Curriculum council, April, 1993. The NCC sees spiritual development as an essential part of a child's development and one that the school should address.

[90] Such as Art. 29 of the UN Convention on the Rights of the Child (to which the U.K. is a signatory), the International Covenant on Economic, Social and Cultural Rights, the Convention against Discrimination in Education and the International Covenant on Civil and Political Rights.

cula, it is quite clear that the children are of the same view as their parents, and are rarely found to be in opposition to their views.[91]

While promoting tolerance and respect for other religious and philosophical viewpoints,[92] schools need, however, to be sensitive to religious sensibilities within the confines of pluralism, and ensure that different religions are viewed positively and not derided, just because their views are regarded as "old-fashioned" or extreme or unpopular. For instance, as Dent points out[93] there is a world of difference in the United States between stating that Judaism is evil, which would be a breach of the Establishment Clause, and running a curriculum in which all the stories portray Judaism and the Jews in a bad light; where all the villains are Jews and all the heroes non-Jewish and where characters frequently deride Jewish beliefs and values.[94] While the latter would arguably be legal, nevertheless such an approach would be undesirable and unacceptable. There is a need not only to tolerate other religions but to treat them positively. The American court in *Mitchell v. McCall*[95] illustrate this very clearly. The child in this case was given permission to dress differently from other children during physical education classes, as the regulation uniform was deemed immodest and unseemly according to the family's religious beliefs. She was not, however, excused, from physical education classes, although this was requested. Her father was concerned that, if she were made to take part in physical education classes with the other children, she would be a "speckled bird" and subject to the contumely of her fellow students. The court held that citizens who held views different from the majority were subject to such inconveniences, and this was especially true:

"of those who hold religious or moral beliefs which are looked upon

---

[91] See, *e.g. Wisconsin v. Yoder* 406 U.S. 205, 32 L Ed. 2d 15, 92 S.Ct. 1526 or *Davis v. Page* 385 F.Supp. 395 (1974) in the U.S., or *Re R.* [1993] 2 FLR 163 in England.
[92] See Dent, "Religious Children and Secular Schools" (1988) 61 S.Cal.L.Rev. 863, who argues that schools do not teach pure tolerance. (After all, no school would want to teach tolerance for the Klu Klux Klan.) Instead, schools teach relativism, a philosophy that all moral values are relative and matters of personal choice.
[93] *ibid.*
[94] Justice Boggs in *Mozert* recognised that the decision would permit this "no matter how offensive or one-sided".
[95] 273 Ala. 604; 143 So. 2d 629 (1962).

with disdain by the majority . . . Solace for the embarrassment that is
attendant upon holding such beliefs must be found by the individual citizen in his own moral courage and strength of conviction, and not in a
court of law".

It would be regrettable if schools and the courts took such a view
today, one which must lead minority religious groups increasingly
to look to the option of setting up their own schools, rather than
remaining within the mainstream of State education. If this is not to
occur, schools need not only to respect and be neutral between one
religion and another, but not to deride and not to be negative in
relation to a child's religion, even where there is general societal
disapproval of the religion. At the same time, children should not
be shielded from exposure to the views and attitudes of the community in which they live, and schools should not participate in the
preservation of ignorance. [96]

---

[96] Some commentators would argue that such an approach, where different conflicting ideas are put before the child is confusing. This may be so, but must be a
problem for any child of "orthodox" religious views of whatever persuasion
unless living in a theocracy espousing the child's religion. This is a problem for all
religions.

Chapter Nine

Conclusion

One of the aims of this book has been to ascertain whether a society without a written constitution can adequately ensure the preservation of religious freedom for its citizens. An attempt has been made to examine the differences in terms of religious freedom for families, between a State with an established Church, and no written, constitutional protection for religious freedom, and a State with no established Church and a constitutional guarantee of free exercise of religion. A second aim has been to explore the extent to which these two States, England and the United States, uphold and implement their obligations under the various relevant international Conventions, Covenants and Declarations to which they are parties. A third aim has been to assess how the legal systems of the two States balance competing religious claims and to assess, if possible, where the boundaries of tolerance lie.

It may be concluded that outside the field of education, the fact that there is an established Church in England makes surprisingly little difference to the ability of a family to live according to their religious beliefs and values. This is largely because the United Kingdom recognises the rights of individuals to belong to, and practice, the religion of their choice. As a signatory to the Covenant on Civil and Political Rights, and as a party to the European Convention on Human Rights, the United Kingdom has bound itself to ensure the religious freedom of its citizens. The rights contained in the various international instruments are to be available to all without distinction of any kind, including distinctions based on religion.

The more noticeable difference between England and the United

States lies in the balance that is struck when religious rights clash with other state interests, or rights. The lack of a written constitution in England, combined with a well developed *parens patriae* jurisdiction, appears to result in a more child-focussed approach in England than in the United States. There is less emphasis on parental rights than is found in the United States, with its constitutional recognition of parental religious and due process rights. The absence of the constricting influence of a written constitution liberates the English judges to provide more protection for the child on those occasions when the rights of parents to bring up children according to their religious beliefs, conflict with what is seen to be in the best interests of the child. This can be regarded as a positive feature of the English legal system. The approach of courts in the United States, such as that taken in the Californian case of *Quiner*,[1] where actual evidence of impairment to the child from religious practices was held to be necessary before a change of custody would be contemplated, or *In the Marriage of Hadeen*,[2] where the court was not prepared to look at the religious practices of the mother and their effect on her children, does not, arguably, provide enough protection for children. Too great a weight is placed on the parents' right to freedom of religion, and too little on the best interests of the child. A clear instance of imbalance between children's best interests and parental rights to religious freedom are seen in the reluctance of the courts, until recently, to override a parents' refusal to allow medical treatment, on religious grounds, for a child who is likely to suffer physical damage as a result. On a number of occasions, courts in the United States have expressed the view that unless there is a showing that the child's condition is life-threatening, they are bound to honour the parents' constitutional rights. Were the United States a party to the United Nations Convention on the Rights of the Child, such decisions would most probably be in violation of Article 3. They are certainly inconsistent with the provisions of the Declaration on the Elimination of all Forms of Intolerance and of Discrimination based on Religion or Belief, Article 5(3) of which provides:

"Practices of a religion or belief in which a child is brought up must not

---

[1] 59 Cal.Rptr. 503 (Cal.App. 1967).
[2] 27 Wash.App. 566; 619 P 2d 374.

be injurious to his physical or mental health or his full development, . . ."[3]

It is in the field of education of children, however, that the effect of a written constitution is most evident, and the impact of establishment of the Church of England most pronounced. To ensure compliance with the constitutional prohibition on establishment of any one religion, and to satisfy the guarantee of the right to free exercise of all religions, the United States requires that schools be secular institutions. This ensures equality between all religions, leaving parents free to provide the religious education of their choice to their children out of school. England, with its dual legislative requirement of religious education,[4] and worship, which is wholly or mainly of a broadly Christian character,[5] in State non-denominational schools, puts the State seal of approval on one particular religion. Such an approach does not ensure equality between religions, nor does it treat all children equally. The explicit "Christianisation" of State schools is disturbing, particularly in the light of the multi-cultural nature of English society, with its sizeable religious minorities. It is arguable that England discriminates between children on the basis of religion and is in breach of its international obligation, in particular under Article 18 of the Covenant on Civil and Political Rights,[6] and Articles 1 and 2 of the Declaration on the Elimination of All Forms of Intolerance and of Discrimination based on Religion or Belief. Elizabeth Odio-Benito's reservation in her report as Special Rapporteur to the Sub-Commission on the Prevention of Discrimination and Protection of Minorities[7] rightly pointed out that establishment of a religion can result in preferences and privileges being given to the followers

---

[3] While Declarations may not constitute binding obligations, they may be cited as customary law. In any event a UN Declaration should be regarded as a standard setter to which all the members of the UN should seek to aspire.

[4] Religious education must reflect the fact that the religious traditions of Great Britain are in the main Christian, while also taking account of the teaching and practices of the other principal religions represented in Great Britain. Education Reform Act 1988, s.8.

[5] Education Reform Act 1988, s.6.

[6] See General Comment adopted by the Human Rights Committee under Art. 40, para. 4, of the International Covenant on Civil and Political Rights CCPR/C/Rev.1/Add.4, September 27, 1993.

[7] See Odio-Benito, *Elimination of All Forms of Intolerance or Discrimination based on Religion or Belief* (1989).

of the established religion, and this creates discrimination. While the intention of Parliament may not have been to discriminate, nevertheless the effect of such provisions may indirectly prejudice certain children. Odio–Benito also pointed out in the same report that "it is important to remember that equality amongst human beings means the absence of discrimination". The role of the established Church, the dominance of Christianity and the place of collective worship and religious education[8] within schools in a multi-ethnic society needs to be re-examined if the United Kingdom is to ensure equality for all its children.

The second aim of this book was to examine the role of international law in ensuring the right of a family to live by their religious beliefs and values. Sadly, a review of judicial decisions in this area, leads one to the conclusion that judges, both in England and the United States, appear largely unaware of relevant international instruments. The notable exception to this can be found in the English courts' references to the European Convention on Human Rights. The lack of reference to these international instruments is largely a result in England, of the dualist legal system, requiring that the instrument be specifically incorporated into English domestic legislation, and in the United States, to the general difficulties of implementation of international instruments.[9] In both jurisdictions, far greater attention needs to be paid to publicising applicable international instruments, and to their effect on domestic law.

The final question is, to what extent will the legislature and the courts allow families to live according to their religious values and beliefs? In respect to the practice of religion, both England and the United States have become more "tolerant" societies. Neverthe-

---

[8] Religious education causes less concern than worship, provided that such education is phenomenological in approach, and that the school chooses a syllabus which allows minority religions to be studied as well. While such education may be desirable, it will, nevertheless, be against the wishes of a number of parents.

[9] This is exacerbated by the practice of breaking up Conventions and Covenants, and other international instruments and implementing them at various times into different pieces of domestic legislation, and by the decisions that certain articles of Conventions are already covered by existing legislation and thus need not be specifically incorported once more into domestic legislation. Judges do not tend to realise, in these instances, that Conventions exist. Where a Convention is absorbed into domestic legislation wholesale, as, for example the Hague Convention on Child Abduction was in England (The Child Abduction and Custody Act 1985), there is a greater realisation that the legislation has arisen from an international instrument.

less, individuals are restricted, from regulating their family life purely in accordance with their religious traditions. The unwillingness to tolerate or accept religious practices arise for a number of reasons. The first is where the State sees the regulation of a certain area of family life as largely a secular, rather than a religious, issue. A particularly clear illustration of this occurs in respect of divorce. In both England and the United States, divorce is a secular, rather than a religious act, requiring compliance with State legislation. Religious divorce is neither prevented nor prohibited, but neither State is prepared to recognise a religious divorce. Thus, a religious divorce has no civil effect, and does not free the parties to contract a second marriage that will be recognised by State law. Secondly, the courts are prepared, on occasion, to question whether certain religious practices, particularly those of the "new Christian sects" or the "new religious movements" are truly "religious" in nature. For example, the religious objections by members of the Plymouth Brethren in England, to the use of computer screens, and the request to withdraw their children from all classes using such screens, was not accepted or recognised as a necessary part of religious practices, and the request was disallowed.

There is, however, a further limitation on religious practices, and the willingness of the court to allow families to regulate their lives according to their religious traditions. It arises where the religious practices are seen to conflict with other fundamental rights and freedoms, or even norms of society, to which the courts and the legislature give greater weight. Thus in the area of marriage, for instance, the need to ensure equality between men and women, overrides religious practice and results in the prohibition of polygamy. But it is in matters concerning children that the balancing of competing rights is most sensitive, and presents courts with their most difficult problems. The practices of a number of the "new Christian sects", established in the nineteenth century and the "new religious movements" established in the twentieth have given rise to judicial disquiet. The courts and the legislature have not always concentrated on ensuring that the rights of children are at least their primary, if not their paramount consideration.[10] Religious freedom

---

[10] Art. 3 of the UN Convention of the Rights of the Child makes the interests of the child only the primary and not the paramount consideration.

has, on occasions, taken priority over children's best interests.[11] This book has been primarily concerned with the increasing level of religious freedom given to families in the twentieth century. While the increasing concern and respect for religious freedom is to be welcomed, both jurisdictions must now concentrate on ensuring that the rights of the child are adequately protected. The rights of the child should not be sacrificed on the altar of religious freedom.

---

[11] For instance, the moving of sex education out of the science section of the national curriculum in England may result in children being left in ignorance of "safe sex" and the risks of AIDS and sexually transmitted diseases. While this approach may respect parents' religious views, it cannot be regarded as in the child's best interests.

Bibliography

Books

Abdulla, *Sisters in Affliction: Circumcision & Infibulation of Women in Africa* (1982). Zed Press, London.

Adams and Emmerich, *A Nation Dedicated to Religious Liberty* (1990). University of Pennsylvania Press, Pennsylvania.

American State Papers on Religious Freedom (1949). Review and Herald Publishing Association, Washington D.C.

Barker, Eileen, *New Religious Movements* (1989). HMSO, London.

Beckford, James, A., *Cult Controversies* (1985). Tavistock Publications, London.

Berkovits, "*Get* and *Talaq* in English Law: Reflections on Law and Policy" in *Islamic Family Law* (Mallet & Conners eds., 1990). Graham and Trotman, London.

Breitowitz, *Between Civil and Religious Law: The Plight of the Agunah in American Society* (1993). Greenwood Press, Westport Conn.

Bromley's Family Law (8th ed., 1991). Butterworths, London.

Butterworths Family Law Service.

Clark, *The Law of Domestic Relations in the United States* (2nd ed., 1988). West Publishing Co., St Paul, Minnesota.

Cobb, S.H., *The Rise of Religious Liberty in America* (1902). Cooper Square Publishers, New York.

Cretney, *Principles of Family Law* (4th ed., 1984). Sweet & Maxwell, London.

Davidson, *Human Rights* (1993). Open University Press, Buckingham.

Dicey and Morris on the Conflict of Laws (12th ed., 1993). Sweet & Maxwell, London.

Ekelaar and Katz (eds.), *Marriage and Cohabitation in Contemporary Societies* (1980). Butterworths, London.

Fawcett, *The Application of the European Convention on Human Rights* (1987). Clarendon Press, Oxford.

Friedman, L.M., *A History of American Law* (1973). Simon & Schuster, New York.

Glendon, *State, Law and Family: Family Law in Transition in the United States and Western Europe* (1977). North Holland Publishing Co., Dordrecht.

Hart, Colin, *From Acts to Action* (1991). Christian and Tyneside Schools Action Research Workers Trust, Newcastle.

Kocourek and Wigmore, Evolution of Law, *Sources of Ancient and Primitive Law* (1915). Little Brown, Boston.

Koegel, *Common Law Marriages* (1992). Bryne & Co., Washington.

Lillich and Newman, *International Human Rights: Problems of Law and Policy* (1979). Little Brown, Boston.

Miller & Flowers, *Toward Benevolent Neutrality* (4th ed., 1992). Markham Press Fund, Waco, Texas.

Muir, *Prayer in the Public Schools* (1967). University of Chicago Press, Chicago.

Murphy, *Church, State and Schools in Britain 1800–1970* (1971). Routledge, Kegan & Paul, London.

Norman, *Church and Society in England 1770–1970* (1976). Oxford University Press, Oxford.

Partsch, "Freedom of Conscience and Expression and Political Freedom" in *The International Bill of Rights: The Covenant on Civil and Political Rights* (Henkin ed. 1981). Columbia Press, New York.

Paulsen, *The Wall Between Church and State* (1963). Phoenix Books, University of Chicago Press, Chicago.

Pearl, *A Textbook on Muslim Personal Law* (1987). Croom Helm, London.

Pfeffer, *Church, State and Freedom* (2nd ed., 1967). Beacon Press, Boston.

Pfeffer, *Religious Freedom* (1977). National Textbook Company, Illinois.

Phillips, *Putting Asunder* (1988). Cambridge University Press, Cambridge.

Poulter, *Ethnic Minorities and the Law* (1986). Butterworths, London.

Poulter, "The Claim to a Separate Islamic System of Personal Law for Muslims" in *Islamic Family Law* (Mallet & Conners eds., 1990). Graham and Trotman, London.

Poulter, *English Law and Ethnic Minority Customs* (1986). Butterworths, London.

Quick and Garran, *Annotated Constitution of the Australian Commonwealth* (1976). Legal Books, Sydney.

Ramsey, *Putting Asunder* (1966). S.P.C.K., Canterbury.

Roth, Cecil, *12 Encyclopedia Judaica* (1972). Macmillan, Jerusalem.

Roth, Cecil, *14 Encyclopedia Judaica* (1972). Macmillan, Jerusalem.

Sawar, Ghulam, *Compulsory Christian Collective Worship and Christian Religious Education in Schools, What can Muslims Do?* Muslim Educational Trust, London.

Sendor, Benjamin, *Legal Guide to Religion and Public Education* (1988). National Organization on Legal Problems of Education. Topeka, Kansas.

Standing Committee of the General Synod of the Church of England, *An Honourable Estate* (1988). Church House Publishing.

Starke, *Introduction to International Law* (11th ed., 1994). Butterworths, London.

Stone, *Road to Divorce in England 1530–1987* (1990). Oxford University Press, Oxford.

Stone, Lawrence, *The Family, Sex and Marriage 1500–1800* (1979). Penguin Books, London.

Story, Joseph, *Commentaries on Equity Jurisprudence* (14th ed., 1918). Little Brown, Boston.

Synagogue Council of America, *Conference on Religious Education and Public Schools* (1944). New York.

Thornberry, *International Law and the Rights of Minorities* (1991). Oxford University Press, Oxford.

Thorpe, *The Federal and State Constitutions* (1991) Vol. 1. W.S. Hein. Buffalo, N.Y.

Union of Muslim Organisations, *Why Family Law?* (1983). London.

Weyrauch and Katz, *American Family Law in Transition* (1983). BNA Books. Washington.

Articles

Anderson, "Presidential Address" (1969), Vol. X. Journal of the SPTL.

Alves, "Just a Matter of Words? The Religious Education Debate in the House of Lords" British Journal of Religious Education, Vol. 13, no. 3, p. 168.

Baade, "Marriage and Divorce in American Conflicts Law: Governmental—Interests Analysis and the Restatement" (Second) (1972) 72 Colum.L.Rev. 329.

Bleich, "Jewish Divorce: Judicial Misconceptions and Possible Means of Civil Enforcement" (1984), Vol. 16, Connecticut Law Review 201.

Boulware-Miller, "Female Circumcision: Challenges to the Practice as a Human Rights Violation" (1985) Harvard Womens' Law Journal 155.

Bradney, "How Not to Marry People: Formalities of the Marriage Ceremony" [1989] Fam. Law 408.

Bratt, "Incest Statutes and the Fundamental Right of Marriage: Is Oedipus Free to Marry" (1984) 18 Fam.L.Q. 257.

Breitowitz, "Plight of the Agunah: A Study in Halacha, Contract and the First Amendment" (1992) 51 Md.L.Rev. 312.

Breyer, "Cinderella, The Horse God and the Wizard of Oz: *Mozert v. Hawkins County Public Schools*" (1991) 20 Journal of Law and Education 63.

Brigman, "Circumcision as Child Abuse: the Legal and Constitutional Issues" (1984–85) 23 Journal of Family Law 337.

Brigman, "Female Circumcision: Challenges to the Practice as a Human Rights Violation" (1985) 8 Harvard Womens' Law Journal 155.

Burt, "Developing Constitutional Rights of, in and for Children" (1975) 39 L. & Contemp.Prob. 118.

Choper, "Religion in Public School: A proposed constitutional standard" (1963) 47 Minnesota Law Review 388, 396–7.

Colby, "When the Family Does Not Pray Together: Religious Rights Within the Family" (1982), Vol. 5, Harvard Journal of Law and Public Policy.

Cole and Scott, "Creation Science and Scientific Research" (1982) 63 Phi Delta Kappa 557.

Comment, "Matching for Adoption: A Study of Current Trends" (1976) 22 Cath. Law 70.

Comment, "Religion and Adoption—Constitutionality of Religious Matching Practices" (1971) 17 Wayne L.Rev. 1509.

Cullen, "Education Rights or Minority Rights" (1993) IJLF 7, 143.

Cumper, "School Admissions Policies: *Choudhury v. Bishop Challoner R.C. School*" (1989) 2 J.C.L. 95.

Dent, "Religious Children, Secular Schools" (1988) 61 S.Cal.L.Rev. 863.

Freeman, M.D.A., "Jews and the Law of Divorce in England" (1981) J.L.A. 276.

Galanter, "Psychological Religious Instruction into the Large Group: Findings from a Modern Religious Sect" (1980) American Journal of Psychiatry, Vol. 137, No. 12, p. 1575.

Galanter, "Religious Freedom in the United States: A Turning Point" (1966) Wisconsin Law Review 216.

Hayter, "Female Circumcision—Is There a Legal Solution?" [1984] J.S.W.L. 323.

Heymann and Barzelay, "The Forest and the Trees: *Roe v. Wade* and its critics" (1973) 53 B.U.L.Rev. 765.

Hollinger, "Beyond the Best Interests of the Tribe: the Indian Child Welfare Act and the Adoption of Indian Children" (1989) 66 U.Det.L.Rev. 451.

Howard, "Transracial Adoption: Analysis of the Best Interests Standard" (1984) 59 Notre Dame L.Rev. 503.

Howery, "Marriage by Proxy and other Informal Marriages" (1944) 13 U.Kan. City L.Rev. 48.

Huard, "The Law of Adoption: Ancient and Modern" (1956) 9 Vand.L.-Rev. 743.

Hull, "Editorial" (Spring 1990) British Journal of Religious Education, Vol. 12, No. 2.

Hull, "Religious education in the state schools of late capitalist society" (1990) British Journal of Educational Studies, Vol. 38, pt. 4, pp. 335–48.

Jaffey, "The Essential Validity of Marriage in the English Conflict of Laws" (1978) 41 M.L.R. 38.

Juenger, "Recognition of Foreign Divorces — British and American Perspectives" (1972) 20 Am.J.Comp.L. 1.

Kaplan, "The First Amendment standard for removal of books from public school curricula" (Winter 1991), Vol. 95 Dickens Law Review 259.

Katz, "Judicial and Statutory Trends in the Law of Adoption" (1962) 51 Georgetown L.J. 64.

Kurland, "Of Church and State and the Supreme Court" (1961) 29 Univ.Chic.L.Rev. 1.

Kurland, "The Irrelevance of the Constitution: The Religion Clauses of the First Amendment and the Supreme Court" (1978) 24 Vill.L.Rev. 3.

Kurland, "The Religion Clauses and the Burger Court" (1984) 34 Cath.U.L.Rev. 1, 2–3.

Laughran, Catherine, "Religious Beliefs and the Criminal Justice System: Some Problems of the Faith Healer" (1975), Vol. 8, Loyola Law Review 396.

Laycock, "A Survey of Religious Liberty in the United States" (1986) 47 Ohio St.L.J. 409.

Maidment, "The Legal Effect of Religious Divorce" (1974) 37 M.L.R. 611.

Malecha, "Faith Healing Exemptions to Child Protection Laws: Keeping the Faith versus Medical Care" (1985) 12 J. Legis. 243.

Mangrum, "Exclusive Reliance on Best Interests may be Unconstitutional: Religion as a factor in Child Custody Cases" (1981–82), Vol. 15, Creighton Law Review 25.

Marshall, "Comment: The religion clauses and compelled religious divorces: a study in marital and constitutional separations" (1985). North Western University Law Review 204.

Neff, "An Evolving International Legal Norm of Religious Freedom: Problems and Prospects" (1977) 7 Calif. Western Int. Law J. (No. 3).

Note, "Child Foster Placement" (1989/1990) 28 Journal of Family Law 152.

Note, "Freedom of Religion and Science Instruction in Public Schools" (1978) 87 Yale L.J. 515.

Note, "Religion Matching Statutes and Adoption" (1976) 51 NYU.L.Rev. 262.

Note, "Religious Matching and Parental Preference" 3 Utah L.Rev. 559 (1986).

Note, "Unconstitutionality of State Statutes: Authorizing Moments of Silence in the Public Schools" (1983) 96 Harv.L.R. 1874.

Novison, "Post-Divorce Visitation: Untying the Triangular Knot" (1983) U.Ill.L.Rev. 121.

Ostling, "Matters of Faith and Death" (April 16, 1984). *Time.*

Parry, "Denying Recognition to Foreign Divorces" (1978) 8 Fam. Law 29.

Pfeffer, "Religion in the Upbringing of Children" (1955) 35 B.U.L.Rev. 333.

Poulter, "Definition of Marriage in English Law" (1979) 42 M.L.R.

Ramsey, "The Legal Imputation of Religion to an Infant in Adoption Proceedings" (1959) 34 NYU.L.R. 649.

Rivera, "Our Straight-Laced Judges: The Legal Position of Homosexual Persons in the United States" (1979) 30 Hastings L.J. 799.

Schachter, "International Law in Theory and Practice" Recuel des Cours (Kluwer, 1982–V).

Schoen, "California Divorce Rates by Age of First Marriage and Duration of First Marriage" (1975) 37 J. of Marriage and the Family 548.

Schwartz, "Religious Matching for Adoption: Unravelling the 'Best Interests' Standard" (Summer 1991) XXV Family Law Quarterly 171 No. 2.

Stewart, "U.S. Ratification of the Covenant on Civil and Political Rights: The significance of the Reservations, Understandings and Declarations" (1993) 14 H.R.L.J. 77.

Stone, "Knowing the Law" (1961) 24 M.L.R. 475.

Strossen, "Secular Humanism and Scientific Creationism: Proposed Standards for Removing Curricular Decisions Affecting Students' Religious Freedom" (1986) 47 Ohio L.J. 333 at 347.

Sullivan, Donna, "Advancing the Freedom of Religion or Belief through the U.N. Declaration on the Elimination of Religious Tolerance and Discrimination" (1988) American J. of International Law, Vol. 882, 487.

Tribe, "Childhood, Suspect Classifications and Conclusive Presumptions: Three Linked Riddles" (1975) 39 L. & Contemp.Prob. 8.

Turner, "New Religious Movements and the Law in Britain" (1987) Quaderni di Dritto e Politica Ecclesiastica 48–55.

Van Geel, "*Mozert v. Hawkins Public Schools*, the Supreme Court and Mr Breyer, a comment" (1991) 20 Journal of Law and Education 63.

Warmflash, "The New York Approach to Enforcing Religious Marriage Contracts: From Avitzur to the *Get* Statute" (1984), Vol. 50, Brooklyn Law Review 229.

West, "The changing battle over religion in public school" (1991), Vol. 26 Wake Forest Law Review 361.

Weyrauch, "Informal and Formal Marriage — An Appraisal of Trends in Family Organisation" (1960) 28 Univ.Chi.L.Rev. 88.

White, "Divorce: Restricting Religious Activity During Visitation" (1985) 38 Oklahoma Law Review 284.

Wicklein, "Religion as a Factor in Adoption Administration" (October 11, 1959) *N.Y. Times*.

Command Papers

Interdepartmental Report, *Adoption: The Future*, Cm. 2288 (1993), HMSO, London.

Lord Chancellor's Department, *Looking to the Future: Mediation and the ground for divorce*, Cm. 2799 (1995) HMSO, London.

Registration: A Modern Service, Cm. 531 (1989).

Registration: proposals for change, Cm. 939 (1990). HMSO, London.

Report of the Departmental Committee on the Adoption of Children (The Houghton Report), Cmnd. 5107 (1972), HMSO, London.

Report of the Royal Commission on Divorce (Chairman: Lord Gorell), Cd. 6478 (1912). HMSO, London.

Report of the Royal Commission on Marriage and Divorce (Chairman: Lord Moyton of Henryton), Cmnd. 9678 (1956). HMSO, London.

Secondary Schools Curriculum and Examination: Initial Government Observations on the Second Report from the Education, Science and Arts Committee, Session 1981–82, Cmnd. 8851 (1982). HMSO, London.

Swann Report, *Education for All: the Report of the Committee of Inquiry into the Education of Children from Ethnic Minority Groups*, Cmnd. 9453 (1995).

Council of Europe

Boyle, "Seminar on Freedomn of Conscience, University of Leiden" (November 12–14, 1992). Council of Europe.

Dye, Patricia, "Active Learning for Human Rights in Intermediate and High Schools in The Challenge of Human Rights Education" (ed. Starkey). Council of Europe.

Report drawn up on behalf of the Committee on Youth, Culture, Education, Information and Sport on the activity of certain new religious movements within the European Community (Rapporteur, R. Cotterell) 1984–85 Document 1–47/84.

Law Commission Reports

Law Commission, *Reform of the Grounds of Divorce — The Field of Choice*, Cmnd. 3123 (1966). HMSO, London.

Law Commission Report No. 53, *Report on Solemnisation of Marriage* (1973). HMSO, London.

Law Commission Report No. 170, *Facing the Future: A Discussion Paper on the Ground of Divorce* (1988). HMSO, London.

Law Commission Report No. 192, *Family Law, the Ground for Divorce* (1990), HMSO, London.

The Joint Report of the Law Commission and the Scottish Law Commission, Law Com. No. 137, Cmnd. 9341 (1984).

Others

Dove, "Of Divorcement: A Sermon preached at St. Paul's Cross the 10th of May 1601" (London 1601).

Exhortation at the beginning of the Marriage service in the *Prayer Book* of 1662 and the omission proposed in 1928. Cambridge University Press.

Freeman, "Divorce and Religious Barriers to Marriage" a Working Paper.

Howson, *Uxore simissa propter fornicationem aliam non licet superinducere* (Oxford, 1602).

Maryland, "Act Concerning Religion" (1649) in *American State Papers on Religious Freedom* (1949). Review and Herald Publishing Association, Washington D.C.

Marriage and Divorce Statistics OCPS 1991 (1993). HMSO, London.

National Curriculum Council: Analysis of SACRE Reports (1992). York.

National Curriculum Council, *Annual National Curriculum Report* (1990). York.

National Curriculum Council, *Spiritual and Moral Development — A Discussion Paper* (April 1993). York.

Religious Education Council, *What Future for the Agreed Syllabus Now?* (1977).

South African Law Commission Working Paper No. 45, *Jewish Divorces* (Project 76). Pretoria.

U.N. Documents

General Comment Adopted by the Human Rights Committee Under Article 40, Paragraph 4, of the International Covenant on Civil and Political Rights U.N. Doc. CCPR/C/21/Rev.1/Add.4 27 September 1993.

General Comment on Article 18 of the Covenant U.N. Doc. CCPR/C/48/CRP.2/Rev.1. 20 July 1993.

Krishnaswami, *Study of Discrimination in the Matter of Religious Rights and Practices*, U.N. Publication No. 60. xiv.2. New York, 1960: U.N. Documents E/CN.4/Sub.2/200/Rev.1. Reprinted in New York University Journal of International Law and Politics, Vol. 11, 1978, p. 227ff.

Odio-Benito, Elizabeth, *Elimination of all forms of Intolerance and Discrimination based on Religion and Belief* (1989). Human Rights Study Series No. 2, U.N. Publication, Sales No. E. 89. XIV.3.

Index